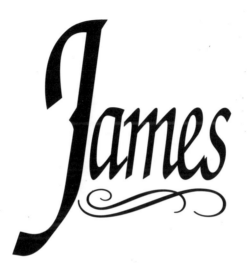

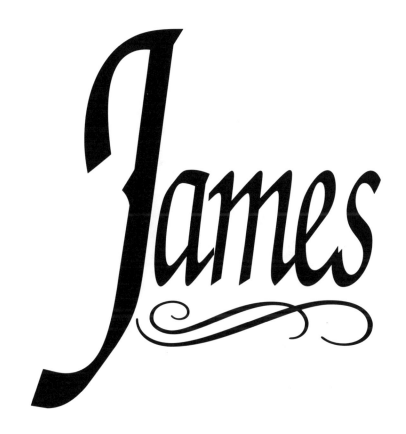

James

D. Edmond Hiebert

MOODY PRESS

CHICAGO

To RUTH
who through the years
has shared with me
in learning the lessons from
the testings of our faith

CONTENTS

PREFACE TO THE REVISED EDITION

In this edition, the *New International Version* is used as the quoted English translation for the epistle of James. Whenever other translations are used they are usually so indicated. With the adaptation of the translation for this revised edition, some revision of a greater or lesser extent has been made of the original, but the thrust of the interpretation of this epistle remains unchanged. Various brief additions, mostly in the nature of practical application, have been incorporated throughout. It is our hope that they will add to the practical value of the study of James.

The renewed intensive study of the epistle of James lying behind this revision, carried out in my eightieth year, has impressed me anew with the pungency and pertinence of this epistle for our own day. May the message of James concerning the nature, testmarks, and reactions of a living faith be vitalized in the lives of the readers.

PREFACE TO THE FIRST EDITION

The title indicates the nature and scope of this volume. The practical epistle of James first assumed special relevance to this writer when it became clear that it presents varied tests of a living faith. My efforts to understand its teachings and to apply them to daily life have extended over many years.

This interpretation of James seeks to bring out something of the riches of the biblical text which a study of the original conveys to the careful student. It is intended for the diligent student who may not be proficient in the Greek, yet is eager to delve into the spiritual wealth of the inspired Word of God.

The English translation quoted is the *American Standard Version,* but the interpretation is based on a study of the Greek text. All Greek words, whenever they are used, have been transliterated[1] and generally placed in parentheses, with their translation appearing in the immediate context.

A detailed outline of the epistle of James, as I perceive its contents, has been included in the interpretation in order to keep the development of the teaching of James clearly before the reader.

My indebtedness to many others in the development of this interpretation of James is evident from the footnotes and Bibliography.

---

1. In the transliterations the usually adopted equivalents for the Greek letters are used, except in the case of *upsilon*, where I have consistently used *u* instead of the more usual *y*.

1

INTRODUCTION TO JAMES

The epistle of James demands that Christian faith must be functional. A living faith is a working faith. The author's central aim is to challenge the readers to test the validity of their faith. Their acceptance of the faith is assumed, and the epistle does not elaborate the doctrinal content of that faith, but they must realize that the gospel makes strong demands for resultant transformed living in daily conduct.

This epistle sternly insists upon Christian practice consistent with Christian belief, heaps scathing contempt upon all empty profession, and administers a stinging rebuke to the readers' worldliness. Its stress upon the gospel's ethical imperative makes the epistle as relevant today as when it was first written. The presence of this practical epistle in the New Testament canon is a magnificent monument to the moral sensitivity and concern of the Christian church.

AUTHORSHIP OF THE EPISTLE

The opening salutation declares that it was written by James, more properly Jacob, but the author's self-identification, which relates only to his spiritual relations, leaves open his exact identity. Traditionally, he has been identified with "James the Lord's brother" (Gal. 1:19), who became the leader of the early church in Jerusalem. Modern critical scholars who reject the traditional view have proposed varied alternatives and commonly date the epistle after the lifetime of the Lord's brother. Maurice Jones remarks, "The gulf which separates the conservative standpoint from that of the more advanced critic is wider in the case of the Epistle of St. James than of any other book in the New Testament."[1]

External Evidence

The earliest known writer to quote by name the epistle of James is Origen (c. A.D. 185-c. 254).[2] He often cited the epistle as "Scripture" and drew freely from its teaching. He was aware that it was not universally acknowl-

edged (*Commentary on John* 19.6) but expressed no personal doubts as to
its canonicity. Occasionally he named James the apostle as the author. In his
Commentary on Matthew (13.55), in discussing the four brothers of Jesus,
Origen treated at some length the righteousness and reputation of James,
whom Paul mentioned in Galatians 1:19, and then referred to Jude, who in
the preface of his letter spoke of himself as the brother of James (Jude 1).
Although not stated, the whole discussion leaves the impression that Origen
connected the epistle of James with the Lord's brother.

The epistle of James is quoted as "Scripture" in *Two Letters Concerning
Virginity* (1.11), a work falsely ascribed to Clement of Rome that was apparently written in Palestine or Syria in the first half of the third century.

Eusebius, in his famous *Ecclesiastical History* (A.D. 325), placed the
epistle of James among the antilegomena, books being disputed by some
section of the church (3.25). Eusebius sharply distinguished the antilegomena from spurious works that were categorically rejected. He acknowledged that the books he listed as disputed "are well known and approved by
many" (3.25). Elsewhere in speaking about James the Lord's brother, "who is
said to have written the first of the epistles general," he remarked that it was
considered spurious by some and that "not many of the ancient have mentioned it," but he concluded, "nevertheless we know that these [the catholic
epistles] are publicly used in most of the churches" (2.23).

Eusebius implies that Clement of Alexandria (c. A.D. 155-c. 220) accepted James and the other general epistles as authentic (*Eccles. Hist.* 6. 14). Wikenhauser notes that "the copious writings of Clement of Alexandria do not
contain a single citation from James" and holds that "despite the evidence of
Eusebius, it is doubtful whether Clement accepted this Epistle as canonical."[3]
Salmon reaches the same conclusion on the basis of the Latin translations of
the works of Clement.[4]

Athanasius, in his thirty-ninth festal letter in A.D. 367, recorded the offi-
cial list of the sacred books. He cited "in the order we now observe, the
Seven Catholic Epistles, which he puts as a group between the Acts of the
Apostles and the Epistles of St. Paul."[5]

No quotations from James are in the known writings of Tertullian (c.
A.D. 160-215), Irenaeus (c. 140-203), Cyprian (c. 200-258), or Hippolytus (d.
236). It is not mentioned in the Muratorian Canon (c. 180), which is held to
represent the accepted view concerning the canon in the church at Rome. It
is not mentioned in the "Cheltenham List" of the canonical books that was
apparently written in Africa in 359.[6] It is also missing in the chief witnesses of
the Old Latin Version.

The epistle of James was late in being accepted in the Syrian church,
but this delay was also true of 1 Peter and 1 John. It was included in the
Peshitta Version, dating from the early fifth century. The epistle was rejected
by Theodore of Mopsuestia (c. A.D. 350-428), but Epiphanius (c. 315-403),
bishop of Salamis in Cyprus, listed it in his canon of the New Testament. Cyril

of Jerusalem (c. 310-86) included all the books of our canon except the Apocalypse in his catalogue and urgently warned against using any other books.

In the West, the earliest clear reference to the epistle of James dates from the middle of the fourth century. The writings of Hilary of Poitiers (c. A.D. 315-404) and Ambrosiaster (c. 339-397) each have a quotation from the epistle. Under the influence of Jerome (345-419) and Augustine (354-430), the epistle gained general acceptance in the West. It was defined as canonical at the synods of Rome (382) and Carthage (397). Jerome, although admitting it to the Vulgate, recorded some uncertainty concerning it. In his *Lives of Illustrous men* (chap. 2) he suggested that it was published by another in the name of James the Lord's brother. The epistle was accepted by Gregory of Nazianzus (330-89), Chrysostom (c. 344-407), and others, but as Harmon observes, "even those fathers who accepted it made but little use of it."[7] Yet as Moo aptly remarks, "It is important to stress that James was not *rejected*, but *neglected*."[8]

Indirect evidence indicating knowledge of the epistle of James goes back to the second century. Striking echoes of the epistle are in Clement's *Epistle to the Corinthians* (c. A.D. 90-100) and especially in *The Shepherd*, by Hermas (c. 90-140).[9] Both Moffatt and Laws accept that the dependence of Hermas on James is clear enough to establish a terminal date for James.[10] Wikenhauser notes that on the basis of the evidence for Clement and Hermas, "Many scholars infer that James was known and esteemed in Rome at an early date, but was later forgotten."[11]

Mitton suggests that the accepted position of this epistle among the general epistles is indirect evidence for the traditional view of authorship. He contends that its position of priority to the epistles by Peter and John, who were among the first apostles of Jesus, "can only be explained on the assumption that its author was regarded as the brother of the Lord, who later became the very influential head of the church at Jerusalem."[12]

External evidence establishes that the epistle of James came slowly into general circulation and was late in winning firm acceptance as canonical. Moffatt concludes that this evidence "is more intelligible upon the hypothesis that James was of late origin than on the view that it was a product of the primitive church."[13] While allowing the possibility of such an explanation, Davids points out that "a theory of limited interest in and circulation of the epistle would also explain the evidence."[14] Conservative scholars believe that the evidence does not conclusively establish a late date, and insist that more weight than usual should be given to the second-century evidence that implies its early existence and influence. Guthrie contends that "the real crux lies in the treatment of this second-century evidence."[15] There seem to be plausible explanations for the obscurity that early surrounded the letter.

With the development of Gentile Christianity with its own distinctive concerns, a letter addressed specifically to Jewish Christian churches would appear to have little appeal to the church as a whole. Its brevity and very practical nature would make the epistle seem to be of minor importance to those whose main interests were doctrinal. Mitton observes,

> Writings which came from the missionary apostles, with a special emphasis on the evangelical doctrines of the Faith, would be more readily valued than an epistle from one whose task in the Church was not primarily evangelical or missionary.[16]

This practical letter could easily be neglected by those concerned with defending the doctrinal realities of Christianity.

Further, a letter addressed to a specific church, and especially one from the founder of that church, would be more likely to be treasured and disseminated than a general letter for which no specific Christian community felt a direct responsibility.

A cause for the neglect of this epistle may have been the fact that the author makes no claim to apostolic authority. Since its author identified himself only as "James," a common name in the ancient world, those unfamiliar with its history would naturally have questions about its true authority or canonicity. Thus the letter was not aggressively promoted by those who had personal questions concerning its authorship and authority. The circulation of the epistle accordingly "was extremely narrow, confined to a tiny segment of the surviving Christian church."[17] The real reason for this was the crash of Jewish Christianity in connection with the destruction of Jerusalem.[18] It marked the termination of the power of Jewish Christianity as exercised by the mother church in Jerusalem under the leadership of James the Lord's brother. Thus Heard remarks that "the original prestige of James, so potent in the earliest days of the church, soon waned when the church of Jerusalem lost its position of leadership, and James became a shadowy figure, known only from a few references in the Pauline epistles."[19]

When the epistle of James became more widely known, it was clear that the work did have spiritual value for the church as a whole. Its discovery by Origen and other church leaders gave it a new lease on life. When the epistle did come to be generally known, questions concerning the identity and authority of the designated author naturally caused reluctance to receive it as canonical. The neglect it had suffered naturally proved to be fertile soil for the future doubts, especially at a time when the church was alert to the need of detecting spurious writings.

Internal Evidence

The evidence concerning authorship drawn from the epistle itself has received widely different evaluations.

Arguments for traditional view. The opening designation, "James, a servant of God and of the Lord Jesus Christ," is ambiguous and might have been used for any of several men named James in the New Testament. The fact that the author felt no need to identify himself, either by his ecclesiastical position or his human relations (cf. Jude 1), suggests that he was so prominent that his readers would know at once who he was. The only James who was such a well-known leader in the early Christian community was James the Lord's brother. The fact that tradition passed over two apostles named James, and ascribed it to the Lord's brother, "suggests that this identification must have had some support in fact and not merely be the outcome of a pious wish to add prestige to the epistle by ascribing it to a person of importance."[20]

If the epistle is not authentic, it appears certain that "a fictitious writer would scarcely have chosen the modest title which commences this Epistle in the endeavor to recommend his exhortations."[21] A spurious letter of James reads, "James, bishop of Jerusalem, to Quadratus."[22] Later, stress was laid on James's relationship to Jesus as "the Lord's brother," but Davids notes that this relationship was "stressed after and only after his death."[23] Elsewhere in the New Testament, Harrison points out, James the Lord's brother (Gal. 1:19) is uniformly mentioned "by his personal name alone (Gal. 2:9, 13; Jude 1; Acts 12:17; 15:13; 21:18)."[24] The authoritative tone of the epistle is consistent with the known position of the Lord's brother in the early Jewish church.

The author's Jewish background, as reflected in the epistle, is consistent with the traditional view. The author is thoroughly familiar with Old Testament and Jewish forms of thought and expression. The address, "to the twelve tribes which are of the Dispersion" (ASV) is characteristically Jewish. He mentions Abraham as "our ancestor" (2:21) and is the only New Testament writer who employs the Old Testament designation "the Lord of Sabaoth" (5:4 *kuriou sabaōth*) in speaking of God. (In Romans 9:29, the only other New Testament occurrence, it is a direct quotation from the Old Testament.) He freely draws his illustrations from the Old Testament (2:21, 25; 5:11, 17-18) and mentions the unity of God as the central fact of the faith (2:19). He is acquainted with Jewish formulas in the use of oaths (5:12). These glimpses of the author are consistent with the picture of the Lord's brother in the rest of the New Testament.

There are remarkable similarities between this epistle and the speech of James at the Jerusalem conference (Acts 15:13-21) and the letter, probably drawn up by James, embodying the conference decision (15:23-29).[25] The epithet "beloved" (*agapētoi*, James 1:16, 19; 2:5; Acts 15:25), as well as the exhortation "Listen, my dear brothers" (James 2:5; Acts 15:13), appears in both the epistle and Acts. The infinitive form of the greeting (*chairein*) in this epistle also is used in the conference letter (James 1:1; Acts 15:17). "To turn" (*epistrephō*) as denoting conversion (James 5:19-20; Acts 15:19) and "to visit" (*episkeptomai*) (James 1:27; Acts 15:14) occur in both James and Acts. The Hebraic expression "your souls" in Acts 15:24 occurs in James 1:21 (cf. 5:20).

Some verbal similarities between this epistle and the words of James in Acts 21:20-23 also have been noted.[26]

Numerous similarities exist between this epistle and the teachings of Jesus, especially the Sermon on the Mount. Compare the following:

James	*Matthew*
1:2	5:10-12
1:4	5:48
1:5; 5:15	7:7-12
1:9	5:3
1:20	5:22
2:13	5:7; 6:14-15
2:14-16	7:21-23
3:17-18	5:9
4:4	6:24
4:10	5:3-4
4:11	7:1-2
5:2	6:19
5:10	5:12
5:12	5:33-37[27]

Mayor further lists a number of parallels for the rest of Matthew as well as Mark and Luke.[28] Nowhere does James say he is quoting Jesus. In fact, he does not give the impression of quoting at all. Rather, his parallels with Jesus' teachings seem to represent the Lord's teachings as they were remembered in the earliest days of the church, before they were enshrined in the gospel accounts. Guthrie further notes that "these parallels are not produced in any mechanical way, but with a real understanding of the point of view from which our Lord proclaimed His teaching."[29] Davids concludes that "collectively, these allusions argue that the author was someone saturated with the teaching of Jesus, and that the work was written before its author contacted written gospel traditions."[30] This situation is fully consistent with the traditional view of authorship, but difficult to conceive if the epistle was written after our gospels were in circulation.

Conditions among the readers as reflected in the epistle are consistent with the traditional view of authorship. The social and economic conditions reflected imply a date some time before the destruction of Jerusalem in A.D. 70. The conflict resulting in the fall of Jerusalem greatly altered conditions for the Jewish people. The simplicity of the ecclesiastical organization suggested in the epistle favors an early date, as does the vivid hope of Christ's second coming. No anachronisms are created by placing the epistle into the lifetime of James the Lord's brother.[31]

Arguments against traditional view. Strenuous objections have been voiced against the traditional view of authorship.

Excellent Greek. The known language milieu of first-century Palestine[32] makes it very probable that James knew Greek from boyhood. Easton recognizes that since "Nazareth lay on a thronged trade route, it may be assumed that most Nazarenes would pick up more or less Greek of some sort or other," but he insists that we cannot "by the wildest stretch of the imagination" accept that James wrote the good Greek of this epistle.[33] But this fails to recognize that the Jews were the most literary of all Mediterranean nations. "The LXX marks the Jewish adoption of Hellenism and it rapidly became the manual of the synagogues and the whole Dispersion west of the Jordan."[34] Seventser concludes his elaborate investigation of this matter with the words

> In view of all the data made available in the past decades, the possibility can no longer be precluded that a Palestinian Jewish Christian of the first century A.D. wrote an epistle in good Greek.[35]

And Moulton asserts,

> There is not the slightest presumption against the use of Greek in writings purporting to emanate from the circle of the first believers. They would write as men who had used the language from boyhood, not as foreigners painfully expressing themselves in an imperfectly known idiom.[36]

The epistle is written in good Greek, but to speak of its "excellent Greek" is to overestimate its literary quality. Robertson asserts, "The author of Hebrews, Luke and Paul far surpass him [James] in formal rhetoric."[37] Zahn points out that the forcibleness of the epistle is "the eloquence that comes from the heart and goes to the conscience, a kind which was never learned in a school of rhetoric."[38]

Although written in accurate Koine Greek, the language of the epistle has a definite Hebrew tinge. "The Greek form of the expression of thought," says Oesterley, "seems to be moulded from a Hebrew pattern, i.e., that the mind of the writer was accustomed to express itself after the manner of one to whom Hebrew ways of thinking were very familiar, and who in writing Greek, therefore, almost unconsciously reverted to the Hebrew mode."[39] Yet Easton, well aware of this Jewish coloring, holds that its literary form points to a non-Palestinian Jew "whose rhetorical training was Hellenistic, but whose religious background was firmly Hebraic."[40] The literary phenomena present a remarkable situation. Liberal students commonly conclude that the phenomena rule out traditional authorship. Advocates of the traditional view advance two different explanations.

One view is that James did acquire the needed familiarity with the Greek to write the epistle as we have it. Acquainted with Greek from boyhood, his position of leadership in the Jerusalem church would make it necessary for him to develop proficiency in its use. There were Hellenists, people completely at home in the Greek, in the Jerusalem church from its very beginning. Daily contact with these Hellenists, as well as frequent practice in public speaking and debate, would give James ample opportunity to develop proficiency in the use of the language. Formal study of the language right in Jerusalem was also a possibility open to James.[41] And James may well have possessed special linguistic aptitudes. Mitton remarks, "James must have been a man of quite extraordinary intelligence and ability to have risen so quickly to the position he achieved. What might have been improbable for a more ordinary person is not so improbable for one of his unusual calibre."[42]

An alternative suggestion is that James used an educated scribe to whom he outlined "what he wanted to say and then left him comparative freedom of expression."[43] Beasley-Murray supports this suggestion with the assertion that "in the Hellenistic age, in which the New Testament was written, scarcely an author gave even his letters their final form in language and style; the dependence of authors on the art of the scribes was well-nigh universal."[44] Sevenster questions this assertion, maintaining that it "probably seldom occurred," and concludes that there is "not one single irrefutably clear example of such" in the New Testament."[45] He points out that the use of key words, wordplays, alliterations, and the arrangement of its contents in short pericopes "make it almost impossible to imagine how a secretary could have composed and written such an epistle at the indication of James."[46] Further, Adamson remarks, "To say that he expected his secretary to create the text from a few notes presumes a secretary more brilliant than the author, a most unlikely presumption."[47]

Either explanation would relieve the problem raised by the language of the epistle. The former is the most natural in view of the known language milieu in the day of James the Lord's brother and the obvious abilities of the leader of the church in Jerusalem. The latter is not conducive to a high view of inspiration.

Scant Christian Content. Oesterley holds that the absence of any reference to the great events in the life of Jesus makes it "almost impossible to believe that one who had known Christ, and had been an eye-witness of His doings and a hearer of His teaching, should maintain such absolute silence on these things when addressing a letter to fellow-believers."[48] Ropes finds it difficult to understand how the Lord's brother could fail to mention the death of Jesus Christ as the means of men's salvation.[49] And Oesterley finds the absence of any mention of Christ's resurrection difficult to account for in view of its importance in the preaching of the early church.[50] Since James himself saw the risen Christ (1 Cor. 15:7), and this event must have made a deep impression on him, it is held to be highly improbable that the writer of this epistle was our Lord's brother. Admittedly, the argument has force, but Heard well replies,

> The very absence of theological interpretation of the life, death and resurrection of Jesus tells against any theory that the epistle is the work of a later anonymous Christian, and it is better to take the silence of James, like that of Jude, as an indication of the way in which the brethren of Jesus proclaimed their faith.[51]

The absence of any reference to these basic Christian doctrines cannot be due to ignorance of them. In writing to fellow believers, the author could assume that his readers were cognizant of them. His ethical purpose did not require him to discuss them. He would feel a natural reticence about discussing these marvelous matters because of his own close personal relations to the Lord. Tasker has well pointed to the capriciousness of this sort of argument by noting that 2 Peter is often considered pseudonymous because its author emphasizes his relationship to Jesus.[52]

Author's claims. Objection to the traditional view of authorship is drawn from the fact that the writer makes no claim to apostleship, nor does he claim to be the Lord's brother. Oesterley thinks that if James the Lord's brother wrote the letter, we should expect mention of his authoritative position to make his letter more effective for his readers in the Dispersion.[53]

James, like Paul, must have realized that a knowledge of Jesus according to the flesh was not spiritually significant (2 Cor. 5:16). After the resurrection appearance of Jesus to James (1 Cor. 15:7), when the true nature of his brother became clear to James, the importance of his human ties with Jesus receded; what was now important to him was the spiritual relationship. While others might give recognition to his human relationship with Jesus, James felt it more appropriate to call himself "a servant . . . of the Lord Jesus Christ" (1:1). The fact that the noted leader of the Jerusalem church was "the Lord's brother" (Gal. 1:19) was not stressed in Christian circles until after the death of James. It was recognized that the physical relationship did not guarantee any higher spiritual insights.

Hellenistic features. The Hellenistic literary features of the epistle have been appealed to as evidence against the traditional authorship. Easton asserts, "The fact that the Epistle of James is written throughout as a paraenesis, with frequent employment of the diatribe, shows that its author must be sought among those whose literary associations were with the Greek rather than with the Hebrew world,"[54] but these features do not establish that conclusion. Harrison well points out that "Paul, the Hebrew of the Hebrews, used the same Hellenistic literary devices, diatribe and all."[55]

Conditions among readers. The distressing conditions among the readers are held to point to a time after the death of James. It is asserted that the sins rebuked require a long period of development; hence, the letter cannot be directed to Christian communities during the early years of the church.

The claim is questionable. Paul found much to rebuke in the Corinthian church a short time after its founding. The opening chapters of Acts (5:1-11; 6:1) show that the Jewish Christians constituting the church in its earliest days were not exempt from some of the sins rebuked. Knowling notes that "the sins and weaknesses which the writer describes are exactly those faults and weaknesses which our Lord blames on His countrymen, and especially in the party of the Pharisees."[56] Davids believes that the moral problems dealt with "might even be the faults of recently converted Jews who needed to realize the implications of their new faith."[57]

Dibelius dismisses this argument as irrelevant. He contends that as paraenetic literature, no firm information concerning the actual condition among the readers can be drawn from its contents.[58]

Literary dependence. Attempts to establish authorship on the basis of assumed literary dependence are precarious.[59] Moffatt asserts, "The dependence of the epistle upon not only 1 Peter, but some of Paul's epistles (especially Romans) is plain."[60]

Actual literary dependence between James and 1 Peter or Romans is by no means certain. Ropes remarks, "Even if literary dependence were admitted to exist, it would be wholly impossible to decide on which side it lay."[61] He holds that the similarities are due to a common stock of thought upon which both writers drew independently. Concerning these claims for literary dependence, Guthrie aptly remarks, "The most that could be supposed with certainty is that the author possessed a mind receptive of common Christian ideas."[62]

Alternative Views of Authorship

Scholars who conclude that the traditional view concerning authorship must be rejected have advanced varied alternative views.

One suggestion is that some unknown teacher published it under the guise of being James the Lord's brother. This view of pseudonymity is beset with great difficulties. Moffatt rightly notes that "the lack of any emphasis upon the apostle's personality and authority tells against the theory."[63] The absence of any heretical views in the epistle affords no plausible motive for a pseudonymous origin. Proponents may decry stamping such a production a forgery, but that does not relieve the view of the moral issue involved.[64]

A variant hypothesis is that it was written by an unknown teacher named James who later was mistakenly identified with James the Lord's brother.[65] This view is advanced to relieve the difficulties of the traditional view, but it is beset with its own difficulties. "An unknown writer, whose name was James, would surely have realized that his readers would confuse him with the well-known James, and unless he intended such confusion, would have given more specific description of his own identity."[66] Under this view, it is difficult to account for the epistle's authoritative tone and encyclical nature. It faces the moral issue of having gained admission to the canon on the basis of false identification of its author. It is founded on an unproven assumption.

In 1896, F. Spitta advanced the novel hypothesis that the epistle was originally a collection of moral instructions written by a Palestinian Jew to the Jews in the Dispersion, and later given a Christian flavor by the addition of a few Christian touches, such as including the name of Jesus Christ in 1:1 and 2:1. The conjecture is highly improbable. "A Christian interpolator would scarcely have contented himself with inserting so little and would probably have left 2:1 clearer."[67] Kümmel points out that this hypothesis ignores "a series of features which are comprehensible only in view of a Christian origin" and refers to 1:18, 21, 25; 2:7; 5:8, 12 as containing teaching which could not have had a non-Christian Jewish origin.[68] McNeile asserts, "The Christianity of the writer gleams behind his words with a subdued light that no redaction could produce."[69] This theory overemphasizes the epistle's Jewish element and neglects its distinctly Christian elements, but it did contribute to the realization that it is not necessary to assume a Hellenistic origin for the epistle.

In 1930, Arnold Meyer in *Das Rätsel des Jakobusbriefes* advanced the fantastic theory that behind our epistle of James lay a Jewish allegorical work based on Jacob's farewell address to his twelve sons, which depicted the traditional vice and virtue of each tribe; our epistle is a revision of this work for Christian purposes. He held that the patriarchal names were interpreted allegorically, and that this ethical allegorical treatment offers the key to the order of the material in our epistle. It is the basis for Easton's interpretation, although he reduces the Jewish document and increases the Christian editing.[70] Meyer's theory is highly ingenious; the proposed connections of thought often are far from apparent. The whole approach is extremely subtle and far from convincing. Tasker justly remarks:

> It is one of the surprising features of contemporary biblical criticism that such a method of exegesis should be regarded as a serious contribution to the problem of the origin of the Epistle of James, or of any other document in the New Testament.[71]

A further theory postulates that the epistle incorporates genuine material from James, probably sermonic in origin, and that an editor translated, adapted, and enlarged on the original material to give the work its present form. Thus Barclay suggests that our epistle is "in substance a sermon preached by James, and taken down by someone else, translated into Greek, added to and decorated a little, and then issued to the Church at large so that all men should possess it and benefit from it."[72] If it is assumed that this process was carried out under the knowledge and approval of James, it is not far different from the view that James employed a scholarly scribe; it simply adds a hypothetical link between the real author and our present epistle.

Davids envisions a more definite, two-stage origin for the present epistle. He suggests, "The editor may have been quite unknown to the author, simply a reviser and compiler of his material, either before or after the author's death. In such a case, the ascription to James the Just is certainly warranted, even though James may never have known the epistle was sent."[73] We may ask, why should such an editor-reviser at a later time issue his own product as the work of James without the knowledge of James, or later when the majority of his intended readers would know that James was already dead? This view raises questions concerning the epistle's inspiration. It provides no better explanation than the traditional view as to why the epistle was so tardy in receiving recognition as rightfully belonging among the church's authentic writings.

AUTHOR OF THE EPISTLE

Picture in Epistle

The author's self-identification as "a servant of God and of the Lord Jesus Christ" (1:1) relates only to his spiritual position. For him, this citation of his servant-relation to God conveyed nothing servile, but rather implied a personal sense of homage and intimacy with the God whose servant he was. It was the central reality in his self-identification. Unlike Jude (1:1), he obviously felt no need to indicate his family relations. He apparently was so well-known that his readers would need no further identification.

Aside from the oblique reference to his position as a teacher in 3:1, the author makes no further direct reference to himself. Yet few writings in the same space reveal more of the person of its author than this epistle. He reveals himself as a vigorous personality, strong and assured in his position. His crisp, concise, authoritative tone commands attention. His brief, pointed sentences, like piercing arrows, invariably hit their mark. He uses "language for which forcibleness is without parallel in early Christian literature, excepting the discourses of Jesus."[74]

A keen observer, he was alert to the operations of nature and repeatedly drew lessons from that area. He was also an attentive observer of human nature. "He knows the fashions of the world, and he notes with unerring clearness and humorous shrewdness the characters of men; he sees their superficial goodness, their indolent selfishness, their vulgarity and the mischief of their untamed thoughtlessness."[75]

He was a man of strong moral convictions whose deep sense of right compelled him to speak out sharply against wrong wherever he encountered it. His words of rebuke are sharp and incisive, yet he is essentially kindly in disposition. He was openly sympathetic with the poor (2:5); his indignation was aroused when they were mistreated (5:4) or scorned and slighted in the

Christian assembly (2:2-4). He held that a living faith must manifest itself in a good life (2:17) and in social concern (1:27).

He held deep Christian convictions. He accepted monotheism as a cardinal principle of the faith (2:19). "He regards God as the 'eternal changeless One' from whom come all good gifts (1:17), and under whose providence is every detail of life (4:15)."[76] He had strong convictions concerning the power and importance of prayer (1:5; 5:14-18) and the indwelling Word (1:18, 21). He was fully aware of the deep roots of sin in human nature (1:13-15), and saw an uncontrolled tongue as a manifestation of indwelling evil (3:6-8). He had a deep, if reticent, love for Christ, whom he called "our glorious Lord Jesus Christ" (2:1). He awaited the return of Christ (5:7).

As a devout Christian, the author's thinking is rooted in a Jewish background. Christian ideas are clothed in Jewish forms. Love for the world is condemned in Old Testament terms as adultery against God (4:4). He never uses the word "gospel," but its place is apparently taken by what he calls "the royal law" or "the law that gives freedom" (2:8, 12). He condemns evil speaking as putting a slight on the law (4:11). He naturally reverts to the Old Testament for illustrations, yet the epistle makes no reference to the observance of Jewish rituals and sacrifices.

Biblical Identity

The Greek name *Iakōbos*, rendered "James" in our English versions, occurs forty-two times in the New Testament. Several different men bear the name.

The James most frequently mentioned in the gospels is James the son of Zebedee (Matt. 4:21; 10:2; 17:1; Mark 1:19, 29; 3:17; 5:37; 9:2; 10:35, 41; 13:3; 14:33; Luke 5:10; 6:14; 8:51; 9:28, 54). He is named twice in Acts (1:13; 12:2). With his brother, John, he was among the earliest disciples of Jesus. He was the first of the twelve apostles to meet martyrdom (Acts 12:2).

Another one of the twelve was James the son of Alphaeus (Matt. 10:3; Mark 3:18; Luke 6:15; Acts 1:13). He was apparently also known as "James the younger" (Mark 15:40)[77] and as the son of Mary (Matt. 27:56; Mark 16:1; Luke 24:10). He had a brother named Joses (Mark 15:40). His name is not connected with any incident in the gospels.

Another member of the twelve is identified as "Judas, *the* son of James (Luke 6:16 and Acts 1:13), more literally, "Judas of James." The parallel expression, "James of Alphaeus," in the lists strongly supports the view that here also "son of," rather than "brother of" (KJV), is the intended rendering. This James is thus simply mentioned as the father of one of the twelve, whom the fourth gospel further identifies as "Judas, not the Iscariot" (John 14:22, Rotherham).

Another James, along with his three brothers, is twice named in the gospels as the "brother" of Jesus (Matt. 13:55; Mark 6:3). These brothers as a group also appear in John 7:3-8 and Acts 1:14. In Galatians 1:19, Paul refers to "James the Lord's brother" as an important individual in the church at Jerusalem, whom he met upon his return to that city three years after his conversion. He further mentions James as the first of three reputed pillars in the Jerusalem church (Gal. 2:9), a leader whose name carried strong influence even in the church at Antioch (Gal. 2:12). Three more references to James in Acts, without any further identification, depict an important leader in the Jerusalem church (Acts 12:17; 15:13; 21:18). His identification with the Lord's brother seems assured on the basis of 1 Corinthians 15:7 and Acts 1:14. He also seems to be the James intended in Jude 1.

Of these four men, James the father of the apostle Jude may at once be eliminated as the possible author of the epistle of James. Nothing further is known of him.

The view that James the son of Zebedee was the author has had few advocates.[78] The scant manuscript evidence in its support is of late origin.[79] Internal evidence in its favor is meager and unconvincing. This James was beheaded under Herod Agrippa I in A.D. 44 (Acts 12:2). There is no evidence that by that date he had attained a special position of leadership among Jewish Christians that would justify this letter. He is not prominent in the first twelve chapters of Acts and is always identified in terms of his father or his famous brother, John. That he was the author of this epistle is very improbable.[80]

This choice between James the son of Alphaeus and James the Lord's brother immediately confronts the preliminary question of their possible identity. The identification, proposed by Jerome in the fourth century, has been the traditional position of Roman Catholic exegetes. Thus, Steinmueller rejects any distinction between James the son of Alphaeus and James the brother of the Lord, maintaining that early ecclesiastical tradition confirms this identification.[81] But Wikenhauser, himself a Catholic, notes that "the Protestants and a growing minority among modern Catholics distinguish the brother of the Lord from the son of Alphaeus" and concludes that the distinction is preferable.[82]

This identification assumes that the Clopas in John 19:25 is to be equated with Alphaeus the father of James (Matt. 10:3; Mark 3:18; Luke 6:15; Acts 1:13). Linguistically, the two names could be derived from the same Aramaic term,[83] yet it is unlikely that the same man would be known by both names in the same company of disciples. In the Syriac versions, made by men who doubtless were acquainted with Aramaic names and their renderings, different forms are used for Alphaeus and Clopas.[84]

This view also assumes that in John 19:25 only three women are named, holding that "his mother's sister" is "Mary the wife of Clopas." Although common, the view is highly improbable.[85] Then there would have been two living sisters bearing the name of Mary in the same family. In light of Matthew 27:56 and Mark 15:40, it is far more probable that John refers to four women, naming them in pairs, and that the sister of Mary, the mother of Jesus, is really Salome, the mother of the sons of Zebedee. The Peshitto Syriac Version inserted a conjunction, showing that the translators understood John to speak of four women.

The gospel references to the brothers of Jesus do not harmonize with the view that one or more of them were among the twelve. Jesus' brothers always are represented as a different set of men than the apostles (Matt. 12:46; Mark 3:31; Luke 8:19; John 2:12; 7:3; Acts 1:14). Their attempt with His mother to check the intensive ministry of Jesus (Matt. 12:46; Mark 3:21, 31) does not agree with the view that they (or some of them) were among His disciples. The people of Nazareth spoke of Jesus' brothers as distinct from His disciples (Matt. 13:55; Mark 6:3). About six months before the crucifixion, just before the Feast of Tabernacles, "even his own brothers did not believe in him" (John 7:5).

Advocates of the identification hold that in Galatians 1:18-19, Paul refers to James the Lord's brother as one of the apostles, but this interpretation of Paul's language is by no means certain. Paul's expression "only [*ei mē*] James" is best understood as having an adversative meaning, "but only"; his addition "if not James's" (Greek) simply seems to mean that he saw no other person important enough to mention along with Peter except James.[86] Even if we allow that Paul here called James an apostle, the term may be used in a wider sense to include other men of prominence in the work of the church (cf. Acts 14:4, 14; Rom. 16:7).[87] The conclusion that James the Lord's brother was not one of the twelve, hence not to be identified with James the son of Alphaeus, is consistent with the fact that, in his introductory greeting, James makes no claim to apostolic authority.

Among those who accept the distinction between James the son of Alphaeus and James the Lord's brother, only comparatively few have attributed the authorship of the epistle to the son of Alphaeus. Calvin regarded this view as not improbable and held that the James mentioned in Galatians 2:9, whom Paul called a "pillar" of the church, was the son of Alphaeus. He did not, however, firmly decide which of the two men wrote the epistle.[88] Apparently Calvin "hesitated about assigning the same degree of authority to an apostle other than Paul, if he was outside the number of the original twelve."[89]

Baxter, a modern advocate of the view that the author was James the son of Alphaeus, insists that to identify the James of Acts 12:17; 15:13-21, and 21:18-25 with James the Lord's brother makes Luke guilty of dropping an apostle without an explanation and putting in his place another leader who was not an apostle.[90] After the list of the twelve in Acts 1, only three of the original twelve are named again in the book. The son of Alphaeus is not named in connection with a single incident in any of the gospels; his name is known to us only from the lists of the twelve. A man who made so little impression on the gospel narratives does not seem to be the strong and forceful personality reflected in our epistle of James. That James the Lord's brother, although not one of the original apostles, should in a short time step into prominence in the early church is understandable in view of his close relationship to the Lord and Jesus' postresurrection appearance to him, as well as his abilities and devout character. The risen Christ's personal appearance to James (1 Cor. 15:7) gave him the fundamental qualification of an apostle (Acts 1:22).

We conclude that of the four men named "James" in the New Testament, only James the Lord's brother fits the picture. Our findings are in harmony with the traditional view concerning the authorship of the epistle of James.

Relation to Jesus

The identification of the author as "the Lord's brother" raises the thorny question of the exact nature of that relationship. The question has been debated through the centuries, and no unanimity has been reached. Three main views have been advocated.[91]

The *Epiphanian theory* holds that these brothers were the sons of Joseph by a former marriage, hence all older than Jesus.[92] Epiphanius (c. A.D. 315-403), bishop of Salamis, strongly endorsed this view in a pastoral letter around 375. The view, current in the second century, received strong expression in the apocryphal gospels.[93] The theory in itself is not intrinsically improbable. It had great appeal in the early church because it safeguarded the virginity of Mary.

In support of this theory, it is held that it explains why on the cross Jesus committed His mother to the care of John (John 19:27). In that tragic hour, the disciple would be more sympathetic toward Mary than her older stepsons. The behavior of these brothers toward Jesus is felt to be more consistent with Jewish custom if they were older than Jesus. In their attempt to interfere with Jesus' ministry (Mark 3:21, 31-34), as well as in their open criticism of Him (John 7:2-9), they did not act like younger brothers. C. Harris further argues that if Mary had other children after the birth of Jesus, "the (practically) unanimous tradition of her perpetual virginity could never have arisen."[94] Keylock replies that the argument is "weak in that it is repeatedly contradicted by the past which is replete with just such developments."[95]

This theory is open to the objection that if these brothers were His seniors, Jesus could not have been the heir to David's throne: His older brothers would have ranked before Him. If these brothers were older than Jesus, their continued presence with His mother is difficult to explain; at the time of Jesus' ministry, we would have expected them to be married and have homes of their own, but the impression left by Scripture is that they constituted one household. Later, they were widely known as Christian workers who were married (1 Cor. 9:5).

The *Helvidian theory,* so named from an obscure advocate in the latter part of the fourth century, holds that these brothers were the sons of Joseph and Mary, hence all younger than Jesus.[96] The treatise of Helvidius, written in Rome, made a deep impression on the Roman church.

In support of this view, it is held that a reader of the New Testament, uninfluenced by historical or doctrinal considerations, would naturally conclude that these brothers were the sons of Joseph and Mary. Except in John 7:3, they appear in connection with Mary, as though they were members of her household. The statement in Matthew 1:24-25 that Joseph "took Mary home as his wife, but had no union with her until she gave birth to a son" naturally means that they lived as husband and wife after the birth of Jesus. Luke's statement (Luke 2:7), that Jesus was Mary's "firstborn" son (*prōtokos*), in light of the gospel records may be construed to imply the existence of children born subsequently. If Luke had meant to teach that Mary had no other children, the word *monogenēs* (used in Luke 7:12 and 8:42 of an "only" child) was available. When Luke wrote, the matter already had been resolved. The reference to Jesus by the people of Nazareth as "the carpenter" (Mark 6:3) naturally suggests that upon the death of Joseph, Jesus, as the oldest son, had taken over the father's occupation as the head of the family.

Tertullian (c. A.D. 160-220) is the first known writer who expressly asserted that the "brethren" were the uterine brothers of Jesus. His statement gives no indication that he was controverting an established tradition favoring the perpetual virginity. On the basis of Origen's statement that the opposite opinion was held by "some," Ropes concludes that this view was held by most persons in the Christian church during the second century.[97]

Opponents of the Helvidian view point out that the majority of ancient writers who discuss the question hold that Mary had no other children. By the time the question came under full discussion, the theory of Mary's perpetual virginity already had begun to project itself into the theology of the church. Ascetic feelings shrank from the thought that the virgin womb of Mary, in which the eternal Word was made flesh, also had been the habitation of other babes. Keylock notes that influential Roman Christian women, committed to the superiority of virginity over marriage, appealed to Jerome to refute the teaching of Helvidius.[98]

It is asserted that the way in which these brothers attempted to interfere with Jesus' ministry is (according to Jewish custom) inconsistent with the view that they were younger. Jacobs tersely replies, "Those who pursue an unjustifiable course are not models of consistency."[99] The fact that Jesus at His death committed His mother to the care of John (John 19:25-27) is held to confirm the view that Mary had no other sons. In that dark hour, none of her sons understood Jesus and could not sympathize with Mary as could John, the beloved disciple. As the son of her sister, Salome, John had closer spiritual ties with Mary than did her unbelieving sons.

The *Hieronymian theory*, originated by Jerome to refute the position of Helvidius, holds that the "brethren" of Jesus were really His cousins, the children of Clopas and Mary, the sister of the mother of Jesus.[100]

This view rests upon the questionable assumption that Clopas and Alphaeus are the same man and that Mary, the wife of Clopas, was the sister of the virgin Mary. If they were the sons of Mary and Clopas, it is inexplicable that they should always be associated with Mary the mother of Jesus rather than their own mother. If they were the cousins of Jesus, we would expect the use of the word *anepsios*, which properly means "cousin." This view assumes that some of these "brothers" were among Jesus' disciples, but John 7:3-8 constitutes a crowning difficulty to that view. Jerome could produce no earlier ecclesiastical support for his novel theory.

This thorny problem will probably never be settled to everyone's satisfaction. We fully concur with Mombert's conclusion:

> The view that Jesus had actual brothers and sisters is as old as any of the other theories, and we believe with Neander, Winder, Meyer, Stier, Alford and Farrar, that it accords best with the evangelical record, and barring dogmatical prejudices or feeling, is at once the simplest, most natural and logical solution of this otherwise hopelessly confused question.[101]

History and Character

Apparently James was the oldest of the brothers of Jesus, since his name stands first in the two lists of their names (Matt. 13:55; Mark 6:3). During Jesus' ministry, His brothers did not understand His true nature and could not associate Him with their messianic views (John 7:2-8), but the appearance of the risen Christ to James (1 Cor. 15:7) dissolved all doubts, and with his brothers he threw in his lot with Christ's followers (Acts 1:14). The appearance of the risen Christ gave James a distinctive position among the larger group of believers (Acts 1:22), no doubt contributing to his rise to prominence in the early church. The further references to James in Acts (12:17; 15:12-29; 21:18-25) and Galatians (1:18-19; 2:6-9) establish his acknowledged importance at different points in the Jerusalem church. James's prominence is evident from Jude's reference to his famous brother in the salutation of his letter (Jude 1); he knew it would clearly establish his own identity.

Our glimpses of James as the leader of the church of the circumcision in Jerusalem indicate his Jewishness. At the Jerusalem conference it was James's speech that conciliated the Jewish brethren (Acts 15:13-21). James explicitly negated the demand of the Judaizers that Gentile believers be required to be circumcised, basing his decision on the divine act narrated by Peter. He also suggested the restrictive clause to the decision of the conference to avoid scandalizing Jewish believers and to remove obstacles to the evangelization of Jews everywhere. He also reminded his hearers that the prophecy concerning Israel's future was relevant for its own time (vv. 15-18).

James's spiritual sensitivity and openness led him, with Peter and John, to recognize Paul's apostolic credentials and his mission to the Gentiles (Gal. 2:6-9). James approved wholeheartedly the division agreed on in the field of labor, and devoted himself to his ministry to those of the circumcision. Apparently, he spent most of his time in Jerusalem, giving guidance to the work of the mother church. Whether James, like his brothers, also undertook preaching missions beyond Jerusalem is not certain (1 Cor. 9:5). That James sought to keep his hand upon the pulse of the spiritual life of Jewish believers beyond Palestine is clear from the salutation of his letter (James 1:1), as well as his words to Paul in Acts 21:21.

When Paul returned to Jerusalem with the collection for the Judean saints, he reported to James and the elders the progress of missionary work among the Gentiles (Acts 21:17-26). In reply, Paul was reminded of the myriads of Jewish believers who were "all zealous for the law" (v. 20). Paul was urged to conciliate their Jewish feelings, aroused by adverse reports, by adopting a plan that would show that he was not opposed to the observance of Jewish rituals. James assured Paul of his adherence to the decision of the Jerusalem conference concerning the Gentiles (v. 25), but his suggestion was motivated by his tender sympathies for the Jewish believers. It seems clear from Galatians 2:11-21 that James personally continued to observe the Jewish dietary regulations. When certain men, upon coming to Antioch, represented themselves as coming "from James" and refused to eat with the Gentile believers, their position produced a strong impact upon the Jewish believers in Antioch. It is not asserted that James sent them, but it seems clear that Peter recognized the correctness of their claim to have the support of James concerning their dietary practices. In the official letter of the Jerusalem conference, apparently largely drafted by James, it was explicitly denied that the men who caused the disturbance in the church at Antioch had been commissioned to make their demands upon the predominantly Gentile church there (Acts 15:24).

James, as a leader of the Judaic church, continued adherence to the Mosaic law, not as a means of salvation but as an accustomed way of life. The Jerusalem conference had settled the question of the relationship of Gentile believers to the law, but it said nothing about Jewish believers. They continued to live as Jews because of their loyalty to their Jewish heritage.

James was no narrow-minded Judaizer. He sided with Paul against the Judaizers at the Jerusalem conference. In the letter embodying the conference decision, he explicitly repudiated the claims of the Judaizers that they represented the position of the Jerusalem church.

James reveals himself as a "man of large influence, impressive character, and intense piety."[102] His life and character inspired deep respect, and men felt that they could lean upon him as a pillar of strength amid conflicting views. Mitton observes that "temperamentally he was cautious and conservative, and reluctant to jeopardize proved values by taking unjustified risks. But once he could see the wisdom of a radical change in policy, he could take it firmly and resolutely. Even then he felt it his duty to carry all sides in the dispute along with him, and in the interests of peace and harmony asked concessions from both sides."[103]

Josephus in his *Antiquities of the Jews* gives a simple and apparently authentic account of James's death. He reports that upon the death of the procurator, Festus, and before his successor Albinus had arrived in A.D. 62, the newly appointed young high priest Ananus II "assembled the sanhedrin of judges, and brought before them the brother of Jesus, who was called Christ, whose name was James, and some others, and when he had formed an accusation against them as breakers of the law, he delivered them to be stoned."[104] His murder was openly condemned by the masses of the Jews.[105]

An account of James by Hegesippus, a second-century Christian writer, places special emphasis upon his Jewish character and prominence within Judaism. He recounts that his life of piety gained for James the title "James the Just" and that he spent so much time in the Temple praying that his knees became as hard as a camel's. When James publicly refused to repudiate the claims of Jesus as the Messiah, the infuriated priests forced him to the Temple roof and threw him over, and since he was not killed, beat him to death with clubs.[106] The account apparently contains legendary elements and exaggerates James's ascetic practices and the scope of his influence among the unbelieving Jews.

READERS OF THE EPISTLE

Identity

The salutatory designation of the readers as "the twelve tribes scattered among the nations" (*tais dōdeka phulais tais en tō diaspora*, literally, "To the twelve tribes, those in the dispersion") has received three different interpretations.

One view is that the epistle was directed to all the Jews living outside Palestine. "The twelve tribes" was a comprehensive designation for the Jews to express the ideal unity of the covenant nation (Matt. 19:28; Acts 26:7), whereas 'the Dispersion" was a technical expression for those Jews who lived outside of Palestine (John 7:35). Thus it is held that this comprehensive Jewish designation was intended to include both Christian and non-Christian Jews. Macknight asserts that "this epistle was designated in part for the unbelieving Jews," and appeals to 4:1-10 and 5:1-6 in support, insisting that "these things could not be said of the believing Jews."[107] Also, "brethren" as a Jewish form of address would readily apply to all Jews.

Such a mixed readership for the epistle is improbable. James at once approaches his readers as "a servant of God and of the Lord Jesus Christ"; for unbelieving Jews, this would at once create an obstacle between the writer and his readers. Rather, "the whole letter assumes a community of faith between the writer and his readers."[108] James thinks of his readers as having been born again by the Word of God (1:18) and "as believers in our glorious Lord Jesus Christ" (2:1). "The noble name of him to whom you belong" (2:7) is almost certainly a reference to the name of Christ. "The Lord's coming" (5:7) as designating their hope is certainly a distinctly Christian formulation. If the writer intentionally included non-Christian Jews, it is strange that the epistle contains no missionary element intended to lead to faith in Christ.

Another view is that the opening designation must be taken figuratively to denote "Christendom in general conceived under the oecumenical symbol of ancient Israel."[109] It is held that James must be interpreted in light of 1 Peter 1:1 where the Christian readers are described as "sojourners of the Dispersion" (ASV). The parallel with 1 Peter is not exact. Peter makes no reference to the "twelve tribes" and, unlike James, uses "Dispersion" without an article (Greek) to characterize his readers as minority groups in their communities in the Roman provinces named. This proposed identification of the readers seems improbable in view of the Jewishness of the epistle of James.

The most probable view is that the epistle is addressed to Jewish Christians living outside of Palestine. The recipients are Christians whose assemblies are designated as a "synagogue" (*sunagōgēn*, 2:2) as well as a "church" (5:14). As Moo notes, "James's use of the feminine 'adultresses' (*moichalides*) in 4:4 would make no sense to anyone who was not well acquainted with the Old Testament tradition likening the Lord's covenant with his people to a marriage relationship."[110]

Monotheism, rather than polytheism, is accepted as the unquestioned basic postulate of the faith (2:19). Machen further observes:

> The faults against which the Epistle is directed—faith without works, words without deeds, censoriousness, ambition, inordinate love of teaching, toadying to wealth and position, contemptuous treatment of the poor, covetousness under the cloak of religion—are typically Pharisaic, and peculiarly Gentile faults like idolatry and impurity, which are so prominent in such an Epistle as First Corinthians, are conspicuous by their absence.[111]

We accept this view as fully harmonious with the entire picture in the epistle.

Locality

Beyond their residence in the Dispersion, the epistle gives no indication as to where the readers were located. Since the epistle was written in Greek, and reveals no firm evidence of having been translated from the Aramaic, it seems clear that the readers were Jewish Christians residing in the Greek, or Western, Dispersion. Gloag held that the readers "in all probability were chiefly congregated in the countries in closest proximity to Judea, namely Phoenicia, Syria, Cilicia, and Proconsular Asia."[112] It seems probable that the epistle was addressed to "the Jewish Christians who were driven from Jerusalem because of the persecution that resulted from the death of Stephen."[113]

The early spread of Christianity into the regions north of Palestine is evident from Acts 9:2; 11:19; 13:1. That they also went as far as Proconsular Asia is not indicated. Thus Dana concluded that "the epistle was written to Jewish Christian congregations in Syria."[114] Following Peter's departure from Jerusalem (Acts 12:23), James became the natural leader of the church in Jerusalem; he naturally would have a deep personal interest in the spiritual welfare of these scattered Jewish believers.

Relation to James

As Jews, the readers had been accustomed to look to Jerusalem for religious leadership. This background conditioned them to look for and accept doctrinal instruction and practical guidance from James, the recognized leader of the Jewish Christians at Jerusalem. The spiritual care of these Jewish Christian congregations would, in a special way, fall to James. Various members of these congregations may have been members of the Jerusalem church before persecution scattered them.

James would come into contact with representatives of these congregations as different members came to Jerusalem for business or to attend Jewish national feasts. His concern for their spiritual welfare soon disclosed disturbing conditions. Those conditions prompted James to use the epistolary method to meet those needs, a method also proposed by him at the Jerusalem conference.

PLACE AND DATE OF THE EPISTLE

Place

Those who reject the view that the epistle is the work of James the Lord's brother place it somewhere in the Gentile world. Different places are suggested. Brandon names Alexandria,[115] Henshaw and Laws point to Rome,[116] whereas Goodspeed believes that Antioch is most probable.[117] These suggestions are grounded in the view that the thought and expressions of the epistle reflect a Hellenistic rather than a Palestinian Judaism.

Acceptance of the traditional view concerning authorship carries with it the conclusion that the place of composition was Jerusalem, James's fixed place of residence. This view is consistent with the allusions to nature in the epistle. The reference to "the early and latter rain" (5:7) "is a climatic peculiarity, familiar to dwellers in Palestine, but not characteristic of areas further to the West."[118] The references to the hot winds (1:11), sweet and bitter springs (3:11), the cultivation of figs and olives (3:12), and the imagery of the nearby sea (1:6; 3:4) are all reminiscent of conditions in Palestine. Furthermore, as Moo notes, "the social conditions of first-century Palestine and Syria certainly provide an appropriate backdrop for the letter of James."[119]

Date

The dates assigned to the epistle by those who reject the traditional view vary greatly. They range between the last quarter of the first century and the middle of the second century.

The dates suggested by those who accept the Lord's brother as the author divide into two groups. Some place it near the end of his life, shortly before his martyrdom in A.D. 62; others place it early, even before the Jerusalem conference. Moffatt, who rejects the traditional view, holds that of these two dates during the life of James, the late date "presents more psychological and historical difficulties than even the earlier date."[120]

Evidence advanced for an early date is the "very slight line which appears to exist between Judaism and Christianity."[121] Aside from the lordship of Christ and the hope of His early return (1:1; 2:1; 5:8), which characterized Christianity from the very beginning, no Christian distinctives appear. Even the word "gospel," to denote the saving message of Christianity, is not used.

The primitive church order is favorable to an early dating. The reference to "the elders of the church" (5:14) is consistent with the view that they were Jewish Christian congregations organized after the pattern of the Jewish synagogues. The warning against many being teachers (3:1) seems to point to an early free type of organization.

The total absence of any reference to Gentiles and their relation to Christanity points to a time before Gentile believers constituted a prominent element in the church. The absence of any reference to circumcision is best understood as pointing to a time before this burning question arose in the church. As the result of Paul's first missionary journey, this became a critical problem and led to the Jerusalem conference (Acts 14:27–15:5). The epistle is silent concerning the social relation between Jewish and Gentile believers, a problem that was acute after the Jerusalem conference (Gal. 2:11-14). The absence of any direct mention of the "faith versus works" controversy is also best understood as pointing to a time before the outbreak of that struggle. Thus, as Moo asserts, "it is difficult to think that James could have written to Jewish Christians, some of whom probably lived in or near Antioch, without any allusion to the problem or the decision of the council."[122]

Proponents of a date just before the death of James insist that the faith-works controversy is implied in James's teaching in 2:14-26 when seen in the light of the corresponding passages in Romans and Galatians. They assume that the epistle of James is a polemic against Paul's teaching or a perversion of his teaching. If James wrote in reaction to Paul's teaching concerning justification by faith, it is replied, he surely would have expressed himself more explicitly concerning his relation to Paul. Dods insists that the discussion in James 2 "does not prove the writer's acquaintance with Paul's position. Rather, it must be accepted as evidence against such acquaintance, for it is incredible that with a knowledge of the Pauline letters he could have said just so much and no more."[123]

The teachings of James and Paul run parallel; they stand back to back, fighting error on both sides of the truth. Paul refuted the need for good works as necessary for justification before God (Rom. 4:4-5; Eph. 2:8 9); James insisted upon the need for good works by the justified as proof of the living nature of saving faith. Paul agreed with James that saving faith manifests itself in a life of good works (Gal. 5:6; Eph. 2:10).

It is more probable that Paul's opponents used the words of James, taken out of context, as a weapon against Paul's teaching of justification by faith. The epistle of James seems rather to belong to a time before the finer distinctions between "works," "good works," and "works of the law" were developed.

Advocates of a date just before the death of James insist that this date is required by "the spread of Christianity through the entire Jewish diaspora."[124] The argument has force only if the designation of the readers in 1:1 is understood as demanding such a widespread location of the readers. If a fairly restricted location for the readers is accepted, an early date for the epistle is not ruled out.

We conclude that the preponderance of the evidence points to an early date for the epistle, some time before the Jerusalem conference. The epistle may thus be dated about A.D. 46, at least not later than 49. This view makes James the earliest book in the New Testament.

THEME AND PURPOSE OF THE EPISTLE

The epistle of James is notoriously difficult to outline. This is confirmed by the great diversity of proposed outlines, which range all the way from two to twenty-five major divisions.[125] The epistle obviously does not set forth a clear structural plan heralding the logical organization of its contents. "A superficial glance at this epistle," says Hendriksen, "may easily leave the impression that every attempt to outline it must fail."[126] Its disjointed character is stressed by scholars who simply view it as a *paraenesis* (from the Greek *parainesis*, meaning "exhortation, advice"), a hortatory composition devoted to ethical instruction. "It was characteristic of *paranesis*," says Songer, "to place together in loose organization a series of exhortations without any concern to develop one theme or line of thought in the entire writing."[127] Thus, Goodspeed describes this book as "just a handful of pearls, dropped one by one into the hearer's mind."[128] Hunter asserts that "it is so disconnected, as it stands, that it is the despair of the analyst."[129]

Others, not yielding to despair, discern a measure of organization in the epistle in that James is seen as discussing a varying number of independent themes. Scroggie finds more than a dozen sermonic themes "being treated almost disconnectedly."[130] Shepherd traces "a series of eight homiletic-didactic discourses" in the book,[131] while Barker, Lane, and Michaels regard the book as consisting of "four brief homilies or messages [which] have been merged into one."[132] Some, like Martin,[133] find three major divisions in the body of the letter.

Still others hold that a unity is conferred upon the whole epistle by a single underlying theme that is ethical rather than doctrinal. Kee, Young, and Froehlich state this overall thrust as follows: "The whole epistle is concerned with one simple truth: It is not enough to 'be' a Christian, if this fact does not show in one's conduct."[134] McNeile finds the unifying thread of the epistle in "the obvious but important truth that a man's faith, his attitude toward God, is unreal and worthless if it is not effective, if it does not work practically in life."[135] Lenski well asserts, "This entire epistle deals with Christian faith and shows how this faith should be genuine, true, active, living, fruitful."[136]

James has much to say about faith, but he is not concerned with developing a theological exposition of the nature of faith. His concern is rather that believers manifest an active faith in daily life. He assumes that a saving faith accepts Jesus Christ as the all-sufficient Savior (1:1; 2:1), but his purpose is to goad his readers effectively to realize that a saving faith is a living, active faith, for "faith without works is dead" (2:20, KJV).

The root difficulty of the readers lies in a distorted conception of the nature of salvation by faith and its relation to daily life as the proving ground for the development of Christian character. Perhaps as an extreme reaction to the legalism to which they had been subjected before their acceptance of Christ, many of them acted as though knowledge of the truth was sufficient. "They conceived faith not as a living contact of the soul with God, effecting a radical change in man's life and producing deeds as its natural fruits (2:17, 18), but simply as a formal consent to certain doctrines (2:19)."[137] James recognized that his readers seriously needed to test themselves to see if their faith was a living faith or a mere lifeless profession. Accordingly, the epistle develops a basic theme: "Tests of a Living Faith." James is not interested in works apart from faith, but he is vitally concerned to show that a living faith must demonstrate its life by what it does.

Following the brief salutation (1:1), James at once plunges into his theme: "the testing of your faith" (1:3). "The problem of testing," Davids observes, "forms the thread which ties the epistle together, although like the thread in any necklace, the pattern of the specific ornaments is more often seen than the thread itself."[138] In 1:2-18, James elaborates on the theme of tests and temptations from different angles. He admonishes his oppressed and tested readers to let their tests produce their intended results as they steadfastly endure. Due to man's fallen nature, such testing may become a temptation, but such temptations are not the work of God and are contrary to God's beneficent activities in human affairs.

James sets forth a series of six basic tests whereby his readers are to test their own faith. In 1:19-27, he notes that faith must be tested by its response to the Word of God. In 2:1-13, he develops the test that faith reveals its nature by its reaction to social distinctions. Faith also must be tested by its production of works (2:14-26). Faith must further be tested by its development of self-control (3:1-18). Their manifestations of a spirit of worldliness led James to devote a long section to the matter of faith's reaction to the world and the various ways whereby worldly-mindedness manifests itself in the lives of believers (4:1–5:12). The concluding test of faith is its resort to prayer under all circumstances of life (5:13-18).

Instead of the usual epistolary conclusion, James ends abruptly with an appeal to restore those who have strayed (5:19-20). This will be an effective manifestation of the beneficial activity of a living faith in their lives.

CHARACTERISTICS OF THE EPISTLE

Omissions

This epistle is distinctive for its omissions. Christ is mentioned as the object of faith and called "our glorious Lord Jesus Christ" (2:1), but no further development concerning His Person and work is found. No mention is made of His incarnation, sufferings, death, and resurrection. Doctrines such as the atonement or the future life are not developed.

The epistle contains no reference to circumcision, the Sabbath, the Temple ritual, and the Jewish feasts, and no warning is made against pagan idolatry with its attendant evils. No indication is given of the presence of Gentile believers in their churches or the impact of Gentile institutions on their lives.

No reference is made to any personal contacts between the author and his readers. Nor does he add any thanksgiving for or commendation of them. Beyond the indirect mention of his work as a teacher (3:1), no autobiographical touches, such as those characterizing the Pauline epistles, are found. Nor does he mention any contemporary historical events or individuals.

Doctrinal Importance

The writer was not devoid of doctrinal convictions, but his pungent, practical letter did not call for their elaboration. His concern was the consistent manifestation of Christian faith in daily life. His insistence upon being "doers of the word, and not hearers only" (1:22, ASV) clearly indicates acquaintance with, and acceptance of, the doctrinal content of that "word." The epistle embodies a great deal of "compressed theology." Expressions such as "He chose to give us birth through the word of truth" (1:18); "the word planted in you" (1:21); "the perfect law that gives freedom" (1:25); "to inherit the kingdom he promised those who love him" (2:5); and "the spirit he caused to live in us" (4:5) are rich in doctrinal implications. However, these expressions underline an ethical rather than a doctrinal emphasis.

The epistle has rich indications concerning God's nature and activity. James affirms the unity of God (2:19; 4:12) but nowhere indicates the trinitarian nature of God. God is the Creator of the universe (1:17; 5:4) and of men (3:9). He is unchangeably good (1:17) and the author of all good (1:17), the source of wisdom (1:5) and prophetic revelation (5:10). He does not tempt men to evil (1:13-14) but gives them His grace (4:6-8), hears their sincere prayers (1:5-7; 5:15-16), and forgives their sins (5:15), but He will judge without mercy those who show no mercy (2:13).

The author reveals a deep if reticent faith in Christ. He was the center and foundation of the author's religious life, as is evident from the full confessional title "our Lord Jesus Christ," the mention of His glory (2:1, ASV), and his acknowledged position as His servant (1:1). His anticipation of Christ's speedy return (5:7-9) forms the basis for a call to present faithfulness and stability. Moo notes that in attributing to the returning Christ "the function of eschatological judge, James plainly implies that Jesus is God." He does so "in asserting within the same letter that 'there is one lawgiver and judge,' and that Jesus Christ, at His return, will act as the judge."[139] In doing so, Davids notes that James reflects "the usual ambivalence of the early church in that lines are not clearly defined; what is attributed to God in one case may be a function of his Christ in another."[140]

The psychological analysis of temptation and sin in 1:12-15 is a distinctive contribution of this epistle. The passage in 5:14-16 is of abiding value for the life of the churches.

Ethical Emphasis

The strong ethical emphasis of the epistle is noteworthy. Distinctive is the fact that "its ethical teaching occupies the whole Epistle and is not, as in the other cases, linked with doctrinal passages."[141] James makes no special effort to ground his ethical injunctions in doctrinal revelation. His denunciations of social injustices have about them the vehemence of the Old Testament prophets. Not without cause has James been called the Amos of the New Testament.

Relation to Christianity

The epistle of James finds its place in the early days of historic Christianity when as yet the distinction between Judaism and Christianity had not been fully brought to view. It offers us a glimpse of the Christian faith as held by Jewish believers during the early chapters of Acts.

Christianity is not thought of as an antithesis to Judaism, but rather as its true consummation. Judaism was the flower, whereas Christianity was the fruit. Christianity was the consummation of the hopes of Judaism—the final manifestation of what was latent in the Jewish revelations. Viewed in this light, the characteristics of the epistle become instructive. Thus, the epistle makes its own distinctive contribution to the New Testament canon, a contribution which we could ill afford to lose.

Style and Language

The author speaks as one conscious of his official authority and resultant responsibility (3:1). Entirely convinced of the truth and importance of his message, his tone is not defensive, and he gives no indication of any feelings that his views are under attack. His authoritative tone is reflected in his use of some 54 imperatives in the epistle's 108 verses, but his spirit is not autocratic.

His language is clear and incisive, energetic and vivid, conveying weighty thoughts in well-chosen words. His sentences are short, simple, and direct. The author reveals a touch of poetic imagination. He has a taste for similes and comparisons and prefers concrete to abstract thoughts, presenting his teaching in picturesque and dramatic form. Obviously he was a lover and keen observer of nature. Howson remarks, "There is more imagery from mere natural phenomena in the one short Epistle of St. James than in all St. Paul's Epistles put together."[142]

A singular feature of the epistle is the use of *paronomasia,* the practice of linking together clauses and sentences by the repetition of a leading word or one of its cognates. In illustration, note 1:3-6: "perseverance" (v. 3) and "perseverance" (v. 4); "not lacking anything" (v. 4) and "if any of you lacks" (v. 5); "he should ask" (v. 5) and "but when he asks" (v. 6); "not doubt" (v. 6) and "he who doubts" (v. 6). See also 1:12, 15, 21-25; 3:2-8; 4:1-3.[143]

Literary Forms

In keeping with the opening epistolary salutation, the book has traditionally been referred to as an "epistle," but it lacks the usual thanksgiving for the readers as well as the customary epistolary conclusion. It does not reveal the usual relations between writer and readers. The material may well have originally been developed by James for his didactic ministry in the church. Obviously, the material was put into its present form as destined for public reading in the congregations addressed.

Its contents connect the book with the genre of hortatory literature. It has close affinities with the Old Testament Wisdom Literature, especially Proverbs, Psalms, and other hortatory sections, as well as some Old Testament Apocrypha. It exhibits close analogies with the Sermon on the Mount and the hortatory portions of Paul's letters. Its hortatory features connect this book with the literary category known as *paraenesis*. Songer lists three common features of this type of literature: (1) ethical maxims were placed side by side without emphasis on their mutual relationship; (2) its basic unit was the imperative sentence; (3) its material was selected to serve the ethical purpose of the writer.[144] This feature of the material has led some to claim that the contents of James consists of an unstructured stringing together of moral exhortations.[145] Davids rightly holds that "the sayings and proverbs are not as unrelated or jumbled together as Dibelius believes."[146] Kistemaker asserts, "Even though these exhortations seem to be loosely connected, James shows progress and development in his presentation."[147]

It has also been pointed out that the literary features of the epistle of James show affinities with the Hellenistic diatribe.[148] Used by the Greek popular moralists, the diatribe was characterized by its use of abbreviated debate with an assumed opponent, the question-and-answer method, and frequent use of the imperative. Its use was widespread, especially in the Jewish synagogues. Although this hortatory style was well-suited to the purpose of James, the epistle cannot be justly characterized as Hellenistic diatribe. In the words of Adamson, "Whereas the diatribe is an entirely Hellenistic product, the Epistle of James is fundamentally and perpetually Semitic and biblical; the stylistic similarities between James and the diatribes are obvious enough, but like those between the synagogue sermons, they are mainly superficial. It is even more obvious that the Epistle as a whole is not a diatribe."[149]

Timeliness

The distinctiveness of the book of James from other New Testament books is a witness to the manysidedness of Christianity. Its contribution is needed to convey the full revelation of the truth in Christ.

The ethical emphasis of James conveys a vital and needed message for today. Salmon underlines the timeliness of this emphasis with the reminder of "how much of the success of Christianity was due to the pains which its teachers took in inculcating lessons which seem to us commonplace."[150] The fuller revelation of the later New Testament epistle does not invalidate James's practical message. "The combination of St. James with St. Paul is a safeguard against much error."[151] As long as there are professed Christians who are prone to separate profession and practice, the message of James will continue to be relevant.

OUTLINE OF THE EPISTLE

I. The opening salutation (1:1)
  A. The author
  B. The readers
  C. The greeting

PART 1: The Theme: The Testings of Personal Faith

II. The trials of the believer (1:2-12)
  A. The proper attitude toward trials (vv. 2-4)
    1. The attitude commanded (v. 2)
    2. The reason indicated (v. 3)
    3. The outcome to be realized (v. 4)
  B. The use of prayer amid trials (vv. 5-8)
    1. The need for wisdom (v. 5a)
    2. The request for wisdom (v. 5b)
    3. The bestowal of wisdom (vv. 5c-8)
      a. The divine response (v. 5c)
      b. The human obligation (vv. 6-8)
        (1) The necessary attitude (v. 6a)
        (2) The rejected character (vv. 6b-8)
  C. The correct attitude toward life by the tried (vv. 9-11)
    1. The attitude of the lowly brother (v. 9)
    2. The attitude of the rich (vv. 10-11)
      a. The reason for the attitude (v. 10a)
      b. The illustration from the flower (v. 11a)
      c. The application to the rich (v. 11b)
  D. The result of enduring trials (v. 12)
    1. The blessedness of endurance (v. 12a)
    2. The reward of endurance (v. 12b)

III. The nature of human temptation (1:13-16)
  A. The source of human temptation (vv. 13-14)
    1. The repudiation of a divine source (v. 13)
      a. The rejection stated (v. 13a)
      b. The rejection vindicated (v. 13b)
    2. The reality of the human source (v. 14)
  B. The consequences of yielding to temptation (v. 15)
  C. The warning against being deceived (v. 16)

IV. The activity of God in human affairs (1:17-18)
  A. The Giver of all good gifts (v. 17)
  B. The Author of the believer's regeneration (v. 18)

PART 2: The Test Marks of a Living Faith

V. Faith tested by its response to the Word of God (1:19-27)
  A. The reactions to the Word (vv. 19-20)
    1. The knowledge possessed (v. 19*a*)
    2. The reaction demanded (v. 19*b*)
    3. The reason stated (v. 20)
  B. The reception of the Word (v. 21)
    1. The stripping off of sins (v. 21*a*)
    2. The appropriation of the Word (v. 21*b*)
  C. The obedience to the Word (vv. 22-27)
    1. The demand for active obedience (vv. 22-25)
      a. The statement of the requirement (v. 22)
      b. The illustration of the requirement (vv. 23-25)
        (1) The negative portrayal (vv. 23-24)
        (2) The positive portrayal (v. 25)
    2. The nature of acceptable obedience (vv. 26-27)
      a. The futility of activity without inner control (v. 26)
      b. Acceptable service with inner control (v. 27)

VI. Faith tested by its reaction to partiality (2:1-13)
  A. The rebuke for partiality (vv. 1-4)
    1. The prohibition of partiality (v. 1)
    2. The illustration of partiality (vv. 2-3)
    3. The question of condemnation (v. 4)
  B. The result of partiality (vv. 5-11)
    1. The inconsistency in their conduct (vv. 5-7)
      a. The divine choice of the poor (vv. 5*b*-6*a*)
      b. The hostile actions of the rich (vv. 6*b*-7)
    2. The breach of God's law (vv. 8-11)
      a. The relations to this law (vv. 8-9)
        (1) The commendation upon its fulfillment (v. 8)
        (2) The sin in its violation (v. 9)
      b. The breaking of this law (vv. 10-11)
        (1) The principle stated (v. 10)
        (2) The principle illustrated (v. 11)
  C. The appeal for consistent conduct (vv. 12-13)
    1. The statement of the appeal (v. 12)
    2. The vindication of the appeal (v. 13)

VII. Faith tested by its production of works (2:14-26)
   A. The character of a useless faith (vv. 14-20)
      1. The uselessness of an inoperative faith (vv. 14-17)
         a. The question concerning inoperative faith (v. 14)
         b. The illustration of inoperative faith (vv. 15-16)
         c. The application made to inoperative faith (v. 17)
      2. The barrenness of orthodox faith without works (vv. 18-20)
         a. The assertion of an objector (v. 18*a*)
         b. The challenge to the objector (vv. 18*b*-19)
            (1) The demonstration of faith by works (v. 18*b*)
            (2) The character of faith without works (v. 19)
         c. The appeal to the objector (v. 20)
   B. The manifestation of saving faith through works (vv. 21-25)
      1. The working of Abraham's faith (vv. 21-24)
         a. The evidence of Abraham's faith (v. 21)
         b. The results of Abraham's working faith (vv. 22-23)
            (1) The perfecting of his faith (v. 22)
            (2) The fulfillment of the Scripture (v. 23*a*)
            (3) The friendship with God (v. 23*b*)
         c. The conclusion from Abraham's example (v. 24)
   C. The union of faith and works (v. 26)

VIII. Faith tested by its production of self-control (3:1-18)
   A. The significance of a controlled tongue (vv. 1-2)
      1. The responsibility of the teacher (v. 1)
      2. The evidence of the perfect man (v. 2)
   B. The need for control over the tongue (vv. 3-6)
      1. The effects of a controlled tongue (vv. 3-5*a*)
         a. The illustrations of proper control (vv. 3-4)
            (1) The horse and the bridle (v. 3)
            (2) The ship and the rudder (v. 4)
         b. The application to the boasting tongue (v. 5*a*)
      2. The damage of an uncontrolled tongue (vv. 5*b*-6)
         a. The illustration of vast damage (v. 5*b*)
         b. The nature of an uncontrolled tongue (v. 6)
   C. The untamable nature of the tongue (vv. 7-8)
      1. The ability to tame animals (v. 7)
      2. The inability to tame the tongue (v. 8)
   D. The inconsistency of the tongue (vv. 9-12)
      1. The statement of the inconsistency (vv. 9-10*a*)
      2. The rebuke for the inconsistency (v. 10*b*)
      3. The condemnation from nature's consistency (vv. 11-12)

E. The wisdom controlling the tongue (vv. 13-18)
  1. The challenge to the wise to show his wisdom (v. 13)
  2. The evidence of false wisdom in control (vv. 14-16)
    a. The manifestation of this wisdom (v. 14)
    b. The character of this wisdom (v. 15)
    c. The outcome of this wisdom (v. 16)
  3. The evidence of the true wisdom in control (vv. 17-18)
    a. The characteristics of this wisdom (v. 17)
    b. The fruit of this wisdom (v. 18)

PART 3: The Reactions of Living Faith to Worldliness

IX. The reaction of living faith to selfish strife (4:1-12)
  A. The condition manifesting worldliness (vv. 1-6)
    1. The description of the condition (vv. 1-3)
      a. The questions exposing the source (v. 1)
      b. The outcome of the condition (v. 2*a*)
      c. The reasons for the condition (vv. 2*b*-3)
    2. The rebuke for the condition (vv. 4-6)
      a. The adulterous character of worldliness (v. 4)
        (1) The question of rebuke (v. 4*a*)
        (2) The significance of their attitude (v. 4*b*)
      b. The authoritative message of Scripture (v. 5*a*)
      c. The divine response to the worldly (vv. 5*b*-6)
        (1) The yearning of the Spirit (vv. 5*b*-6*a*)
        (2) The verification from Scripture (v. 6*b*)
  B. The exhortation to the worldly (vv. 7-12)
    1. The call to return to God (vv. 7-10)
      a. The statement of the basic demand (v. 7)
        (1) Nearness to God (v. 8*a*)
        (2) Personal cleansing (v. 8*b*)
        (3) Open repentance (v. 9)
        (4) Godly humility (v. 10)
    2. The injunction against censoriousness (vv. 11-12)
      a. The statement of the prohibition (v. 11*a*)
      b. The justification for the prohibition (vv. 11*b*-12)

X. The reaction of living faith to presumptuous planning (4:13-17)
  A. The rebuke of their self-sufficient attitude (vv. 13-14)
    1. The delineation of the attitude (v. 13)
    2. The presumption in the attitude (v. 14)
  B. The indication of the proper attitude (v. 15)
  C. The evil of their present attitude (vv. 16-17)
    1. The evil of their boasting (v. 16)
    2. The sin of their inconsistency (v. 17)

XI. The reaction of living faith to injustice (5:1-11)
    A. The judgment coming upon the oppressive rich (vv. 1-6)
        1. The announcement of the judgment (v. 1)
        2. The description of the judgment (vv. 2-3)
        3. The charges against them in the judgment (vv. 4-6)
            a. The oppression of the poor laborers (v. 4)
            b. The self-indulgence of the rich (v. 5)
            c. The violence against the righteous (v. 6)
    B. The exhortation to the afflicted brethren (vv. 7-11)
        1. The call for patience in view of the parousia (vv. 7-8)
        2. The warning against blaming one another (v. 9)
        3. The examples of suffering and endurance (vv. 10-11)
            a. The example of the prophets (v. 10)
            b. The example of Job (v. 11)

XII. The reaction of living faith to self-serving oaths (5:12)

PART 4: The Reliance of Living Faith on God

XIII. The reliance of living faith on God (5:13-18)
    A. The resort to prayer in diverse circumstances (v. 13)
    B. The resort to God in sickness (vv. 14-16a)
        1. The calling of the elders to pray for the sick (v. 14)
        2. The results of the prayer of faith (v. 15)
        3. The duty of mutual confession and prayer (v. 16a)
    C. The power of a godly man's petition (vv. 16b-18)
        1. The statement concerning its power (v. 16b)
        2. The illustration of its power (vv. 17-18)

XIV. The abrupt conclusion: The restoration of the erring (5:19-20)
    A. The assumed restoration of one erring (v. 19)
    B. The assured results of the restoration (v. 20)

NOTES

1. Maurice Jones, *The New Testament in the Twentieth Century*, pp. 313-14.
2. The dates are those given in J. D. Douglas, ed., *The New International Dictionary of the Christian Church.*
3. Alfred Wikenhauser, *New Testament Introduction*, p. 474.
4. George Salmon, *An Historical Introduction to the Study of the Books of the New Testament,* p. 449.
5. J. Cantinat, "The Catholic Epistles," in A. Robert and A. Feuillet, *Introduction to the New Testament*, pp. 565-66.
6. Joseph B. Mayor, *The Epistle of St. James. The Greek Text with Introduction and Comments*, pp. xlix-l.
7. Henry M. Harmon, *Introduction to the Study of the Holy Scriptures*, pp. 711-12.
8. Douglas J. Moo, *The Letter of James,* Tyndale New Testament Commentaries, p. 17. Moo's italics.
9. For the references in Greek, see Mayor, pp. lii-liii, lvii-lxii.
10. James Moffatt, *An Introduction to the Literature of the New Testament*, p. 467; Sophie Laws, *A Commentary on the Epistle of James,* Harper's New Testament Commentaries, pp. 22-23.
11. Wikenhauser, p. 475.
12. C. Leslie Mitton, *The Epistle of James*, p. 219.
13. Moffatt, p. 468.
14. Peter Davids, *The Epistle of James*, The New International Greek Testament Commentary, p. 8.
15. Donald Guthrie, *New Testament Introduction*, p. 738.
16. Mitton, pp. 227-28.
17. James B. Adamson, *James, The Man and His Message*, p. 51.
18. Cf. Adamson, pp. 47-48.
19. Richard Heard, *An Introduction to the New Testament*, p. 165.
20. Mitton, p. 223.
21. R. J. Knowling, *The Epistle of St. James,* Westminster Commentaries, p. xxv.
22. Theodor Zahn, *Introduction to the New Testament,* 1:148. Also see the information cited there.
23. Davids, p. 9, n. 31.
24. Everett F. Harrison, *Introduction to the New Testament*, p. 386.
25. See Adamson, pp. 21-24 and note 111 on p. 22.
26. Alexander Ross, *The Epistles of James and John,* The New International Commentary on the New Testament, pp. 14-15.
27. Compare a similar listing in Ralph P. Martin, *James,* Word Biblical Commentary, pp. lxxv-lxxvi.
28. Mayor, pp. lxxxiv-lxxxvi.
29. Guthrie, p. 744.
30. Davids, p. 16.
31. See the elaborate treatment in Adamson, pp. 25-52.
32. See R. H. Gundry, "The Language Milieu of First-Century Palestine," *Journal of Biblical Literature* 83 (1964):404-8; see also J. N. Sevenster, *Do You know Greek? How Much Greek Could the First Jewish Christians Have Known?*
33. Burton Scott Easton and Gordon Poteat, "The Epistle of James," in *The Interpreter's Bible,* 12:6.
34. G. H. Rendall, *The Epistle of James and Judaic Christianity*, quoted in Adamson, p. 36.
35. Sevenster, p. 191.
36. James Hope Moulton, *A Grammar of the New Testament Greek*, 1:8.

37. A. T. Robertson, *A Grammar of the New Testament Greek in the Light of Historical Research*, p. 123.
38. Zahn, 1:111.
39. W. E. Oesterley, "The General Epistle of James," in *The Expositor's Greek Testament*, 4:393.
40. Easton and Poteat, p. 5.
41. See Adamson, p. 36, n. 12 for supporting sources.
42. Mitton, p. 228.
43. G. R. Beasley-Murray, *The General Epistles, James, 1 Peter, Jude and 2 Peter*, Bible Guides, p. 19.
44. Ibid.
45. Sevenster, p. 12.
46. Ibid, pp. 13-14.
47. Adamson, p. 37.
48. Oesterley, p. 398.
49. James Hardy Ropes, *A Critical and Exegetical Commentary on the Epistle of St. James*, The International Critical Commentary on the Holy Scriptures of the Old and New Testaments, pp. 33-34.
50. Oesterley, p. 398.
51. Heard, p. 165.
52. R. V. G. Tasker, *The General Epistle of James*, Tyndale New Testament Commentaries, p. 20.
53. Oesterley, p. 397.
54. Easton and Poteat, p. 4.
55. Harrison, p. 389.
56. Knowling, p. xiii.
57. Davids, p. 18.
58. Martin Dibelius, "James, A Commentary on the Epistle of James," in *Hermenia—A Critical and Historical Commentary on the Bible*, pp. 2, 21-22, 46.
59. For a convenient display of the material upon which the discussion is based, see Mayor, chap. 4.
60. Moffatt, p. 466.
61. Ropes, p. 23.
62. Guthrie, p. 753.
63. Moffatt, p. 472.
64. See Guthrie, Appendix C. "Epistolary Pseudepigraphy," and R. D. Shaw, *The Pauline Epistles, Introduction and Expository Studies*, pp. 477-87, and the literature cited in both.
65. A. M. Hunter, *Introducing the New Testament*, pp. 164-65; James Moffatt, *The General Epistles, James, Peter and Jude*, p. 2.
66. Guthrie, p. 755.
67. Moffatt, *Introduction to the Literature of the New Testament*, p. 474.
68. Werner Georg Kümmel, *Introduction to the New Testament*, rev. ed., p. 409.
69. A. H. McNeile, *An Introduction to the Study of the New Testament*, p. 194.
70. Easton and Poteat, vol. 12.
71. R. V. G. Tasker, *The General Epistle of James*, The Tyndale New Testament Commentaries, p. 35.
72. William Barclay, *The Letters of James and Peter*, The Daily Study Bible, p. 39.
73. Davids, p. 13.
74. Zahn, 1:111.
75. W. Boyd Carpenter, *The Wisdom of James the Just*, p. 12.
76. G. T. Manley, ed., *The New Bible Handbook*, p. 396.

77. Literally, *"James the Little,"* probably in reference to his stature, or possibly his age.

78. For a negative evaluation of the view, see E. H. Plumptre, *The General Epistle of St. James,* The Cambridge Bible for Schools and Colleges, pp. 6-10.

79. Zahn, 1:101-2; 106-7, and Ropes, p. 45.

80. "But even this view has had its (few) supporters, especially from the Spanish Roman Catholic Church—and notably Isidore of Seville (c. 636)—who claim him St. James of Compostella, as patron saint." Adamson, p. 9, n. 50.

81. John E. Steinmueller, *A Companion to Scripture Studies,* 3:324 25.

82. Wikenhauser, p. 480.

83. S. Barabas, "Alphaeus," in *The Zondervan Pictorial Encyclopedia of the Bible,* 1:118.

84. Robert Johnstone, *Lectures Exegetical and Practical on the Epistle of James,* p. 59.

85. See George E. Evans, "The Sister of the Mother of Jesus," *Review and Expositor,* October 1947, pp. 475-85, and John W. Wenham, "The Relatives of Jesus," *The Evangelical Quarterly* 47, 1 (January 1975):6-15.

86. See the discussion in R. C. H. Lenski, *The Interpretation of St. Paul's Epistles to the Galatians, to the Ephesians, and to the Philippians,* pp. 61-62; Martin, p. xxxviii.

87. Karl Heinrich Rengstorf, "Apostolos," in *Theological Dictionary of the New Testament,* 1:422-23.

88. John Calvin, *Commentaries on the Catholic Epistles,* p. 277.

89. Tasker, p. 22.

90. J. Sidlow Baxter, *Explore the Book,* 6:292-93.

91. For the history of these views, see Ropes, pp. 54-59, and Leslie R. Keylock, "Brothers of Jesus, The," in *The Zondervan Pictorial Encyclopedia of the Bible,* 1:658-66; John W. Wenham, "The Relatives of Jesus," *The Evangelical Quarterly* 47 (January 1975):6-15.

92. This is the view of the Greek Orthodox and other Eastern churches, and has some strong defenders among modern Protestant scholars. See J. B. Lightfoot, *Saint Paul's Epistle to the Galatians,* pp. 252-91; Knowling, pp. lxiv-lxvii, and H. Maynard Smith, *The Epistle of S. James Lectures,* pp. 33-37.

93. For these apocryphal sources, see Keylock, p. 660.

94. Charles Harris, "Brethren of the Lord," in *A Dictionary of Christ and the Gospels,* 1:237.

95. Keylock, p. 664.

96. This is the view of numerous modern Protestant scholars. See Samuel J. Andrews, *The Life of Our Lord upon the Earth,* pp. 111-23; John Eadie, *Commentary on the Epistle of Paul to the Galatians, Based on the Greek Text,* pp. 57-100; Mayor, in chap. 1; Johnstone, pp. 56-65, and H. E. Jacobs, "Brethren of the Lord," in *The International Standard Bible Encyclopaedia,* 1:518-20.

97. Ropes, p. 54.

98. Keylock, p. 662.

99. Jacobs, p. 520.

100. This is the established view of the Roman Catholic church. A growing minority of modern Catholic scholars reject it.

101. Addition by J. Isidor Mombert, as quoted in John Peter Lange and J. J. Van Oosterzee, "The Epistle General of James," in *Lange's Commentary on the Holy Scriptures,* 23:22.

102. Wilber T. Dayton, "James," in *The Zondervan Pictorial Encyclopedia of the Bible,* 3:395.

103. Mitton, p. 226.

104. Josephus, *Antiquities of the Jews,* 20.9.1.

105. Ibid.

106. Eusebius, *Ecclesiastical History,* 2.23.

107. James Macknight, *A New Literal Translation from the Original Greek of All the Apostolical Epistles with a Commentary and Notes,* 5:333.

108. Salmon, p. 454.

109. Moffatt, p. 464.

110. Moo, *The Letter of James*, p. 30.
111. J. Gresham Machen, *The New Testament, An Introduction to Its Literature and History*, p. 235.
112. Paton G. Cloag, *Introduction to the Catholic Epistles*, p. 48.
113. Simon J. Kistemaker, *New Testament Commentary: Exposition of the Epistles of James and the Epistles of John*, p. 18.
114. H. E. Dana, *Jewish Christianity*, p. 107.
115. S. G. F. Brandon, *The Fall of Jerusalem and the Christian Church*, p. 238.
116. T. Henshaw, *New Testament Literature in the Light of Modern Scholarship*, p. 357; Laws, *The Epistle of James*, pp. 25-26.
117. Edgar J. Goodspeed, *An Introduction to the New Testament*, p. 295.
118. Mitton, p. 236.
119. Moo, p. 35.
120. Moffatt, p. 470.
121. E. C. S. Gibson, "The General Epistle of James," in *The Pulpit Commentary*, 49:ix.
122. Moo, p. 34.
123. Marcus Dods, *An Introduction to the New Testament*, p. 193.
124. Lange and Van Oosterzee, 23:28.
125. Robert G. Gromacki, *New Testament Survey*, p. 341, and Easton and Poteat, p. 18.
126. William Hendriksen, *Bible Survey. A Treasury of Bible Information*, p. 329.
127. Harold S. Songer, "James," in *The Broadman Bible Commentary*, 12:102.
128. Goodspeed, p. 290.
129. A. M. Hunter, *Introducing the New Testament*, p. 96.
130. W. Graham Scroggie, *The Unfolding Drama of Redemption. The Bible as a Whole*, 3:290.
131. Massey H. Shepherd, Jr., "The Epistle of James and the Gospel of Matthew," *A Journal of Biblical Literature* 75 (1956):41.
132. Glenn W. Barker, William L. Lane, and J. Ramsey Michaels, *The New Testament Speaks*, p. 329.
133. Martin, *James*, pp. ciii-civ.
134. Howard Clark Kee, Franklin W. Young, and Karlfried Froehlich, *Understanding the New Testament*, p. 379.
135. McNeile, p. 189.
136. R. C. H. Lenski, *The Interpretation of the Epistle to the Hebrews and of the Epistle of James*, p. 538.
137. George A. Hadijiantoniou, *New Testament Introduction*, p. 305.
138. Davids, p. 35.
139. Moo, p. 43.
140. Davids, p. 41.
141. Guthrie, p. 767.
142. John S. Howson, *The Character of St. Paul*, p. 8, n.
143. For a full display of the evidence in the Greek, see Mayor, pp. ccxxii-ccxxiv.
144. Harold S. Songer, "The Literary Character of the Book of James," *Review and Expositor* 66 (Fall 1969):383-386.
145. Dibelius, pp. 5-11.
146. Davids, p. 23.
147. Kistemaker, p. 10.
148. Ropes, pp. 10-16.
149. Adamson, p. 104.
150. Salmon, p. 467.
151. Quoted in Mitton, p. 245.

2

I. THE OPENING SALUTATION

1:1 James, a servant of God and of the Lord Jesus Christ, to the twelve tribes scattered among the nations: Greetings.

The opening verse at once stamps this document as an epistolary communication. Since an epistle written on papyrus material was rolled up rather than folded, it was convenient to begin with an introductory statement indicating its origin and destination. The conventional epistolary salutation consisted of three parts: the name of the author in the nominative, the designation of the reader or readers in the dative, and some form of greeting to the recipient.[1] The opening salutation of James conforms to the prevailing epistolary practice of the time. Whatever may have been the initial use of the material used in this epistle, it is clear that the author employed it to fulfill an epistolary purpose.

A. THE AUTHOR

Our English monosyllabic "James" blurs the fact that the author bore the familiar name of the Hebrew patriarch Jacob. The name was common among Palestinian Jews during the first century. The Septuagint transliterates the patriarch's name as *Iākob*, and this form is always retained in the New Testament when the reference is to the patriarch personally.[2] Whenever a contemporary individual with this Hebrew name appears in the New Testament story, it is always given in the Hellenized form *Iakōbos*, the terminal *-os* being simply the Greek nominative case ending.[3] The older Latin translated this name as *Iacobus*, which in turn was altered to *Jacobus,* whereas in later popular Latin *Jacomus* came to be used as an alternative form.[4] From this evolved our English monosyllabic "James." Thus, in English we have two names, Jacob and James, both stemming from the common Hebrew name Jacob. Our English versions always render the Greek form *Iakōbos* as James.[5]

The author's self-identification, "a servant of God and of the Lord Jesus Christ," indicates only his scriptural relationship and says nothing of his human relationships or of his ecclesiastical position. This is understandable and significant if, as we hold,[6] the author was "the Lord's brother" and the leader

51

of the early Christian church in Jerusalem. He prefers to speak only of his status as a Christian man. When after His resurrection Jesus appeared to James (1 Cor. 15:7), and James became convinced of His true nature as the Messiah, the spiritual identity of the One whom he had previously regarded as his physical brother became so important to him that the physical relations receded into the background. While others in the church might have referred to him as "the Lord's brother" (Gal. 1:19), he preferred to speak of himself as a "servant" rather than the "brother" of the Lord Jesus Christ. Mayor observes:

> We find here an example of the refusal "to know Christ after the flesh" which appears in ii. 1; the same willingness to put himself on a level with others which appears in iii. 1,2.[7]

James also refrains from any claim to apostleship. Galatians 1:19 has been taken to mean that Paul called James an apostle. This interpretation of Paul's words is questionable. He was not an apostle in the technical sense of the term. Although James did have the apostolic qualification of being an eyewitness of the resurrection (Acts 1:22; 1 Cor. 15:7), he did not accompany Jesus during His public ministry as an acknowledged disciple. He was present when Matthias was chosen to fill the place of Judas (Acts 1:14-15), but the other apostles did not consider James to have the necessary qualifications (Acts 1:21, 23). Winkler further notes that James "did not perform the proper apostolic work: he was not *sent forth* to testify to the resurrection of Jesus, but remained at Jerusalem."[8] Yet it may be that James, as one to whom the risen Lord had appeared, was at times spoken of as an apostle in the wider sense of the term. Certainly, James felt "no need of any such title to command the attention of Christians, among whom he exercised unquestioned authority."[9]

The appositional phrase "a servant of God and of the Lord Jesus Christ" does not actually serve to establish the identity of the writer to his readers, because it does not distinguish him from other Christian workers named James. Those who did not already know his identity would not be able to determine just who he was from these words. Rather, this modest self-designation implies that the writer's personal identity already would be known to his readers. By contrast, Jude felt it desirable to establish his identity by noting that he was "the brother of James" (Jude 1).

In the original phrase, contrary to our conventional English order, the term "servant" stands at the end: "of God and of the Lord Jesus Christ a servant." This order makes prominent the identity of his heavenly Masters. For James, the fact of this relationship was of primary importance. He could conceive of no higher honor than being the servant of such Masters. He thus stresses his personal, spiritual relationships. The term "servant" does "not denote any outstanding qualification other than the mere expression of his utter devotion and total subservience to his Master."[10]

In calling himself a "servant," James used the common Greek term *doulos*, which means a slave, a bondservant, one who is in a permanent relation of servitude to another. Bennett remarks that the term emphasizes "the supreme and absolute authority of the master and the entire submission of the slave."[11] Among the Greeks, with their strong sense of personal freedom, the term carried a degrading connotation. This is likewise true for the modern English reader. In making an English rendering, there is some difficulty in seeking to retain the original force of the term while avoiding undesirable modern overtones. Literal renderings such as "bond-servant,"[12] "bondman,"[13] or "slave,"[14] while retaining the thought of being bound to a master and obligated to do his will, for the modern reader also carry the implications of forced enslavement. For James, the use of the term did not convey the thought of an unwanted, compelled servitude. Most of our modern English versions continue to use "servant" to avoid implications of involuntary servitude,[15] yet this term does not adequately convey the basic picture of the master-slave relationship present in the original.

The early church was well aware of the true nature of the master-slave relationship. Both Paul and Peter gave instructions to believers who were the possession of human masters (Eph. 6:5-8; Col. 3:22-24; 1 Peter 2:18-21). Christianity found the term *doulos* appropriate in setting forth the essence of the believer's true relationship to God. It aptly set forth the Christian consciousness that believers are totally dependent upon God, belong wholly to Him, and are convinced that His will is the only true rule for all of His people. Because believers voluntarily and joyously accepted this relationship, the term was commonly used in the New Testament of the believer's relationship to God without any implication of involuntary servitude. For them the term did not suggest any degradation, but only their total surrender to their spiritual Master. Stevenson points to this word *doulos* as another one of those words which Christianity has "transmuted into the most glorious key-notes of the Gospel."[16]

Adamson points out that "for the Jew, if not for the Greek, there was nothing servile in the relation of man to God" in the term "servant."[17] The relationship implied in the term was sufficiently elastic to cover the service that a son gives his father as well as that which a master requires of his slave. Prompted by his faith and love toward his heavenly Master, James, in identifying himself as "a servant of God and of the Lord Jesus Christ," presented himself to his readers as representative of a pious Jewish Christian. It was because of his recognized personal piety that James assumed the right to address his readers, his spiritual brothers, who likewise had acknowledged themselves as the servants of these heavenly masters. This appositional description places James on a level with his readers and is an expression of Christian brotherhood in whose interest James felt prompted to write.

James reverently refers to Jesus under His full name, "the Lord Jesus Christ." All three nouns are used without an article as proper names. He is named elsewhere in this epistle only in 2:1, where the confessional "our" is added. The reticence of James concerning Jesus Christ is in keeping with the fact that in the words of James recorded in Acts 15:13-21 and 21:20-25, Jesus' name is not mentioned.

All three names serve to unfold the true nature of this Master. "Jesus" is His human name. It was the name given Him before His birth and speaks of His saving work in incarnation (Matt. 1:21). *Iēsous* is the Greek form of the Hebrew name *Joshua* meaning "salvation." This name embodies the entire gospel story concerning the historic Man of Nazareth. "Christ" (*Christos*) is the Greek rendering for the Hebrew "Messiah" (Ps. 2:2; Acts 4:26), both meaning "the anointed one." For Jewish readers, the term *Christos*, whether placed before or after "Jesus," meant that He was the fulfillment of the Old Testament messianic promises. For James and the early church, the name "Jesus Christ" embodied the faith that the messianic redemption was realized in the incarnate Jesus.

Thus, "Jesus is the Christ" became the earliest Christian confession (Acts 2:36; 3:20; 5:42; cf. John 20:30-31). This faith arose in the hearts of His disciples from their associations with Jesus during His earthly ministry (John 1:41; Matt. 16:16) and received unshakable confirmation from His resurrection and ascension (Acts 2:32 36). The Christian church proclaimed this incarnate and risen Savior as its "Lord" (*kurios*). As her Savior and Master, He received her full allegiance and whole-hearted service. For Jewish readers, the title "Lord" carried with it implications of deity. In the Septuagint, it is the translation for the ineffable Name (Yahweh) and speaks of His sovereignty. Various quotations from the Old Testament referring to Jehovah are applied directly to Jesus in the New Testament, where they were "understood of the new Lord of the Christian church."[18] The term *kurios* occurs fourteen times in this epistle (1:1, 7, 12; 2:1; 4:10, 15; 5:4, 7, 8, 10, 11 twice, 14, 15). Only here and in 2:1 does James connect it directly with Jesus Christ, and it is not always clear in the other places whether his reference is to God or to Christ. Easton insists that apart from 1:1, 2:1, and 5:14, "in all the other eleven instances in James—including even 5:7, 8—it is God, not Christ, who is the Lord."[19] Lenski disputes this claim and holds that "only in 5:4 in the combination 'Lord Sabaoth,' does James use 'Lord' as a designation for 'God'; elsewhere he writes 'God' when he means God."[20] The reference must be decided in light of the context, but this very uncertainty concerning the intended reference in the usage of the term underlines that, for James, there was no sharp line of distinction between Jesus Christ and God. Davids notes that this reveals "the usual ambivalence of the early church in that lines are not clearly defined; what is attributed to God in one case may be a function of his Christ in another. Yet it is a consistent picture."[21]

B. THE READERS

James addressed his message "to the twelve tribes scattered among the nations." In the original (*tais dōdeka phulais tais en tē diaspora*) the use of the repeated article with the prepositional phrase "to the twelve tribes, those in the Dispersion" stresses that the readers belonged to the twelve tribes, yet were located in the Dispersion in contrast to the Palestinian Holy Land.

"The twelve tribes" is a Jewish expression denoting the Jewish people as a whole (Matt. 19:28; Acts 26:7). While precise tribal divisions had often been lost, in New Testament times many Jews were able to establish their tribal descent (Matt. 1:1-16; Luke 1:5, 2:36; Phil. 3:5). The expression "the twelve tribes" was used to indicate Jewish faith in the unity of the people of Israel "as being ecclesiastically the exclusive representatives of the ancient Israel."[22] The Old Testament prophets announced the reunion of Israel and Judah under the coming Messiah (Isa. 11:11-13; Jer. 3:18; 50:4; Ezek. 37:15-23; Zech. 10:6-12), and there was a strong Jewish expectation that when the Messiah came, He would reestablish the chosen people in their correct tribal divisions (Ezek. 48:1-29).[23] Although the Jews clung to the belief of the solidarity of the people of Israel, they were deeply aware of the absence of visible unity. Various displacements befalling them had scattered them far and wide. This fact is recognized in the NIV rendering "scattered among the nations" of the Greek world (*en tē diaspora*, "in the Dispersion"). "The Dispersion" had become a technical term used to denote the Jews living outside Palestine, scattered in the Gentile world. The term appears twice elsewhere in the New Testament, in John 7:35 in the literal meaning and in 1 Peter 1:1 in a figurative sense. The term is a compound form, composed of the preposition *dia*, basically meaning "through," and the noun *spora*, "a sowing." The term thus conveys the picture of the scattering abroad of the Jews as seed.

The scattering of the Jews into all parts of the known world was a well-known fact. Those Jews who resided east of Palestine, and among whom the Aramaic language had commonly displaced the Hebrew, were thought of as the Eastern Dispersion. By contrast, the Western Dispersion denoted the Jews living in the Greek-speaking part of the world. This included Egypt, Syria, Asia Minor, Greece, and even Rome.

Oesterley asserts that there had developed "a real distinction between the Jews of the Dispersion and the Palestinian Jews. The latter were for the most part peasants or artisans, while the former congregated almost wholly in cities and were practically all traders (cf. iv. 13)."[24] Through their contacts with other people, the Jews of the Dispersion generally had a larger outlook on life and a greater openness to new ideas, whereas their contacts with the surrounding paganism generally made them more strongly convinced of the immeasurable superiority of Judaism over the pagan religions. As the gospel spread in the Gentile world, it was seen that wherever there was a colony of Jews with their synagogue, their message of ethical monotheism had become a strong preparatory force for Christianity. Scattered abroad as seed, they had "become the seed of a future harvest."[25]

James does not indicate the intended scope of his readers in the Dispersion. Was he addressing readers throughout the Dispersion or some restricted part of the Dispersion? Further, did he intend his wording of his readership to be taken literally or figuratively? His expression is capable of varied interpretations. Adamson notes that the designation of the recipients "has been taken to refer, e.g., to (1) unconverted Jews, implying a later Christianized ascription; (2) the Jewish nation; (3) Gentile Christians (see 1 Peter 1:1), perhaps of the third or fourth generation; (4) Christian Jews; (5) the church as the new Israel."[26]

Some of these varied views are reflected even in the renderings of our modern English versions. The *American Standard Version,* "to the twelve tribes which are of the Dispersion," is representative of those translations which render the words of James more or less literally. A figurative interpretation of the words of James is boldly introduced into the rendering of the popular modern version *Good News for Modern Man, Today's English Version*: "Greetings to all God's people, scattered over the whole world." By contrast, the rendering of Lilly, "to the Jewish Christians dispersed throughout the world," interprets the Dispersion literally and takes it as limited to the Jewish believers.[27] We agree with Lilly's interpretation of the identity of the readers as being Jewish Christians but question his implied scope of the address. The *New English Bible* interprets the intended scope of the Dispersion as total in rendering "to the Twelve Tribes dispersed throughout the world," but this is probable only if the address is taken figuratively to denote the Christian church.

We hold that from the contents of the epistle, it is essential to accept that the recipients of the letter were Jewish Christians. Further, we hold that the readers addressed were a very limited part of the total Dispersion and that most probably they were located in the area just north of Palestine.[28] The NIV "scattered among the nations" implies a broader scope.

C. THE GREETING

The greeting to the readers consists of one word: *chairein* ("greetings"), which is simply the present active infinitive of the verb *chairō,* meaning "to rejoice, be glad." This verb in the imperative was regularly used in Greek salutations, as in Luke 1:28 or Matthew 26:49.[29] In the greeting in letters, the infinitive was commonly used. It is possible that this epistolary infinitive implies the addition of a verb, such as *legei,* "he says."[30] This is the view suggested in the margin of the *American Standard Version,* "wishes joy." More probably, the infinitive was regarded as imperatival. Moulton notes that the infinitive with imperative force "was familiar in Greek, especially in laws and in maxims."[31] It was the common form in secular Greek letters, as shown by papyrus letters from all periods. The apocryphal books show that it was in common use among Greek-speaking Jews.[32] None of the other New Testament epistles uses this imperatival infinitive in the opening salutation, but it is used in the letter of the Jerusalem Conference preserved in Acts 15:23-29 and probably written by James. (It also appears in the letter written by the Roman chiliarch Claudius Lysias, as given in Acts 23:26-30.) James was simply using the conventional greeting of his time. The familiar Christian greeting found in the Pauline epistles, "Grace and peace to you from God the Father and the Lord Jesus Christ" (2 Thess. 1:2), was not known before Paul's day and probably was his own inspired coinage. But this writer seems totally unaware of that fuller Christian greeting.

Mayor sees in this greeting a strong argument against the view that the book of James is pseudonymous and written near the end of the century. He asks:

> Is it conceivable that, after the introduction of the fuller Christian salutation, any one professing to write in the name of the most honoured member of the church at Jerusalem would have fallen back on the comparatively cold and formal *chairein?*[33]

We agree that the form of the salutation strongly points to an early date for this epistle.[34]

When the verb *chairō* is used as a greeting, its conventional force seems well represented by our term "greetings." The root meaning of the word is "joy." In view of his use of the noun *charan* ("joy") in verse 2, it may well be that James intended his form of greeting to prepare the readers for the discussion of joy amid trials that immediately follows. Thus, perhaps it is another instance of the use of *paranomasia* in the epistle, a feature clearly seen in the following verses (1:2-6).[35]

This three-part opening salutation, consisting of just fifteen words in the original, is one of the shortest of all the New Testament epistles.[36] Its brevity stands in striking contrast to some of Paul's expanded salutations, as, for example, those in Romans (1:1-7) or Galatians (1:1-5). This conciseness is characteristic of James.

NOTES FOR
James 1:1

1. "The introduction to the epistle, then, is the equivalent of an envelope that shows the names and addresses of sender and recipients." Simon J. Kistemaker, *New Testament Commentary: Exposition of the Epistle of James and the Epistles of John*, p. 28.

2. *Iakōb* occurs twenty-five times in the New Testament in reference to the patriarch, and twice in Matthew's genealogy (1:15-16) of Jacob the father of Joseph, the husband of Mary.

3. This Hellenized form occurs forty-two times in the Greek New Testament.

4. "James," in *The Oxford English Dictionary*, 5:549.

5. David H. Stern in his recent translation, *Jewish New Testament*, intended to express its Jewishness, renders "From: *Ya'akon*, a slave of God and of the Lord *Yeshua* the Messiah," p. 311.

6. See Introduction.

7. Joseph B. Mayor, *The Epistle of St. James. The Greek Text with Introduction, Notes and Comments*, p. 29.

8. Edwin T. Winkler, "Commentary on the Epistle of James," in *An American Commentary on the New Testament*, p. 13.

9. F. W. Farrar, *The Early Days of Christianity*, p. 324.

10. R. Duane Thompson, "The Epistle of James," in *The Wesleyan Bible Commentary*, 6:205.

11. W. H. Bennett, *The General Epistles, James, Peter, John, and Jude,* The Century Bible, A Modern Commentary, p. 145.

12. NASB.

13. J. N. Darby, *The "Holy Scriptures," A New Translation from the Original Languages.*

14. Berkeley; Montgomery; Williams; and Goodspeed.

15. Among them, RSV; NEB; TEV; NIV; Moffatt; Cuthbert Lattey, *The New Testament in the Westminster Version of the Sacred Scriptures*, and William F. Beck, *The Holy Bible, An American Translation.*

16. Herbert F. Stevenson, *James Speaks for Today*, p. 12.

17. James B. Adamson, *James, the Man and His Message*, p. 7.

18. William F. Arndt and F. Wilbur Gingrich, *A Greek-English Lexicon of the New Testament and Other Early Christian Literature*, p. 460.

19. Burton Scott Easton and Gordon Poteat, "The Epistle of James," in *The Interpreter's Bible*, 12:21.

20. R. C. H. Lenski, *The Interpretation of the Epistles to the Hebrews and of the Epistle of James*, p. 540.

21. Peter H. Davids, *The Epistle of James, A Commentary on the Greek Text*, p. 41.

22. Bennett, p. 146.

23. James Hardy Ropes, *A Critical and Exegetical Commentary on the Epistle of St. James*, The International Critical Commentary, pp. 118-19.

24. W. E. Oesterley, "The General Epistle of James," in *The Expositor's Greek Testament*, 4:419-20.

25. Brooke Foss Westcott, *The Gospel According to St. John, The Authorized Version with Introduction and Notes*, p. 122.

26. Adamson, p. 11, n. 64.

27. Joseph L. Lilly in James A. Kleist and Joseph L. Lilly, *The New Testament Rendered from the Original Greek*, pt. 2, p. 593.

28. See Introduction.

29. In 2 John 10-11, the verb of greeting is in the infinitive because of the indirect discourse.

30. A. T. Robertson, *A Grammar of the Greek New Testament in the Light of Historical Research*, p. 394.

31. James Hope Moulton, *A Grammar of New Testament Greek*, 1:179.

32. See the references in Ropes, p. 128.

33. Mayor, p. 31.

34. See Introduction.

35. See Introduction.

36. Hebrews and 1 John have no epistolary salutation. Even the abbreviated salutation in First Thessalonians, according to the critical text, is longer. Technically, the salutation of 3 John, if limited to v. 1, is the shortest (ten words), but the form is irregular and, according to Paul's practice, vv. 1-4 would have composed the three-part salutation.

PART 1 (1:2-18)

THE TESTINGS OF PERSONAL FAITH

Following the concise opening salutation, James at once plunges into a discussion of his theme. Absent is the customary thanksgiving to God for his readers; nor does James offer a prayer for their needs. The epistle contains no indication of his personal contacts with his readers. The approach throughout is direct, and his words are incisive and to the point. When his final admonition has been delivered, he ends as abruptly as he began.

His mention of "faith" in his opening sentence (vv. 2-3) makes it clear that, for James, faith is central to the Christian life and is its true energizing principle. It has been said that Paul was the apostle of faith, John the apostle of love, and James the apostle of works, but this simplistic analysis fails to do justice to all three of them. It is a misinterpretation of the thrust of the epistle of James to say that his chief concern is works. For James, there can be no vital Christianity apart from a living faith. James is concerned with the fact that Christian faith is more than mere profession. Throughout the epistle, his concern is "to impress on his readers the fact that Christianity is not a *faith* merely, but through the power of faith, a *life*."[1] A saving faith is a living and active faith; it proves that it is alive by what it does.

The reality of a living faith is demonstrated by its reaction under adversity. "Faith is such a vital matter to the children of God that it must be put to the test, first in order to prove that it is genuine, and second, to purge and strengthen it."[2] The central thrust of the epistle of James is his treatment of various tests of a living faith. "The testing of your faith" (v. 3) may well be taken as the indication of its theme.

Such a proving that faith is genuine naturally calls for a discussion of the character of such a testing process. He therefore begins with a discussion of the "trials" (*peirasmoi*) that believers inevitably encounter. The noun *peirasmos* denotes a testing being directed toward an end, to discover the nature or quality of the object or person tested. The verbal form *peirazō* denotes the action of putting something or someone to the test. Such a test may be applied with either a good or bad intention. In a good sense, the test may be applied in order to demonstrate the strength or good quality of the object tested. When the testing is applied with the evil aim that the object will be led to fail under testing, then the thought of temptation comes in. Since it is a melancholy fact that men often break down under the testings of life, the term *peirasmos* is often used with the meaning of temptation, a solicitation to evil. Under either meaning, the term "has always the idea of probation associated with it."[3] Both the noun and the verb are rare in secular Greek,[4] but they are common in the Septuagint and the New Testament. Since the Scriptures are concerned with moral values, the concept of testing is an essential one in the Bible.

In human experience, the two aspects of testing and temptation may be closely related. That which is intended as a test may in fact become a temptation for the person tested because of his inner response to the situation. Well aware of this close connection in actual experience, James deals with both aspects of *peirasmoi* in this opening section of his epistle. In verses 2-12 he deals with the nature and use of external tests that come to the believer in daily life, while in verses 13-16 he deals with the experience of temptation to evil. In verses 17-18 he shows that God's beneficent activities toward the believer establish that He cannot be associated with *peirasmos* in the sense of solicitation to evil. God does test the faith of His people, but He does not allure them to evil.

NOTES FOR
Part 1

1. Robert Johnstone, *Lectures Exegetical and Practical on the Epistle of James*, p. 71.
2. Philip Mauro, *James: The Epistle of Reality*, p. 31.
3. See "*Peirazō*" in James Hope Moulton and George Milligan, *The Vocabulary of the Greek Testament Illustrated from the Papyri and Other Non-Literary Sources*, p. 501.
4. Heinrich Seesemann, "*Peira, peiraō, peirazō, peirasmos*," in *Theological Dictionary of the New Testament*, 6:23-24.

3

II. THE TRIALS
OF THE BELIEVER

1:2-12 Consider it pure joy, my brothers, whenever you face trials of many kinds, ³because you know that the testing of your faith develops perseverance. ⁴Perseverance must finish its work so that you may be mature and complete, not lacking anything. ⁵If any of you lacks wisdom, he should ask God, who gives generously to all without finding fault, and it will be given to him. ⁶But when he asks, he must believe and not doubt, because he who doubts is like a wave of the sea, blown and tossed by the wind. ⁷That man should not think he will receive anything from the Lord; ⁸he is a double-minded man, unstable in all he does.

⁹The brother in humble circumstances ought to take pride in his high position. ¹⁰But the one who is rich should take pride in his low position, because he will pass away like a wild flower. ¹¹For the sun rises with scorching heat and withers the plant; its blossom falls and its beauty is destroyed. In the same way, the rich man will fade away even while he goes about his business.

¹²Blessed is the man who perseveres under trial, because when he has stood the test, he will receive the crown of life that God has promised to those who love him.

In these verses James deals with the term *peirasmoi* in its good sense of testing: the testings of believers. He insists that they must have a proper attitude towards trials (vv. 2-4), urges that they resort to prayer for wisdom amid their trials (vv. 5-8), reminds those being tried that they must have a correct estimate of life (vv. 9-11), and states the result of enduring trials (v. 12).

A. THE PROPER ATTITUDE TOWARD TRIALS (vv. 2-4)

The opening words of James "are like an unexpected bugle call, and the bugler sounds an heroic note."¹ He urges his readers to assume a joyous attitude amid their trials (v. 2), indicates the reason for the commanded attitude (v. 3), and delineates the outcome to be realized (v. 4).

1. The Attitude Commanded (v. 2)

"Consider it pure joy, my brothers, whenever you face trials of many kinds." The arresting command "Consider it pure joy" indicates the attitude called for. The aorist imperative conveys a sense of urgency, while the tense points to a definite action. The use of the aorist tense rather than the present, which we might have expected, may mean that as a definite act they are to adopt this as their attitude toward their trials, or the thought may be that it must be their attitude as each separate experience of testing is encountered. The former is probably the intended meaning, bidding them once and for all to adopt this as their attitude toward trials. The verb "consider" (*hēgēsasthe*) means "to consider, deem, regard as" and calls for a mental evaluation adopted as the result of due deliberation, the conscious acceptance of a definite inner attitude. They are to regard their experiences of testing as the ground for "pure joy" (*pasan charan*, "all joy"), which stands emphatically at the beginning, "all joy account it" (Rotherham).[2]

"All joy" has been taken to mean joy in the highest degree, "count yourselves supremely happy" (*New English Bible*); others take it as meaning unmixed joy, "consider it pure joy" (*New International Version*). So understood, the meaning is "not that suffering is the occasion for all the joy there is, but that it should occasion only joy, unmixed with other reactions."[3] New Testament usage of "all" (*pas*) tended to support the latter meaning (Phil. 2:29; 1 Tim. 2:2; Titus 2:10; 3:2; 1 Pet. 2:18). It is probable that James intended "all joy" to balance "trials of many kinds," with all the varied testings to have their counterpart in every kind of joy. "The joys are as varied as the manifold tests themselves."[4] The command of James seems clearly rooted in the teaching of Jesus (Matt. 5:10-12; Luke 6:22-23).

Before finishing his startling command, James inserts a personal address: "my brothers." This form of direct address, a favorite with James,[5] marks his personal feelings toward his readers. He accepts them as members with him of one spiritual community, as fellow members of the family of God. Therefore, "what James has to say applies only to born-again Christians."[6] The possessive "my" expresses his own consciousness of his equality with them as brothers and that as their brother he is concerned about their trials. Farrar remarks, "The perpetual recurrence of this word shows that the wounds which St. James inflicts are meant to be the faithful wounds of a friend."[7] He eagerly draws his readers to himself as he seeks to minister to their needs. In the pagan world, the term was used of a fellow member in some restricted secular group or of members of a particular religious society. Among the Jews, the term was used to denote a fellow Israelite. The early Christians readily employ the term as expressive of their consciousness that as believers in Christ they were all members of one spiritual family. The use of this designation in the early church was apparently stimulated by the teaching of Jesus in Mark 3:35 and Matthew 23:8.

The attitude called for is to be displayed "whenever you face trials of many kinds." As Blue notes, "Most people count it all joy when they escape trials. James said to count it all joy in the midst of trials."[8] Here the rendering "temptations" (KJV; ASV) is rather unfortunate and confusing.

The context makes it clear that the term (*peirasmoi*) is not now used with the sense of solicitation to evil but rather in the objective sense of trials. The reference cannot be to inner temptations to sin as in 1:13-14, since such experiences could not be urged as a ground for rejoicing.

James assumes that his readers will readily distinguish the intended meaning of the term. This objective sense of the term as denoting testings or trials of daily life is evident from the verb rendered "face" as denoting undesirable events that assail us from without. The verb (*peripiptō*) occurs only twice elsewhere in the New Testament. In Luke 10:30, Jesus used it of the man who went down from Jerusalem to Jericho and "fell among" thieves. In this compound verb, the preposition *peri*, "around," pictures the man as being surrounded by the thieves on all sides, with no way of escape, and thus unavoidably "falling" victim to their assaults. It also occurs in Acts 27:41 of the ship that unexpectedly encountered a sandbar where two seas met, and running into it, was shipwrecked.

The expression of James indicates that such trials are sure to come, for he says "whenever," not *if*. The aorist tense expresses our encounter with such trials as individual experiences. The use of the indefinite temporal construction (*hotan* with the subjunctive),[9] "whenever ye [may] fall into," indicates that they tend to come at an undetermined time. Their arrival cannot be pinpointed beforehand. They may be expected at anytime.

It is further suggested that these trials are unavoidable. Like the thieves who surrounded the man on the Jericho road, such adverse situations unexpectedly surround the believer with no escape. The compound verb, which pictures these trials as encircling the believer, implies that the reference is not to minor little irritations but to larger adverse experiences that cannot be avoided. The reference is to various adversities, afflictions, and calamities that are hard to bear. The reference is not specifically to religious persecutions, although they were a prominent part in the experiences of the readers. Martin, indeed, holds that these trials "are better understood as signs of oppression and persecution endured for one's religious convictions."[10] James's expression "trials of many kinds" seems best understood to include both "the difficulties that are common to all people as well as the specific adversities that Christians must face as a result of their faith."[11]

The adjective "of many kinds" (*poikilois*) does not describe the great number but the diversity or manifold forms of the trials. In the original, prominence is given to this variety by the position of the adjective at the end of the clause and by separation from its noun, "whenever into trials ye may fall of many kinds." The original meaning of the adjective was "manycolored, variegated," like Joseph's coat of many colors (Gen. 37:3, LXX). It was used of stones of many colors or of a piece of cloth that that had been embroidered with many different colors. The adjective thus stresses the great variety or diversity of the trials that befall believers. In Matthew 4:24 it is used of the great variety of torments of body and mind among the people whom Jesus healed; in Hebrews 2:4 it is used of the variety of the manifestations of God's power in connection with the preaching of the gospel. God's grace is sufficient for every trial, whatever its color.

Whenever such trials strike, James calls upon his readers to "consider it pure joy." "To have joy," Epp well remarks, "does not necessarily mean we will be hilarious and laughing about the trials we are experiencing, but it means we will have a deep-seated confidence that God knows what He is doing and that the results will be for His glory and our good."[12] It is occasionally asserted that James asks his readers to *enjoy* their trials, but James did not say that. He was too realistic to make such a demand. He well knew that when such experiences strike, they are not joyous but grievous (Heb. 12:11). He did not say that they must *feel* it all joy or that trials *are* all joy. James was not inculcating a stoic resignation, which when engulfed by trials wears a forced smile and seeks to ignore the pain. Rather, James is calling for a positive Christian attitude toward trials that he views as opportunities, under God's grace, for growth and development in the Christian life. Christian faith must apprehend that beneficial results are to be derived from such experiences and so accept them as occasions for rejoicing.

While believers should look at the bright side of their trials, such trials are not to be sought or needlessly rushed into. The call of James is consistent with the prayer that Jesus taught His disciples, "Lead us not into temptation" (Matt. 6:13, KJV). The words of James apply whenever his readers "face" such trials unsought. Mayor well remarks:

> One who is conscious of his own weakness may without inconsistency pray that he may be kept out of temptation, and yet, when he is brought into it through no fault of his own but by God's providential ordering, he may feel such trust in Divine support as to rejoice in an opportunity of proving his faithfulness.[13]

2. The Reason Indicated (v. 3)

James at once adds his reason for his surprising command: "Because you know that the testing of your faith develops perseverance." Motyer notes, "James comes to us as one facing, not concealing, the facts . . . . his appeal is not for the adoption of a superficial gaiety but for a candid assessment of certain truth."[14] The participle rendered "because you know" (*ginōskontes*, "knowing") is in grammatical agreement with the imperative "consider" (v. 2) and introduces the knowledge that enables them to evaluate their trials as occasions for rejoicing. The present tense participle indicates that his readers were not ignorant of the truth being set forth but had to continue to realize it in personal experience. The verb used (*ginōskō*) suggests a "knowledge grounded in personal experience."[15] As they adopt the attitude called for amid their trials, they will come to personal realization "that the testing of your faith develops perseverance."

The term "testing" (*to dokimion*) has been differently understood. As a noun its usual meaning is "a means or instrument of testing." Their trials are the agents that test their faith and reveal its true nature. In the words of Johnstone,

> Affliction lets down a blazing torch for him into the depths of his own nature—and he sees many things which he little expected to see. He finds his faith weak where he thought it strong, his views dim where he thought them clear.[16]

And these trials lead to a purging and purifying of this faith.

Others, on the basis of papyrus usage, hold that the original is not a noun but an articular adjective used as an abstract substantive to denote "that which is approved, genuine" by testing.[17] This view is represented in the translation of C. B. Williams, "for you surely know that which is genuine in your faith." Then the meaning is that which is genuine or approved in their faith, as revealed by testing, produces perseverance. And this revelation of the nature of their faith, as precious like gold, is a true reason for a joyous attitude amid trials. We accept "genuine" as the meaning in 1 Peter 1:7, the only other occurrence of the precise term in the New Testament, but prefer to retain the idea of "testing" in James as better suited to the context.

"Your faith" recognizes the readers as fellow believers with James. The use of the article with "faith" (*tēs pisteōs*, "the faith") makes it specific, and in light of verse 1 can only mean their faith as Christians. The fuller statement in 2:1 completely establishes that Christian faith is in view. Clearly "the faith" is not used objectively to denote the content of the gospel, but subjectively to denote their personal acceptance of, and assured confidence in, the gospel. This initial reference to "faith" in this epistle[18] makes clear that James held faith to be of central importance in the Christian life, the very foundation of a vital relationship to God. It is therefore unlikely that in the famous discussion in 2:14-26 of the relationship of works to faith, James had any intention of depreciating the importance and function of faith in the Christian life.

James asserts that the testing of their faith has an impact upon the very core of their spiritual being. That testing process "develops perseverance." The present tense, "develops" (*katergazetai*), pictures it as a continuing process. The verb is an emphatic compound form. The simple verb *ergazetai* ("worketh"), used in 1:20 and 2:9, is strengthened by the prefixed preposition *kata* ("down") giving the verb a perfective force; the work is continued until the task has been "worked down" to a successful conclusion— the production of "perseverance."

The rendering of this noun as "patience" (KJV; ASV) does not adequately convey the force of the original, *hupomonē*, composed of the preposition *hupo* ("under") and the verb *meno* ("to stay, abide, remain"). It thus presents the picture of being under a heavy load and resolutely staying there instead of trying to escape. The reference may be to the act of endurance (2 Cor. 1:6; 6:4) or to the frame of mind that bravely endures the trials and pressures encountered (Rom. 5:3; 2 Thess. 1:4). The latter is the meaning here. Ropes calls it "staying-power."[19] It is the virtue of steadfastness, constancy, and endurance. It is a virtue that grows under trial and testing. Mayor notes that Philo called it "the queen of virtues."[20] It is not a passive attitude of quiet submission or resignation but rather a brave manliness that confronts the difficulties and contends against them. Thayer calls it "the characteristic of a man who is not swerved from his deliberate purpose and his loyalty to the faith and piety by even the greatest trials and sufferings."[21] It is that tenacity of spirit which holds up under pressure while awaiting God's time for dismissal of the test or for His reward.

Triumphant faith finds power to persevere by "looking steadfastly on Jesus, the leader and completer of faith, who, in view of the joy lying before him, endured [the] cross" (Heb. 12:2; Darby).

3. The Outcome to be Realized (v. 4)

In this verse James turns to a more remote result of cheerfully bearing the trials of his life. Instead of giving the full sequence of events in their successive order as Paul does in Romans 5:3-5, James breaks the chain at the mention of "perseverance" to give expression to another exhortation: "Perseverance must finish its work" (*hē de hupomonē ergon teleion echetō*, literally, "But the perseverance its perfect work let have"). The word "let" in our English rendering must not be taken as merely denoting permission (there is no word for it in the Greek), since it is the only way we have of giving expression to the Greek imperative in the *third* person. It is a command, intent on putting his readers on guard against the danger mentioned—allowing the chain of results to be interrupted.

It is characteristic of James's style that he repeats the word "perseverance," or endurance, in verse 4. In verse 3 it was used without the article, but now it has the article, "the perseverance" already mentioned in verse 3.[22] The conjunction *de*, omitted in the NIV, has been given two different renderings. The rendering "and" views its force as transitional, serving to add a further aspect to the picture. Others give it an adversative force and render it "but": "But let endurance have its perfect work" (Montgomery). Then it points to a conceived danger to be avoided. Sore trials are hard to bear uncomplainingly, and it is easy to give way to an attitude that hinders endurance from exercising its proper effect and thereby incur serious loss. The latter seems more in harmony with the author's use of the imperative.

With his present imperative, James reminds his readers that it is their continuing duty to enable perseverance or endurance to "finish its work," to achieve its intended goal. James does not identify what that "perfect work" is. The reference may be to the development of perfect endurance: "Let endurance show itself perfectly in practice."[23] More probably the reference is to the development of perfect character as perseverance or endurance is allowed to work out its intended effect in our lives. Maturity of character is not the result of the number of trials encountered but the way in which those trials are met, allowing them to achieve their divinely intended impact on us. "Mature Christians are the end-product of testing."[24]

A double purpose-clause states the final outcome they must realize: "so that you may be mature and complete, not lacking anything." "So that you may be" indicates that the intended outcome is in the realm of character development. The present tense "may be" implies that this is not merely an eschatological goal but involves a present, progressive attainment.

The intended outcome is stated both positively and negatively: positively, "so that you may be mature and complete." The adjective "mature" (*teleios*) is a favorite with James;[25] it was probably borrowed from the teaching of Jesus (Matt. 5:48; 19:21). Rather than absolute perfection (cf. 3:2), the term implies the ethical character of the mature believer. It denotes something that has attained its proper goal. In connection with animals or people, it indicates adult growth and maturity—the opposite of babyhood. Thus James is thinking of a personality that has reached full development. "The word describes a 'maturity,' a ripeness and richness of knowledge and character, such as might be supposed to mark the full-grown man, as contrasted with the babe in Christ."[26] Unfortunately, many believers succumb to spiritual infantile paralysis and remain in a state of childish backwardness in their spiritual life.

The second adjective, "complete" (*holoklēroi*), is a compound form composed of *holos* ("whole, complete") and *klēros* ("a lot, a portion received by lot), and thus denotes "that which retains all that was allotted to it." It was used for things that were complete and intact, such as animals that were sound and possessing all their parts, and thus acceptable for sacrifice on the altar. Here it is used in an ethical sense to include all those virtues that should characterize the mature believer. "Christ is not satisfied with less than our full-rounded personality."[27] In this second adjective (which occurs only twice in the New Testament: 1 Thess. 5:23; James 1:4) there is the suggestion that "perfection is not just a maturing of character, but a rounding out as more and more 'parts' of the righteous character are added."[28]

The two adjectives supplement each other. Using the KJV terminology, Knowling remarks:

In the "perfect" character no grace is merely in its weak imperfect beginnings, but all have reached a certain ripeness and maturity, while in the "entire" character no grace which ought to be in a Christian man is wanting.[29]

James intensifies the picture by adding a corroborating negative, "not lacking anything." This practice of supplementing the positive with a negative is also seen in 1:5-6. The negative is the exact counterpart of the second adjective, but it probably was intended to balance both positive adjectives just used. The expression may quite literally be rendered "in nothing being left behind." It may thus picture James's concern that in no area of their development should they fail to reach the goal and that no part of their personality should fail to develop, leaving them in an unbalanced state. There is to be the absence of deficiency.

Viewed in light of the total result, James's demand that his readers should reckon it a cause for joy whenever they fall into affliction is not seen to be fantasy but sober teaching in light of Christian experience (cf. Rom. 5:3-5; 1 Pet. 1:5-6). The attitude James calls for is vastly superior to the natural human reaction of complaining and brooding in self-pity or the adoption of an attitude of stoic resignation and grim fortitude. This "hard saying" by James "is really a merciful one, for it teaches us to endure the trials in the spirit that will make us feel them least."[30]

B. THE USE OF PRAYER AMID TRIALS (vv. 5-8)

Oesterley holds that "there is no thought connection" between this paragraph and what has preceded,[31] but most interpreters agree with Barclay that "there is a close connection between this passage and what had gone before."[32] An external link is provided by the repetition of the thought of "lacking" from verse 4. An inner thought connection seems intended from the fact that these verses form a clear part of the general discussion concerning trials and temptations in verses 2-18. Based on the author's thread of thought, Carpenter holds that the connection "is more psychological and experimental than logic and argumentative."[33]

That some thought sequence is implied is clear from the use of the particle *de* in verse 5 which implies that something further is to be added. The thought connection is that if any one of the readers feels the inability to look at his trials as just indicated, let him turn to God in prayer for the needed wisdom. James well knew that to look at the providential vicissitudes of life as just demanded (vv. 2-4) requires God-given wisdom. In this paragraph, James realistically recognizes the need for wisdom (v. 5*a*), directs that the tested believer should ask God for the needed wisdom (v. 5*b*), and assures that the requested wisdom will be granted if the attitude for effective praying is present (vv. 5*c*-8).

1. The Need for Wisdom (v. 5*a*)

The conditional statement "If any of you lacks wisdom" does not imply doubt concerning the reality of the need. Rather it assumes the reality of the need and views it as a standing fact.[34] The first step in gaining such wisdom is the consciousness of our need for it. "If any of you" indicates that this consciousness of a wisdom shortage must come as an individual recognition. There is no suggestion that there were individual exceptions to this need. The degree of the need may vary, but all believers have a need for this wisdom. As Burdick notes, "James speaks of a period of testing before perseverance has completed its work."[35]

The believer needs "wisdom" to see his trials in a true light and to profit spiritually from them. James knew from Psalm 73 and the book of Job that the trials that often overwhelm the godly create struggles and require God-given wisdom to resolve them. For James, wisdom is more than wide knowledge or the mental sagacity that can express itself in subtle rhetorical distinctions or abstruse arguments. As a Jew, James viewed wisdom as related to the practice of righteousness in daily life. It is the moral discernment that enables the believer to meet life and its trials with decisions and actions consistent with God's will. Johnstone defines it as "that queenly regulative discretion which sees and selects worthy ends, and the best means of attaining them."[36]

The great Old Testament example of this wisdom is Solomon, whose God-given wisdom enabled him to devise a means to determine which of two women claiming to be the mother of a child was in fact his real mother (1 Kings 3:16-28). James has just set forth a piece of such wisdom in verses 2-4 in relation to the trials of life, but this wisdom has a wider application and relates to all areas of conduct where such discernment is needed (cf. 3:13-17). The fear of the Lord is the beginning of such wisdom (Prov. 9:10), for the wise man recognizes that he is morally accountable to God for all his decisions and actions in life. This consciousness prompts him to turn to the eternal fountain of wisdom in all circumstances of life.

2. The Request for Wisdom (v. 5*b*)

"He should ask God" at once directs the needy believer to the true source of wisdom. The use of the present imperative (*aiteitē*) makes clear that James is not merely offering a piece of true wisdom but is commanding his tested readers to practice prayer for wisdom as a Christian duty. The third person singular verb marks it as the duty of each individual believer. The present tense states it as a standing duty to be performed whenever there is a conscious need. "Let him be asking of God" (Rotherham). "Prayer brings God near in His full resourcefulness."[37] Any failure to ask implies that the believer is blind to his need, but he who has a constant longing for wisdom will persistently pray for it. As Winkler remarks, "A sense of spiritual poverty is a blessing when it leads the humble soul to God."[38]

The verb "ask" (*aiteitō*) gives prominence to the thought that it is a prayer for something to be given rather than for something to be done.[39] The desired gift is "wisdom" and is to be given by God as its only true Teacher. Such a request is characteristically Christian. Songer notes that in first-century Judaism, wisdom was thought of as embodied "in the Jewish Scriptures (Torah) and that man gained it by study."[40] For the Christian, divine wisdom is embodied in the Scriptures, but his study of those Scriptures must be connected with his constant prayer for divine illumination. Sadler notes that such prayer for wisdom is foreign to the view of a noted pagan like Cicero:

> In one of Ciccro's moral books, in speaking of the things which we could properly ask of the gods, he enumerates such things as wealth, honour, or health of body, but he adds it would be absurd to ask wisdom of any god, for it would be totally out of his power to give such a thing to his worshippers.[41]

The Christian can confidently make his request for wisdom from "God, who gives generously to all without finding fault." The Greek (*para* with the ablative *theou*) pictures the needed wisdom as richly present "alongside of God" and to be procured from Him as its true source by asking for it. The giver of the requested wisdom is "God, who gives" (*para tou didontos theou*). The Greek construction is open to two interpretations. The participle with the article (*tou didontos*) may be taken as a substantive, with *theou* standing in apposition, "from alongside the Giving One, namely God." More probably, the article relates directly to God, and the participle between them, as attributive, stresses that "giving" is the inherent nature of God. The present tense of the participle sets forth God's generous nature as continually giving. He has revealed Himself as a God who is continually giving to men. No statement of the gifts is made; His giving comprehends everything that is good. Blanchard asserts, "It is characteristic of the unbeliever to see God with a clenched fist; it is characteristic of the believer to see Him with an open hand."[42] It is this view of the nature of God that encourages the believer to come boldly to God with his requests.

"To all" sets the scope of God's giving. It is not limited to a favored few but is available to all who ask. Such asking is motivated by the double fact that God gives "generously . . . without finding fault." Both phrases refer to the mode of the divine giving, not His gifts. The intended meaning of the positive characterization, "generously" (*haplōs*), has been differently understood. This adverb occurs only here in the New Testament, but the adjective is not rare. The basic meaning of the adjective is "simple, single," as in Matthew 6:22 and Luke 11:34, where the reference is to a "single eye." Accepting this meaning for the adverb, the teaching of James is that God gives with a single motive: to further the welfare of the asker. He gives without ulterior motives, harboring no calculated desire to get something in return.

Bauernfeind thinks that the adverb here most probably means "whole-heartedly."[43] Martin asserts that this adverb "stands in contrast to *dipsuchos* (in v. 8), "double-minded," and reassures us that God is not of two minds about His giving.[44] Others hold that the meaning is that God gives freely and without restraint, hence generously or "liberally."[45] The first meaning well shades into the second, "since the gift which is willing and unconditional tends also to be liberal."[46] Both meanings are true of God's giving; He gives to all wholeheartedly and with singleness of purpose, and He also gives with a wealth of liberality.

The negative assertion "without finding fault" further elaborates God's giving. The negative with the present tense participle indicates that God permanently abstains from such a practice. He does not respond to our petition and then heap insults upon us for asking. He "does not offensively recall the benefits already given, or rebuke the applicant who asks for more."[47] He does not give in a way that humiliates the receiver. He does not scold because we have inadequately used His former gifts or rebuke us for our repeated lack of wisdom. "God's generosity is measured by what He designs and not by what we deserve."[48] Rather, when we again ask His help, His gracious response makes us wonder why we were so tardy in asking Him.

This does not mean that God never rebukes our sins. He never condones sin. He reproves us for our failure to depend upon Him in our need, and rebukes our distrust of His bounty in supplying our needs.

3. The Bestowal of Wisdom (vv. 5c-8)

James promises that God will not fail to respond to the request for wisdom (v. 5c), but he at once adds that there is a definite obligation upon the supplicant to ask in faith when making his request (vv. 6-8).

a. *The divine response* (v. 5c). The positive assurance "and it will be given to him" encourages prayer for wisdom. The future indicative places God on record that He will respond favorably when we turn to Him in our need. The assertion seems clearly reminiscent of the teaching of Jesus (Matt. 7:7-11; Mark 11:23-25; Luke 11:9-13). The identity of the promised gift is left unnamed, but the context makes clear that the specific reference is to the wisdom requested by the believer who is conscious of his wisdom shortage.

b. *The human obligation* (vv. 6-8). This assurance of answered prayer does not mean "that God is some kind of a dispensing machine into which we put a prayer and out comes whatever we select.[49] The promise of answered prayer makes its spiritual demands upon the one asking. James points to the necessary attitude for effective praying (v. 6a) and vividly portrays the man who does not get his prayer answered (vv. 6b-8).

(1) *The necessary attitude* (v. *6a*). The required attitude is stated both positively and negatively. "But when he asks, he must believe and not doubt." The original is, more literally, "But let him be asking in faith, nothing doubting" (Rotherham). The use of the present imperative (*aiteitō*) indicates that James sets forth a standing demand on God's part if prayer is to be answered. The singular number indicates that each one individually must meet the condition to get his prayer answered. No exceptions are made.

The demand that our prayers must be offered in "faith" underlines James's view that there can be no acceptable prayer without faith. For James, as for the author of Hebrews, faith is of the very essence of spiritual life (Heb. 11:6). This stress upon the importance of faith in prayer again echoes the teaching of Jesus (Matt. 21:22; Mark 11:24).

"Faith" here is not merely a body of doctrinal truth to which we adhere but rather the wholehearted attitude of a full and unquestioning committal to and dependence upon God, as He has revealed Himself to us in Christ Jesus. It is the proper human response to the goodness of God. When we approach God with our petitions, we must believe not only in His ability to grant our requests but also in His ability to answer in harmony with His character and purpose. Believing prayer takes its stand upon the character of God.

The nature of prayer in faith is underlined by the added negative "and not doubt." Doubting conveys the picture of a divided mind, being torn in two directions. The individual is in a state of oscillation between the competing desires within him. The present tense denotes that this "halting between two opinions" has become habitual, while the middle voice indicates that the conflict is rooted in his competing personal desires. Although he has given expression to his petition to God, he is not at rest in himself concerning what he has asked. Now he wants the things asked for, and then again he desires something else. His uttered request has not terminated the inner indecision between the competing desires. His inner yearnings are divided between God and the world (4:3-4). It is not merely a state of mental indecision but an inner moral conflict. He is divided between the desire to say yes to his request and the desire to say no to it, with the inclination to say no gaining the upper hand. It is an inner unwillingness to rely wholly upon God. As Stier aptly remarks, "A doubting petitioner offers not to God a steady hand or heart, so that He cannot deposit in it His gift."[50]

(2) *The rejected character* (vv. *6b-8*). The true character of such a man is vividly portrayed, "because he who doubts is like a wave of the sea, blown and tossed by the wind" (v. *6b*). The opening "because" (*gar*) indicates that the evil of such doubting is now to be illustrated. The preceding present participle rendered "and not doubt" (*mēden diakrinomenos*) depicted the activity being condemned; now "he who doubts" (*ho diakrinomenos*) repeats the preceding participle with the definite article to portray the individual himself as a characteristic doubter. "The man who prays without faith has

a radical defect in his character."⁵¹ The portrayal of his defective character is intended as a dissuasion against doubting.

Such a doubter "is like a wave of the sea, blown and tossed by the wind." It is a lively picture of the constant unrest of the doubting soul. Here we have the first of a number of similies⁵² employed by James. He had a marked ability to make his teaching vivid by the use of illustrations and comparisons. Before the risen Christ appeared to him (1 Cor. 15:7), James had been a doubter concerning the messianic claims of his Brother, and he well understood the nature of such a condition.

The verb rendered "is like," occurring only here and 1:23 in the New Testament, expresses the continuing resemblance⁵³ of the doubter to "a wave of the sea." The word "wave" (*kludōn*) does not mean an individual wave (*kuma*) but a succession of waves—one long ridge of water after another being swept along by the wind. Ropes suggests the rendering "the billowing sea."⁵⁴ Both here and in Luke 8:24, the only occurrences of the noun in the New Testament, it is used in connection with the wind. The doubter is like the turbulent sea, "wind-driven and storm tossed" (Rotherham). The present tense of these two participles portrays the continuing impact of the wind upon the sea. Ropes remarks that James has in mind "the ordinary instability of the heaving sea, not the unusual violence of a storm."⁵⁵ When the wind blows from one direction the billowing waves move with it; when the wind comes from the opposite direction they again move with it. The billows, fanned by the wind, also rise and fall as they move along. "In the figure," says Vincent, "the emphasis falls on the *tossing*; not only moving before the impulse of the wind, but not even moving in regular lines; tossed into rising and falling peaks."⁵⁶ This combination of lateral and vertical movement gives a vivid picture of four-dimensional instability. "The point to be enforced," Martin notes, "is that the doubter is as insecure and unsteady as a boat rocked in turbulent seas."⁵⁷

The passive voice of the participles further conveys the thought that the billows respond to forces from without. The water has no inner stability to stand against the outer forces. So also the doubter, lacking a firm inner will of his own, is deficient in his ability to attain any fixed goals. He is totally "untrustworthy with regard to gaining any end that needs determined perseverance in a certain course."⁵⁸

This picture of the instability of the sea is one that James would be familiar with from his acquaintance with the Sea of Galilee as well as the eastern shores of the Mediterranean. Being alert to spiritual lessons from nature, James saw in this scene of instability "a wonderfully apt symbol of a mind that cannot fix itself in belief."⁵⁹ Divine wisdom cannot dwell in a personality so unstable and unable to carry out a determined course of action.

In verse 7, James presents a further persuasive against doubting: "That man should not think he will receive anything from the Lord." The opening *gar*, "for," omitted in the NIV, is best taken as introducing a second reason he must ask in faith without doubting (v. *6a*). The first reason (v. *6b*) was a description of the doubter; now the reason is stated as a command, forbidding the doubter to have any illusions about receiving an answer to his prayer. "That man" (*ekeinos*) has a note of personal rejection in it; by its use James disassociates himself from the man and places him at a distance. He instinctively refuses to be in the same class with such a doubter. The verb "think" (*oiesthō*), which occurs elsewhere in the New Testament only in John 21:25 and Philippians 1:17, implies "a subjective judgment which has feeling rather than thought for its ground."[60] It carries the collateral notion of an unwarranted judgment: "let not that man suppose."[61] The negative *mē* with the present imperative demands that he must stop entertaining any thought of receiving an answer to his prayer.

"That man should not think he will receive anything from the Lord" states the unwarranted supposition. "Anything" is properly limited to the things for which he has asked. He is not necessarily excluded from those common benefits which the Lord, the giver of all good, bestows upon all men indiscriminately (Matt. 5:45), but as a faithless doubter he can expect to receive no specific answer to his prayer. "Faith unlocks the divine storehouse, but unbelief bars its doors."[62]

Here "the Lord" is generally taken to mean God the Father, but in view of 1:1, Lenski sees no reason for denying that the reference is to the Lord Jesus Christ.[63] Either view is possible, yet in view of 5:7, 14-15 there is no reason to hold that James could not think of prayer being addressed to Christ Jesus. Since neither the Father nor the Son is expressly indicated in the context, we may perhaps assume that James is thinking of the Trinity in its unity.

Since no verb is expressed in verse 8 in the original, the grammatical connection may be taken in either of two ways. It is possible to supply a copulative verb, "is," and read it as a separate sentence: either "he is a double-minded man" (NIV), or "a double-minded man *is* unstable in all his ways" (KJV). The alternative is to regard all of verse 8 as standing in apposition with "that man" (v. 7), setting forth a further graphic description of his character. The latter construction, perhaps best marked by a dash at the end of verse 7, is preferable. It is more forceful and fully in keeping with James's abrupt style.

"Double-minded" (*dipsuchos*) has been called "one of the most expressive words in the letter."[64] It occurs only here and in 4:8 in the New Testament, and has not been found in pagan authors before the time of James. Moulton and Milligan suggest that James may have coined the term.[65] It readily took root in the vocabulary of ecclesiastical writers.[66] The word is literally "two-souled," and James may have formed it on the basis of the Hebrew in 1 Chronicles 12:33 and Psalm 12:2: "a heart and a heart." Here James uses the noun "man" (*anēr*) before the adjective, making the adjective more emphatic than it would be if used alone.[67] In verse 7, he uses the more general term for "man" (*anthrōpos*), but the change to *anēr*, which generally denotes a man as contrasted to a woman, seems simply due to the desire for variety, without any intended difference between the two terms.

The vivid expression "a man two-souled" (Gk.) denotes the doubter's divided attitude. He acts as though two distinct souls or personalities are in his body, in perpetual conflict with each other. The one is turned Godward, while the other is turned toward the world; the one believes God, but the other disbelieves. He is "a walking civil war in which trust and distrust of God wage a continual battle against each other."[68] He is the pattern for Bunyan's "Mr. Facing-both-ways." In trying to move in two directions at once, he is like the mythological horseman who mounted his horse and rapidly rode off in both directions.

His double-mindedness reveals itself in his conduct as a whole; he is "unstable in all he does." The adjective "unstable" (*akatastatos*) is a compound verbal occurring only here and in 3:8 in the New Testament.[69] It is built on the verb *histēmi*, "to place or stand," with the preposition *kata*, "down," while the alpha privitive, like our English *un*, gives the whole a negative quality; it conveys the thought of being unsettled, unstable—not having been put down to stand solid.

Lacking a solid foundation, such a man is unsteady and wobbling "in all he does." Never able to settle down, he is "irresolute at every turn" (20th Cent.). "In all he does," literally "in all his ways," is a Hebraism depicting his personal conduct (Psa. 91:11; 145:17; Prov. 3:6; Jer. 16:17). The plural "all his ways" encompasses all the varied aspects of his life. His fickle and vacillating attitude in the realm of faith projects itself into all the areas of his life, making him unreliable in all of his dealings. "The man who does not trust God cannot be trusted by men."[70] There is a close connection between the way a man prays and the way he lives. "Since the resting place of our will is the will of God found in prayer, a division at the centre destroys unity and force of character, and this produces instability in the whole range of conduct."[71]

C. THE CORRECT ATTITUDE TOWARD LIFE BY THE TRIED (vv. 9-11)

Here again Oesterley sees "no connection with what has preceded."[72] Others, like Plumptre, hold that the use of the conjunction *de* in the original clearly implies "that there is a sequence of ideas of some kind."[73] Yet the precise connection is not clear. The rendering "but" (ASV) suggests that James intended an antithesis to what has just gone before, indicating a contrast to the double-mindedness condemned in verse 8. Such double-mindedness will be avoided by the believer, whether rich or poor, who has the needed wisdom to evaluate properly his station in life. Others, like Lenski, hold that *de* is not adversative, but simply "the common transitional particle,"[74] hence the absence of any connecting particle in the NIV. Then this brief paragraph relates back to the theme in verses 2-4 and contains another piece of spiritual wisdom being offered to the tested believer. This seems the better view, although the reality of a contrast to the double-mindedness of verse 8 need not be rejected.

This brief paragraph offers another nugget of spiritual truth that the tested believer needs. James well knew that the heroic steadfastness under trial for which he has called (v. 4) is furthered by the believer's correct evaluation of his material circumstances. He is not merely concerned about the circumstances of poverty and wealth as tests of faith but with the believer's response to those conditions. James realized "that a person's attitude toward material things is a good index of his spiritual condition."[75] He makes no move toward eliminating these economic differences but points to the common faith in Christ as the true equalizing factor.

1. The Attitude of the Lowly Brother (v. 9)

"The brother in humble circumstances ought to take pride in his high position." The verb rendered "take pride in" (*kauchasthō*) stands emphatically at the beginning of the sentence. The verb denotes a strong personal reaction, a feeling of pride or exultation in the condition mentioned. It encompasses the individual's total reaction, both his inward feeling and the outward expression of exultation. Zodhiates remarks that the word means "to profess loudly something that you have a right to be proud of."[76] The present imperative calls upon the believer to adopt this as his characteristic response. James did not agree that a gloomy downcast attitude is the normal and expected response of the believer to economic stringencies. "The pessimist," declares Robertson, "is not a representative of Christianity."[77]

The verb *kauchaomai*, "take pride in," occurs only here and in 4:16 in the New Testament outside of Paul's writings. Paul uses it thirty-six times, generally in a good sense, but Paul, like James in 4:16, recognized that there is also a wrong boasting in which men may engage. In this context, the verb denotes "not the arrogant boasting of the self-important, but the joyous pride possessed by the person who values what God values."[78] Such an attitude is the best safeguard against succumbing to despondency when assailed by trials.

The call to have this attitude is first directed to "the brother in humble circumstances," more literally "the brother, the lowly one." The identification is generic, denoting any individual who belongs to this class.[79] The double designation underlines that James freely accepts this poor believer as a worthy member of the Christian brotherhood in spite of his humble circumstances. The adjective rendered "in humble circumstances" (*tapeinos*) basically means "low-lying," but in the New Testament it is always used figuratively. It may have either a material or an ethical import, and in each instance it must be evaluated according to its context. Some, such as Songer, hold that the term here is the equivalent of "pious" to denote an inner spiritual quality.[80] It is generally accepted that the reference here is to the individual's humble external circumstances.[81] (In 4:6, James uses the adjective in the sense of an inner character trait.) Here, as in Luke 1:52, the adjective means "poor" in terms of wealth, since it stands in opposition to "rich" in the next verse. His humble financial circumstances also would relegate him to a lowly social position. The repetition of the article with the adjective places it in apposition to "the brother" as a sort of climax,[82] stressing this fact concerning the brother. Many poor believers were in the early churches (Acts 2:45; 4:35; 1 Cor. 1:26-28; 2 Cor. 8:1). James well knew how oppressive and disheartening such circumstances could be.

James did not pity this poor brother but called upon him to contemplate "his high position" (more literally, "his height"). Barnes understands the term to denote that the poor man, due to a change in his fortunes, has become rich.[83] It is much better to accept that James uses the term here to denote his present exalted spiritual position as a Christian. He is urged to let wisdom open his eyes to the spiritual height to which he has been lifted as a child of God. He may be financially poor, looked down upon by the world, and considered a nobody, but in the eyes of God he has a position of lofty dignity. As a believer, let him evaluate his present circumstances in light of assured eschatological consummation. His hope for the future is to influence his present evaluations. "Since it is incomparably the greatest dignity to be introduced into the company of angels, nay, to be made the associates of Christ, he who estimates this favour of God aright, will regard all other things as worthless."[84] His exaltation in Christ is beyond present visualization. He must glory in what he has become as a member of God's family. "Instead of resenting his poverty and being discontented with his obscurity, let him remember that he is a prince.[85] As a son of the King, he is an heir to the future kingdom in glory. He need not be disheartened by his present poverty, or regard it as an evil; he is the possessor of spiritual riches that more than counterbalance his material poverty.

> A tent or a cottage, why should I care?
> They're building a palace for me over there;
> Tho' exiled from home, yet, still I may sing:
> All glory to God, I'm a child of the King.
> Hattie E. Buell

A vivid example of this power of Christianity to transform one's evaluation of life may be seen in the story of the Cornish miner-preacher Billy Bray (1794-1868). Although often hungry and ill-clad, he was a forceful and colorful preacher who constantly exulted in his high position as a son of the King.[86]

2. The Attitude of the Rich (vv. 10-11)

"But the one who is rich should take pride in his low position." These words are a direct continuation of the sentence begun in verse 9. In seeking to establish the intended identity of "the rich," much has been made of the fact that James did not repeat the word "brother" or use a verb to state his duty. Two views are advocated: (1) that this rich man is a non-Christian; (2) that both the rich and the poor are Christians.

Various scholars conclude that James views him as a non-Christian.[87] Dibelius holds that the elaborate picture of the rich man given "not without satisfaction" and depicting "*only* his downfall" cannot be applied to a Christian.[88] He concludes that if James "was thinking here of Christians as well, then these are people whom he considers no longer to be included in a proper sense within Christendom."[89] Easton asserts that "in view of 2:5-7 and 5:1-6, it does not seem that James would approve of any rich man at all."[90] The reading of such an Ebionitic attitude into the epistle of James seems highly doubtful. That in the early churches there were rich men, fully accepted and appreciated in their circles, is beyond doubt (cf. 1 Tim. 6:17-19). The view that James, in light of his strong terms against the rich in 5:1-6, must always regard the rich as wicked unbelievers outside the church, has little or no force. There is no justification for the claim that the "rich man" here belongs to the oppressive rich denounced in 5:1-6. In the present passage, all that is implied is a clear contrast between the two classes.[91]

If we accept James's speaking of non-Christians, then his words are intensely ironic: "Let him glory in what is really his shame." Although James can use irony, he seems to be entirely sincere in his statement here. To avoid this note of irony, Alford proposes that the indicative rather than the imperative be supplied: "he glories in his debasement."[92] Such an unexpressed change of mode in James's statement does not suit the structure of his sentence. Mayor calls the proposed change in mode "extremely harsh" and insists that "no interpretation is admissible which does not supply the imperative *kauchasthō*."[93] If the rich man is held to be a non-Christian, the passage is probably best understood as eschatological: in the Judgment Day, the lowly brother will be exalted and the rich man will be brought low.

We accept as most probable the view that both the rich and the poor man are thought of as Christians by James. This is the most natural meaning of the structure of the sentence in the original, as displayed in Lenski's very literal rendering: "Now let him boast, the brother, the lowly one, in his high position; on the other hand, the rich one, in his lowly position!"[94] The balanced structure implies that both articular adjectives, "the lowly one" as well as "the rich one," relate to the same noun— "the brother." His beautiful parallel structure indicates that James thought of both as brothers and that the imperative verb goes with both. From the teaching of Jesus (Matt. 19:23; Luke 18:23-27), James knew the danger that wealth might be to a rich believer and felt it incumbent to issue the warning to those who were rich in material possessions. The word "rich" (*plousios*) denotes "one who does not need to work for a living."[95]

The rich brother is admonished to take pride in "his low position." The expression may have reference to his humiliation as an experience. If taken quite literally, the meaning may be "the humiliation of the rich man, by his being stripped of his riches and possessions."[96] This seems implied in Goodspeed's rendering, "to rejoice at being reduced in circumstances." Others suggest that the experience of humiliation is social; the rich man as a Christian is now ostracized by his former rich friends and treated as a social outcast.[97]

It seems best to accept that the statement is figurative, pointing to the attitude that the rich brother must adopt. Moffatt well asserts, "The lowering of the rich brother is as inward as the raising of the poor brother."[98] The parallel in James's statement supports this view; if the exaltation of the poor brother has a spiritual basis, the experience of the rich brother being brought into a humble station should also be understood spiritually. Cadoux notes that James

> can hardly mean, let him glory in the loss of his wealth, for such loss without change of mind would be no true reason for glorying, nor does the desirable frame of mind depend on the loss. It would seem that here to be "made low" is to find something of incomparably greater value than his wealth, something that by its greatness makes him feel small, so that disillusioned in his old ground of glorying, he attains a basis for a better glory.[99]

The attitude of both the poor and the rich brother is the result of the spiritual wisdom each has attained. The results look in opposite directions.

> As the poor brother forgets all his earthly poverty, so the rich brother forgets all his earthly riches. By faith in Christ the two are equals.[100]

The rich brother has come to realize that at the cross he stands on a level with the poor brother. Both have been given a new status in Christ, and it is their true ground for glorying.

The command to the poor brother is tersely stated, but the command to the rich brother receives strong amplification. James states a reason for the command to the rich brother (v. 10*b*), illustrates it from the fate of the field flower (v. 11*a*), and applies it to the end of the rich (v. 11*b*).

a. *The reason for the attitude* (v. 10*b*). The reason for the demand upon the rich brother is "because he will pass away like a wild flower." He must have the indicated attitude because of the brevity and uncertainty of life. This is also true for the poor man, but James presses it upon the conscience of the rich, because while living in the midst of plenty he is more prone to forget it than the poor brother. He needs grace to realize that his earthly fortune is not the true basis for his security.

James declares the rich man to be as transitory as "a wild flower," (literally, "flower of grass"). It is another of James's similes drawn from nature. The expression "as the flower of the grass" is from Isaiah 40:6, where it is the Septuagint rendering of the Hebrew "the flower of the field." The picture is not to be restricted only to grass but includes any green herbage. The reference is to the various field flowers in Palestine that bloom in great abundance each spring with the spring rains (cf. Matt. 6:28 30). James was well aware that the life of these beautiful wild flowers was brief. With the commencement of the dry summer season, they rapidly passed away. Their brief duration became a common Oriental symbol of the transitoriness of life (Pss. 90:5-6; 102:11; 103:15; Isa. 51:12; 1 Pet. 2:24). Isaiah 40:6-8 presents a picture of the transitory nature of human life in general, but here James applies it specifically to the rich. He skillfully uses the picture to encourage the rich brother to foster that lowly mindedness which looks beyond temporal material things to spiritual values.

b. *The illustration from the flower* (v. 11*a*). The transitoriness of life is clearly set before the rich brother in what follows. "For the sun rises with scorching heat and withers the plant; its blossom falls and its beauty is destroyed" vividly draws out the comparison in narrative form. "For" introduces the picture as justification for the comparison of the rich man with a flower (v. 10*b*). The four verbs, "arises," "withers," "falls," and "is destroyed," picture the rapid succession of events. All are in the aorist tense, which generally presents the action as a definite historical event. Here the aorists are gnomic, portraying the successive events as characteristic of what always happens in such cases.[101]

The words rendered "the sun ariseth with scorching heat" are open to two interpretations. "With scorching heat" is literally "with the burning," with no defining noun added. The rendering of Rotherham, "The sun hath sprung up with its scorching heat," is representative of those who hold that the reference is to the hot Palestinian sun with its scorching effect upon the green herbage; on the other hand, the ASV rendering, "The sun ariseth with the scorching wind," represents the view that the reference is to the burning wind, the sirocco, the scorching wind blowing in from the Arabian Desert. The dreaded sirocco could be like a hot oven destroying the green vegetation in a few hours.

In support of the former view is the fact that the word used means heat rather than wind; also, it is the sun that brings the scorching heat but not necessarily the scorching east wind. Fausset observes, "The 'burning heat' of the sun is not at its *rising*, but rather at noon; whereas the scorching *Kadim* wind is often at sunrise (Jonah 4.8)."[102] Mayor thinks that the presence of the article favors the latter view. It is also supported by the general usage in the

Septuagint (Jer. 18:17; Ezek. 19:12; Hos. 13:15; Jonah 4:8). In Matthew 13:6 and 20:12 the reference is only to the scorching heat. Apparently, in James's thinking, the scorching wind cannot be wholly ruled out.

Under either view the inevitable result was that the grass withered and "its blossom falls." The verb "falls" (*exepesen*) means "to fall off, fall out" and is an exact description of "the dropping of the petals or corona out of the calyx, as an effect of drought."[103] When this happens "its beauty is destroyed." The words of James are literally "and the beauty of the face of it perished." The word "beauty" (*euprepeia*), which does not occur elsewhere in the New Testament, denotes the flower's outward attractiveness. The expression "the beauty of its face" reveals that James had "something of the same appreciation of the loveliness of God's creation which we find in the words of Jesus, who said that the simple beauty of the wild flowers exceeded that of the splendour of Solomon's court."[104] Smith suggests that the words of James reflect his personal sympathy with the withering flowers: "For him each flower has a face. He notes its tender gracefulness. He feels the pathos of decay, and sighs over the falling petals."[105] James must have often observed how the field flowers with their beauty and intricacy soon wilted, disintegrated, and passed away. Their beauty offered no security against the adverse elements. The fate of these flowers solemnly declared to James the fact of the transitoriness of human life.

c. *The application to the rich* (v. 11*b*). James formally applied the illustration: "In the same way, the rich man will fade away even while he goes about his business." "In the same way" (*houtōs kai*, literally "thusly also") underlines the parallel; the adverb "in the same way (*houtōs*) marks the similarity between the flower's fate and the passing of the rich man, while "also" (*kai*) notes the applicability of the picture. "The rich man" (*ho plousios*) is identical with the expression in verse 10 and apparently has the same meaning here. It is true that the poor brother will also die, but Lenski comments that the poor "never blooms like the one who has wealth. Thus the figure is applied only to the latter."[106] It is a strong reminder to the wealthy that permanence is not to be found in the material things of this world. Ropes referred this fading away to the loss of his wealth,[107] but the reference is to the rich man himself; nothing is said of his wealth.

The remark that the rich man "will fade away" continues the imagery of the flower; his passing is similar to that of the rapidly fading flower. "Even while he goes about his business" implies that his disappearance from the earthly scene will come while he is busy with his varied activities. "While he goes about his business" (*en tais poreiais autou*, literally, "in his goings") may refer to a literal trip or journey. In Luke 13:22 the noun is used of Jesus on His journey to Jerusalem. With this meaning, the implication is that the rich man will come to his end while on one of his business trips (cf. 4:13). The term is also used metaphorically of one's way of life (cf. the expression in v. 8 above). Then the reference is to the varied activities of the rich man in general. Ropes insists that "to take it of literal journeys is wholly inappropriate to the context."[108] The metaphorical view is the more probable. Under either interpretation, the words of James imply that the rich man will pass away while he is still restlessly busy with his material pursuits and not anticipating that his end is at hand.

D. THE RESULT OF ENDURING TRIALS (v. 12)

Although Dibelius regards this verse as "an isolated saying which is connected neither with what follows nor with what precedes,"[109] it is generally recognized as forming the fitting conclusion to the discussion concerning trials begun with verse 2. This relationship with what precedes rather than what follows is indicated by the repetition of terminology ("trials," v. 2; "testing," "perseverance," v. 3) as well as the fact that the testing here is to be endured ("perseveres"), whereas the temptations in verses 13-15 are to be resisted.[110] This verse crowns the whole discussion with the promise of reward in the future life. The teaching in verse 2 to count their trials as joy is here completed with the assurance concerning the ultimate effect of trials bravely endured. It assures a blessedness both here and hereafter. Therefore, it is better to conclude the paragraph with verse 12 or make a separate paragraph of it.

1. The Blessedness of Endurance (v. 12*a*)

"Blessed is the man who perseveres under trial," not *escapes* trial. The word rendered "trial" is the same used in verse 2 and has the double meaning of "testing" and "temptation" (see pp. 89-96). The former is still the meaning here, since an inner enticement to evil would call for resistance rather than endurance. Verse 12 places a limitation upon the statement in verse 2. Falling into various trials can be considered "pure joy" only when those trials are effectively endured. Only then is the experience of undergoing testings a blessing rather than a disaster.

The beatitude, like those of Jesus (Matt. 5:3-11; Luke 6:20-22), contains no expressed verb ("is"). It is neither a wish, "May he be blessed," nor a prosaic statement of fact, but a ringing verdict. It is the opposite of the "woes" in Luke 6:24-26 and needs no connecting copula. The predicate noun, "man" (*anēr*), is again used in the same general sense as in verse 8 above, with no thought of restricting the beatitude to the male sex. The noun[111] is without an article, thus making it of general application, "any one who" has the indicated character.

The word "blessed" (*makarios*) could be translated "happy" or "fortunate." It implies a congratulatory element as recognizing the desirability of the condition felicitated. In the New Testament it is always a strongly religious concept denoting an inner quality of life, a joy and happiness not dependent upon favorable external circumstances. It commonly denotes "the distinctive religious joy which accrues to man from his share in the salvation of the kingdom of God.[112] It points to a state of soul that the believer begins to experience in his life, even amid adverse outward circumstances, but its full bliss will be realized only in the future life.

The blessedness consists not in being free from trials, or yet in the fact that he is being subjected to testing, but that he "perseveres" under trial in the manner indicated in verses 2-4. The present tense denotes that he bravely and steadfastly remains under the trying ordeal until it is ended. It implies that "pressures and problems exist right now and are the norm for the lives of the brethren."[113] The meaning is not that he will never sink in defeat under a certain trial. Failure can be repented of and reversed. Rather, the tense portrays him as characteristically enduring the varied tests and refusing to give up. Such perseverance is the sign of genuine faith. In verse 2 the trials were referred to as plural to denote their great variety; here, the noun is a collective singular, pointing to trial as the characteristic feature of present human experience.

2. The Reward of Endurance (v. 12*b*)

"Because when he has stood the test, he will receive the crown of life that God has promised to those who love him." The conjunction "because" (*hoti*) introduces the reason for the blessedness of endurance under trial. The promised reward will be given when the time of testing has been completed. The adjective *dokimos* ("has stood the test") was used of the testing of coins and metals to establish their genuineness. To be rewarded, the believer must not only be "tested" but also be "attested" as having shown himself genuine. The aorist participle "having been proved" (Darby) denotes that the testing has effectively demonstrated his character as firm and reliable. Each new test the believer successfully endures adds fresh proof of fidelity to God and contributes to approved character.

"He will receive" states that the bestowal of the reward is still future, but the future tense does not imply that the reward is uncertain, since the individual has established his approval by God before that day. The time is not the present time of trial, or even death, but the time of the second advent (2 Tim. 4:8).

The approved believer will receive "the crown of life." James does not say that the one who successfully endures trials thereby earns eternal life. Eternal life is not earned through human effort and achievement; it is received as a gift through faith in Christ Jesus in this life (John 1:12; Eph. 2:8 9). In the day of reward, the approved believer will not receive life, but "the crown of life," eternal life as the final consummation of our salvation in eternity. The genitive "of life" is best taken as an appositional genitive, the crown which consists of eternal life in the full, final sense of the term. It is God's gracious reward to those who have been rendered fit for that life by their approved character. The article with "life" (*tēs zōēs*) points to that eternal life in all its fullness awaiting the attested believer. Burdick remarks, "Since it is a reward for an accomplishment subsequent to initial faith, it must refer to a still higher quality of life."[114] It is not merely escape from eternal condemnation, but the believer's eternal enjoyment of life as the approved of God in His presence.

In Pauline usage, the figure of the crown (*stephanos*) generally has the background of the victor's crown bestowed upon the winner in the Greek athletic contests. It may well be questioned whether James, with his strong Jewish background, had that picture in mind. Certainly, James would not be totally unfamiliar with the picture of the athletic games, since such athletic contests were actually staged in Jerusalem itself during the days of Herod the Great.[115] Because of the orthodox Jewish abhorrence of such games, it is not probable that James would consciously employ the figure. Nor would such a figure be pleasing to his Jewish readers, but the imagery of the crown was familiar from Jewish literature. In the Septuagint, the word *stephanos* was used to symbolize a special honor or as representative of happiness and prosperity (Ps. 21:3; Prov. 12:4; 16:31; Lam. 5:16; Ezek. 16:12; Zech. 6:11) and also of a royal crown (2 Sam. 12:30; 1 Chron. 20:2). Clearly James was not thinking of a fading crown, such as was given to victors in the athletic contests, but of a crown that was living and imperishable.

It has been questioned whether James viewed this crown as symbolizing victory or sovereignty. While reference to the kingdom in 2:5, and the Septuagint usage of the term of a royal crown, both point to the latter meaning, the concept of this verse leaves room for the thought of victory. Moo remarks, "The crown is the emblem of spiritual success, given by the King of the universe to those who 'keep their faith' in the midst of suffering and temptation. *Life* should be taken as identifying the reward—'the reward that is life.'"[116] This crown is connected with a divine promise "that God has promised to those who love him." In the original, no noun is expressed with the verb; the subject is simply the pronoun in the verb, "which he promised to them that love him."[117] That the promise was divinely given was regarded as self-evident by James. The absence of any expressed subject is fully in keeping with the Jewish practice of reverentially omitting the divine name when no misunderstanding would arise, but it is not clear whether James had in mind the Lord Jesus Christ or God the Father. Views differ. In light of 1:1 and 1:7, the former seems preferable. Lenski complains that those who oppose this view "seem to ignore Jesus and to substitute God, as if James thought of Jesus as little as possible."[118]

The aorist tense of the verb "promised" simply records the historical fact that the promise was given. If the reference is taken to be to God the Father, some Old Testament promise must be considered, but the Old Testament does not record such a promise. Deuteronomy 30:15-20 has been pointed out as the possible source, although Easton suggests Zechariah 6:14 (LXX) as a possibility.[119] If the promise is held to be given by Jesus Christ, the gospels likewise record no such promise. The expression "the crown of life" occurs elsewhere in Scripture only in Revelation 2:10, which was written after the epistle of James. In the gospels, the nearest approach to such a promise seems to be Matthew 19:28. It is generally suggested that James is referring to some unrecorded saying of Jesus that was orally preserved in the early church (cf. Acts 20:35). Others, like Lenski, hold that no specific promise in the gospels needs to be sought because James had in view "all the Lord's promises of heavenly glory."[120]

The indicated promise was given "to those who love him." This is the first mention of "love" in the epistle of James. The present articular plural participle portrays a group characterized as loving God. The "blessed man" is thus united with those identified by their continuing love for God. "Those loving God" is a well-known designation for God's people both in the Old Testament (Ex. 20:6; Pss. 97:10; 145:20) and the New (Rom. 8:28; 1 Cor. 2:9; 2 Tim. 4:8; 1 Pet. 1-7-8). Their love for God is the outcome of their faith in Him, which produces willing endurance for Him (1:2-4). Love is the essence of true faith. Where there is no love for God, death reigns. The verb "love" (*agapō*) denotes the noble love of understanding and purpose that prompts the believer to aspire to implicit obedience to God's commandments (John 14:15; 15:10; 1 John 2:5-6; 5:3).

The promised reward cannot be earned. It is God's gift to those who truly love Him. Indeed, "it is unattainable by those who do not serve God from a heart of love and devotion."[121] An obedience that is motivated by a personal desire to win a reward is the very antithesis of Christian spirituality. The rewards that God promises to those who love Him are of such a nature that only someone prompted by unselfish love for the Lord would be able to appreciate them.

NOTES FOR
James 1:2-12

1. H. Maynard Smith, *The Epistle of S. James, Lectures*, p. 45.
2. Joseph Bryant Rotherham, *The Emphasized New Testament*.
3. Sophie Laws, *A Commentary on the Epistle of James*, p. 50.
4. J. W. Roberts, *A Commentary on the General Epistles of James*, p. 40.
5. It occurs fifteen times as a form of address in this epistle.
6. Spiros Zodhiates, *The Epistle of James and the Life of Faith*, 1:21.
7. F. W. Farrar, *The Early Days of Christianity*, p. 326, n. 8.
8. J. Ronald Blue, "James," in *The Bible Knowledge Commentary, New Testament*, p. 820.
9. H. E. Dana and Julius R. Mantey, *A Manual Grammar of the Greek New Testament*, p. 281.
10. Ralph P. Martin, *James*, Word Biblical Commentary, p. 15.
11. Douglas J. Moo, *The Letter of James*, Tyndale New Testament Commentaries, pp. 59-60.

12. Theodore H. Epp, *James, the Epistle of Applied Christianity*, p. 40.
13. Joseph B. Mayor, *The Epistle of St. James. The Greek Text with Introduction, Notes and Comments*, p. 187.
14. J. A. Motyer, *The Tests of Faith*, p. 21.
15. Joseph Henry Thayer, *A Greek-English Lexicon of the New Testament*, p. 118.
16. Johnstone, pp. 73-74.
17. This is the meaning of the variant reading *dokimon* found in a few manuscripts.
18. The noun "faith" (*pistis*) occurs sixteen times; the verb "believe" (*pisteuō*) twice.
19. James Hardy Ropes, *A Critical and Exegetical Commentary on the Epistle of St. James*, The International Critical Commentary, p. 135.
20. Mayor, p. 34.
21. Thayer, p. 644.
22. Grammatically known as the article of previous reference.
23. William F. Arndt and F. Wilbur Gingrich, *A Greek-English Lexicon of the New Testament and Other Early Christian Literature*, p. 307.
24. Moo, p. 61.
25. He uses it five times—1:4 (twice), 17, 25; 3:2. In all the Pauline epistles, it occurs only seven times.
26. Johnstone, p. 75.
27. Zodhiates, p. 31.
28. Peter H. Davids, *The Epistle of James, A Commentary on the Greek Text*, p. 70.
29. R. J. Knowling, *The Epistle of St. James*, Westminster Commentaries, p. 8.
30. Alfred Plummer, "The General Epistle of St. James and St. Jude," in *An Exposition of the Bible*, 6:572.
31. W. E. Oesterley, "The General Epistle of James," in *The Expositor's Greek Testament*, 4:222.
32. William Barclay, *The Letters of James and Peter*, The Daily Study Bible, p. 52.
33. W. Boyd Carpenter, *The Wisdom of James the Just*, p. 105.
34. The first class conditional sentence. See A. T. Robertson and W. Hersey Davis, *A New Short Grammar of the Greek Testament*, pp. 350-51.
35. Donald W. Burdick, "James," in *The Expositor's Bible Commentary*, 12:168.
36. Johnstone, p. 78.
37. A. F. Mitchell, "Hebrews and the General Epistles," in *The Westminster New Testament*, p. 184.
38. Edwin T. Winkler, "Commentary on the Epistle of James," in *An American Commentary on the New Testament*, p. 17.
39. Thayer, p. 18.
40. Harold S. Songer, "James," in *The Broadman Bible Commentary*, 12:108.
41. M. F. Sadler, *The General Epistles of SS. James, Peter, John, and Jude, with Notes Critical and Practical*, p. 7.
42. John Blanchard, *Not Hearers Only. Bible Studies in the Epistle of James*, p. 44.
43. Otto Bauernfeind, "*Haplous, haplotēs*," in *Theological Dictionary of the New Testament*, 1:386.
44. Martin, p. 18.
45. Ropes, p. 140.
46. Roberts, p. 47.
47. Winkler, p. 17.
48. Blanchard, pp. 44-45.
49. Ralph A. Gwinn, *The Epistle of James*, Shield Bible Study Series, p. 18.
50. Rudolf Stier, *The Epistle of St. James*, p. 238.
51. H. W. Fulford, *The General Epistle of St. James*, p. 41.

52. See Blue, "James," in *Bible Knowledge Commentary, New Testament*, for a list of thirty references to nature in the book of James, p. 817.
53. The form *eoiken* is the perfect tense, but it has the force of the present. See Thayer, p. 175.
54. Ropes, p. 141.
55. Ibid., p. 142.
56. Marvin R. Vincent, *Word Studies in the New Testament*, 1:726.
57. Martin, p. 19.
58. Johnstone, p. 85.
59. Oesterley, p. 423.
60. Thayer, p. 276.
61. Robert Young, *The Holy Bible Consisting of the Old and New Covenants Translated According to the Letter and Idioms of the Original Languages*, p. 157.
62. Curtis Vaughan, *James, A Study Guide*, p. 24.
63. R. C. H. Lenski, *The Interpretation of the Epistle to the Hebrews and of the Epistle of James*, p. 540.
64. Martin, p. 20.
65. Moulton and Milligan, p. 166.
66. For early ecclesiastical usage, see Mayor, pp. 40-41; Laws, pp. 58-59.
67. Ropes, p. 143.
68. Barclay, p. 54.
69. The noun *akatastasia* is used five times in the New Testament and means "disturbance, disorder, unruliness."
70. Oesterley, p. 424.
71. Mitchell, p. 185.
72. Oesterley, p. 424.
73. E. H. Plumptre, *The General Epistle of St. James*, The Cambridge Bible for Schools and Colleges, p. 51.
74. Lenski, p. 541. Cf. Arndt and Gingrich, pp. 170, 172.
75. Clayton K. Harrop, *The Letter of James*, p. 25.
76. Zodhiates, p. 46.
77. A. T. Robertson, *Practical and Social Aspects of Christianity: The Wisdom of James*, p. 68.
78. Moo, p. 67.
79. Dana and Mantey, p. 144.
80. Songer, p 109.
81. Ropes, p. 145; Mayor, p. 43; Oesterley, p. 425; Davids, p. 76; Martin, p. 25.
82. A. T. Robertson, *A Grammar of the Greek New Testament in the Light of Historical Research*, pp. 776-77.
83. Albert Barnes, *Notes on the New Testament, Explanatory and Practical—James, Peter, John, and Jude*, p. 21.
84. John Calvin, *Commentaries on the Catholic Epistles*, p. 285.
85. R. W. Dale, *The Epistle of James and Other Discourses*, p. 15.
86. F. W. Bourne, *The King's Son: A Memoir of Billy Bray*.
87. Martin Dibelius, "James. A Commentary on the Epistle of James," in *Hermenia—A Critical and Historical Commentary on the Bible*, pp. 83-88; Burton Scott Easton and Gordon Poteat, "The Epistle of James," in *The Interpreter's Bible*, 12:25; Plummer, p. 576; Kistemaker p. 43; Laws, pp. 63-64.
88. Dibelius, p. 85.
89. Ibid., pp. 87-88.
90. Easton and Poteat, p. 25.
91. The use of *"de ho . . . ho de"* clearly marks the antithesis.

92. Henry Alford, *The Greek Testament*, vol. 4, pt. 1, p. 278.

93. Mayor, p. 43.

94. Lenski, p. 541.

95. Arndt and Gingrich, p. 679.

96. James Macknight, *A New Literal Translation from the Original Greek of All the Apostolical Epistles with a Commentary and Notes*, 5:344.

97. C. Leslie Mitton, *The Epistle of James*, p. 39.

98. James Moffatt, *The General Epistles, James, Peter, and Judas*, The Moffatt New Testament Commentary, p. 15.

99. Arthur Temple Cadoux, *The Thought of St. James*, p. 48.

100. Lenski, p. 543.

101. Dana and Mantey, p. 197.

102. Robert Jamieson, A. R. Fausset, and David Brown, *A Commentary, Critical and Explanatory, on the Old and New Testaments*, 2:485.

103. Arthur Carr, "The General Epistle of St. James," in *Cambridge Greek Testament*, p. 17.

104. Mitton, p. 42.

105. H. Maynard Smith, p. 54.

106. Lenski, p. 544.

107. Ropes, p. 149.

108. Ibid.

109. Dibelius, p. 88.

110. Ropes, p. 150.

111. The uncial manuscripts A and 044, and several minuscules, change *anēr* to *anthrōpos* in order not to exclude women.

112. F. Hauck, *"Makarios, Makarizō, makarismos,"* in *Theological Dictionary of the New Testament*, 4:367.

113. Roy R. Roberts, *The Game of Life, Studies in James*, p. 20.

114. Burdick, "James," in *Expositor's Bible Commentary*, 12:171.

115. Josephus, *Antiquities of the Jews*, 15.8.1.

116. Moo, p. 70.

117. The earlier and better textual witnesses have no noun, but in later manuscripts "Lord," with or without the article, or "God" (*ho theos*), were added to express the unnamed subject.

118. Lenski, p. 547.

119. Easton and Poteat, p. 26.

120. Lenski, p. 547.

121. Moo, p. 71.

4

III. THE NATURE
OF HUMAN TEMPTATION

1:13-16 When tempted, no one should say, "God is tempting me." For God cannot be tempted by evil, nor does he tempt anyone, [14]but each one is tempted when, by his own evil desire, he is dragged away and enticed. [15]Then, after desire has conceived, it gives birth to sin, and sin, when it is full-grown, gives birth to death. [16]Don't be deceived, my dear brothers.

The Greek word rendered "temptation" (*peirasmos*) has the ambiguity of meaning both "testing" and "temptation" (see pp. 63-64). Having dealt with the testings and trials of the believer in verses 2-12, James now turns to the thought of temptation, the inner solicitation to evil. The two aspects may be closely related in human experience. Because of a wrong inner reaction, the testings that God meant for our good may become an occasion for sin. The shift in meaning from the objective to the subjective aspect is clear from the contents of this paragraph. Instead of the noun *peirasmos* combined with adjectives suggesting the thought of anticipated approval (vv. 3, 12), James now uses the verbal form (*peirazō*) and combines it with the thought of sin. He deals with the source of man's temptation (vv. 13-14), portrays the result of yielding to temptation (v. 15), and adds a warning against being deceived (v. 16).

A. THE SOURCE OF HUMAN
TEMPTATION (vv. 13-14)

James realized that some individuals, when subjected to hard trials, were prone to think unfairly about God. They were inclined to blame God for their failure. James rejects the claim that God was tempting them (v. 13) and insists that the true source lies in man's lustful nature (v. 14).

1. The Repudiation of a Divine Source (v. 13)

James categorically forbids the claim that temptation comes from God (v. 13*a*) and vindicates his rejection of such a claim (v. 13*b*).

a. *The rejection stated* (v. 13*a*). "When tempted, no one should say, 'God is tempting me.'" The prohibition, stated in the singular, demands that "no one," not a single individual, however severe his testing, is to make such a claim. The present imperative with the negative implies that some individuals were suggesting this, but all such claims must be terminated. Whether made directly or indirectly, James sharply rebukes anyone harboring such an excuse for his failure.

"When tempted," rendering a present passive participle (*peirazomenos*), stands emphatically forward: "While being tempted, let no one be saying." The claim is advanced while the individual is being subjected to temptation. The present tense pictures the temptation as continuing. It is implied that the one being tempted is on the point of yielding.

The excuse advanced for yielding is "God is tempting me." James states the spurious assertion in the very words of the individual, *hoti*[1] *apo theou peirazomai*, "Of God I am being tempted." Scholars such as Mayor[2] and Ropes[3] suggest that the use of the preposition *apo* conveys the thought of remote source, whereas the use of *hupo*[4] would have denoted direct agency. So understood, the quoted charge does not crudely blame God as directly tempting him but charges that God, through His creative action and providential direction of affairs, is behind the situation that produced the temptation. God is responsible for bringing him into such a situation. But Davids,[5] following Dibelius,[6] questions this suggested refinement of the charge and insists that "this is simply a case of *apo* beginning to take over functions of *hupo*.[7] Then the temptation is viewed as being "by God." Under either view, the blame for the temptation is placed on God.

Perverse human nature is ever prone to blame someone else for its sins. That cowardly tendency is as old as the sinful human race. In the Garden of Eden after the Fall, Adam asserted, "The woman you put here with me—she gave me some fruit of the tree and I ate it" (Gen. 3:12). Admittedly, the woman was the immediate agent leading to the forbidden act, but God Himself, since He had given the woman to be with him, was the real cause.

This tendency to blame others for our moral failures is universal. Ropes notes that the idea was expressed among the Greeks at various periods.[8] The claim was also known in Jewish circles. Proverbs 19:3 says, "A man's own folly ruins his life, yet his heart rages against the Lord." Ecclesiasticus 15:11-13 asserts,

> Say not thou, It is through the Lord that I fell away;
> For thou shalt not do the things that he hateth.
> Say not thou, It is he that caused me to err;
> For he hath no need of a sinful man.
> The Lord hateth every abomination,
> And they that fear him love it not.

Ropes quotes Philo as saying, "When the mind has sinned and removed itself far from virtue, it lays the blame on divine causes, attributing to God its own change."[9] It has been noted that this teaching also prevailed in the Qumran community (*Manual of Discipline*, 3:13ff). Several early Christian writers also felt it necessary to oppose this impious claim.[10] People today may not be so bold as to blame God directly, but they do so indirectly. Some seek to hide behind their heredity or their slum environment or their evil companions. Some even flippantly claim, "The devil made me do it." But all such claims are simply futile efforts to escape personal responsibility for their actions.

Some of those addressed by James may have sought support for their claim from a misapplication of such Old Testament passages as Genesis 22:1 and 2 Samuel 24:1 (cf. 1 Chron. 21:1) or the phrase in the Lord's Prayer "And lead us not into temptation" (Matt. 6:13). This is a misreading of God's purpose in permitting man to be tested. James is not denying that God does indeed subject men to testing, but he does deny the claim that God tests men with an evil intent to lead them into sin. Testings are necessary to develop the desired moral maturity and strength in His people, but He does not solicit men to evil. In 1 Corinthians 10:13, Paul points out that God does not permit man to be tempted beyond the power of genuine faith to endure, but along with the temptation He provides the way of escape. Lenski aptly remarks,

> When God sent Jesus to be tempted by Satan, and when now he lets Satan tempt us, we should not blame God, but should remember that God's own Spirit helped Jesus to crush Satan and that he now helps us to vanquish him.[11]

b. *The rejection vindicated* (v. 13*b*). "For God cannot be tempted by evil, nor does he tempt anyone." "For" introduces a twofold reason for the rejection of this claim. It rests on the character and activity of God.

The claim is inconsistent with God's character because "God cannot be tempted by evil." "Cannot be tempted" translates the verbal adjective *apeirastos*, which does not occur elsewhere in the New Testament or the Septuagint. Moffatt suggests that it was coined by James.[12] This negative adjective is derived from the verb *peirazō*, "to tempt," used three times in this verse alone. Such verbal adjectives can be either active or passive in meaning. The active would mean "not tempting to evil," while the passive means "not tempted by evil." The context here calls for the passive meaning; the active would make the following statement sheer repetition. "He Himself is in His purity *untemptable* of evil."[13] The word for "evil" is a neuter plural adjective without an article and denotes things that have the moral quality of being base and degrading, the opposite of the morally good, the wholesome and beneficial.

91

Alford insists that the form used by James is simply the equivalent of the classical *apeirētos* or *apeiratos*, derived from the verb *peiraō*, meaning "to try, to experience." He suggests the rendering "unversed in," having no experience of evil.[14] Under this view, the meaning is that God is unexperienced in things evil. This is the view in the margin of the *American Standard Version*, "God is untried in evil." This explanation is possible, but the resultant sense is less likely in view of the strong emphasis on temptation in this paragraph. Mayor insists that the meaning of this verb must be determined from the general force of the verb *peirazō*, "to tempt."[15]

The words of James are an important declaration concerning God's nature. Seesemann notes that it is "a statement about the nature of God which we do not find elsewhere in the Bible."[16] It is thoroughly in keeping with the biblical presentation of the divine nature as good, perfect, and unchangeably holy. God is unsusceptible to evil; evil never has any appeal for Him. It is repugnant and abhorrent to Him. The fact that God is untemptable of evil is the foundation for the Christian belief in a moral universe. Carpenter well observes:

> In the stainless purity of His character lies our security. If saints can give thanks at the remembrance of His holiness, struggling men may take courage also, since God's purity is not against us, but for us in our conflict with evil. It is madness to throw away this sheet anchor of faith. This anchor holds.[17]

Johnstone calls attention to the contrast between this picture of God and the character of the gods in pagan mythology:

> The gods of heathen imagination are always conceived both as liable to temptation to moral evil, and as themselves tempters. The conception of their character comes from man's wicked heart, and the stream cannot rise higher than its source.[18]

The claim that God tempts men is also contrary to God's actions. "Nor does he tempt anyone." "Nor" (*de*) reminds that this is a further fact that must be added. The argument is that His character makes such conduct impossible. The fact of human temptation is a sad reality, but God "himself" (*autos*, passed over in NIV), because of what He is, never solicits anyone to do what is morally wrong. It is corrupted human nature that turns into evil that which God meant for our good.

2. The Reality of the Human Source (v. 14)

"But" (*de*) introduces the positive fact: "each one is tempted when, by his own evil desire, he is dragged away and enticed."

The singular "each one" (*hekastos*) stresses that the universal experience of being tempted is an individual matter, assailing each individually.

None is exempt from the experience. The present tense "is tempted" points to the repeated experience of being tempted as characteristic of each human being.

"By his own evil desire" names the true source of man's temptation. God is not to be blamed, for the trouble lies in the combustible material that each man carries within himself. Temptation has its source not in the outer lure but in the inner lust. "By" (*hupo*) implies direct agency and serves to personify "his own evil desire" as the active agent of temptation. "His own" underlines the individual peculiarity of the temptation in the case of each person. The word *epithumias*, rendered "evil desire," is in itself a neutral term simply denoting strong desires or cravings. The desires may be either good or bad. In the New Testament, the word is used in a good sense in Luke 22:15, Philippians 1:23, and 1 Thessalonians 2:17, but generally it carries an evil connotation. The context must decide the meaning. Desires are necessary for human survival, but human experience shows that man's desires and cravings are predominantly evil. They are evil whenever they are self-centered and contrary to God's will. James's assertion assumes depravity of human nature. It is consistent with Jesus' teaching in Mark 7:21-23 that the things "from within, out of men's hearts" defile the person. The practical purpose of James does not call for a philosophical explanation of the origin of this nature.

The word order in the original, "each one is tempted by his own evil desire being drawn out and enticed," permits "by his own evil desire" to be closely connected either with the preceding verb or with the following participles. The former connection is represented in the rendering of Lilly: "Each individual is tempted by his own passion inasmuch as he is allured and enticed by it."[19] This connection makes prominent the fact that lust is the personal agent in the temptation. So NIV. Generally, the phrase is taken closely with the following participles. Thus, Young's literal rendering is: "Each one is tempted, by his own desires being led away and enticed."[20] Then the words "by his own evil desire" stand emphatically forward and stress how lust operates in temptation. The participles, connecting directly with the personal subject of the verb, picture the reactions of fallen man when exposed to temptation. Davids remarks, "The grammar is deliberately vague," so that the phrase "by his own evil desire" "fits well with either the verb or the participles."[21] The latter connection seems preferable as more in keeping with the vivid picture of James.

The two participles rendered "is dragged away and enticed" picture two phrases of the same process. Both are in the passive voice and indicate how lusts affect the tempted individual. Both terms were used in connection with the activity of the fisherman, and then came to be used of the wiles of the harlot. James here personifies the operation of lust and probably has in mind the picture of the harlot as given in Proverbs 7:6-23, but there is no reason to restrict the picture of James to sexual sins.

The first term, "is dragged away" (*exelkomenos*), is a compound form of the preposition *ek*, "out," and the verb *helkō*, "to draw, drag." It expresses the intensity of lust forcefully drawing the tempted individual toward the object of desire and pictures the movement of the tempted one toward it. The second term, "enticed" (*deleazomenos*), which occurs elsewhere in the New Testament only in 2 Peter 2:14, 18, conveys the picture of catching with bait (*delear*). It depicts the juicy worm being dangled in front of the fish. His inner craving to appropriate it for himself prompts him to bite, but he is deceived and caught. Instead of enjoying the anticipated pleasure, he is caught on the hook concealed within. It is an apt picture of the deceptiveness of lust. When a person is confronted with alluring temptation, he sees only the attractiveness of the desired object. Only when his will has sanctioned the performance of the sinful act do the tragic consequences come into operation. "We are free to choose, but not free to choose the consequences of our choice, for those are determined by the eternal purpose and laws of God."[22]

The picture of James stresses the operation of our psychological nature in temptation. Here James says nothing about the part that the devil may have in temptation. He was well aware of Satan's vicious activities, for he said, "Resist the devil, and he will flee from you" (4:7; cf. also 3:6). James is emphasizing man's personal responsibility for sinning by refuting the effort to place the blame on God.

B. THE CONSEQUENCES OF YIELDING TO TEMPTATION (v. 15)

"Then, after desire has conceived, it gives birth to sin, and sin, when it is full grown, gives birth to death." The consequences of yielding to temptation demonstrate that the enticement to do evil cannot be from God (v. 13).

"Then" points to a sequence. The inner craving demands action. It must either be acted on or be resolutely repulsed. When indulged, a chain of results surely follows.

"After desire has conceived" again personifies the lust as a harlot; it resumes the mention of "his own evil desire" in verse 14. The craving is an inner reaction of the individual's own nature, but when it is indulged it becomes malignant and is destructive of personal well-being. Our nature may involuntarily and instinctively feel a longing for a certain object when it is presented, but the craving becomes sinful when it is encouraged and acted upon, the will surrendering to the enticement of the harlot and uniting with it in a guilty union. When the will consents to the illicit union, the lustful feeling becomes impregnated with sin. "Conceived" (*sullabousa*) is a compound form, derived from the preposition *sun*, "together," and the verb *lambanō*, "to take." Hence it has the basic meaning of clasping. In a sexual sense, it denotes the woman's resultant conception. In James's figurative use here, it may well suggest the man's will bending toward the evil suggestion and seizing it.

The result is that impregnated lust "gives birth to sin." McGee tersely remarks, "There cannot be a stillbirth."[23] Thus lust (*epithumia*, fem. gender) is the mother of sin. "Sin" used without the article is general—an actual sin of one kind or another. Its exact identity is immaterial. Each lust gives birth to its own kind of sin. "Sin" (*hamartia*) is "the most comprehensive term for moral obliquity" in the New Testament.[24] Its basic meaning is "a falling short of the target, missing the mark." Trench observes that it contemplates sin "as a failing and missing the true end and scope of our lives, which is God."[25] In New Testament usage, the concept conveyed is not merely negative; it is a positive act "in which a person is knowingly disobedient to the perfect will of God, something to which in a measure at least he gives his consent."[26] The word may denote the principle of sin, the inner sinful element producing acts of sin. In James's statement, the reference is clearly to an act of sin.

"And sin, when it is full grown, gives birth to death." "And" (*de*) indicates that this further result must be added to complete the picture. "Sin," literally "the sin," takes up the story of the particular "sin" just mentioned. That sin, having been born, has its own life and development. Unless its life and growth are terminated by repentance, sin will have its sure development until it becomes "full grown" (*apotelestheisa*). As an aorist passive participle, the term suggests the thought of something having been effectively brought to its goal, brought to completion. The rendering "full grown" views the sin as having reached its full maturity. Mayor holds that sin becomes "full grown when it has become a fixed habit determining the character of man."[27]

Matured sin "gives birth to death." The verb *apokueō* is a different term than that used for the birth of sin just before (*tiktō*). Whereas the latter is the usual word for childbirth, it has been suggested that the former denotes "some monstrous deformity, a hideous progeny,"[28] but this claim is doubtful since in 1:18 (the only other occurrence of the verb in the New Testament) James uses it for the new birth of the believer through the Word of God. Moulton and Milligan hold that the two verbs are ordinary synonyms, but the preposition *apo* in the former gives it a perfective force, to bring forth from the womb.[29] The figure is not completely carried through since there is no mention of sin's conceiving, but the verb implies a second birth: sin becoming the mother of death.

Therefore James gives the story of three generations: the grandmother is lust, the mother is sin, and the daughter is death. However, some hold that James means that when lust conceives, the developing embryo is sin, and when the matured embryo comes forth from the womb, the child that is born is death. Burdick well remarks, "The details of the illustration must not be pressed too far. The author's intention is simply to trace the results of temptation when one yields to it. The order is evil desire, sin, death."[30]

The "death" that sin brings forth is mentioned "in all its undefined terror."[31] The statement is "intended to cover every form of disintegration and final collapse to which man is heir."[32] The primary reference seems to be to spiritual death, but physical death is certainly included and ultimately eternal death also. The basic meaning of "death" (*thanatos*) is separation. Physical death is the separation of the soul from the body; spiritual death is the separation of the spirit of man from God because of sin; eternal death is the separation of the self-conscious personality from God forever. Eternal death is not cessation of existence but rather the loss of that life of fellowship with God that alone is worthy of the name. Death in all its forms is traceable to sin.

C. THE WARNING AGAINST BEING DECEIVED (v. 16)

James immediately follows his stark picture of death with an affectionate warning to his readers. "Don't be deceived, my dear brothers." The verb "deceived" means "to lead astray, cause to wander," and in the passive, as here, "to go astray, to let oneself be misled, be deceived." The *mē* with the present imperative demands that the readers must not allow this danger of being led astray to continue. "Stop being deceived!" The ringing warning indicates how seriously James is concerned about the safety of his readers.

The warning may be connected with what immediately precedes (vv. 13-15) or with what follows (vv. 17-18). If the former, the warning is to not be deceived about the source and consequences of sin. If the latter, it is a call to beware of casting suspicion on God and His beneficent activities. The verse has a transitional function and, like a bridge, provides connections in both directions, but what has gone before seems primarily in view. The same formula occurs elsewhere to establish the rejection of a false opinion, as in 1 Corinthians 6:9; 15:33, and Galatians 4:7. "It introduces an appeal to Christian consciousness and experience to confirm the writer's statement."[3]

To harbor the false concept that God tempts people is to cast grave suspicion on His character. It is a grievous doctrinal error that must have dangerous consequences for daily conduct. "My dear brothers" is the first of three occurrences of this full address in James (1:19; 2:5). The warning is prompted by his strong affectionate relationship to his readers. The verbal *agapētoi*, here rendered "dear," is more literally "beloved" and marks the close relationship between writer and readers. They are the recipients of his heartfelt love. As members of the family of God, they must not allow a false view of God to quench their filial relations to the Head of the Christian family.

NOTES FOR
James 1:13-16

1. The *hoti* is recitative—the equivalent of our English quotation marks.
2. Joseph B. Mayor, *The Epistle of James*, p. 40.
3. James Hardy Ropes, *A Critical and Exegetical Commentary on the Epistle of St. James*, p. 155.

4. *Apo* was changed to *hupo* in Codex Aleph and some minuscules.
5. Peter H. Davids, *The Epistle of James*, p. 82.
6. Martin Dibelius, *James. A Commentary on the Epistle of James*, p. 90.
7. Davids, p. 82. He says, "The slight textual uncertainty probably reflects orthographic similarity rather than differentiation in use."
8. Ropes, pp. 154-55.
9. Ibid., p. 154. Also, see Debilius, pp. 90-91.
10. Mayor, p. 48.
11. R. C. H. Lenski, *The Interpretation of the Epistle to the Hebrews and of the Epistle of James*, p. 549.
12. James Moffatt, *The General Epistles, James, Peter, and Judas*, Moffatt New Testament Commentary, p. 18.
13. Rudolf Stier, *The Epistle of St. James*, p. 248.
14. Henry Alford, *The New Testament for English Readers*, p. 1595.
15. Mayor, p. 50.
16. Heinrich Seesemann, *"Peira, perraō, peirazō, perrasmos,"* in *Theological Dictionary of the New Testament*, 6:29.
17. W. Boyd Carpenter, *The Wisdom of James the Just*, p. 129.
18. Robert Johnstone, *Lectures Exegetical and Practical on the Epistle of James*, p. 101.
19. James A. Kleist and Joseph L. Lilly, *The New Testament Rendered from the Original Greek with Explanatory Notes*, p. 594.
20. Robert Young, *The Holy Bible, New Testament, p. 157.*
21. Davids, p. 84.
22. Spiros Zodhiates, *The Epistle of James and the Life of Faith*, p. 62.
23. J. Vernon McGee, *James*, p. 33.
24. W. E. Vine, *An Expository Dictionary of New Testament Words with Their Precise Meanings for English Readers*, 4:32.
25. Richard Chenevix Trench, *Synonyms of the New Testament*, p. 240.
26. C. Leslie Mitton, *The Epistle of James*, p. 49.
27. Mayor, p. 53.
28. E. G. Punchard, "The General Epistle of James," in *Ellicott's Commentary on the Whole Bible*, 8:359.
29. James Hope Moulton and George Milligan, *The Vocabulary of the Greek Testament Illustrated from the Papyri and Other Non-Literary Sources*, p. 65.
30. Donald W. Burdick, "James," in *The Expositor's Bible Commentary*, 12:172.
31. R. J. Knowling, *The Epistle of St. James*, Westminster Commentaries, p. 22.
32. John Wick Bowman, *The Letter of James*, The Layman's Bible Commentary, 24:102.
33. Edwin T. Winkler, *Commentary on the Epistle of James, An American Commentary on the New Testament*, p. 24.

5

IV. THE ACTIVITY
OF GOD IN HUMAN AFFAIRS

1:17-18 Every good and perfect gift is from above, coming down from the Father of the heavenly lights, who does not change like shifting shadows. ¹⁸He chose to give us birth through the word of truth, that we might be a kind of first fruits of all he created.

These verses pick up the theme of God's character as a giving God, touched upon in verse 5, and develop it as a refutation of the claim that God tempts men (vv. 13-15). James presents a double picture of God's beneficent activity in human affairs. The first picture is comprehensive, depicting God as the giver of every good gift (v. 17); the second is specific, portraying Him as the true source of human regeneration (v. 18). Both assertions are made without any connecting particles to tie them to what has just been said. This use of *asyndeton*, the absence of connecting particles, which stresses "a logical expression of coherence of thought,"¹ declares these truths as independent realities.

A. THE GIVER OF ALL GOOD GIFTS (1:17)

James emphatically declares that God is the true source of all good gifts: "Every good and perfect gift is from above, coming down from the Father of the heavenly lights." The NIV rendering compresses the original (*pasa dosis agathē kai pan dōrēma teleion*) by omitting one of the two nouns rendered "gift" with its adjective "every." The ASV, "Every good gift and every perfect gift," expresses the double original. The two nouns rendered "gift" use the same verb root but have a different suffix. The first (*dosis*), adding the suffix of action to the verb root, means the act of giving; the second (*dōrēma*), adding the common suffix denoting result, means "the thing given," the gift itself. The first noun may be either passive in meaning, "gift," or active, "giving," as in Philippians 4:15, its only other occurrence in the New Testament. Some, like Ropes² and Vincent,³ hold that the double expression supports the passive meaning and that the different forms were used only for rhetorical effect. Davids insists, "Because of the poetic and pro- verbial nature of the text, no distinction ought to be drawn between *dosis* and *dōrēma*, for they simply make for proper style."⁴ This is clearly the view behind the NIV rendering.

It is clear that the noun *dosis* did have the meaning of "gift" in classical usage,⁵ but Moulton and Milligan quote no example of its usage in the papyri with a passive meaning.⁶ In keeping with papyrus usage, it seems better to hold that James, in employing different forms, intended a clear distinction in their meaning. This is in harmony with its usage in Philippians 4:15. In 1:25, James uses another noun formed with the same suffix (*poiēsis*) with the ac- tive meaning. This view is well represented in the rendering of Rotherham, "Every good giving and every perfect gift is from above."

The two adjectives further distinguish the two concepts. "Good" (*agathē*) describes the giving as "useful" and "beneficial" in its effect, and "perfect" (*teleion*) marks the gift as "complete" and lacking nothing to meet the needs of its recipient. In each expression, the emphasis falls on the adjec- tive. Standing after the nouns, the adjectives are best taken as predicates, "every act of giving (which is) good and every gift (which is) perfect." Smith remarks that the former expression "indicates the nature of a person, lavish in his generosity," whereas the latter "represents the value of the gift re- ceived."⁷ The perfection of the gift received flows from the goodness of the One bestowing it (Luke 11:13). Although all good gifts that men enjoy come from God, the context suggests that James is thinking specifically of His gifts "with special reference to their action on the soul of man; for he is exhibiting the truth which stands opposed to the error that God is the author of sin."⁸ God alone is the ultimate source of all such gifts.

In the original, "every good gift and every perfect gift" has a poetic sound, being a nearly perfect hexameter line. It often is concluded that James was quoting from some unknown hymn.⁹ Blackman seems to suggest that this trace of the author's feeling of affinity with Greek culture presents some diffi- culty concerning the Jacobean authorship of the epistle.¹⁰ A conscious quota- tion is a possibility, but the poetic cadence of the expression does not prove it. It may simply be that the words of James naturally fell into a metrical form, an occurrence not uncommon in good prose. The poetical flow of the words may simply mean that James, like Jesus, had a natural feeling for metrical rhythm.

James insists that every such gift "is from above, coming down from the Father of the heavenly lights." The NIV inserts the adjective "heavenly," not in the Greek text, since the reference seems to be to the lights in the heavens, sun, moon, and stars. The word order in the original (*anōthen estin kata- bainon*, "from above is coming down") offers a slight grammatical problem. Should the participle after "is" be set off by a comma and construed as a predicate offering a supplemental statement, or should the participle be taken with "is" as a paraphrastic construction? In support of the latter is the parallel construction in 3:15 and the fact that the older interpreters accepted the paraphrastic construction.[11] This view is behind the rendering of the *New English Bible*, "All good giving, every perfect gift, comes from above." The majority of our English versions accept the participle as a predicate, presenting a complementary thought. This is the meaning of the NIV rendering.

Mayor holds that this construction best preserves the rhythm and balance of the sentence.[12] Although the difference is not great, we accept the latter view as more probable. Then, two thoughts rather than just one are involved. James first asserts that all such gifts have their source "above," the heavenly sphere as contrasted to the earthly (3:15; John 3:31; Col. 3:1-2). He then supplements this with the truth that these gifts are descending from above in a continual stream.

These gracious gifts are viewed as continually "coming down from the Father of lights" (ASV). The present participle (*katabainon*) views each gift as originated and designed in heaven and then as descending in an unending succession. The God who sends them is first named in the verse. Davids holds that the identification is a typical Jewish circumlocution. "James, like a good Jew, avoids using the name of God where he does not feel it is necessary."[13]

"Lights" in the original has the definite article, "the lights," and the primary reference is to the well-known celestial lights, the heavenly luminaries that are the sources of light for our earth. As "the Father" of these lights, God is their source of being, and they reflect the glory of their Creator (Pss. 19:1; 136:7). As their Creator and Sustainer, He is not to be identified with them. These luminous celestial bodies must not be worshiped as God, but they testify to the Creator's luminous nature. Their glory and dignity declare the nature and essence of God, that "God is light" (1 John 1:5). He is also the Father of all our spiritual illumination (2 Cor. 4:6). This identification of God as "the Father of the lights" (Gr.) does not occur elsewhere in Scripture, but it was known in Jewish circles. Philo (30 B.C.-A.D. 50) used the expression (*Apo. Mos.* 36) and frequently spoke of God as "Father of the universe."[14] Among the Dead Sea Scrolls, the *Damascus Document* speaks of God as "Prince of Lights."[15]

God's creative relation to these variable heavenly lights prompts James to assert the immutable nature of God, "who does not change like shifting shadows." The first part of the Greek text behind this rendering (*para hō ouk eni parallagē ē tropes aposkiasma*) asserts the changeless nature of God. The exact meaning of the whole expression is not fully clear and has been the occasion of much discussion. The first part of the expression (*para hō ouk eni parallagē*) asserts the constancy of His being. In His presence there is no indication of any inner variation. This is obvious from a position *para hō*, "alongside of," God. The assertion "does not change" (*ouk eni parralagē*), according to Lightfoot, negates "not the fact only, but the possibility."[16]

(Cf. Gal. 3:28; Col. 3:11.) It is doubtful how far the idea of impossibility can be pressed for the original expression (*ouk eni*), and the rendering "can be" may be somewhat strong. It is generally held today that the expression simply conveys the negative fact "there is."[17] Representative of this view is the *New American Standard Bible,* "with whom there is no variation." With this, most modern versions agree.

The noun rendered "variation" (*parallagē*) in the NASB occurs only here in the New Testament. Basically, it denotes a change or variation from an established course or pattern. Thus James seems to suggest that unlike the light of the heavenly bodies, God's light—expressive of His very being—is without change. The noun was at times used as an astronomical term (cf. our English "parallax"), but it is not certain whether James had an astronomical meaning in mind that his readers (being ordinary people) would fail to understand. James simply seems to be using the term to signify the variation in the intensity of light given by the sun and moon, the primary sources of natural light for our world. God is the Creator and Sustainer of these variable lights, as the Giver of good gifts to men, but there is no variation in Him.

Behind the concluding phrase of verse 17 in the original (*ē tropēs aposkiasma*) lies a textual problem. The Greek manuscripts and ancient versions show a wide array of variant meanings[18] due to the obscurity of the passage. The King James rendering, "neither shadow of turning," is based on the text that is found in all printed editions of the Greek text except the recent edition by Tasker.[19] This common text, *ē tropēs aposkiasma*, is literally "or of turning a shadow," in English "or a shadow of turning." Since the interpreters have found this reading difficult, attention has been directed to the variants in the manuscripts.

The only variant with any significant support, favored by Ropes [20] and adopted in Tasker's edition, reads *hē tropēs aposkiasmatos*, which may be rendered "no change, the one (which consists of) turning of a shadow."[21] Ropes holds that this reading "makes excellent sense," but Dibelius finds that the reading supported by Ropes "makes no real sense." Since he is not satisfied with the commonly accepted reading, Dibelius resorts to a conjectural reading: *ē tropēs ē aposkiasmatos*, which inserts a second *ē*, "or"; he renders "and knows neither turning nor eclipse."[22] The conjectural reading of Dibelius has found little approval, and the reading supported by Ropes and adopted by Tasker has not won the general acceptance of scholars. It is generally agreed that "the least unsatisfactory reading" is the commonly used text.[23] We accept it as the most probable text. With this reading, James makes a double negative statement concerning God's character. In the proposed alternatives, the description is conceived as a whole, as in the NIV rendering.

Having asserted that God's character is not subject to the variation that characterizes the heavenly lights, James further insists that God is not characterized by "shadow that is cast by turning" (ASV). Neither of the Greek nouns, "shadow" (*aposkiasma*) or "turning" (*tropēs*), occurs elsewhere in the New Testament. The latter was used of the solstice and generally of movements of the heavenly bodies from one place to another. Hence it came to denote simply "change" or "turning." The genitive case seems to have a casual force, thus the rendering "shadow that is cast by turning."[24]

The picture is larger than the changing shadow on the sundial caused by the rotating earth. Kistemaker remarks, "As the earth, sun, moon, and stars move in their ordained courses, we observe the interplay of light and darkness, day and night, the longest and the shortest day of the year, the waning and the waxing of the moon, eclipses, and the movement of the planets. Nature is subject to variation and change. Not so with God!"[25] In Him there is never such turning because of any change in His nature or purpose. Epp asserts that "this phrase goes even a step further by emphasizing that God does not even give the appearance of change."[26] The light from Him is constant and unvarying. "In him is no darkness at all" (1 John 1:5). There is never any dimming of the light of God's holiness that would make it possible for Him to become the tempter of men.

In verses 14 and 17, James has given us a remarkable picture of God's character. James is concerned not only with what God is thought of as doing or not doing; he is also concerned with what God is. His portrayal of God's character is an important feature of this epistle.

B. THE AUTHOR OF THE BELIEVER'S REGENERATION (v. 18)

The good gifts of God find specific illustration in His bestowal of the new birth upon believers. "He chose to give us birth through the word of truth, that we might be a kind of first fruits of all he created." James recognizes this as a "greater witness to God's goodness than that which is written upon the dome of heaven."[27] "He chose" (*boulētheis*) renders an aorist participle, standing emphatically first, making prominent the cause of our regeneration. Rotherham renders it "Because he was so minded." The term stresses that the new birth roots in "the resolute will of God as the motivating force which gives new life."[28] Sin brought death (1:25), but God resolutely willed not to let us perish in sin. His deliberate will to save us was not forced by any outside necessity. Having willed it, God acted freely to save us—a fact wholly inconsistent with the claim that God tempts an individual to sin.

"He chose to give us birth" asserts how God's will expressed itself. "Give us birth" (*apekuēsen*) is the same verb used in verse 15. There is pictured a terrible bringing forth of sin unto death; here we have God's will acting to bring us forth as new beings. The aorist tense looks back to the time of our conversion and records the fact of our spiritual birth as a historical reality. It has been noted that this verb, which means "bring forth, give birth to," properly applies only to the female. Davids notes that "two pieces of data resolve the problem: (1) Female imagery is sometimes applied to God in scripture (Num. 11:12; Deut. 32:8; Deut. 32:18*a* in the Septuagint; Psalms

7:14; 90:2; Isa. 66:13), and (2) James needed an action parallel to desire in 1:15."[29] In this epistle, James emphatically calls for Christian conduct as proof of the reality of our new birth, but he clearly insists that this new life must first be wrought in us by God.

"Through the word of truth" names the divine means used in our regeneration. Some suggest that "the word" primarily refers to Christ Himself, as in John 1:1, but the context does not suggest such a reference. Neither "word" nor "truth" has the article in the original; the stress is on the quality of each. The "word" used as the instrument of regeneration denotes a divine message, spoken or written. God used "the message of truth" (Williams). The genitive "of truth" may be appositional, "a message which consists of truth"(cf. John 17:17), but it seems better to take the genitive as objective, "a message which proclaims truth." Under either view it is a direct reference to the gospel, a message that embodies the divine truth of God in the Person and work of Jesus Christ. Faithfully proclaimed under the power of the Holy Spirit, this message works regeneration in the hearts of those who receive it (Rom. 10:17; 1 Cor. 4:15; 1 Thess. 2:13; 1 Pet. 1:23-25). There is no substitute for the proclamation of the gospel.

Some scholars suggest that the "us" brought forth by the word of truth does not refer to the regeneration of believers but to the creation of mankind as the first fruits of the whole creation. Then the reference is to creation rather than redemption. This view was first advocated by Spitta in support of his claim that this epistle was originally a Jewish document. (See Introduction, p. 23.) In his posthumous commentary on *The Epistle of James*, Hort supported the view that the reference was cosmological rather than soteriological. This view has received the support of some subsequent writers.[30] Davids replies, "Yet is it not the case that redemption in the N.T. is often seen as a new creation, the creation terminology being used for effect? It is this fact that has persuaded most recent commentators that the regeneration reference is intended."[31] Ward well remarks, "If James has creation in mind at all he is thinking of the new creation."[32] The verb "give birth" (*apokueō*) has the basic idea of a mother's giving birth, and is not appropriate to the cosmological view. Ropes asserts, "The figure of begetting was not used for creation, whereas it came early into use with reference to the Christians, who deemed themselves 'sons of God.'"[33] Nor does the expression "by the word of truth" readily suggest the creative words "Let us make man" (Gen. 1:26), but it does suggest the gospel. The reference to personal salvation through the implanted word in verse 21 strongly supports the soteriological meaning here.

God's regenerating work in believers looked forward to a glorious goal: "that we might be a kind of first fruits of all he created." "That we might be" (*eis to einai hēmas*) indicates purpose, but that does not imply that the purpose is as yet unrealized. The divine purpose that we should be His first fruits was fulfilled. The new birth that the readers, along with James, have experienced has given them the position and character as "first fruits." The addition "a kind of" (*tina*) serves "to soften the metaphorical expression."[34] Alford sees in the expression an argument for an early date for this epistle, regarding it as an "apologetic explanation" for introducing a figure that afterward became common in the Christian church.[35]

The figure of the "first fruits"[36] is drawn from the Old Testament Law that designated the first portion of the harvest as belonging to God, that was to be offered to Him before the rest could be used for ordinary purposes (Exod. 23:19; Lev. 23:9-11; Deut. 18:4). These first fruits were the specimens and pledge of the full harvest. Paul used the term of the first converts in a province as the promise of the coming harvest in the area (Rom. 16:5; 1 Cor. 16:15). The figure would be especially meaningful and challenging to the Jewish Christians to whom the figure was being applied.

When James speaks of "we" as the first fruits, it seems natural that he is applying the term specifically to his Jewish Christian readers. They were the first sheaves of the gospel harvest and the earnest of what would yet be reaped. As the first ripe samples of that harvest, they proclaimed the new order of spiritual things that God was bringing upon the world scene.

What did James envision as the intended scope of that new order? What is included in "all he created" (*tōn autou ktismatōn*, "His creations")? The noun denotes that which is the product of God's creative activity. The term occurs three other times in the New Testament (1 Tim. 4:4; Rev. 5:13; 8:9), and only here does the context require that the reference is to human beings, at least chiefly so. The unusual position of "his" in the original stresses that all the creatures in view belong explicitly to God. If the meaning here is restricted to people, then the reference is to that vast multitude of believers who shall yet be brought to a saving faith in Christ (Acts 15:14-18). The fact that the term is commonly used of the material creation makes it possible that James has a larger transformation in view. Mayor holds that the term chosen by James indicated that the intended scope includes "not only men, but all created things."[37] Then these believers are to be viewed as the earnest of the transformation awaiting the present creation (Matt. 19:28; Rom. 8: 19-22; Rev. 21:1). Creation will yet share in the freedom now being experienced by God's saints.

Davids again draws the application: "The God who is redeeming creation is a gracious God. Such a gracious God is not one who is trying to lead people to fall, but one who would use his giving to preserve them in the test."[38]

NOTES FOR
James 1:17-18

1. A. T. Robertson, *A Grammar of the Greek New Testament in the Light of Historical Research*, p. 443.
2. James Hardy Ropes, *A Critical and Exegetical Commentary on the Epistle of St. James*, International Critical Commentary, p. 158.
3. Marvin R. Vincent, *Word Studies in the New Testament*, 1:731.
4. Peter H. Davids, *The Epistle of James, A Commentary on the Greek Text*, p. 86.
5. William F. Arndt and F. Wilbur Gingrich, *A Greek-English Lexicon of the New Testament and Other Early Christian Literature*, p. 204.
6. James Hope Moulton and George Milligan, *The Vocabulary of the Greek Testament Illustrated from the Papyri and Other Non-Literary Sources*, p. 169.
7. H. Maynard Smith, *The Epistle of S. James*, p. 62.
8. Robert Johnstone, *Lectures Exegetical and Practical on the Epistle of James*, p. 114.
9. Ropes, p. 158; Joseph B. Mayor, *The Epistle of James*, p. 54; Martin Dibelius, *James, A Commentary on the Epistle of James. Hermeneia*, pp. 99-100.
10. E. C. Blackman, *The Epistle of James*, Torch Bible Commentaries, p. 57.
11. See R. J. Knowling, *The Epistle of James*, Westminster Commentaries, p. 24.
12. Mayor, p. 56.
13. Peter H. Davids, *James, New International Biblical Commentary*, p. 52.
14. See Dibelius, p. 100 and the references in note 160.
15. Ibid., and notes 161-162.
16. J. B. Lightfoot, *Saint Paul's Epistle to the Galatians*, p. 150. This view holds that *eni* is a strengthened form of *en*, which, used without a verb with the negative *ouk*, carries the force of "there is no place for, is not possible." See also Joseph Henry Thayer, *A Greek-English Lexicon of the New Testament*, p. 216.
17. This view considers *eni* as a contraction of *enestin*, "there is." See Arndt and Gingrich, p. 265; Ropes, p. 162; R. C. H. Lenski, *The Interpretation of the Epistle to the Hebrews and of the Epistle of James*, p. 554. The uncials Aleph and P and a number of minuscule manuscripts changed *ouk eni* to the more familiar *ouk estin*, "there is not."
18. For these variants, see United Bible Societies, *The Greek New Testament*, 3d ed.
19. R. V. G. Tasker, *The Greek New Testament, Being the Text Translated in the New English Bible 1961*.
20. Ropes, pp. 162-65.
21. It has the support of the important uncials Aleph (original hand) and B and Papyrus 23, dating from the early 3d cent.
22. Dibelius, pp. 100-103.
23. Bruce M. Metzger, *A Textual Commentary on the Greek New Testament*, pp. 679-80.
24. A. T. Robertson, *Practical and Social Aspects of Christianity. The Wisdom of James*, p. 83.
25. Simon J. Kistemaker, *New Testament Commentary. Exposition of the Epistle of James and the Epistles of John*, p. 53.
26. Theodore H. Epp, *James, the Epistle of Applied Christianity*, p. 86.
27. E. G. Punchard, "The General Epistle of James," in *Ellicott's Commentary on the Whole Bible*, 8:360.
28. Gottlob Schrenk, "*Boulomai, boulē, boulēma*," in *Theological Dictionary of the New Testament*, 1:632.
29. Davids, *James, New International Biblical Commentary*, p. 52.
30. See L. E. Elliot-Binns, "James 1:18: Creation or Redemption?" in *New Testament Studies* 3, 2 (Jan. 1957):148-61, and the literature cited there.
31. Davids, *The Epistle of James, A Commentary on the Greek Text*, p. 89. See also Ropes, pp. 166-67; Dibelius, pp. 104-7; and Blackman, pp. 58-61.

32. Ronald A. Ward, "James," in *The New Bible Commentary, revised*, p. 1225.

33. Ropes, p. 166.

34. F. Blass and A. Debrunner, *A Greek Grammar of the New Testament and Other Early Christian Literature*, p. 158.

35. Alford, p. 284.

36. The English uses the idiomatic plural, but the form (*aparchē*) in the Greek New Testament is always the collective singular.

37. Mayor, p. 61.

38. Davids, *The Epistle of James*, p. 90.

PART 2 (1:19–3:18)

THE TEST MARKS OF A LIVING FAITH

In the first section of his epistle, James introduced and developed his basic theme: the testings of personal faith. He began with a ringing call to his readers to maintain the needed constructive attitude amid their testings, assuring them that their varied testings served to verify their possession of a living faith, and furthered its maturity and productivity. He reminded them of the availability of God-given wisdom rightly to evaluate their testing experiences, whatever their station in life might be, and assured them of the blessedness of perseverance under trial.

James was fully aware that the meaning of the basic Greek term involved in the discussion (*peirasmos*) could mean either testing or tempting, as well as the fact that in human experience these two realities are often closely related. Therefore he categorically denied the claim that the experience of temptation is also to be attributed to God. Such a claim is refuted by the beneficent nature and activity of God. God is the true source of all good and of our spiritual regeneration through His word. The believer's faith relationship with such a beneficent and loving heavenly Father rightly requires that this professed relationship with Him through personal faith must be tested to confirm its living nature and to promote its maturity and productivity.

In Part 2, James proceeds to set forth four test marks of a living faith. He insists that a living faith is confirmed by its response to the Word of God (1:19-27), by its reaction to the presence of partiality in social relations (2:1-13), by its production of good works (2:14 26), and by its production of self-control in the life of the believer (3:1-18).

6

V. FAITH TESTED BY
ITS RESPONSE TO THE WORD OF GOD

1:19-27 My dear brothers, take note of this: Everyone should be quick to listen, slow to speak and slow to become angry, ²⁰for man's anger does not bring about the righteous life that God desires. ²¹Therefore, get rid of all moral filth and the evil that is so prevalent, and humbly accept the word planted in you, which can save you.

²²Do not merely listen to the word, and so deceive yourselves. Do what it says. ²³Anyone who listens to the word, but does not do what it says is like a man who looks at his face in a mirror ²⁴and, after looking at himself, goes away and immediately forgets what he looks like. ²⁵But the man who looks intently into the perfect law that gives freedom, and continues to do this, not forgetting what he has heard, but doing it—he will be blessed in what he does.

²⁶If anyone considers himself religious and yet does not keep a tight rein on his tongue, he deceives himself and his religion is worthless. ²⁷Religion that God our Father accepts as pure and faultless is this: to look after orphans and widows in their distress and to keep oneself from being polluted by the world.

The reference to the regenerating "word of truth" in verse 18 appropriately provides the subject for the first test of a living faith that James develops in this epistle. Having been brought to life by means of the Word, a genuine faith will rightly relate to that Word. The "word" in this paragraph seems clearly to have the same meaning as in verse 18 above—the message of God's truth as embodied in the Person and work of Jesus Christ. It must be dominant in nurturing, guiding, and disciplining the life that God implanted by means of the Word. In this paragraph, its nature and function appear under three different figures: as seed (v. 21), as a mirror (v. 23), and as a law that gives freedom (v. 25). In developing this test of faith, James calls for the proper reaction to the Word (vv. 19-20), notes the condition for effective reception of the Word (v. 21), and discusses the nature and importance of obedience to the Word (vv. 22-27).

A. THE REACTIONS TO THE WORD (vv. 19-20)

Since God used the Word to make us the first fruits of His creatures (v. 18), it must be accorded the proper attention and response. James begins with a recognition of the readers' knowledge concerning the Word (v. 19*a*), calls for appropriate reactions to the Word (v. 19*b*), and advances a reason for the demanded purpose (v. 20).

1. The Knowledge Possessed (v. 19*a*)

The opening phrase of verse 19, "My dear brothers, take note of this" (*Iste, adelphoi mou agapētoi*), presents a textual problem as to the form of the opening Greek word. The Greek manuscripts use two different words as the initial word of the sentence. The King James Version, "Wherefore, my beloved brethren," follows the Textus Receptus, which uses *hōste*, while the NIV rendering given above is based on the reading *iste*, a variant form of the familiar Greek verb *oida*, "to know." Most modern critical editions of the Greek New Testament accept *iste* as more probably the original reading.[1] The two Greek words, differing only in the initial letter, could easily be confused by the copyists. The reading of the Textus Receptus forms a smooth connection with what has just gone before, but the reading accepted in the critical editions is more difficult and unexpected. In the process of recopying the text, it is more probable that the reading *iste* was changed to the easier and more familiar *hōstē* than the other way. The verbal form *iste* occurs only twice elsewhere in the New Testament. We accept *iste* as more probably the original reading.

The verb *iste* may be either the imperative or the indicative mode. Both views have their advocates. Varied interpreters, such as Ropes,[2] Lenski,[3] Dibelius,[4] and Davids,[5] view it as an imperative. Then it is an admonition to the readers and is apparently intended to focus attention on the following imperative. Thus Laws asserts, "The author calls for particular attention to what he is about to say."[6] The NIV rendering is representative of this view, indicated by the use of the colon. Others, such as Alford,[7] Reicke,[8] and Wolff,[9] prefer the indicative as more in keeping with the context. This view receives support from the presence of *de* with the second verb, indicating that a further matter is to be presented. Under this view, the opening verb looks back to what was said in verse 18 and reminds the readers "that they are definitely aware of the heavenly source of their regeneration (new birth)."[10] They already know its regenerating power. Thus the added *de* makes clear that they must not stop there; they must allow the Word to continue to function in daily life. The *American Standard Version*, "Ye know *this*, my beloved brethren," makes these words a separate sentence. Views will continue to differ, but we accept the indicative as more probable.

The NIV rendering, "My dear brothers, take note of this," reverses James's order by placing the direct address before the verb. Only twice (2:1;

5:19) out of fifteen occurrences of the use of "brothers" as a vocative does James place it first in the sentence. Here "my dear brothers," as standing in apposition to the subject of the preceding verb (*iste*), identifies and restricts those who have this asserted knowledge. With his affectionate "my brothers" James draws them to his heart as members of the same spiritual family. It softens any suggestion of harshness in his commands to them and assures them that "he wants them to feel that he is not a superior, commanding them, but an equal, exhorting them."[11] They are the objects of his brotherly concern, and this should strengthen their desire to accept his call unto attainment of the ideal for the Christian life.

2. The Reactions Demanded (v. 19*b*)

"Everyone should be quick to listen, slow to speak and slow to become angry." The particle *de*,[12] omitted in the NIV as unsuited to the preceding imperative verb, is best taken as implying divergence between their knowledge and practice as Christians. James would remind them that their knowledge of the new birth through the Word must lead to a new life directed by the Word. Dibelius, who regards verse 19 as an independent wisdom-saying, rejects this close connection with verse 18 and renders *de* as "Now."[13] Aside from the view that James is paranetic literature largely composed of isolated sayings, there is no call to reject an intended connection with what has preceded. The suggested contrast is in keeping with the basic thrust of the entire epistle.

The exhortations that follow were common in Jewish ethical literature. Comparable warnings are in Proverbs and Ecclesiastes:

> A patient man has great understanding,
> but a quick-tempered man displays folly.
> Proverbs 14:29

See also Proverbs 10:19; 13:3; 15:1; 17:27-28; 29: 11, 20.

> Be not hasty in thy spirit to be angry;
> for anger resteth in the bosom of fools.
> Ecclesiastes 7:9 (KJV)

See also Ecclesiastes 5:1-2.

Noncanonical Jewish literature likewise contains interesting parallels. Ecclesiasticus advises:

> Be not hasty in thy tongue,
> And in thy deeds slack and remiss (4:29).
> Be swift to hear,
> And with patience make thine answer (5:11).

Rabbinic parallels also appear: "Silence is a fence for wisdom." "Even a fool, as long as he keeps silent, is regarded as wise." "Speech is worth one Selah, but silence two." "All my days I have grown up among the wise, and I have found nothing better for men than silence."[14] Such remarks obviously relate to social intercourse and are general in their scope and import.

Easton[15] and Dibelius[16] hold that this saying of James is also to be taken as a perfectly general exhortation, an example of an isolated wisdom-saying. The connection indicated with *de* and the contents of verses 21-22 more naturally indicate that the primary reference is to the believer's response to the message of the Word. Songer holds that while the counsels of James are valuable in human relations, "the primary reference is probably to hearing in worship."[17]

The use of the third person singular imperative, "everyone should be," indicates that the command is stated as a duty incumbent upon each believer. The present tense underlines it as a continuing duty. All members of the Christian community, whatever the extent of their knowledge of the Word or the degree of their spiritual maturity, need the exhortation. The imperative, as an appeal to the will, calls for their personal acceptance of the duty. The effective functioning of the Word in daily life demands their active cooperation.

A triple duty is indicated: "quick to listen, slow to speak and slow to become angry." The two aorist infinitives, "to listen" and "to speak," denote a standing unitary duty. The adjectives "quick" and "slow" do not describe the nature of the action but the attitude governing it.

"Quick to listen" requires that they be eager and attentive, ready to receive and assimilate the message heard. "Listening," Kistemaker notes, "is the art of closing one's mouth and opening one's ears and heart."[18] Their first duty is to use the opportunity to increase their knowledge of the Word of truth. "To listen" implies a public reading of the Word and oral instruction in the Christian faith. Our acceptance of an early date for this epistle (see Introduction, pp. 35-36) carries with it the conclusion that the New Testament had not yet been written. Therefore, "the Christians were dependent upon the preaching of traveling missionaries . . . and of local teachers (Acts 13:1) for their knowledge of the gospel."[19] To listen eagerly to the message was the first duty of discipleship.

"Slow to speak" does not mean slowness in speaking but is a call for restraint upon hasty and ill-considered reactions to what is heard. It would allow time for a fuller apprehension and thoughtful evaluation of what had been heard. It offered a valuable safeguard against shallow, immature, and immoderate reactions. "A continual talker cannot hear what anyone else says and by the same token will not hear when God speaks to him."[20] The need for this exhortation apparently arose out of the free and largely unstructured nature of the early Christian assemblies, permitting personal participation in, and ready interaction with, others sharing in the service (1 Cor. 14:26 33).

Hasty reaction to what was felt to be objectionable, or individual zeal for what was held to be the truth, might lead to rash assertion and overstatement, which often tended to obscure the truth. Let them remember that freedom of expression involves grave responsibility.

"Slow to become angry" rebukes the danger involved in a flash reaction. Rash and reckless speech is prone to wound; it is likely to provoke animosity. "Intemperate religious zeal is often accompanied with a train of bad passions, and particularly with great wrath against those who differ from us in opinion."[21] James's warning suggests "scenes of wrangling, of attempts at self-display, of the manifestation of unchristian tempers in the midst of debates on Christian truth."[22] Mitchell calls it "the wrath of argumentation."[23] Such wrathful reactions are manifestations of carnal zeal under a religious guise. Such furious reactions to the views of others have always been a discredit to the cause of Christ.

The Greek noun (*orgē*), here rendered "become angry," implies more than a passing surge of irritation or displeasure. It denotes a strong and persistent feeling of indignation and active anger. Another Greek word, *thumos*, also means anger. It denotes the turbulent, passionate outburst of anger, whereas the term used here points more to the deliberate, persistent attitude of hostility.[24] In Matthew 5:22 the verbal form suggests the persistent harboring of the feeling of resentment.

Human anger is an instinctive reaction against that which is evil and injurious. The feeling of anger is not always wrong (cf. Mark 3:5). The individual who is never aroused and deeply stirred at evil is gravely deficient in moral character. James's words do not forbid all anger, but this instinctive feeling needs careful control lest it blaze forth in unjustified and injurious reactions. The attitude of Scripture is consistently negative toward the indulgence in human wrath.[25]

3. The Reason Stated (v. 20)

"For" introduces the reason for the warning against yielding to anger: "Man's anger does not bring about the righteous life that God desires." James assumes that his readers were aiming at promoting the righteousness of God, but he insists that wrath is not a proper tool to further that goal. James must have been aware that not all of his readers would agree with his warning against wrath. Bennett observes, "Those admonished would have justified themselves by saying that they were angry on account of false teaching and unworthy habits."[26] It is James's conviction that human wrath does not further spiritual ends, "even when it appears in the garb of religious zeal."[27]

"Man" (*andros*) in its specific connotation denotes the male sex. Mayor suggests that its use here "was probably determined by the facts of the case; the speakers would be men, and they might perhaps imagine that there was something manly in violence."[28] The original setting may lend some support to the suggestion, but it need not be assumed that James intended his warning for men only (cf. 1:8, 12). The term is without the article and is qualitative: "man's anger." It is human wrath, standing in sharp contrast to "the righteous life that God desires" (*dikaiosunēn theou*, literally "righteousness of God"). The expression may be differently understood. Clearly the reference is not to God's own righteousness (possessive genitive), nor does it seem to denote justifying righteousness, a righteousness bestowed by God that places man in right relationship with God (subjective genitive). Rather, the reference is to the upright conduct that God prescribes and demands of man, which meets His approval. Thus the NIV rendering, "The righteous life that God desires." Moo notes that this phrase consistently has this meaning in biblical Greek with the verb "do" (*poieō*) or "practice" (*ergazomai*).[29] Such a righteous life is "of God" because it is defined by Him. "Righteousness" is without the article and is qualitative, characterizing a life that is just or right in the eyes of God. Such conduct can only be the product of justifying righteousness.

The negative (*ouk*) and the present indicative verb assert an abiding negative fact: "Man's anger does not bring about the righteous life." The verb "bring about" (*ergazetai*) may mean that man's wrath never actively performs that which constitutes right dealing in God's sight. Under this view "worketh righteousness" is the opposite of "worketh sin" (see 2:9). Human anger never practices the things that God can approve. The verb can also mean that man's wrath never produces or brings about the righteousness that is God-approved.[30] Then the meaning is that whenever man gives way to anger, he never furthers the righteousness he professedly strives for; anger blocks his goal of fostering righteousness. Either view is possible, but the latter seems more probable[31] Human anger is not an appropriate means for the production of righteousness, even if it professes a conscientious endeavor toward that end. It does not produce the desired righteousness in self or in others. The history of Christendom is replete with examples of this fact.

B. THE RECEPTION OF THE WORD (v. 21)

"Therefore" (*dio*), an inferential conjunction meaning "for this reason," looks back to verse 20 and indicates that a different response is needed. The suggestion is that wrath has operated in their relations because they have not effectively dealt with the evils in their own hearts. A double activity on their part is required. Negatively, they must remove the hindering sins; positively, they must welcome the Word and permit it to carry out its saving work in their lives.

1. The Stripping Off of Sins (v. 21*a*)

The negative aspect of the demand is "get rid of all moral filth and the evil that is so prevalent." "Get rid of" renders a plural participle (*apothe-*

menoi) that is grammatically dependent upon the following plural imperative "accept" and partakes of its imperatival force. Since both the participle
and the verb are in the aorist tense, the action of the participle is best understood as being antecedent to that of the verb.[32] Before the Word can be effectively welcomed into their lives, the hindering sins must be dealt with.

"Get rid of" contains the figure of the stripping off of garments. In Acts
7:58 it is used in the literal sense, but generally in the New Testament the
term is used metaphorically. It was a familiar term in ethical exhortations
inculcating the duty of divesting oneself of certain undesirable qualities or
deeds (Rom. 13:12; Eph. 4:22; Col. 3:8; 1 Pet. 2:1). The aorist tense calls for a
definite break with these things. In keeping with the ethical usage of the
term, James is calling for a definite change in lifestyle on the part of his
readers.

A twofold stripping is called for: "all moral filth and the evil that is so
prevalent." Laws suggests, "Since James is concentrating in context on warnings about speech, it is probably fair to particularise his condemnation as of
vulgar and malicious talk."[33] His use of "all," most naturally taken with both
nouns, is comprehensive in its scope and may denote either "every kind of"
or "every instance of." The latter is preferable as stressing the comprehensiveness of the removal. "God is never satisfied with partial purity, partial
goodness, partial righteousness."[34] No articles are used, and the statement is
qualitative; all that has the indicated moral quality.

The noun "filth," occurring only here in the New Testament, continues
the metaphor of clothing. (James also uses the adjective of clothing in 2:2.) Its
literal meaning is "dirt, filth," but metaphorically it denotes moral uncleanness or impurity, that which defiles human nature. It was at times used in the
more restricted sense of "avarice" or "greediness," but the general sense is
more appropriate here. They must rid themselves of all filthiness, all that is
morally defiling, as inconsistent with Christian life.

They must also remove "the evil that is so prevalent" (*perisseian kakias*,
literally, "abundance of evil"). The expression has been differently understood. The genitive "of evil" (*kakias*) identifies the moral character of that to
be removed. It has a general meaning denoting what is bad or evil in quality,
hence "wickedness" or "vice" in general as opposed to virtue. It also has a
specific meaning: "malice, ill-will, malignity," the attitude of mind that desires the injury of others. Either meaning is possible here. The general meaning is more probable as being more in keeping with the comprehensiveness
of the demand. The genitive is appositional, identifying the nature of that
which is "so prevalent" or "overflowing" (*perisseian*). This latter term has
been differently understood. The normal meaning of this noun is "abundance" (Rom. 5:17; 2 Cor. 8:2; 10:15).

Thus the term suggests the vast quantity of wickedness that must be
removed. This is represented in various versions: "abounding of wickedness" (Darby);[35] rank growth of wickedness" (RSV); "the evil that is so preva-

lent" (NIV). Arndt and Gingrich suggest the rendering "all the evil prevailing (around you)."[36] This is the rendering adopted by C. B. Williams[37] and implies that they must discontinue all conformity to the prevailing evils around them. Still others suggest that the intended force is the "residue, remainder." This view is represented in the *New American Standard Bible*: "and *all* that remains of wickedness." This is the regular meaning for the cognate term *perisseuma* but is not the natural significance for *perisseia*. This view leads Calvin to conclude "that these are the innate evils of our nature, and that . . . we are never wholly cleansed from them in this life, but that they are continually sprouting up, and therefore he requires that care should be constantly taken to eradicate them."[38] The NEB rendering, "the malice that hurries to excess," conveys the thought of the rapid growth of evil. This might be mistaken to mean it is a call to remove only the evil that is in excess. It is best to retain the basic meaning "so prevalent" to denote that there is a lot of it, and all of it must be removed.

2. The Appropriation of the Word (v. 21*b*)

The positive duty is: "humbly accept the word planted in you, which can save you." James might have balanced the preceding "put off" by insisting that humility must be "put on" as the soul's appropriate garment. Instead, he drops the figure of clothing and introduces an agricultural figure of seed and soil. He insists upon the appropriation of the Word as providing the secret of victory.

The original word order placing "humbly" (*en prautēti*, literally "in humility") before the verb "accept" stresses the needed inner attitude toward the Word. Humility is the opposite of wrathfulness (vv. 19-20). Humility or meekness is an inner attitude, not of spineless weakness or haughtiness. Instead of brashly asserting themselves in anger, they need to be humble and teachable in order to rightly receive the divine message.

The aorist imperative "accept" conveys a sense of urgency. Effectively getting rid of evil is accomplished by a definite acceptance of the Word. The verb denotes more than the historic act of reception: it includes the thought of "a welcoming or appropriating reception."[39] Thus Williams well renders it "In humble spirit welcome the message." It is the word used of the noble Bereans who "received the message with great eagerness and examined the Scriptures every day to see if what Paul said was true" (Acts 17:11). The readers needed to go beyond a passive acquiescence to the statements of the Word and, by a definite volitional response, welcome it as an active, working force in their lives. They had to offer their hearts as the good soil in which the "implanted word" could readily grow.

The expression "the word planted in you" occurs only here in the New Testament. The compound verbal adjective "planted in" (*emphuton*), denoting that which has been planted within, is capable of two general meanings.

It may denote that which is inborn, or native. The Word of God is not native to the human heart. The word can also denote a subsequent implantation, which is clearly the meaning here. Although the Word is not native to the human heart, it is well suited to be planted therein. As a living seed, its nature is to root itself deeply into the soil of the believing heart. Implanted at regeneration, the living Word actively roots itself in the heart as a vital part of the new nature. In Romans 6:5, this adjective is used of the believer's being "united with" the indwelling Christ. The rendering "engrafted" (KJV) is not quite adequate, since the Word is not a bud grafted into us.[40] Rather, the figure is that of seed sown in the heart. The power of this seed to root itself deeply is not an automatic process. The imperative verb denotes that a welcoming human response is involved.

The dynamic character of this Word is indicated in the words "which can save you" (*ton dunamenon sōsai*, "the one being able to save"). This appositional designation declares the innate nature of the Word of God. It affirms its continual ability to save. This character of the Word must motivate the readers to welcome the Word and allow its full operation in their lives. It is the work of God and His Word to save, but this saving work demands the cooperation of those being saved. It has been rightly noted that "with all James' preoccupation with 'works' he does not lose sight of the saving power of the 'word' to effect salvation and to lead to daily conduct that is in keeping with a person's profession of faith."[41]

The aorist active infinitive "to save" (*sōsai*) simply states the saving function of God's Word, delivering believers from the destructive consequences of sin. The present tense would have pictured the process, but the aorist simply views the process as an accomplished whole. James has already mentioned their new birth in verse 18, but the full import of this saving activity is eschatological—the believer's full and final salvation at the return of Christ. Implied is the present process of salvation from sin as the believer grows and matures spiritually (1 Cor. 1:18; 2 Cor. 3:18).

"You," as the recipients of this saving activity, is literally "your souls." It is commonly accepted as a Hebraism to denote the whole person, the real self (cf. Num. 23:10, ASV marg.; Acts 2:41; 27:37; Heb. 10:38; 1 Pet. 3:20). Certainly James did not intend to exclude the body from this salvation. He may have intentionally used "your souls" to emphasize the spiritual nature of the salvation, a salvation involving the soul as the seat and center of the human personality, and transcending earthly existence. Johnstone remarks that the use of "your souls" was apparently intended

> to bring out prominently the radical and therefore gloriously complete nature of the deliverance. It is no mere amelioration or adornment of the outward life, but reaches that inmost and noblest part of our nature, out of which are "the issues of life," and by the condition of which, accordingly, is determined the condition of the whole man; for the body follows the state of the soul, to destruction or to salvation.[42]

C. THE OBEDIENCE TO THE WORD (vv. 22-27)

Wholehearted acceptance of the Word must result in active obedience to the Word. Such obeying of the Word constitutes the essence of a living faith. These verses express James's central concern. Verses 22-25 state and illustrate the need for active obedience to the Word, and verses 26-27 portray the true nature of religious obedience.

1. The Demand for Active Obedience (vv. 22-25)

The conjunction *de*, not in the NIV rendering, is not adversative but continuative,[43] indicating that something further must be said. Receiving the regenerating Word (1:18) is only the beginning. Attentive listening to the Word must be followed by active obedience. James states (v. 22) and illustrates (vv. 23-25) the required obedience.

a. *The statement of the requirement* (v. 22). "Do not merely listen to the word, and so deceive yourselves. Do what it says." The NIV rendering reverses the order in the Greek, which is well represented in the ASV rendering, "Be ye doers of the word, and not hearers only, deluding your own selves." Kistemaker explains the reversal: "The New International Version reverses the order because in actual experience, hearing comes before doing. Also, the phrase *and so deceive yourselves* applies only to hearing."[44] This reversal blurs the fact that James's appeal is basically positive, using a verb only with the positive aspect of the statement; the reversal demands that the verb be repeated. It also eliminates the chiasm in verses 22-25: positive—negative; negative—positive. Having stressed true hearing of the Word (vv. 19-21), his fundamental aim is now to foster active obedience to the Word.

Such a call to active "doing the Word" would be nothing new to the readers, since "doing the Word" was a familiar maxim in Jewish ethical literature. The use of the present imperative underlines this demand as a continuing duty. It does not imply that his readers have never done so, but they must never stop being doers. The verb here is *ginesthe*, which basically means "to become." Rotherham literally renders it "Become ye doers."[45] Mayor suggests that here it means "show yourselves more and more."[46] Then the meaning is a call to demonstrate the reality of their profession. It may be best to simply accept *ginomai* as a substitute for the common verb "to be" (*eimi*),[47] since the second person plural of this verb (*este*) never seems to be used as an imperative in the New Testament.[48] A fair rendering would be "Continue to be doers of the Word." Williams renders it "Keep on obeying this message."

"Doers" (*poiētai*) is a favorite word of James. Four of its six occurrences in the New Testament are in this epistle (1:22, 23, 25; 4:11). In Romans 2:13 it is also rendered "doers," but in Acts 17:28 it has the special classical sense of "poets." The use of the noun rather than a verbal form calls attention to the individual characterized as carrying out the demands of the Word.

James wants his readers to be individuals who habitually submit to and comply with the requirements of the Word of God.

This call to be active doers is underlined by the negative restatement "not merely listen to the word" (*kai mē akroatai monon*, "and not merely hearers"). "Merely" indicates that this demand to be doers in no way disparages the importance of being "hearers" of the Word. "Hearers" again implies public reading and oral instruction. The term appears thrice in this passage (vv. 22, 23, 25) and elsewhere in the New Testament in Romans 2:13. Among the Greeks, it was a common term for persons who were attendants at a lecture but not disciples of the lecturer. They were hearers who in life did not follow the instructions given. It is a common human failing from which Christians are not exempt. If all who are auditors of the Word on Sunday would put it into practice during the week, what a difference that would make! Roberts tartly remarks, "Our churches are filled with spiritual sponges who soak up the information, sit, sour, and eventually stink!"[49]

The subtle error involved in being "hearers only" is "and so deceive yourselves." The present deponent[50] middle participle (*paralogizomenoi*) denotes a process of self-deception by means of fallacious reasoning. Their conclusion, that attentive hearing of the Word was the fulfillment of all that was required, had led them astray from the path of truth. In resting satisfied with possessing the means of grace without applying it, they were the victims of their own deception. "It is sad to be deceived, most miserable to be self-deceived. Many still determine their godliness by the quality of hearing (for instance sermons) or reading (even God's word) instead of action and obedience."[51] Jesus warns explicitly against this error (Matt. 7:21-27; cf. Rom. 2:17-25).

b. *The illustrations of the requirement* (vv. 23-25). James adds a vivid negative (vv. 23-24) and positive (v. 25) illustration of obedience to the Word.

(1) *The negative portrayal* (vv. 23-24). By introducing the negative portrayal with *hoti*, "because," not in NIV, James advances a grim reason for the warning against self-deception in verse 22. The point at issue is carefully restated: "Anyone who listens to the word and does not do what it says is like a man who looks at his face in a mirror and, after looking at himself, goes away and immediately forgets what he looks like." The NIV rendering clearly presents the picture for the modern reader and thus does not fully reveal the form of the original, which is grammatically a conditional sentence. The ASV, "For if any one is a hearer of the word and not a doer," more literally reproduces the force of the original. "If" (first class condition) assumes the existence of an unnamed individual whose hearing of the Word is not united with personal obedience to it. James characterizes the individual as a "listener" and not a "doer." James notes not merely his conduct but the character of the individual as revealed by his conduct. The individual is a personal illustration of the danger warned against in verse 22.

119

"But does not do what it says" marks his fatal failure to let the message find active operation in daily life. His inaction brings his faith into question. Jesus told His followers, "If you love me, you will obey what I command" (John 14:15). "The Christian faith," Kistemaker notes, "is always active and stands in sharp contrast to other religions that practice mediation and general inactivity."[52]

"Is like a man" (*houtos eoiken andri*), more literally "this one is like a man," vividly sets such an individual before the gaze of the readers. Such an individual "is like a man who looks at his face in a mirror, and after looking at himself, goes away and immediately forgets what he looks like." The word "man" (*andri*) generally denotes the man as contrasted to the woman, but here its use seems to be quite general (cf. 1:8, 12, 20), as for example in Luke 11:31-32. Nor is there any basis for holding that the portrait drawn applies only to the male sex. "Looks at," rendering a present active participle, "beholding," denotes linear action and apparently suggests this as a characteristic activity of the individual. There is no reference to abiding, as in verse 25. The verb implies that the beholder took note of what he saw, and the picture implies that the look revealed something that needed attention. That the observation was careless and hasty is not stated in the verb, but it may be inferred from the entire picture of this man.

"His face" (*to prosōpon tēs geneseōs autou*) is literally "the face of his genesis," and has been differently understood. It may mean "the face he was born with" (Beck[53]), "his natural face" (ASV), or "the face of his (present) existence," that is, he "sees himself as he is" (TEV).[54] Under either meaning, the reference is to mere material perception—"his natural face." In view of the elements in the parallel more fully drawn out in verse 24, others suggest an implied spiritual truth. Thus, Wolff suggests that the expression "is used here to contrast the reflection in the mirror of the natural face which belongs to this transitory life, with the reflection in the word of God, of the ideal human character."[55] Perhaps it is best not to give any particular stress to "genesis," accepting that the reference is to his physical face with the implication that it might need some attention.

The "mirror" used to see his face was probably a small hand mirror, but Kistemaker holds that ancient mirrors "rested horizontally on tables so that the person who wished to see his reflection had to bend and look down."[56]
Ancient mirrors were generally polished bronze, sometimes silver or even gold. "Glass mirrors were not available until late Roman times."[57] Mirrors of glass coated with quicksilver date to the thirteenth century.[58] The reflection of ancient mirrors was often imperfect, as Paul implies in 1 Corinthians 13:12, but generally they were adequate for an individual to gain a good view of himself.

The illustration of this "no doer" is drawn out in verse 24 in three verbs. The first, "looking at himself," as well as the third, "forgets," are in the aorist tense. These aorists are gnomic, or timeless, picturing the events as they usually happen and are rightly translated in the present tense in the English.[59] The first verb implies that his look in the mirror reveals something that calls for action on his part, but before any action is taken the man "goes away and immediately forgets what he looks like." "Goes away" (*apelē-luthen*) is a perfect tense between the two aorists and denotes that his departure, before action was taken, has become a continuing state. With the revelation in the mirror no longer before him, his mind centered its interest on other things and "immediately" (*eutheōs*) he forgot what he had seen. This failure to act demonstrated the evanescent nature of the impression made by the view in the mirror. This picture of inaction in the physical realm aptly illustrates the superficial and temporary effect of his listening to God's Word without letting it direct his conduct.

(2) *The positive portrayal* (v. 25). "But" (*de*) marks the contrast between the negative picture's being condemned and the true positive impact he aims to stimulate. The simile is now dropped, and the figure merges with reality. The illustration is given with the use of substantival participles, conveying the impression of the man himself being observed in action: "But the man who looks intently into the perfect law that gives freedom, and continues to do this, not forgetting what he has heard, but doing it." The participles are gnomic aorists, describing the events that characteristically take place whenever there is active obedience to the divine Word.

"The man who looks intently" (*ho parakupsas*) pictures this individual as bending over the mirror with eagerness and intentness in order to examine more minutely what is revealed therein. "Into" (*eis*) suggests a penetrating look. The verb may denote a cursory look, but that meaning is excluded here by the following participle, "and continues to do so" (*parameinas*), which is closely connected with the first participle as being under the government of the same article. Both are compound forms with the preposition *para*, "beside, alongside of," suggesting proximity. Such looking into the mirror was intended to lead to action, usually remedial in its nature. James pictures this individual as bent over the mirror and gripped by what he saw; he continued to do so and did not forget what he saw. This feature marks his crucial distinction from the first man.

Although the figure of the mirror is still in mind at the opening of the verse, the reality emerges with the statement that this man looks into "the perfect law that gives freedom" (*eis nomon teleion ton tēs eleutherias*). The context makes clear that the reference is to "the implanted word" in verse 21 or simply "the word" in verse 22. Now it is given a different designation. "Law," without the article, has a qualitative force: the object being examined or looked into has the authoritative nature of law. In calling the Word "a law," James refers to that authoritative body of truth that is the foundation of the Christian faith. It is the message contained in the apostolic preaching and

121

now embodied in the New Testament. Christians accept this body of truth as the authoritative standard by which life is to be regulated. This title for the Word of God is in keeping with James's stress upon the importance of doing the things found in the Word.

This "law" James characterizes as "perfect." This law is final and complete, embodying the full and effective revelation of God in Christ Jesus. In the words of Knowling,

> This Law is "perfect," not only because it may be contrasted with the burden and yoke of the Law in its Pharisaic observance, but because it completes and realizes the object and meaning of the Mosaic law, Matt. v. 17, cf. Jer. xxxi. 33; because it sums up all the commandments in the one command and principle of love: "he that loveth his neighbour hath fulfilled the law," cf. Rom. xiii. 8ff; Gal. vi. 2.[60]

Unlike the imperfect metal mirror in the previous illustration, this law is able to give the beholder a true and undistorted revelation of himself. Its perfection justifies the appositional description of it as the law "that gives freedom" (*ton tēs eleutherias*, literally "the (law) of the freedom" or "liberty"). This paradoxical designation makes specific the preceding general concept of law.

> It is when the law is seen to be perfect that it is found to be the law of liberty. So long as the law is not seen in the beauty of its perfection, it is not loved, and men either disobey it or obey it by constraint and unwillingly. But when its perfection is recognized, men long to conform to it, and they obey, not because they must, but because they choose.[61]

The genitive "of liberty" is subjective, denoting that this law "gives" the experience of freedom in the lives of those who voluntarily observe it. The definite article with "liberty," "the liberty," points to the well-known Christian freedom from bondage that the believer knows through faith in Christ (John 8:31-36). As he submits himself to its transforming power, this law of liberty works in his life a disposition and ability to do God's will joyfully (Phil. 2:12-13). It does not promote antinomianism but prompts obedience without compulsion. In 2:12, the only other place in the New Testament where the designation "law of liberty" occurs, James associates it with the law of love. The believer is not free from the obligation to do God's will as revealed in His Word, but love works in him the desire to do his Father's will. Men are free when they want to do what they ought to do. This is the "splendid paradox" produced by a living faith in the gospel through the indwelling Holy Spirit.

A third aorist participle rounds out the picture of the person as one "not forgetting what he has heard, but doing it." This is his crowning excellence and sharply distinguishes him from the preceding "no doer" (vv. 23-

24). Instead of finite verbs, James used a participle and two nouns to portray what this individual has become, indicated negatively and positively. These two aspects, in the original, are symmetrically formed and call attention to what the person is, not merely what he does.

Negatively, he is not guilty of the fatal failure of the previous individual, "not forgetting what he has heard" (*ouk akroatēs epilēsmonēs genomenos*, literally "not a hearer of forgetfulness having become"). He is a "hearer" like the previous person, but a further noun in the genitive (*epilēsmonēs*) marks the contrast—he is not a hearer characterized by "forgetfulness." This noun occurs only here in the New Testament. This negative picture characterizes him by the important fact that he does not let the things seen in the Word lightly escape his attention. It is one of those rare instances where a negative habit is of primary importance in his Christian life. It is essential for the effective operation of the positive characterization that completes the picture.

Positively, he continues "doing" what he has learned, being "a doer of the word" (*poiētēs ergou*). He is marked by persistent performance of what he has learned in being a receptive hearer of God's word. The emphasis is not on certain notable deeds he performs but on his characteristic obedience to God's known will.

James concisely evaluates this individual: "he will be blessed in what he does." "He" (*houtos*, "this one") summarizes and sets the man before the readers as worthy of their admiring attention and imitation. Only a man of this character enjoys the true liberty of the gospel. He is assured of God's blessing and qualifies for the blessing of the wise man pictured by Jesus in Matthew 7:24-25.

The future "will be blessed" is a statement of assurance. He will share in the blessing of the future life, but God's blessing already is experienced here. The blessing lies in his "doing." "The life of obedience is the element wherein the blessedness is found and consists."[62] The voluntary doing of God's will is the secret of true happiness. The singular noun "doing" (*poiēsis*), used only here in the New Testament, views his whole life as a consistent doing. God wants more than isolated acts of obedience; the believer's entire life must be devoted to the incessant doing of His will.

2. The Nature of Acceptable Obedience (vv. 26-27)

James does not use a connecting particle for either of these two verses,[63] thus making them prominent as independent assertions, but there is a relationship to what has gone before. In verses 22-25, James rebuked a "hearing" of the Word that did not lead to "doing." Here he rebukes a religious "doing" that leaves the inner life unchanged. The practice of dividing people into two categories is continued. Verse 26 portrays religious activity without inner control, while verse 27 pictures religious obedience as involving outward service as well as self-control.

a. *Futility of activity without inner control* (v. 26). In portraying inadequate religious obedience, James first pictures a representative individual
and then presents his verdict. "If anyone considers himself religious and yet
does not keep a tight rein on his tongue, he deceives himself" paints the
picture. The conditional statement (first class) assumes the actual existence
of such an individual, while the indefinite pronoun *tis*, "any one," leaves the
identity indefinite. The individual in view "considers himself religious." The
rendering "seem to be religious" (KJV) may be understood to denote the
reputation he has in the community.[64] It may be questioned how he could
have this reputation when his uncontrolled tongue belied his religious pretensions. The picture is not that of a conscious hypocrite but of a self-deceived religionist. The verb (*dokei*) denotes "the subjective mental estimate
opinion about a matter which men form."[65] The reference is to the erroneous
opinion the man has of himself.

The adjective "religious" (*thrēskos*) occurs only here in the New Testament, while the noun (*thrēskeia*), the last word in verse 26 and the first in
verse 27, occurs in Acts 26:5 and also in Colossians 2:18, where it is used for
"worshipping of the angels." No form of the term occurs in the Septuagint.
Josephus used it freely of the public and ceremonial worship in the Temple
at Jerusalem. Paul used it of his rigorous ceremonial worship as a Pharisee
(Acts 26:5), but in Colossians 2:18 it has a bad connotation due to the added
genitive "of angels." The term denotes the zealous and diligent performance
of the outward and ceremonial aspects of worship.

The precise religious practices James has in mind are not certain, but
they would include personal prayer and fasting and regular attendance at the
worship services. Assuming a Jewish community, conformity to the ritual of
the law may also have been involved. Clearly James applies the designation
"religious" to an individual whose "piety" consists in the scrupulous performance of the religious rites of worship and who feels satisfied that thereby
he is obedient to the demands of the Word. Rotherham renders it "If any
thinketh he is observant of religion." James is not opposed to such a careful
adherence to the external expression of worship, but he knew that there is "a
valid distinction between the inner religious disposition and its outer expression in worship."[66] Brown well remarks, "For a man who had been brought
up amid the most elaborate ritual, and who still clung to Temple obser-
vances, the language of these verses [1:26-27] is certainly very remarkable."[67]

The man who esteems himself as religious "and yet does not keep a
tight rein on his tongue, deceives himself." The two verbs render two present active participles that modify the subject of the verb and thus picture the
true state of the man while he rests satisfied in his opinion of himself.

The negative fact is his characteristic failure to "keep a tight rein on his
tongue." The compound verbal form (*chalinagōgeō*), which occurs only
here and in 3:2 in the New Testament, means to guide and to hold in check

with a bridle (*chalinos*). The man's tongue is like a wild horse that he does not hold in check. "Exactly how his speech offended is not indicated, whether it be by his cutting criticism of others, by uncleanness, by dishonesty, or by other means."[68] It is implied that a sincere acceptance and personal application of the Word of God will result in curbing the tongue. James makes no comment on how his unbridled tongue reveals its untamed nature; the crucial fact is that it remains untamed. "Bridling the tongue," Johnstone asserts, "is a peculiarly excellent test of genuine religion"[69] (cf. 3:6-9). His failure to control his tongue is an index of his inner spiritual destitution; the gospel has not wrought a transformation in his inner life. "To guide the tongue, hold it in check, restrain it, is a task so difficult that he who has the grace to accomplish it has grace to accomplish anything. Such self-control is a fruit of the Spirit (Gal. 5:23)."[70]

The positive fact is the man's self-deception: "he deceives himself" (*alla apatōn kardian heautou*, "but deceiving his own heart"). The adversative "but" (not in NIV) marks the contrast between what he does not do and what he does do. In view of his failure to bridle his tongue, his evaluation of himself as religious can only be explained as due to self-deception. He fails to see the inconsistency between his assumed acceptance before a holy God and his evil words directed against those around him. The verb for "deceive" (*apataō*) is more common than the term used in verse 22, where the reference is to self-deception due to erroneous reasoning. Here the deception comes from the erroneous evaluation of his conduct, leading him astray from the path of reality. He harbors the delusion that performance of the external rites of religion is all that is needed. He is deceived by "himself" (*kardian heautou*, "his own heart"). "Heart" denotes the seat and center of his own personality and stresses the moral nature of his error.

James's verdict is "his religion is worthless." "His" (*toutou*, literally "this one's") looks back and marks the precise identity of the subject of the verdict. "Worthless" (*mataios*) does not mean that it is hollow and without content (which would be *kenē*), but that it is futile because it fails to bring him to the goal for which religion is intended. His concern with the external leaves the inner nature unchanged; it is futile because it does not bring into operation the power of the gospel upon the whole man. In the Septuagint, this adjective is used of pagan idols and idol worship (2 Chron. 11:15; Isa. 44:19; Jer. 2:5; 10:3; Ezek. 8:10). A professed Christianity that centers on the external expressions of faith—attendance at worship, rote prayers, church membership, participation in the ordinances—but is devoid of the regenerating power of the gospel—is as futile and unprofitable as idol worship. These outward aspects are important as expressions of personal faith, but they are useless apart from the Spirit's inner work. "James sees the unbridled tongue and the deceived heart as concomitants of an empty religion. Religion . . . requires a life."[71] A living religion is a life-changing force.

b. *Active service with inner control* (v. 27). James accepts the need for "religion," but insists that "religious observance pure and undefiled with our God and Father" (Rotherham) must unite the inner and outward effects of the gospel. A living religion must know the reality of the divine life within as well as experience its energizing activity in the production of deeds "pure and faultless" in daily conduct.

Such life will produce an obedience to the Word that is "pure and faultless" before God. For Jewish readers, these adjectives might carry ceremonial suggestions, but James uses them here with a moral and ethical sense. The two terms view the same obedience from a positive and negative standpoint. "Pure" denotes that which is intrinsically free from moral pollution or corruption, whereas "faultless" (*amiantos*) or "undefiled" negatively declares that it has not been soiled or stained by contact with moral evil, hence not "worthless" as unacceptable before God. For James, moral purity has replaced the concern for ritualistic purity.

"Religion that God our Father accepts" must be in harmony with the divine standard (*para tō theō kai patri*, "before the God and Father"), and so acceptable in His presence—acceptable religious observance related to "God our Father." The Greek has no pronoun "our," but the definite article uniting the nouns may have that force. The formula, familiar from Paul's epistles, is distinctively Christian. As "God," He is omnipotent, sovereign, and will authoritatively deal with our religious practices. He is also our "Father," not merely an impartial Judge but a loving Father, who has the interest of His children at heart. This fact should encourage us to relate the evaluation of all our religious practices to Him. "If we worship God, who is father and who loves His creatures, while we ourselves are heartless and merciless, we should be able to see ourselves that there is something incongruous in our worship."[72] As Epp remarks, "James was contrasting a religion that can fool others with a religion that God knows is genuine."[73]

In saying that such acceptable religion "is this" (*hautē estin*), James is not attempting to give a full picture but rather "focuses on two elements of true piety that illustrate the doing of the word 1:22-25."[74] "This" serves to summarize and interrelate the otherward and selfward aspects of acceptable religion: "to look after orphans and widows in their distress and to keep oneself from being polluted by the world." The two points are not exhaustive but representative as setting forth the two aspects of genuine religion. The transforming power of the gospel must manifest itself in the believer's social and personal ethics. Moffat notes that "charity" and "chastity" were "the two features of early Christian ethics which impressed the contemporary world."[75]

Genuine religion has a positive social concern: "to look after orphans and widows in their distress." "To look after" (*episkeptesthai*), "to look in on, go see," denotes more than a friendly social call. In classical Greek, it was commonly used of visiting the sick, whether by a doctor or a friend.[76] In

Jewish usage, it commonly denoted to visit with the aim of caring for and supplying the needs of those visited (Job 2:11; Jer. 23:2; Ezek. 34:11; Zech. 11:16; Matt. 25:36, 43). The term implies concern and personal contact with the needy; it involves more than a matter of charity by proxy. The present tense indicates that for James "it is not a question of isolated acts, but of a fundamental attitude."[77]

"Orphans and widows" are representative of the two most needy classes in ancient society and, as such, were rightly viewed as claiming the believer's sympathetic action. Neither term has an article here, and the reference is to any who are characterized as belonging to either of these two unfortunate classes. The first group, the "orphans," are those who have been deprived of their parents, either through death or abandonment.[78] "Widows," those bereft of their husbands, were especially helpless in ancient society. In the New Testament the two terms are combined only here, but the combination is frequent in the Old Testament (Ex. 22:21; Deut. 10:18; Isa. 1:17; Jer. 5:28; Ezek. 22:7; Zech. 8:10) as denoting the two classes needing help and sympathy. They were subject to "distress," the pressure of difficult circumstances, not only because of their grief and loneliness but also because of the unscrupulous exploitation of unprincipled individuals (Zech. 7:10; Mark 12:40). In expressing compassion toward these typically needy classes, Christians reflect the attitude of God Himself (Deut. 10:18; Ps. 68:5). As Epp points out, "Basically, this means doing something for those who cannot return the favor. If we express concern only for those who are able to reciprocate, we are not loving as Christ loved"[79] (cf. Luke 14:12-14). Such love-prompted social concern has often been a means of furthering the gospel.

"And to keep oneself from being polluted by the world" balances the need for social concern with the obligation for personal purity. There is no connecting "and" in the Greek; the arresting asyndeton makes prominent this inner duty. The original word order, "unspotted himself to be keeping from the world," makes prominent the personal moral quality being insisted upon. "From being polluted" (*aspilon*), "unspotted," depicts a condition of personal purity that remains unblemished from contact with surrounding pollution. It is the term used of Christ Himself in 1 Peter 1:19. Roberts comments, "Believers, in the clean acts of compassion, are to be Christ-like."[80] The position of the reflexive pronoun "himself" before the present infinitive makes prominent the personal obligation. Living in this world but not "of the world," the believer must be alert to the danger of having the contamination of the world "rub off" on him.

Though the believer's preservation is in the fullest sense the work of God (1 Thess. 5:23; 1 Pet. 1:5; Jude 1, 24), "it is characteristic of St. James to lay stress on the co-operation of man's will."[81] Constant vigilance is required of the believer to remain undefiled "by the world" (*apo tou kosmou*). This prepositional phrase is best taken as indicating the true source of the contamination to be avoided.[82] By "the world," James does not mean the material creation but the world of unredeemed humanity as alienated from God and in rebellion against His will. It is the present world-system as dominated by the spirit of "the prince of this world" (John 14:30). It stands in antithesis to "God our Father," to whom the believer has pledged his allegiance. James, like Paul and John, was fully aware of the "wide-spread disposition and power in mankind for evil in opposition to God."[83] The maintenance of personal holiness does not call for bodily separation from humanity but for a constant alertness against accepting the purposes and practices of a Christ-rejecting world. "The friendship of the world is enmity with God" (James 4:4, ASV).

These verses must not be misread as teaching a religion of good works that assures acceptance with God and makes faith in the gospel unnecessary. Rather, James is insisting upon right conduct that results from a right relationship with God through the transforming Word of God. Sympathy with suffering and separation from sin demonstrate the operation of living faith in the heart.

This first test mark of a living faith developed by James is foundational to the further tests to be presented. Such a living faith accepts God's Word as setting forth the objective content of its faith as well as the motivating power for Christian living. Faith's living appropriation of God's Word assures continuing growth in Christian faith and conduct and provides an effective measuring line for the testing of, and God-pleasing response to, the varied demands and experiences of daily life.

NOTES FOR
James 1:19-27

1. Zane C. Hodges and Arthur L. Farstad, *The Greek New Testament According to the Majority Text*, retain *hōste*. For the textual evidence see United Bible Societies, *The Greek New Testament*, 3d ed.; Nestle-Aland, *Novum Testamentum Graece*, 26th ed.

2. James Hardy Ropes, *A Critical and Exegetical Commentary on the Epistle of St. James,* The International Critical Commentary on the Holy Scriptures of the Old and New Testaments, p. 168.

3. R. C. H. Lenski, *The Interpretation of the Epistle to the Hebrews and of the Epistle of James*, p. 557.

4. Martin Dibelius, "James, A Commentary on the Epistle of James," in *Hermeneia—A Critical and Historical Commentary on the Bible*, pp. 108-9.

5. Peter H. Davids, *The Epistle of James, A Commentary on the Greek Text*, p. 91.

6. Sophie Laws, *A Commentary on the Epistle of James,* p. 80.

7. Henry Alford, *The Greek Testament*, vol. 4, pt. 1, p. 285.

8. Bo Reicke, "The Epistles of James, Peter, and Jude," in *The Anchor Bible*, 37:19-20.

9. Richard Wolf, *General Epistles of James and Jude*, p. 29.

10. Roy R. Roberts, *The Game of Life. Studies in James*, p. 33.

11. J. Nieboer, *Practical Exposition of James*, p. 98.

12. *De* was omitted in the Textus Receptus as unsuited to the reading *hōste*.

13. Dibelius, pp. 108-9.

14. Quoted in Paul Billerbeck, *Die Briefe Des Neuen Testaments Und Die Offenbarung Johannis Erläutert Aus Talmud und Midrasch*, p. 753.
15. Burton Scott Easton and Gordon Poteat, "The Epistle of James," in *The Interpreter's Bible*, 12:30.
16. Dibelius, p. 109.
17. Harold S. Songer, "James," in *The Broadman Bible Commentary*, 12:112.
18. Simon J. Kistemaker, *New Testament Commentary, Exposition of the Epistle of James and the Epistles of John*, pp. 56-7.
19. Edward H. Sugden, "James," in *The Abingdon Bible Commentary*, p. 1332.
20. Donald W. Burdick, "James," in *The Expositor's Bible Commentary*, 12:174.
21. James Macknight, *A New Literal Translation from the Original Greek of All the Apostological Epistles with a Commentary and Notes*, 5:350.
22. Robert Johnstone, *Lectures Exegetical and Practical on the Epistle of James*, pp. 135-36.
23. A. F. Mitchell, "Hebrews and the General Epistles," in *The Westminster New Testament*, p. 192.
24. Richard Chenevix Trench, *Synonyms of the New Testament*, pp. 130-33.
25. Gustav Stählin, "Orgē. The Wrath of Man and the Wrath of God in the NT," in *Theological Dictionary of the New Testament*, 5:419-21.
26. W. H. Bennett, *The General Epistles, James, Peter, John, and Jude,* The Century Bible, A Modern Commentary, p. 153.
27. John Wesley, Adam Clarke, Matthew Henry et al., *One Volume New Testament Commentary.*
28. Joseph B. Mayor, *The Epistle of St. James*, p. 62.
29. Douglas J. Moo, *The Letter of James*, p. 79.
30. William F. Arndt and F. Wilbur Gingrich, *A Greek-English Lexicon of the New Testament and Other Early Christian Literature*, pp. 306-7.
31. This is the proper force of the compound form, *katergazetai*, used in the Textus Receptus.
32. H. E. Dana and Julius Mantey, *A Manual Grammar of the Greek New Testament*, p. 230.
33. Laws, p. 81.
34. Frank E. Gaebelein, *The Practical Epistle of James*, p. 50.
35. J. N. Darby, *The 'Holy Scriptures,' A New Translation from the Original Languages*; RSV; and NIV.
36. Arndt and Gingrich, p. 656.
37. Charles B. Williams, *The New Testament, A Private Translation in the Language of the People.*
38. John Calvin, *Commentaries on the Catholic Epistles*, p. 295.
39. Joseph Henry Thayer, *A Greek-English Lexicon of the New Testament*, p. 131.
40. The proper word for this would be *emphuteuton.*
41. Ralph P. Martin, *James, Word Biblical Commentary*, p. 49.
42. Johnstone, pp. 140-41.
43. Dana and Mantey, p. 244.
44. Kistemaker, p. 60.
45. Joseph Bryant Rotherham, *The Emphasized New Testament.*
46. Mayor, p. 66.
47. Arndt and Gingrich, p. 159.
48. Cf. 3:1; also Matt. 6:16; 24:44; 1 Cor. 14:20; Eph. 5:21.
49. Roberts, p. 44.
50. A Greek verbal form, which in usage has a middle or passive voice but retains an active meaning.
51. Wolff, p. 32.
52. Kistemaker, p. 60.

53. William F. Beck, *The Holy Bible, An American Translation.*

54. TEV.

55. Wolff, p. 32.

56. Kistemaker, pp. 60-61.

57. Harold D. Koos, "Mirror," in *The Wycliffe Bible Encyclopedia*, 2:1139.

58. James Straham, "Mirror," in *Dictionary of the Apostolic Church*, 2:42.

59. Dana and Mantey, pp. 197-98.

60. R. J. Knowling, *The Epistle of St. James*, Westminster Commentaries, p. 33.

61. Alfred Plummer, "The General Epistles of St. James and St. Jude," in *An Exposition of the Bible*, 6:582.

62. Henry Alford, *The New Testament for English Readers*, p. 1600.

63. A few manuscripts have *de*, "but," in verse 26, and *gar*, "for," in verse 27; neither has sufficient support to be regarded as authentic.

64. The words "among you" (*en humin*), appearing in the Textus Receptus, have little manuscript support and are best omitted.

65. Trench, p. 304.

66. Ronald A. Ward, "James," in *The New Bible Commentary, Revised*, p. 1226.

67. Charles Brown, "The General Epistle of James," in *A Devotional Commentary*, p. 41.

68. Burdick, 12:176.

69. Johnstone, pp. 159-160.

70. Wolff, p. 35.

71. Ralph A. Gwinn, *The Epistle of James*, Shield Bible Study Series, p. 33.

72. J. W. Roberts, *A Commentary on the General Epistle of James*, p. 82.

73. Theodore H. Epp, *James, The Epistle of Applied Christianity*, p. 114.

74. Davids, p. 103.

75. James Moffatt, *The General Epistles, James, Peter, and Judas*, The Moffatt New Testament Commentary, p. 30.

76. Hermann W. Beyer, "*Episkeptomai, episkopeō*," in *Theological Dictionary of the New Testament*, 2:601.

77. Ibid., 2:603.

78. Heinrich Seesemann, "*Orphanos*," in *Theological Dictionary of the New Testament*, 5:487.

79. Epp, pp. 114-15.

80. Roberts, p. 54.

81. E. H. Plumptre, *The General Epistle of St. James,* The Cambridge Bible for Schools and Colleges, p. 63.

82. If it is connected with the infinitive "to keep" (*tērein*), then it is a call for the believer's constant separation from the world, but Bruce C. Johanson points out that "nowhere in the New Testament does *apo* relate directly in syntax to the verb *terein* ["to keep"]. "The Definition of 'Pure Religion' in James 1:27 Reconsidered," *The Expository Times* 84 (January 1973):119.

83. Ibid.

7

VI. FAITH TESTED BY
ITS REACTION TO PARTIALITY

2:1-13 My brothers, as believers in our glorious Lord Jesus Christ, don't show favoritism. ²Suppose a man comes into your meeting wearing a gold ring and fine clothes, and a poor man in shabby clothes also comes in. ³If you show special attention to the man wearing fine clothes and say, "Here's a good seat for you," but say to the poor man, "You stand there," or, "Sit on the floor by my feet," ⁴have you not discriminated among yourselves and become judges with evil thoughts?

⁵Listen, my dear brothers: Has not God chosen those who are poor in the eyes of the world to be rich in faith and to inherit the kingdom he promised those who love him? ⁶But you have insulted the poor. Is it not the rich who are exploiting you? ⁷Are they not the ones who are slandering the noble name of him to whom you belong?

⁸If you really keep the royal law found in Scripture, "Love your neighbor as yourself," you are doing right. ⁹But if you show favoritism, you sin and are convicted by the law as lawbreakers. ¹⁰For whoever keeps the whole law and yet stumbles at just one point is guilty of breaking all of it. ¹¹For he who said, "Do not commit adultery," also said, "Do not murder." If you do not commit adultery, but do commit murder, you have become a lawbreaker.

¹²Speak and act as those who are going to be judged by the law that gives freedom ¹³because judgment without mercy will be shown to anyone who has not been merciful. Mercy triumphs over judgment!

In content and style, these verses constitute a distinct paragraph setting forth the second test for a living faith. The passage is unified by its vigorous protest against manifestations of favoritism by believers in Jesus Christ. Verse 1, embodying the theme of this test, connects with the preceding section as an unfolding of the religion that is "pure and faultless" (1:27). This passage is characterized by the literary style of diatribe. James administers a strong rebuke to partiality (vv. 1-4), shows the evil consequences of such partiality (vv. 5-11), and appeals to the readers to live according to the law of liberty (vv. 12-13).

A. THE REBUKE FOR PARTIALITY (vv. 1-4)

The address "My brothers" marks the transition to a new section. It is the author's reminder that "Christ's disciples have an intimate and sacred bond of union in the common relationship they bear to the glorious Lord."[1] It forms a fitting basis for his rebuke for partiality. James prohibits further expressions of partiality in their midst (v. 1), gives a specific illustration of such partiality (vv. 2-3), and concludes with a question of condemnation (v. 4).

1. The Prohibition of Partiality (v. 1)

"As believers in our glorious Lord Jesus Christ, don't show favoritism." This rendering accepts the verb (*echete*, "have, hold") as imperative and, with the negative (*mē*), as forming a prohibition, "do not be holding." As believers in such a Lord, they must cease all further manifestations of partiality in their midst. Westcott and Hort in their Greek text[2] punctuate the verse as a question, a view presented as an alternative in the *American Standard Version* margin.[3] Goodspeed renders it, "Do you try to combine faith in our glorious Lord Jesus Christ with acts of partiality?"[4] Songer holds that James's diatribe style "makes it more likely that the verse is a question."[5]

Most interpreters agree that the imperative is more probable. The imperative, which is found in all ancient versions,[6] is more forceful and in keeping with James's hortatory style. If the verse is a question, the *gar*, "for," not in NIV, of verse 2 is more difficult to explain. Also, if the verse is a question, the negative *mē*, implying a "no" answer, is ironic since James in verse 6 emphatically asserts their guilt.[7] It is best to take the verse as an imperative, demanding that they terminate all further practices of partiality. The second person plural (*echete*) confronts the readers directly with this demand.

The Greek places the phrase rendered "don't show favoritism" (*en prosōpo lēmpsais*) emphatically forward, as shown in Rotherham's literal rendering, "Do not with respect for persons be holding the faith of our Lord Jesus Christ."[8] The original order calls attention to this evil with peculiar pungency. This compound noun that literally means "a receiving of face" is based on the Septuagint rendering of a Hebrew phrase meaning "to lift up the face" (Lev. 19:15; Ps. 82:2). The compound noun does not occur in secular Greek or the Septuagint and is apparently a term developed early in the Christian church. It came to be a well-known term to denote the partiality of a judge raising the face of someone to his unjust advantage. It denotes "a biased judgment based on external circumstances such as rank, wealth, or race, disregarding the intrinsic merit of the person involved."[9] This was a common failing of Oriental judges, and the Old Testament strictly prohibited it (Lev. 19:15; Deut. 1:17; 2 Chron. 19:6-7; Prov. 24:23). The early church, with its strong sense of justice and personal worth, was keenly aware of this evil practice.

In 2:9, James uses the verbal form and stamps such respect of persons as sin. This evil is not found in God (Rom. 2:11; Eph. 6:9; Col. 3:25), and

Peter's experience compelled him publicly to testify to that fact (Acts 10:34). James uses the noun in the plural, "acts of partiality," thus including the varied ways in which partiality may be shown. This condemnation of "respect of persons" does not prohibit the recognition of factual distinctions between people, or showing honor and respect to those to whom it is justly due (1 Pet. 2:17).

All such acts of calculated favoritism are inconsistent with their acknowledged identity "as believers in our glorious Lord Jesus Christ." As "believers in our Lord" (*echete tēn pistin tou kurio hēmōn*, more literally "holding the faith of our Lord"), James appeals to those who are actively adhering to the One in whom "the faith" centers. "The faith" points to the well-known faith of Christians as embodied in the gospel. It is a distinctive faith as centered "in our glorious Lord Jesus Christ." The "our" is confessional and denotes that James unites himself with those who adhere to "Jesus Christ" as their "Lord." (For a discussion of these designations, see pages 53-54). Only here and in 1:1 is "the Lord Jesus Christ" explicitly named in this epistle, but see 2:7, 5:7, 9, 14-15. James insists that Christian practice must be consistent with the realities of our Christian faith.

The uniqueness of James's identification of the Person in whom Christian faith centers lies in the expression rendered "glorious" (*tēs doxēs*, literally "of the glory"). In the Greek, the article and the noun form the conclusion of an unbroken series of seven words all in the genitive; varied connections for these concluding words have been advocated. Some, such as Macknight[11] and Zahn,[12] would relate this expression with "the faith" to mean "the faith in the glory of our Lord Jesus Christ," thus making it a reference to the glorification of Christ. The five intervening genitives in the original make this connection improbable. Another view is to connect "of glory" with "the Lord" and then smooth out the connection by repeating "the Lord," "the faith of our Lord Jesus Christ, *the Lord* of glory" (ASV). This view is possible and has received considerable acceptance, but as Lenski points out, "the whole name and title, 'our Lord Jesus Christ,' is a standard unit, which means that one word in it cannot well be modified in this way."[13] Others give these words a predicate force and render them "believing as you do in our Lord Jesus Christ, who reigns in glory" (NEB). Of these three renderings, the second seems the most probable.

A further suggested solution to this difficult string of genitives is to take "of the glory" as adjectival and render "our glorious Lord Jesus Christ" (NIV). Martin supports this rendering as "the simplest solution of a difficult set of words" and points to parallels in 1:25 and 2:14.[14] In support, Davids notes that this view, "while awkward . . . allows one to explain the word order as a qualifying (and amplifying) addition to the standard title."[15]

Still others hold that a significant solution is available in accepting that this concluding genitive (*tēs doxēs*) stands in apposition to all the preceding genitives, "the faith in our Lord Jesus Christ, the Glory." Thus, Weymouth renders "your faith in our Lord Jesus Christ who is the Glory."[16] Suggested by

Bengel,[17] this view has received the support of scholars such as Mayor,[18] Oesterley,[19] Lenski,[20] Moffatt,[21] and others. Gibson objects to this view because of "the absence of any parallel expression elsewhere,"[22] but Tasker replies, "Although such a title is not found elsewhere, what is implied in it is a truth unfolded in several passages (see especially Lk. ii. 32; Jn. i. 14, xvii. 5; Heb. 1.3)."[23] Ramsey remarks, "This interpretation makes good sense, and it fits the Greek better than the others."[24] Laws concludes that "this solution seems best to take account of the structure of the verse."[25]

If the author of this epistle is James the Lord's brother, as we hold, this title is really his confession of faith concerning the true identity of Jesus Christ. As long as James was not convinced that Jesus really was the Messiah, he was unwilling to accept His claims. However, after his encounter with the risen Lord (1 Cor. 15:7), his doubts vanished and he wholeheartedly acknowledged Jesus Christ as the incarnate glory of God. James "breaks through his habitual reserve in speaking of the Master, and shows us something of his devotion to Christ."[26] The very greatness of his Christology made him hesitant to speak about it.

In New Testament usage, the noun "glory" (*doxa*) denotes the "divine and heavenly radiance" manifesting God's visible presence.[27] In the Old Testament, this divine manifestation of His presence was seen in the Shekinah, or "glory" cloud, over the Tabernacle (Ex. 40:34; Num. 14:10), and it filled Solomon's Temple (1 Kings 8:11; 2 Chron. 7:2). New Testament Christology associates this glory of God with the Person of Jesus Christ, and James thinks of Christ Himself as "the glory" in the midst of His people (cf. John 1:14; Heb. 1:3). The Old Testament taught that "the glory of the Lord will be revealed" (Isa. 40:5, NASB), and the New Testament holds before believers the hope of the "appearing of the glory of our great God and Savior, Christ Jesus" (Titus 2:13, NASB).

2. The Illustration of Partiality (vv. 2-3)

James continues in verse 2 with the use of *gar*, "for," (not in the NIV) as providing justification for the rebuke in verse 1. Martin suggests that this conjunction may be "translated here 'to illustrate' and shows that James connects the thought of 2:1 with what follows."[28] It introduces a concrete example of favoritism whereby they will be able to recognize it as sin. "Suppose" (*ean*) introduces a third class condition, indicating that the illustration is hypothetical, but surely the picture drawn is not entirely unrelated to known circumstances among the readers.[29] While hypothetically stated, the illustration suggests a situation that the readers would immediately recognize and that would strike their conscience.

Verse 2 depicts the arrival of a rich and a poor man while the readers are assembled: "Suppose a man comes into your meeting wearing a gold ring and fine clothes, and a poor man in shabby clothes also comes in." The repetition of the verb "comes" views each man's arrival as a separate event.

They may have arrived at practically the same time, but James mentions their coming separately since the arrival of each became a test of the group's attitude.

The precise nature and purpose of "your meeting" (*sunagōgēn humōn*, literally "your synagogue") is not clearly defined by James, the emphasis being on the readers' reaction toward the arrival of the two men. The use of this unusual term makes clear that a religious gathering of some kind is in view, but its precise purpose has been understood in two different ways. James has commonly been understood to picture a meeting for united public worship. So understood, neither man apparently was a member of the local assembly, and both seem to have been strangers. Having heard of this worship service, both men have decided personally to visit the service. Ropes holds that both visitors undoubtedly are non-Christians.[30] For personal reasons, they have decided to gain further acquaintance with this assembly.

Some scholars[31] hold that the meeting in view is rather a judicial assembly of the church, an occasion when the members have gathered for a judicial purpose, meeting as a religious court to deal with a dispute among its members (cf. Matt. 18:15-17; 1 Cor. 6:1-11). So understood, both men are members but "both litigants are strangers to the process."[32] As the two men arrive, "one thing is clear to the church from the start: the wealthy man must not be offended."[33]

In response to this second view, Laws remarks that "it is doubtful if the terms in which James sketches his supposed situation will allow for so precise a definition of it."[34] This view involves the questionable assumption that both of the two men coming into the meeting are members. As Moo remarks, "the text most naturally suggests that the two man were visitors, and this would be unlikely in a Christian judicial assembly."[35] The early church worship services were open to the public, and visitors were welcome (cf. 1 Cor. 14:23-25). We conclude that the most probable understanding of the scene James assumes is a regular worship assembly. Accepting this view, Kistemaker remarks, "The point of the example is to show that in a gathering of believers snobbery prevailed."[36]

James calls the place of meeting "your synagogue."[37] The term is the well-known designation for a Jewish congregation or group meeting for worship (Matt. 4:23; Acts 17:1). The compound noun, composed of *sun*, "together," and *agō*, "to lead or bring," basically means a gathering together and may denote either the people gathered together (Acts 6:9) or the place of assembly (Luke 7:5). Here the reference is to the place of assembly, as is evident from the mention of assigned seats. The readers are Christians (1:1; 2:1), and the pronoun "your" makes clear that it is not a non-Christian Jewish synagogue, since the readers are viewed as being in control of arrangements. Dods holds that the term suggests "a place so distinctively Jewish as to be naturally called the synagogue."[38] At the time when James wrote, the Jewish Christians apparently continued to speak of their place of assembly as their "synagogue," so James used the term that would be most familiar to them. Early Christian literature shows that the term was used at times of Christian assemblies,[39] but from 5:14 it is clear that Christians also used the word "church." It seems most natural to accept this epistle as belonging to an early date, since at the time, Jewish Christians made no sharp distinction between the two terms.

Others propose to strip the term "synagogue" of any strictly Jewish connotations and interpret it simply to mean "assembly" without any implications as to the background of the congregation.[40] Only if the designation of the readers in 1:1 is taken symbolically to denote the whole church is such a view probable here. Songer advances the suggestion that James used the term "synagogue" in irony here to deepen his indictment that because of its partiality, "the prejudiced church had lost one of the major characteristics distinguishing it from Judaism."[41] But such subtle irony is not evident from the text.

Although James does not actually call the first visitor "rich," his status and social dignity was at once evident from his impressive appearance. He was a man "wearing a gold ring and fine clothes." The deference accorded him was solely on the basis of his external appearance. "A gold ring" (*chrusodaktulios*) is a compound adjective, not found elsewhere in the New Testament or the Septuagint, and literally means "gold-fingered." The term does not suggest just one ring but rather a finger laden with gold rings. The wearing of a ring was customary among the Jews (Luke 15:22), but in Roman society, the wealthy wore rings on their left hand in profusion. A sign of wealth, rings were worn with great ostentation. There were even shops in Rome where rings could be rented for a special occasion. No doubt this ostentatious practice also spread to the provinces and would be known to James's readers. The practice of wearing rings as a manifestation of luxury and display invaded the churches. Clement of Alexandria (c. 155-c. 220) in his *Paidagogos* felt it necessary to urge Christians to wear only one ring because it was needed for purposes of sealing.[42] The Apostolic Constitutions (c. 381) warned Christians against fine clothing and rings, since these were all signs of lasciviousness.[43]

The man's "fine clothes" were further evidence of his wealth. "Fine" (*lampra*) means "bright" or "shining" and refers either to the glittering color of his clothes or his sparkling ornaments, probably the former. Luke used the adjective for the "elegant robe" in which Herod Antipas and his soldiers mockingly arrayed Jesus (Luke 23:11), and also for the "shining clothes" of the angel who appeared to Cornelius the centurion (Acts 10:30). The reference is probably to the shining white garments often worn by wealthy Jews.

"And a poor man in shabby clothes also comes in" turns the attention to the entry of the second visitor that day. His "shabby clothes" at once made evident to all that he was a poor man. He displayed no rings, and his garment was "shabby" (*rhupara*), "dirty," worn, and unsightly (cf. 1:21). As a poor laboring man, he probably had only one garment, and it was work-stained and begrimed. The adjective stands in direct contrast to the "fine" clothes of the rich man.

In the original, verse 3 is a direct continuation of the conditional sentence begun in verse 2. The use of *de* (not represented in the NIV) indicates that more needed to be added to complete the picture James has in mind. In beginning a new sentence, the NIV rightly uses "if" (*ean*) to continue the hypothetical picture. The two visitors are now seen as the occasion for the diverse response of the people to their presence.

"If you show special attention to the man wearing fine clothes and say, 'Here's a good seat for you'" vividly portrays the response his presence evoked. The verb "show special attention to" (*epiblepsēte*) basically means "to look upon," but from the context, it gains the force of "looking upon with favor." The second person plural verb makes clear that the eyes of the congregation were fixed admiringly upon this visitor. They were awed by his "fine" or "elegant" clothes. (The repeated article with the adjective, "the clothes, the shining," stresses his striking appearance. The repeated reference to his clothes underlines that their favorable response was prompted solely by his external appearance, "only the outward and the perishing attracting attention."[44]

Their favorable response to the opulent visitor was given verbal expression, "and say" (*eipēte*). The second person plural verb does not mean that it was the verbal response of the entire group, but that the speaker well expressed their united sentiment. The speaker is left unidentified. It is possible that he was the group's leader or someone appointed to meet visitors —perhaps a deacon.[45] The fourth-century Apostolic Constitutions ordered that the bishop should place the deacons in charge of seating the people and directed that if the service already was in progress, the bishop would not interrupt the service to direct a rich visitor to "an upper place."[46]

"Here's a good seat for you" expresses the cordial reception given the rich man. The use of the emphatic personal pronoun (*su*) directs the invitation to him personally. He is asked to be seated, while "here" points out the place to him. The exact force of the adverb rendered "a good seat" (*kalōs*) is not certain. In the papyri, it is often used with the sense of "please," an expression of courtesy.[47] That meaning is possible here, but the context makes it more probable that the reference is to the place offered him. The seat is appropriate and fitting for a man of his status. The expression conveys the thought of convenience and comfort, but the thought of honor need not be wholly excluded.

"But say to the poor man" turns attention to the second visitor. "But" (*de*) denotes this as a second example of partiality. The poor man is likewise addressed personally (*su*) and brusquely told, "You stand there," or, "Sit on the floor by my feet." He is given a choice, but either alternative reveals indifference to his comfort or feelings. The speaker is inclined to order the man to stand "over there" in an inconspicuous place, or, if he prefers to sit, he can take a place "on the floor by my feet" (*hupo to hupopodion*, literally "under my footstool"). The alternative for him is to sit cross-legged on the floor. If the reference to his "footstool" is taken literally, the words imply that "the speaker has a footstool as well as a good seat."[48] Then the stool is not even offered to the poor man; he is told curtly to sit "under [hupo] my footstool," not underneath it but beside it on the floor. Dibelius suggests that the reference to the footstool is probably figurative. Since the head of a man sitting on the floor would be at the level of the feet of those on the platform, the expression would imply nothing more than sitting on the floor.[49] This is natural only if the speaker himself sat on the platform. More likely is the assumption that the man giving the order was himself seated, not on the platform with the leaders, but in the audience, apparently in a good location near the entrance.

The manuscripts reveal considerable variation in the exact wording to the poor man. The Textus Receptus gives a double place designation, "Stand thou *there*, or sit *here* under my footstool" (KJV). This reading states that the place where he may sit is nearer to the speaker than the place where he may stand. Modern textual critics agree that the second-place designation, "here," was probably introduced into the second part in order to provide a parallel to the seat offered the rich man. Neither the manuscripts nor the modern textual critics are agreed on the place for "there" (*ekei*). Some read, "You stand, or sit there under my footstool,"[50] whereas others read, "You stand there, or sit under my footstool."[51] The latter reading is probably original; it best explains the origin of the other readings.

3. The Question of Condemnation (v. 4)

This verse forms the conclusion of the conditional sentence begun in verse 2. The question invites the readers to probe their conscience. The negative *ou* implies that they will need to admit that his evaluation of their conduct is correct. The aorist verbs simply designate the results in light of the action just illustrated. Sadler well exclaims, "How very old the pew scandal is!"[52]

Less probable is the view that the verse is a declarative statement.[53] The two parts are connected with "and" (*kai*), while the first verb is negative (*ou*) and the second verb is positive. If the statement is declarative, they are absolved in the first part but charged in the second. Then an adversative conjunction other than *kai* should have been used. If the words are a question, the negative at the beginning (*ou*) naturally goes with both verbs and expects an affirmative answer. It is more natural to read the verse as a question; this is the commonly accepted interpretation.

The question, "Have you not discriminated among yourselves?" has been differently understood. The reference may be to their inner attitude or outward conduct. "Among yourselves" points to outward action, but the words can also mean "in yourselves" as denoting inner wavering. The compound verb "discriminated" (*diekrithēte*) basically means to separate or divide between two. It is a common verb, and was used with varied meanings. In James 1:6, it means "to doubt," to be at variance with oneself, a meaning for the verb confined to the New Testament. Vincent holds that New Testament usage supports the view "that, in making a distinction between the rich and the poor, they expressed a doubt concerning the faith which they professed, and which abolished such distinctions."[54] They had accepted for themselves the abolition of class distinctions (cf. 1:9-11), but in dealing with others they perpetuated such distinctions. They were double-minded (1:8). They were at odds with themselves and were not whole in their faith. Thus, Laws holds that it is their "personal, internal dividedness that is the target of James' attack."[55] Such inner dividedness inevitably results in divided, blameworthy conduct. Others hold that the reference is to the objective fact that they have discriminated and made unjustified divisions in their assemblies.[56] James points to the logical result of their practice of favoritism. He is challenging them to admit that they are guilty of social discrimination. Although either view is possible, the objective meaning seems more in keeping with the context.

In making their distinctions between the rich and the poor man, did they not realize that they had "become judges with evil thoughts?" In calling them "judges," James suggests that they have needlessly constituted themselves "judges" in the situation. Their acts of favoritism, based on external matters of dress alone, were less than judicious. Did it not reveal that they were judges "with evil thoughts" (*dialogismōn ponērōn*)? The genitive describes the quality of the judges: they were motivated by evil thoughts. They had acted according to "the worldly consideration of expediency which made them pay court to the rich and slight the poor."[57] Such principles James stamps as "evil" (*ponērōn*), having the ethical quality of being vicious, injurious, and destructive. Partiality is an evil that exhibits the character of the one who practices it.

B. THE RESULTS OF PARTIALITY (vv. 5-11)

Partiality produces evil consequences. It demonstrates inconsistency in conduct (vv. 5-7) and constitutes a breach of the law of love (vv. 8-11).

In dealing with these matters, James is eager to have their full attention: "Listen, my dear brothers" (v. 5a). This impassioned plea, aimed at reaching their hearts, is characteristic of a vigorous speaker (cf. Acts 15:13). Before rebuking the folly of their thoughts and conduct, James affectionately addresses them as "my dear brothers." It assures them that he is motivated by love and seeks the welfare of the Christian brotherhood (cf. 1:16, 19).

1. The Inconsistency in Their Conduct (vv. 5-7)

Their favoritism involves a double inconsistency. It is inconsistent with God's choice of the poor (vv. 5b-6a) and with the hostile actions of the rich (vv. 6b-7).

a. *The divine choice of the poor* (vv. 5b-6a). James fully states the glaring contrast: "Has not God chosen those who are poor in the eyes of the world to be rich in faith and to inherit the kingdom he promised those who love him? But you have insulted the poor." The two men in verses 2-3 were representative of two classes, "the rich" and "the poor." The statements concerning both classes are general and admit to exceptions in either class. Their snobbish treatment of the poor man is now viewed in a wider spiritual context.

The form of the question, "Has not God chosen . . . ?" implies an affirmative answer. When they stop to think about it, they will readily admit that their contemptuous treatment of the poor man stands in sharp contrast to God's sovereign choice of the poor for Himself. The aorist tense records the past fact of God's choice; His action has created a presumption in their favor, making them the objects of His kindness and favor.

The divine election does not mean that *all* the poor will be saved, but it does assure that their poverty does not place them at a spiritual disadvantage in comparison to the rich. They are better placed than the rich to understand God's saving purpose and to be drawn to Him (Mark 10:32-35). Nor does their election imply any merit in their poverty; their choice unto salvation is due to God's unmerited action in grace. When men become Christians, it is not due to their own unaided decision to accept the gospel but to the fact that God has chosen and drawn them unto Himself (John 15:16; 1 John 4:10; Rom. 9:11).

"Poor in the eyes of the world" denotes those who are lacking in earthly possessions by the world's estimation. "Poor" (*ptōchos*) basically means those who are conscious of their material needs, often reduced to the need to beg. In the New Testament, the term is used in a broad sense to denote "the poor" in contrast to "the rich." In Jewish thinking, the term became closely associated with "the pious." "In the O.T. God's promises were often addressed especially to the poor of the nation because it was in this class that godliness had maintained itself. Poor and humble had almost become synonymous."[58] Perhaps, as James thought of the economic status of the majority of the church members, this close association of "poor" with "pious" may have been in his mind. He well knew that God never tired in selecting the materially poor to be rich in spiritual things (cf. 1 Cor. 1:26-29). Church history demonstrates that comparatively more poor people than rich have responded to the gospel.

God's choice of the poor has opened up to them great opportunities "*to be* rich in faith, and to inherit the kingdom." The first part relates to this present life, whereas the second looks to the future kingdom. The Christian life has both a present and future aspect, neither complete without the other.

The words "to be" were added by the translators to denote that they regarded "in faith" as a predicate; God's choice looked forward to those chosen to become "rich in faith." If, however, these words are taken as standing in apposition to the "poor in the eyes of the world," then James sets forth a future characteristic of the chosen. The world may view them as poor, but God views His chosen as rich in faith. Their material poverty and their spiritual riches coincide. It seems best, with our translators, to accept the words "to be rich in faith and to inherit the kingdom" as predicates to express what God's electing grace had in view for them.

"Rich in faith" does not mean that their faith is their wealth. "Faith," denoting their personal trust in God and His gospel, is rather the sphere or realm wherein their wealth is known and enjoyed. Their wealth consists of their salvation and all the blessings accompanying it. Faith "is the open hand of the soul, to receive all the bounteous supplies of God."[59] James is fully aware of the fundamental importance of faith in the Christian life. This spiritual wealth is not earned by good works but is appropriated by faith.

God also has chosen the poor "to inherit the kingdom" (*kai klēronomous tēs basileias*, literally "and heirs of the kingdom"). Being an heir is attained not through meritorious effort but through a personal relationship with the Ruler of the kingdom. This is the only mention of "the kingdom" in the epistle, but the concept would be familiar to the readers. The reference here is to the eschatological kingdom. Christ inaugurated His kingdom during His first advent, and now He rules in the lives of those who have accepted Him as their Sovereign. The kingdom in its full manifestation is still in the future, awaiting the return of the King in glory (Matt. 25:31; 1 Cor. 15:50-54; 2 Tim. 4:1; Titus 2:11-13).

Those who know the present riches of God's saving grace are assured that they are also heirs of "the kingdom he promised." Being now the sons of God by faith, they are also His heirs (Rom. 8:17). They may now be poor and insignificant "nobodies" in the world's view, but they also possess the glorious prospect of inheriting the kingdom with their sovereign Lord (Matt. 25:34). They are "heirs" because of their relationship to the King, established through faith; their assured inheritance is not the fruit of personal exertion but of what they are now. They already possess the title deed to the kingdom on the basis of the divine promise. In classical Greek, the verb "promised" (*epanggellomai*) was used "of voluntary offers, and so is fitly used here and elsewhere in the N. T. of the Divine promises."[60] God's faithfulness to His promises makes the promise secure to every believer. The aorist tense looks back to the fact that God made the promise to believers. "Their heirship was not a sudden thought, but a long-premeditated gift, a fact which in itself should make them see the high worth of every Christian."[61]

The heirs are characterized as "those who love him," (*tois agapōsin*). The same designation occurs in 1:12 in connection with the promised crown of life, implying that "the crown of life" and the coming "kingdom" are practically synonymous expressions, both relating to the eschatological future. The designation calls attention to the human side in God's great redemptive program. It is a reminder that the inheritance is not secured because they are materially poor. Such love for God is the evidence of eternal life (1 John 4:7-8), the result of receiving by faith the revelation of God's redemptive love in Christ (1 John 4:14-19). These words, characterizing the heirs, "do not include those of the poor who are without faith, and do include those of the rich who have not succumbed to their wealth."[62]

"But you have insulted the poor" (v. 6a). James recalls abruptly that their treatment of the poor man was very different from God's. The emphatic pronoun "you" (*humeis*) sharpens the factual contrast. God has "chosen" the poor, but they "have insulted" him. They have acted in contempt toward the poor man by ordering him to stand "over there" in an inconspicuous place or to sit on the floor. It was an act of rank discourtesy. They should have realized that of the two visitors, the poor man was the more likely prospect as a convert. Their action could only lead this poor man to conclude that these Christians were no different than non-Christians and that their Christianity was not for him.

b. *The hostile actions of the rich* (vv. 6b-7). Without employing any transitional particle, James next requests his readers to evaluate their partiality toward the rich man. He does so by asking three questions[63] concerning the hostility of the rich. The questions imply an affirmative reply, asking their confirmation that his picture is correct.

The first two questions in the NIV relate to acts of hostility in daily life: "Is it not the rich who are exploiting you? Are they not the ones who are dragging you into court?" Instead of the circumlocution used to identify a wealthy visitor in verses 2-3, James now speaks of "the rich" as a distinct class known for their oppressiveness and their legal harassments of believers. The expression does not mean that all rich people were thus guilty. The rich visitor to whom they paid such servile deference was simply representative of the rich as a class. Two hostile actions are recalled, based on sad experience with varied rich individuals.

"Are exploiting you" (*katadunasteuousin*) is a compound verb conveying the picture of a potentate exercising his power over those under his control in a hurtful and oppressive manner. In Acts 10:38, its only other occurrence in the New Testament, the verb is used of the devil's tyrannical rule over his victims. The term, frequently used in the Septuagint of the exploitation of the poor and needy (Jer. 7:6; Ezek. 22:29; Amos 4:1; Zech. 7:10), does not denote religious persecution but social and economic exploitation by the unprincipled rich who were "lording it over" them. James 5:4, 6 gives a fuller picture of their oppressive acts. The present tense of the verb denotes repeated experiences of such oppression. It is an inveterate social evil that has plagued human relations in all ages.

As a further aspect of their hostility, "are they not the ones who are dragging you into court?" "They" (*autoi*, "they themselves") is emphatic and underlines that they are the very class to whom they showed open favoritism in their assembly. The strong verb "are dragging" indicates that they were being hauled forcibly into court (Acts 16:19). The picture is not that of direct religious persecution,[64] which also might be instigated by a mob on some poor zealot, but of judicial persecution. The rich were using the courts to exploit the poor, either through appeal to unjust legal enactments or by their power with the judges to deprive the poor of their just rights. Religiously motivated hostility probably entered into their actions. The courts could be either Roman or Jewish—here, apparently the Jewish synagogue-courts.

The readers, Jewish Christians of the Dispersion (1:1), apparently lived in predominantly Jewish communities, but as Christians they were a minority group in the community. Until the destruction of the Jewish state in A.D. 70, the Jews were permitted a large measure of judicial independence by the Romans. They "administered justice to a certain extent among themselves, according to their own sacred law, even in Roman cities of the Eastern provinces."[65] (Cf. Acts 9:2; 18:12-17; 26:11.)

The question, "Are they not the ones who are slandering the noble name of him to whom you belong?" (v. 7), reveals bitter religious hostility on the part of the rich. The verb rendered "are slandering" (*blasphēmousin*) may mean "to slander, revile, defame" when directed against men (Rom. 3:8; 1 Cor. 10:30; Titus 3:2). When directed against that which is sacred, it is rightly translated "blaspheme" (Acts 13:45; 18:6; 26:11; 1 Tim. 1:13). Here the reference is to verbal blasphemy against "the noble name" of the One to whom Christians belong. Sugden points out, "As blasphemy is associated with the divine name, this passage implies that James accepted the divinity of Jesus."[66] This question concerning "the rich" establishes that they were not Christians. The passage best suits the view that they were wealthy Christ-rejecting Jews. Their blasphemous utterances against Jesus Christ may be viewed as expressed in the court in order to intensify the hostility of the judge toward the Christians, but it need not be confined to the courts. It may well be their reaction to the testimony of believers to Christ in daily life.

"The noble name" is most probably the name of Jesus. Since "Christ" denotes the Messiah, it is not probable that these unbelieving Jews would revile the name of the expected Messiah. "The noble name," an expression used only here in the New Testament, indicates the high esteem in which James and his readers held that name. Since one's name represents the bearer of the name, Jesus early came to be referred to among Christians as "the Name" (Acts 5:41; 15:14; 3 John 7). "Noble" (*kalon*) means "beautiful, honorable, excellent." "By this epithet, the disgracefulness of the blasphemy is emphasized."[67]

"Of him to whom you belong" marks the personal relationship of the readers to that name. The verb is in the aorist passive and may be literally rendered "that was called upon you" (Young). The expression is a Hebraism denoting that they belong to the one whose name they wear (Deut. 28:10; 2 Chron. 7:14; Isa. 4:1; Jer. 14:9; Amos 9:12). So Christians belong to Christ. The *New English Bible* renders it "the honoured name by which God has claimed you." The aorist tense looks back and suggests an actual invocation of the name of Jesus over believers, and it is commonly held that the reference is to their baptism. The expression is a gentle reminder that they belong to Christ Jesus and are not at liberty to practice partiality, for it dishonors that honorable name.

2. The Breach of God's Law (vv. 8-11)

Their partiality also stands under condemnation as a breach of God's royal law. James points out the alternative relations to this law (vv. 8-9) and stresses the seriousness of its violation (vv. 10-11).

a. *The relations to the law* (vv. 8-9). James commends any fulfillment of this law on the part of his readers (v. 8) but insists that its violation is unmistakably sin (v. 9).

(1) *The commendation upon its fulfillment* (v. 8). "If you really keep the royal law found in Scripture, 'Love your neighbor as yourself,' you are doing right." The connective particle *mentoi*, here rendered "really," clearly marks a specific connection with what has preceded.[68] Yet its intended force is not certain. This particle, which occurs eight times in the New Testament (John 4:27; 7:13; 12:42; 20:5; 21:4; 2 Tim. 2:19; James 2:8; Jude 8), means "really, actually," and, with an adversative force, "though, to be sure, indeed."[69]

A common interpretation is that James is anticipating an excuse on the part of his readers that their treatment of the rich man was in reality an expression of love for their neighbor. Then James's ironic reply is, if that was really their motive he has no objection. Roberts even suggests that James may have known "that this was already being used as an excuse."[70] Then James goes on to remind them that it does not excuse their treatment of the poor man, but James's words offer slight justification for such an interpretation.

Alford holds that James is not replying to "a fancied objection on the part of others, but is guarding his own argument from misconstruction": what he has said about the rich is true, but they must not assume that he suggests they should hate them and drive them from their assemblies.[71] Johnstone points out that in every other place in the New Testament, this particle "introduces something which modifies what has preceded, or is in some way divergent from the line of observation previously pursued, having the force of 'but,' 'nevertheless,' 'however.'"[72] He maintains that it is best to understand that "the apostle merely pauses for a moment in his strain of exposure and rebuke of sin, to throw in the kindly remark that, though addressing his readers generally in this strain, still he knew there were many among them who did not merit condemnation, in reference to the matter in hand."[73] This view is in keeping with the form of the conditional sentence (first class) that assumes the actual fulfillment of the law of love. Speaking with a tone of calm impartiality, he is willing and eager to give credit where credit is due.

"If you really keep the royal law" states the concession James is willing to grant to those whose conscience clears them of any guilt of actual partiality. The present indicative verb "keep" (*teleite*) acknowledges that they do fulfill this law by putting it into practice and carrying it to its intended goal. He magnifies this law by designating it as "royal." This adjective is made prominent by the Greek order, "a law ye are keeping royal." The original contains no article, thus stressing the quality of the law as being truly "royal," or kingly, in its character.

The expression "a royal law" occurs only here in the New Testament. Varied reasons for the designation have been suggested: "(a) as describing the law of love as sovereign over all others (cf. Mt. 22:36-40; Rom. 13:8 9; Gal. 5:14); (b) as fitted for kings and not slaves (cf. vv. 5, 12); (c) as given by the King."[74] Huther dismissed the last suggestion as "farfetched."[75] The first is the most common suggestion, but perhaps the term "royal" is intended to denote that this law is "supreme," being the highest formulation of law that man can conceive. Epp remarks, "The terminology that James used is a reminder that it ought to be practiced by the 'royal priesthood'" (1 Pet. 2:9).[76] This "royal law" is often equated with the law of love, which James at once quotes, but more probably the reference is to the whole law of God, of which the law of love is the crucial element. As Davids notes, "The use of *nomos* instead of *entolē* makes it appear decisive that the whole law rather than a single commandment is intended."[77] There is no basis for equating this "royal law" with the Ten Commandments.

The words "found in Scripture" (*kata tēn graphēn*, "according to the Scripture," NASB) seem best taken not merely as indicating that it is recorded in Scripture, although James clearly has Leviticus 19:18 in mind, but as pointing to the standard for its fulfillment. When they act in harmony with this "royal law" (*kata* with the accusative) they will realize that they are keeping the law of love as recorded in Leviticus 19:18. When this injunction "Love your neighbor as yourself" is actively obeyed, all the manward duties set forth by the law will be effectively performed. In Mark 12:29-31, Jesus quotes Deuteronomy 6:4-5 and Leviticus 19:18 as the two laws in which all the other laws find their true fulfillment.

The use of the second person singular verb marks this as an individual duty. The law of love must operate in each individual believer; it cannot be fulfilled by proxy. The "love" (*agapēseis*)[78] called for is an intelligent and purposeful love, a love that voluntarily and sacrificially seeks the welfare of its object, "your neighbor." In Leviticus 19:18, the "neighbor" is limited to "one of your people," but in Jesus' teaching the scope of the term was enlarged. In the parable of the Good Samaritan (Luke 10:30-37), Jesus revealed that the term is not to be limited by considerations of race but incorporates every human being, including foreigners (Luke 10:25-37) and enemies (Matt. 5:44), whom our circumstances enable us to benefit. The love expressed to the neighbor is to be "as yourself," best taken to denote both its degree and its manner. It marks a standard that is impossible to realize apart from the indwelling love of Christ in the believer (John 13:34-35). "Consistent obedience to this precept throughout the church," Johnstone observes, "would be of itself an evangelistic power immeasurably surpassing anything else she could bring into action."[79] Christianity's adoption of, and demand for, such a love has transformed social and domestic relations wherever it has been carried into practice.

"You are doing right." The conclusion of the "if" clause asserts that their actual fulfillment of the law of love is a noble and commendable practice. A life of service thus motivated will surely receive the "well done" of the Lord at the judgment seat. James, like the rest of the New Testament writers, has no quarrel with the morality of the Old Testament. Roberts observes:

> There is little difference between the morality of the law and the gospel, though there is a difference in application. If one actually was trying to fulfill the concept of love as laid down in the law, he would be doing excellently.[80]

(2) *The sin in its violation* (v. 9). "But" (*de*) marks the sharp contrast to the commendation just given. "But if you show favoritism, you sin." "If" (again the first class condition) recognizes that the violation of the law of love is a factual situation among them. Acts of partiality and obedience to the law of love are incompatible. James knew that sin springs from lack of love. The compound verb "you show favoritism" (*prosōpolēmpteite*), used only here in the New Testament, tersely states the evil practice.

The evil was not some unfortunate action into which they had accidentally fallen but was a deliberate practice. As Roberts pungently remarks, "Partiality is not a *trifling fault*, it is a *foul travesty* of the law of God fully exposed in the Scriptures!"[81] Since partiality was strictly forbidden by the Mosaic law (Lev. 19:15), by engaging in it "you sin" (*hamartian ergazesthe*, literally "sin you are working"). The original order stresses that what they are doing is not merely a breach of manners but nothing less than "sin," a tragic falling short of, and actual diversion from, the divine standard set forth in the law. The verb means "to work, to perform" and depicts a deliberate, premeditated action. It betrays a perverse inner attitude.

James relates their practice to the Mosaic law: "and are convicted by the law as lawbreakers." "By" (*hupo*) indicates agency; the law is personified and pictured as a witness whose testimony exposes them each time they practice partiality. This fact justifies the stern verdict just given. "Convicted" denotes that the law brings in the evidence to prove that they are wrong. The charge is sustained on the basis of evidence. Their guilt calls for repentance. The article with "law" (the article of previous reference) looks back to "the royal law" mentioned in verse 8. Whether the reference is to the law of God as a whole or to the law of love in particular, in either case they stand condemned. Since the Mosaic law prohibits partiality (Lev. 19:15; Deut. 1:17; 16:19), and the law of love is violated when anyone is treated with discourtesy and snobbery, they cannot escape the verdict that they are "lawbreakers" (*parabatai*), people who are guilty of having passed over a forbidden boundary.

Their partiality is not a trivial fault to be dismissed lightly as of no consequence, but a clear case of disobedience to a known demand of the Law. Adamson notes that "to the rabbis such transgression was 'rebellion,' and broke 'the fence of the Torah.'"[82] Behind the noun "lawbreakers" lies the picture of the law laying out the way of righteousness in which a man should walk. But they have not stayed on the marked road; they have stepped defiantly over the boundary to engage in a forbidden practice. If the word "sin" conveys the negative truth that they have not measured up to the requirements of the Law but have fallen short, "lawbreakers" marks the positive side of sin in that they have deliberately violated the restrictions of the law.

b. *The breach of this law* (vv. 10-11). The conjunction "for" introduces a confirmation of the evil of their partiality from the seriousness of their violation of God's Law. James was well aware of the tendency of human nature to offer an excuse for some breach of the law, especially when the failure was in relation to some minor matter. He reminds them that they cannot claim, "What is one commandment disobeyed, compared to so many obeyed?"[83] This is evident from the unitary nature of this Law. The principle is stated in verse 10 and illustrated in verse 11.

(1) *The principle stated* (v. 10). "For whoever keeps the whole law, and yet stumbles at just one point is guilty of breaking all of it." The indefinite relative pronoun "whoever" (*hostis*) has a generic force, "anyone who" belongs to the class of those who "keep the whole law, and yet stumble at just one point." No one can claim that he is an exception to this principle. The verbs "keeps" and "stumbles" are both aorist subjunctives and indicate that James presents the situation as a mental concept rather than a historical scene;[84] but his omission of the particle *an* indicates that he does not view it as an improbable situation but as a real possibility.

The first aspect of the picture is that this individual "keeps the law" by carefully guarding it against violation. The aorist simply states this as his characteristic action. "The whole law" (*holon ton nomon*) stands prominently before the verb, "the law as a whole he keeps." Although recognizing that the law involves varied injunctions, the singular designation denotes its unitary nature. The varied laws unite to form a whole, expressing the will of the one Lawgiver.

While characteristically observing the requirements of the law, a second aspect concerning the individual must be noted, "and yet stumbles at just one point." "And yet" (*de*) here clearly marks an adversative fact; "but" marks a crucial contrasting feature. "[He] stumbles" declares his failure to keep all parts of the law, in that he trips over the boundary that clearly marks the way of obedience. Zodhiates remarks that the verb "stumbles" does not suggest a deliberate, purposeful act: "We certainly don't stumble purposely as we walk."[85] Because of carelessness or inattention, perhaps due to enemy distraction, he actually trips and fails in his performance of the demands of the law. Thus, the verb used metaphorically "means to make a mistake, go astray, sin."[86] It stamps him as a transgressor of the Law. "At just one point" (*en heni*) may be rendered "in one law" (masculine) or "in one thing" (neuter). Grammatically either rendering is possible, but since the word "law" seems never to be used of a single commandment in the New Testament, [87] the latter is generally accepted as more probable. His failure to obey the law may be in connection with any particular matter which the law demands.

"Is guilty of breaking all of it" categorically states the sweeping result. "Is" (*gegonen*) renders a perfect tense and asserts that his failure has brought him into the abiding condition of being guilty "of all," all the things demanded by the law. "Guilty" does not mean that James charges the man with having actually violated all the other parts of the law. Nor does it mean that all violations of the law are equally serious. "Guilty" (*enochos*) is literally "in the power of" and means that the transgressor has been "brought into the condemning power of" the whole.[88] In the words of Davids, "although penalties may vary, one is counted a criminal no matter which particular section of the code one may have broken."[89] He who deliberately violates one part of the law, while observing the rest, reveals in himself "a sinful disposition which will manifest itself in many other ways when there is convenient opportunity and adequate inducement."[90]

Our obedience to God's will cannot be on a selective basis; we cannot choose that part that is to our liking and disregard the rest. God's will is not fragmentary; the entire law is the expression of His will for His people; it constitutes a grand unity. To break out one corner of a window pane is to become guilty of breaking the whole pane. He who crosses a forbidden boundary at one point or another is guilty of having crossed the boundary. The guilt of violating any part of that law "is proportioned to the greatness, the moral excellence, and glory of Him against whom the offence is committed, and who made us for loyal obedience to Himself."[91]

To violate any part of the God-given Law is an offense against the divine Lawgiver. It breaks our relationship of obedience to Him and reveals in us the spirit of the lawbreaker. It shows lack of true reverence for the Lawgiver and His law and breaks our personal relationship of obedience to Him as His disciples. In thus following our will rather than the will of our Master, we have violated the beneficent purpose of the whole law. The prohibition of partiality as part of the law was intended for the welfare of God's people. "A man cannot commit the sin of willfully despising human personality and be pleasing to God any more than he can violate another commandment and still retain God's favor."[92]

This principle of the unity of the law was also taught by the rabbis. "If he do all, but omit one, he is guilty for all severally" (shabbath. 70.2).[93] But as Billerbeck points out, more frequently the rabbis reversed this teaching and held that obedience to certain specific laws was as good as obedience to the whole, usually in connection with the observance of the Sabbath.[94] "The Sabbath weighs against all the precepts; if they keep it, they were reckoned as having done all" (Shemoth Rabb. 25).[95] There was a constant tendency among the rabbis to make the ceremonial cover up moral and spiritual lapses. But Scripture does not allow us to make such compensatory value judgments concerning the various demands of the law. In Galatians 5:3 Paul declares that those who place themselves under the law are obligated to obey the whole law.

(2) *The principle illustrated* (v. 11). "For" introduces the illustration of the unitary nature of the law. "For he who said, 'Do not commit adultery,' also said, 'Do not murder.'" "He who said" is apparently another Jewish circumlocution for God. Laws notes that the two aorist tense verbal forms, "who said" and "also said," suggest "a single event rather than the continuing speech of law or scripture, and the probable thought is therefore of the definite past speaking of God on Sinai."[96] God explicitly set forth both of these laws. The one Lawgiver underlines the unity of the laws He established. The two laws cited, the first two precepts of the second table of the Decalogue, are both negatively stated: the negative *mē* with the aorist subjunctive[97] expresses a peremptory prohibition; not even a single act of adultery or murder can be condoned. But the interest of James centers not on the individual commands but on the fact that the same God gave both. They equally express the will of the one Lawgiver. Songer suggests that the selection of these two commands enables James "to deepen the blackness of the sin of partiality by associating it with adultery and murder."[98] Both are equally a glaring violation of the law of love. "He who thinks that on one side he is standing in the obedience of holy love, but falls out of it on the other, is not standing firmly at all."[99]

The order here used reverses the sixth and the seventh commandments. This order may be due to the Septuagint, since this reverse order is found in some but not all the manuscripts of the Septuagint. Both orders appear elsewhere in the New Testament when both commandments are quoted.[100] No subtle meaning in the order used here need be sought.

James insists that it is folly to assume that if one of these commands is kept, the other may be violated with impunity. The use of *de*, not in the NIV, introduces the proof, and the conditional statement again assumes the reality of the picture. The use of the negative *ou* in the conditional clause fixes attention on the fact that no adultery is being committed. "But" (*de*) points to the contrasting sad reality, "but do commit murder." The present tense pictures the vicious deed as being committed. This illustration of murder may be viewed as theoretical, or it may be that James "understands the commandment against murder in the broadened and deepened sense which Jesus gave it in the Sermon on the Mount (Matt. v 21f.)."[101]

The devastating truth is, "you have become a lawbreaker." The perfect tense (*gegonas*) states the abiding result. "From the generalizing 'whosoever' of v. 10 James advances to the direct personal 'thou' in v. 11."[102] The guilt is individual and personal. He has become a "lawbreaker" (cf. 2:9), having overstepped the boundary set by "the law" of which the sixth commandment is an integral part. If the two commandments are reversed he would, of course, be equally guilty of violating God's law. Blue well concludes, "Utilizing the extreme instances of adultery and murder, James showed the absurdity of inconsistent obedience."[103]

In calling for his readers' consistent obedience to the commands of God, James is not to be understood as demanding their total obedience to all the ritualistic matters of the Mosaic law. As David observes, "the examples James selects show he is not at all concerned with ritual commands or minutiae. Rather, he selects the central ethical commands of the decalogue as examples."[104] Both of the commands cited are intimately related to the observance of the fundamental law of Christian love. James is concerned that their conduct be governed by their personal relationship to Christ Jesus who told His followers, "If you love me, you will obey what I command" (John 14:15). As Moo observes, "it is not the Old Testament law *per se* that he urges perfect compliance with, but 'the royal law' (v. 8), 'the law of liberty' (v. 12)—a law that takes up within it the Old Testament law, but as understood through Jesus' fulfilment of it."[105]

C. THE APPEAL FOR CONSISTENT LIVING (vv. 12-13)

James concludes this section with a ringing appeal to conform their lives to the law of liberty. His primary reference is in relation to their treatment of the poor, but the appeal is applicable to all of life. He states his appeal (v. 12) and enforces it with a solemn reminder concerning the coming judgment (v.13).

1. The Statement of the Appeal (v. 12)

"Speak and act as those who are going to be judged by the law that gives freedom."

The imperatives mark this as a duty, not a desirable option. The appeal concerns their speech and action, both of which were involved in the example of partiality in verses 2-3 above. James is deeply conscious of the importance of both in the believer's life, and both are given fuller treatment.

The two commands, "speak and act," are more literally rendered "so speak and so act." The use of the adverb "so" (*houtos*) before each verb indicates James's earnestness and places equal emphasis on the importance of speech and deeds. "So speak" directs attention not to the content of the spoken word but rather to the motivating power behind their speech; he is concerned that this should be equally true of their deeds. This adverb of manner is not to be disjointed from the following comparative particle "as" (*hōs*) introducing the motivating reality behind their speech and deeds. James is insistent that all of Christian conduct be motivated by the realization of future judgment (cf. 2 Cor. 5:9-10).

The imperatives are in the present tense, "so be speaking and so be doing," calling for habitual action. Let them constantly regulate both word and deed by the fact that as Christians they "are going to be judged by the law that gives freedom." The construction rendered "are going to be judged" (*mellontes krinesthai*) denotes a future event which is sure to happen, being divinely appointed (Rom. 14:10*b*-12; 2 Cor. 5:9-10). "Judged" here does not have the meaning of "condemned" (cf. 4:11) but rather conveys the thought of standing before the Judge, who will assess their character and conduct "by the law that gives freedom" (*dia nomou eleutherias*, "by a law of liberty"). This expression occurs elsewhere in the New Testament only in James 1:25, but the thought is clearly indicated in John 8:32-36. The absence of an article with either noun gives prominence to the character of this law that will be the standard of God's judgment. The designation is James's way of distinguishing this law from the Mosaic law, especially as interpreted by the rabbis. The reference is to "the word of truth" (1:18) that has been implanted in the believer's heart (1:21) and works in him the spontaneous desire to do the will of God. Wolff remarks, "As long as the law remains external, as long as it has not become an internal principle, an impulse of love, law and liberty are at odds. When the law is written on the heart, internalized, which is the distinct mark of the new covenant (Jer. 31:31ff), then law and liberty go hand in hand."[106] Thus the NIV interpretatively renders "the law that gives freedom." It "is not a law of liberty because it liberates us from obedience to God's holy Commandments, or as even from a single point in any of them; the Gospel itself and true faith impel us to this obedience."[107] It is a divinely wrought motivation in the hearts of "those who love him" (1:12; 2:5). Thus, as Epp points out, "the judgment referred to here is a judgment of believers and is for rewards, not for determining salvation."[108] The reference is to the judgment seat of Christ (Rom. 14:10*b*-12; 2 Cor. 5:10). First Corinthians 3:10-15 makes clear that those who fail to allow the indwelling Spirit to work this love-prompted change in their lives will find the reality of the judgment seat a solemn experience indeed.

The consciousness that we will be judged by this law should be a powerful motive for present Christian living. It should effectively promote the cultivation of personal holiness. If our words and deeds are guided by faith-inspired love, we will desire the welfare of others and avoid injury and insult through acts of partiality. If now our relations with others are governed by the law of love, God will also deal with us according to that law in the Day of Judgment. Mayor observes:

> It will be a deeper-going judgment than that of man, for it will not stop short at particular precepts or even at the outward act, whatever it may be, but will penetrate to the temper and motive. On the other hand it sweeps away all anxious questioning as to the exact performance of each separate precept. If there has been in you the true spirit of love to God and love to man, that is accepted as the real fulfilment of the law. The same love which actuates the true Christian here actuates the Judge both here and hereafter.[109]

2. The Vindication of the Appeal (v. 13)

"Because" (*gar*) introduces facts that vindicate the appeal just made. "Because judgment without mercy will be shown to anyone who has not been merciful." Laws remarks that the switch from the second person in verse 12 to the third person "suggests that what is being given is a general principle rather than a specific guide."[110] The absence of the finite verb "will be shown" in the original underlines the axiomatic nature of the statement. The article with "judgment" (*hē krisis*) is the article of previous reference and looks back to the judgment indicated in verse 12. It is certain that in the future judgment day there will be no mercy for him who has shown no mercy in dealing with others. He has thereby taken himself out of the merciful judgment at God's hands that our Lord promised to the merciful (Matt. 5:7; 18:23-35; Luke 16:19-31). "Not been merciful" (*mē poiēsanti eleos*, literally, "not did mercy") denotes the absence of any conscious, deliberate act of mercy toward another. The practice of mercy is not natural to the unregenerated, self-centered human heart. But in the circle of the redeemed the showing of mercy toward others will manifest itself as the expression of Christian love. "Mercy" is the outward manifestation of pity and compassion in kindly action toward the misery of another. It looks not at what the man deserves but what he needs. Such mercy is not shown in voluble words but in sincere action (1 John 3:17-18).

Such refusal to practice mercy will be like a boomerang in the Day of Judgment. A merciless attitude toward others determines the development of our own character and will condition the judgment we ourselves will receive. In that day God will deal with such a one "without mercy" (*aneleos*), a negative adjective found only here in the New Testament. Their treatment of the poor man (v. 3) was not prompted by a spirit of mercy. This statement unveils the serious implications of the practice of partiality, and James speaks frankly to expose its true evil.

"Mercy triumphs over judgment!" states the opposite and favorable side in relation to the coming judgment. The absence of any connecting particle intensifies the antithesis. "The asyndeton allows the words to be taken in their widest generality, as embodying the very essence of the Christian law of liberty, affirming the universal principle of God's judgment . . . and supplying the rule for the believer's daily life."[111] The abstract terminology enumerates the principle.

The verb "triumphs" stands forward emphatically as the first word in the statement. This compound verb (*katakauchatai*), appearing elsewhere in the New Testament only in 3:14 and Romans 11:18,[112] means "to boast against, exult over," and pictures mercy as exulting in its victory over condemnation. Mercy does not triumph at the expense of justice; the triumph of mercy is based on the atonement wrought at Calvary. Vaughan rightly remarks that the meaning is not "that by showing mercy to man we procure mercy from God. That would make salvation a matter of human merit and would contradict the whole tenor of Scripture."[113] The practice of mercy toward others is the evidence that God's grace has produced a transformation in a person. Having himself received God's mercy, he will be able to stand in the judgment that otherwise would overwhelm him. He will be "full of glad confidence," having "no fear of judgment."[114] By his conduct the merciless man reveals that he has never vitally apprehended God's mercy himself (Matt. 18:23-25). But "the man who by a merciful character proves his having a vital faith in God's mercy, is through Christ safe" and can face the coming judgment with "a blissful sense of safety."[115]

Moffatt inserts the words of James 4:11-12 after verse 13, holding that "at some early period the passage was misplaced; its proper and original position is here," after 2:13.[116] But the claim is entirely devoid of textual support, and thus it is arbitrary to transpose the passages in the epistle as we have it.

NOTES FOR
James 2:1-13

1. Edwin T. Winkler, "Commentary on the Epistle of James," in *An American Commentary on the New Testament*, p. 32.
2. Brooke Foss Westcott and Fenton John Anthony Hort, *The New Testament in the Original Greek*, p. 318.
3. "Do ye, in accepting persons, hold the faith . . . glory?"
4. Edgar J. Goodspeed, *The New Testament, An American Translation*.
5. Harold S. Songer, "James," in *The Broadman Bible Commentary*, 12:114.
6. W. E. Oesterley, "The General Epistle of James," in *The Expositor's Greek Testament*, 4:435.
7. It is possible to connect the negative closely with the noun "respect of persons," as in the RSV, "show no partiality as you hold the faith." But then the noun must be strained to have a verbal force, as this version does.

8. Rotherham.

9. Richard Wolff, *The General Epistles of James & Jude*, p. 37.

10. The genitive, "of our Lord," is objective, the faith that centers in Him, not the faith that He exercised while here on earth.

11. James Macknight, *A New Literal Translation from the Original Greek of All the Apostolical Epistles with a Commentary and Notes*, 5:356.

12. Theodor Zahn, *Introduction to the New Testament*, 1:151.

13. R. C. H. Lenski, *The Interpretation of the Epistle to the Hebrews and of the Epistle of James*, p. 572.

14. Ralph P. Martin, *James*, Word Biblical Commentary, p. 60.

15. Peter H. Davids, *The Epistle of James. A Commentary on the Greek Text*, pp. 106-7.

16. Richard F. Weymouth, *The New Testament in Modern Speech*.

17. John Albert Bengel, *New Testament Word Studies*, 2:702-3.

18. Joseph B. Mayor, *The Epistle of St. James. The Greek Text with Introduction, Notes and Comments*, pp. 77-79.

19. Oesterley, pp. 435-36.

20. Lenski, pp. 571-72.

21. James Moffatt, *The General Epistles, James, Peter, and Judas*, The Moffatt New Testament Commentary, pp. 31-32.

22. E. C. S. Gibson, *The General Epistle of James*, The Pulpit Commentary 49:28.

23. R. V. G. Tasker, *The General Epistle of James*, The Tyndale New Testament Commentaries, pp. 56-57.

24. Arthur Michael Ramsey, *The Glory of God and the Transfiguration of Christ*, p. 149.

25. Sophie Laws, *A Commentary on the Epistle of James*, p. 95.

26. J. R. Drummelow, ed., *A Commentary on the Holy Bible by Various Writers*, pp. 1034-35.

27. Gerhard Kittel, "*Doxa*," in *Theological Dictionary of the New Testament*, 2:237.

28. Martin, p. 60.

29. Dibelius insists that because James is paraenetic literature, this illustration cannot be used to infer actual conditions in the churches; it is used simply for deterrent effect. See Martin Dibelius, "James. A Commentary on the Epistle of James," in *Hermeneia—A Critical and Historical Commentary on the Bible*, pp. 128-30.

30. James Hardy Ropes, *A Critical and Exegetical Commentary on the Epistle of St. James*, The International Critical Commentary on the Holy Scriptures of the Old and New Testaments, p. 191. See also Zahn, 1:87-89.

31. See Roy Bowen Ward, "Partiality in the Assembly: James 2:2-4," *The Harvard Theological Review* 62, 1 (Jan. 1969):87-97; Davids, *The Epistle of James*, p. 109; Davids, *James*, The New International Biblical Commentary, pp. 57-58; Martin, p. 61.

32. Davids, *The Epistle of James*, p. 109.

33. Davids, *James*, The New International Biblical Commentary, p. 57.

34. Laws, p. 101.

35. Douglas J. Moo, *The Letter of James*, pp. 89-90.

36. Simon J. Kistemaker, *New Testament Commentary, Exposition of the Epistle of James and the Epistles of John*, p. 73.

37. In our English translations the rendering "your synagogue" occurs only in Jones, *The Jerusalem Bible*, and Stern, *Jewish New Testament*, designed to express its Jewishness.

38. Marcus Dods, *An Introduction to the New Testament*, pp. 192-93.

39. Wolfgang Schrag, "*Sunagōgē*," in *Theological Dictionary of the New Testament*, 7:840-41; Dibelius, pp. 132-34; Zahn, 1:94-95.

40. Moffat, pp. 31-32; and TEV.

41. Songer, p. 115.

42. Clement of Alexandria "The Instructor" 3.11, in *The Ante-Nicene Fathers* 2:285.

43. "Constitution of the Holy Apostles" 1.3., in *The Ante-Nicene Fathers*, 7:392.

44. R. J. Knowling, *The Epistle of St. James*, Westminster Commentaries, p. 43.

45. Allen Cabaniss divides the contents of the epistle according to the usual grouping of the peoples in the Christian community and holds that 2:1-26 is addressed to the deacons; the speaker is then one of the deacons. See his "A Note on Jacob's homily," *The Evangelical Quarterly* 47, 4 (Oct.-Dec. 1975):219-22.

46. "Constitutions of the Holy Apostles" 2.57-58, in *The Ante-Nicene Fathers*, 7:421-22.

47. James Hope Moulton and George Milligan, *The Vocabulary of the Greek Testament*, p. 319.

48. Robert Jamieson, A. R. Fausset, and David Brown, *A Commentary, Critical and Explanatory, on the Old and New Testaments*, 2:487.

49. Dibelius, p. 132, n. 47.

50. So Westcott and Hort; United Bible Societies, *The Greek New Testament*; and R. V. G. Tasker, ed., *The Greek New Testament*.

51. Erwin Nestle and Kurt Aland, *Novum Testamentum Graece*; and United Bible Society, *The Greek New Testament*, 3d ed.

52. M. F. Sadler, *The General Epistles of SS. James, Peter, John, and Jude, with Notes Critical and Practical*, p. 26. See also John Scanzoni, "The Man with the Gold-ringed Finger," *Eternity* 14, 8 (Aug. 1963):11-13.

53. Thus Robert Young, *The Holy Bible Consisting of the Old and New Covenants Translated According to the Letter and Idioms of the Original Languages*, reads: "Ye did not judge fully in yourselves, and did become ill-reasoning judges." Also TEV renders it, "Then you are guilty of creating distinctions among yourselves and making judgments based on evil motives."

54. Marvin R. Vincent, *Word Studies in the New Testament*, 1:739.

55. Laws, p. 102.

56. E. C. Blackman, *The Epistle of James*, Torch Bible Commentaries, p. 79; and Dibelius, p. 136.

57. Mayor, p. 82.

58. Richard Wolff, *General Epistles of James and Jude*, Contemporary Commentaries, p. 40.

59. Thomas Manton, *An Exposition of the Epistle of James*, p. 195.

60. Knowling, p. 46.

61. A. F. Mitchell, "Hebrews and the General Epistles," in *The Westminster New Testament*, p. 198.

62. James B. Adamson, *The Epistle of James*, p. 109.

63. So in the NIV rendering. Grammatically the questions asked constitute two distinct questions, the first being a double question. This is clear in the quite literal rendering in the ASV: "Do not the rich oppress you, and themselves drag you before the judgment-seats? Do not they blaspheme the honorable name by which you are called?"

64. If it was religious persecution, we would rather have expected the verb *diōkō*, as in Matt. 5:10; Luke 21:12; Acts 7:52; and Gal. 1:13.

65. W. M. Ramsay, *The Church in the Roman Empire Before A.D. 170*, p. 349.

66. Edward H. Sugden, "James," in *The Abingdon Bible Commentary*, pp. 1333-34.

67. Vincent, 1:740.

68. The KJV, following the lead of Tyndale, left the particle untranslated, apparently regarding it simply as the equivalent of *men* to balance the *de* in v. 9.

69. William F. Arndt and F. Wilbur Gingrich, *A Greek-English Lexicon of the New Testament and Other Early Christian Literature*, p. 504.

70. J. W. Roberts, *A Commentary on the General Epistle of James*, p. 96.

71. Henry Alford, *The Greek Testament*, vol. 4, pt. 1, p. 294.

72. Robert Johnstone, *Lectures Exegetical and Practical on the Epistle of James*, p. 183.

73. Ibid., p. 21.

74. T. Carson, "The Letter of James," in *A New Testament Commentary*, p. 574.

75. J. E. Huther, *Critical and Exegetical Handbook to the General Epistles, James, Peter, John, and Jude*, p. 82.

76. Theodore H. Epp, *James, the Epistle of Applied Christianity*, p. 128.
77. Davids, *The Epistle of James*, p. 114.
78. The future indicative in expression of commands is common in the LXX and the New Testament. See F. Blass and A. Debrunner, *A Greek Grammar of the New Testament and Other Early Christian Literature*, p. 183.
79. Johnstone, p. 188.
80. Roberts, p. 96.
81. Roy R. Roberts, *The Game of Life, Studies in James*, p. 66. Roberts's italics.
82. Adamson, *The Epistle of James*, p. 116.
83. Spiros Zodhiates, *The Work of Faith*, p. 182.
84. The manuscripts show some confusion here between the aorist subjunctive and the future indicative. Whenever *an* is omitted, this confusion is constant in the manuscripts.
85. Zodhiates, p. 184.
86. Arndt and Gingrich, p. 734.
87. Mayor, pp. 88-89; Ropes, p. 199.
88. Alford, p. 295.
89. Davids, p. 116.
90. W. H. Bennett, *The General Epistles, James, Peter, John, and Jude*, The Century Bible, A Modern Commentary, p. 159.
91. George Smeaton, *The Doctrine of the Atonement as Taught by Christ Himself*, p. 21.
92. A. F. Harper, "The General Epistle of James," in *Beacon Bible Commentary*, 10:212.
93. Quoted in Ropes, p. 200. See further Laws, pp. 111-12.
94. Paul Billerbeck, *Die Briefe Des Neuen Testaments Und Die Offenbarung Johannis Erläutert Aus Talmud Und Midrash*, p. 755.
95. Mayor, p. 89, n. 1.
96. Laws, p. 114.
97. When one in authority says, "Not you may do so," the prohibition is binding. It is a common expression of prohibition. See H. E. Dana and Julius R. Mantey, *A Manual Grammar of the Greek New Testament*, p. 171.
98. Songer, p. 116.
99. Rudolph Stier, *The Epistle of St. James*, p. 331.
100. Order 7th, 6th: Matt. 5:21, 27; Luke 18:20; Rom. 13:9. Order 6th, 7th: Matt. 19:18; Mark 10:19.
101. Bo Reicke, "The Epistle of James, Peter, and Jude," in The Anchor Bible, 37:29.
102. Lenski, p. 582.
103. J. Ronald Blue, "James," in *The Bible Knowledge Commentary, New Testament*, p. 825.
104. Davids, p. 117.
105. Moo, p. 96.
106. Wolff, *General Epistles of James and Jude*, p. 45.
107. Lenski, p. 584.
108. Epp, p. 130.
109. Mayor, p. 90.
110. Laws, p. 117.
111. Mayor, p. 92.
112. James used the simple form of the verb in 1:9 and 4:16. A few manuscripts use the compound form in 4:16.
113. Curtis Vaughan, *James, A Study Guide*, p. 54.
114. Joseph Henry Thayer, *A Greek-English Lexicon of the New Testament*, p. 331.
115. Johnstone, p. 200.
116. Moffatt, p. 37. See also James Moffatt, *A New Translation*.

8
VII. FAITH TESTED BY
ITS PRODUCTION OF WORKS

2:14-26 What good is it, my brothers, if a man claims to have faith but has no deeds? Can such faith save him? ¹⁵Suppose a brother or sister is without clothes and daily food. ¹⁶If one of you says to him, "Go, I wish you well; keep warm and well fed," but does nothing about his physical needs, what good is it? ¹⁷In the same way, faith by itself, if it is not accompanied by action, is dead.

¹⁸But someone will say, "You have faith; I have deeds."

Show me your faith without deeds, and I will show you my faith by what I do. ¹⁹You believe that there is one God. Good! Even the demons believe that—and shudder.

²⁰You foolish man, do you want evidence that faith without deeds is useless? ²¹Was not our ancestor Abraham considered righteous for what he did when he offered his son Isaac on the altar? ²²You see that his faith and his actions were working together, and his faith was made complete by what he did. ²³And the scripture was fulfilled that says, "Abraham believed God, and it was credited to him as righteousness," and he was called God's friend. ²⁴You see that a person is justified by what he does and not by faith alone.

²⁵In the same way, was not even Rahab the prostitute considered righteous for what she did when she gave lodging to the spies and sent them off in a different direction? ²⁶As the body without the spirit is dead, so faith without deeds is dead.

This closely reasoned passage develops one theme: faith and works and their interaction. Faith and works are mentioned together ten times in the thirteen verses of this paragraph, but the stress throughout is on their interrelationship. The rhetorical questions of verse 14 state the theme of this third test of faith. James insists that a living faith will authenticate itself in the production of works. There is no antagonism between faith and works. They are not totally distinct concepts but rather two inseparable elements in salvation.

James insists that "works are not an 'added extra' to faith, but are an essential expression of it."[1] In this passage James is echoing the teaching of Jesus in Matthew 7:21-27.

This treatment was apparently necessitated by the tendency of some of the readers to go from one extreme to the other. Before their conversion to Christianity, these Jewish Christian believers had shared the prevailing Jewish emphasis upon the efficacy of works; after they saw and accepted the evangelical message that salvation is by grace through faith without meritorious works, they went to the opposite extreme. They were now prone to assume that works were not needed at all. James was seeking to combat a moral indolence that was seeking to fasten itself upon their assurance of the doctrinal correctness of their faith.

This paragraph is one of the most difficult, and certainly the most misunderstood, sections in the epistle. It has been a theological battleground; James often has been understood as contradicting Paul's teaching that salvation is by faith alone apart from works. None can deny that there is an apparent verbal connection between Paul's teaching "that a man is justified by faith apart from observing the law" (Rom. 3:28; cf. Rom. 4:1-12; Gal. 3:6-14) and James's assertion that "by works a man is justified" (James 2:24, ASV). Because of this passage, Luther, to whom the doctrine of justification by faith alone was a precious truth, depreciated the whole epistle and termed it "a right strawy epistle" and without evangelical character.[2] But it is now commonly agreed that there is no actual conflict between the teaching of James and Paul.[3] Their teachings run parallel and do not cross. "They are not antagonists facing each other with crossed swords; they stand back to back, confronting different foes of the Gospel."[4] Paul is combatting a Jewish legalism that insisted upon the need for works to be justified; James insists upon the need for works in the lives of those who have been justified by faith. Paul insists that no man can ever win justification through his own efforts but must accept by faith the forgiveness that God offers him in Christ Jesus. James demands that the man who already claims to stand in right relationship with God through faith must by a life of good works demonstrate that he has become a new creature in Christ. With this, Paul thoroughly agreed. Paul was rooting out "works" that excluded and destroyed saving faith; James was stimulating a sluggish faith that minimized the results of a saving faith in daily life. "Both James and Paul view good works as the proof of faith—not the path to salvation."[5]

In this passage James insists that genuine faith must prove itself by its production of works. He demonstrates that an inoperative faith is useless (vv. 14-20), provides scriptural proof that saving faith manifests itself in the production of works (vv. 21-25), and concludes with a summary statement concerning the union of faith and works (v. 26).

A. THE CHARACTER OF A USELESS FAITH (2:14-20)

James insists that an inoperative faith is useless (vv. 14-17) and that even an orthodox faith if it produces no works is barren of saving power (vv. 18-20).

1. The Uselessness of an Inoperative Faith (vv. 14-17)

With the abruptness of a vivacious speaker, James introduces this further test of a living faith without any connecting particle to tie it to what has preceded. It is possible to view this discussion as a further delineation of the faith in "our Lord Jesus Christ" (2:1);[6] or it may be thought of as a development of the kind of character that will stand in the coming judgment (2:12-13).[7] But the absence of any connecting link indicates that his condemnation of an inoperative faith is an independent concern for James. He asks two rhetorical questions to set forth the uselessness of an inoperative faith (v. 14), gives a vivid illustration of such a useless faith in the face of human need (vv. 15-16), and makes a summary application to the relationship between faith and works (v. 17).

a. *The questions concerning inoperative faith* (v. 14). "What good is it, my brothers, if a man claim to have faith but has no deeds?" The abrupt question challenges the readers to contemplate the supposed value of a faith that is without works. Instead of an opening declaration of the uselessness of such a faith, James with his question seeks to involve his readers in a thoughtful consideration of its true value. The address "my brothers," placed in the middle of his question, indicates his tenderness and concern in dealing with this vital matter. It is his hope that they will not be like the people pictured.

"What good is it," literally "What the profit," challenges the readers to identify the specific gain that will result from the situation depicted. The nature of the "profit" or benefit in view relates to salvation, as is clear from the second question. James is not implying that faith as such is useless; the question is limited to the kind of faith described in the hypothetical picture,[8] "if a man claims to have faith but has no deeds?" "A man" (*tis*), "anyone," is impersonal; the concern is not with the personal identity but with the inner relation to faith of such an individual. The object, "faith," stands emphatically forward, "if 'faith' any one may speak of having,"[9] marking it as the focal concern in the discussion. James gives no indication here of the nature of this professed "faith," but his question implies that faith is the basic ingredient of the Christian life. Clearly James uses the term "in a broad and general sense, covering any degree of acceptance of Christian truth."[10] James is well aware of the inadequacy of this professed faith, but "like a practical man, he proposes a practical test."[11]

"Claims" (*legē*) is in the present tense, indicating that this individual repeatedly advances his claim that he has faith. The hypothetical form, "may be saying," does not imply that the claim is hypocritical; an inactive faith may be sincerely held. In assenting to Christian truth, the man regards himself a Christian. For the discussion, James accepts the man's claim; but by his use of the hypothetical form, James avoids any assertion that the man does have faith. Since faith is invisible, his possession of faith is dependent upon his verbal testimony alone.

The positive claim must be tested by the negative fact: "but has no deeds." The present tense underlines the continuing lack of "deeds" as characteristic. The plural "deeds" points to the numerous individual deeds that should have revealed the reality of his faith in daily conduct. By "deeds" James does not mean legalistic works as a means of salvation but rather the ethical and social activities that spring out of true piety. Huther notes that such individuals "indeed believed, but they did not receive Christ in themselves as a principle of a new life; the object of their faith remained to them purely external, and thus they wanted [lacked] those works which spring from living faith."[12] James is attacking a verbal profession of faith that produces no change in conduct. Maclaren tartly observes, "The people who least live their creeds are not seldom the people who shout the loudest about them. The paralysis which affects the arms does not, in these cases, interfere with the tongue."[13]

The second question, "Can such faith save him?" reveals that this is no mere academic question but an issue that involves individual salvation. The negative *mē* at the head of the question implies that the answer must be a resounding no. The definite article with "faith" (*hē pistis*), "the faith," which unfortunately was omitted in the King James rendering, makes clear that James is not disparaging the power of a living faith to save. In the words of Johnstone, "That faith can save a man, and that nothing else can, is written throughout the Scripture as with a pencil of light."[14] And James heartily agrees. The definite article, which here may be given either a possessive force ("his faith")[15] or a demonstrative force ("that faith" or "such faith"),[16] is the article of previous reference and looks back to the inoperative faith pictured in the first question. Such a faith is characterized by a standing inability to "save him," the individual who rests content with his profession. The aorist infinitive *sōsai* ("to save") primarily looks to the future culmination of the believer's salvation. The reference is to acquittal in the coming Judgment Day. "The criterion then will not be profession but performance."[17]

Zodhiates well remarks, "This verse is a pronouncement of the practicality of the Christian faith. Christianity is not getting a few notions into our heads, but it is a change of the seat of all our affections and dispositions, a change of the heart. True, we begin with the head, but we travel to the heart, and from the heart we travel to the hand."[18]

b. *The illustration of inoperative faith* (vv. 15-16). With masterly skill James draws a vivid picture of inoperative faith, "giving a concrete illustration of the abstract principle stated in v. 14."[19] The Textus Receptus has a connective *de* after "if."[20] But modern critical editors agree in omitting it. The illustration, which Ropes calls "a little parable,"[21] is again presented as a hypothetical scene (third class). However, the scenes of chronic poverty in the Jerusalem church (Acts 4:35; 6:1; 11:29-30) must have provided ample material to James's mind to construct this picture. See 1 John 3:17-18 for a similar picture. Zodhiates observes, "It is the imperfections of this world which provide a great opportunity to test the genuineness of our faith."[22]

James first portrays the human need: "Suppose a brother or sister is without clothes and daily food" (v. 15). Although some, such as Sadler, insist the "brother or sister" here "must mean all who are in abject poverty,"[23] it is generally accepted that the reference is to fellow believers. As fellow members of the household of faith, the obligation toward them is all the more pressing (Gal. 6:10). The disjunctive expression "brother or sister" underlines that sex does not enter into the reality of the obligation. Ross comments, "Sisters must receive equality of treatment with brothers in the Church of Him with whom there is neither male nor female (Gal. 3:28). [24] The use of these terms in the early church to denote spiritual relationships (Rom. 16:1; 1 Cor. 7:15; 9:5; Philem. 2) roots back to Jesus' teaching in Matthew 12:46-50 and Mark 3:31-35.

The pictured need is twofold: "without clothes and daily food." Although the disjunctive "or" distinguishes the singular subjects, the verb and participle are in the plural.[25] Without the disjunctive "or" it would be natural to assume that James was thinking of a husband and wife who were members of the church community. James assumes that such experiences of poverty naturally involve both brothers and sisters. The verb rendered "is" (*huparchōsin*) seems to add a subtle touch to the picture. The common verb *eimi* ("to be") would simply have stated the present fact; this verb, which basically means "to make a beginning," has a backward look; it suggests that the need discovered was a past condition extending into the present. Vincent suggests the paraphrase "If a brother or sister, having been in a destitute condition, be found by you in that condition."[26] Under this interpretation, the situation is not new, although probably not previously made known to others.

"Without clothes" need not be taken absolutely. The term was used of people wearing only an undergarment (1 Sam. 19:24; John 21:7), or, more generally, it might denote those who were poorly clad (Job 22:6; 31:19; Isa. 58:7; Matt. 25:36). The latter seems the intended meaning here. Thus the RSV renders "is ill clad," and the NEB has "is in rags."

Insufficient food is the accompanying need: "and [without] daily food." The exact expression occurs only here in the New Testament. It suggests "the day's supply of food" rather than the supply that is needed day by day. It depicts "the indigence which failed to obtain a supply for even a single day."[27] The double need presents a picture of extreme destitution. When encountered, the individual is both cold and hungry.

A vivid portrayal of the response of inoperative faith follows: "If one of you says to him, 'Go, I wish you well; keep warm and well fed,' but does nothing about his physical needs" (v. 16). "One of you" leaves the speaker unidentified but presents him as belonging to the circle of the readers. It is intended to shake his readers. Are they guilty of or tolerating such a heartless reaction?

"Go, I wish you well" (*hupagete en eirēnē*, literally "Go in peace") was a warm and kindly expression of farewell among the Jews (1 Sam. 1:17; 20:42; 2 Sam. 15:9; Mark 5:34; Acts 16:36). It implies a prayer-wish suggesting that the individual is being dismissed with a feeling of personal peace and well-being, assured that God will meet his needs. We cannot miss the irony, but the words were not spoken in conscious mockery by the speaker. Jesus used the expression in dismissing those who had come seeking His help (Luke 7:50; 8:48), but He used it after He had met the needs of those thus dismissed. The added instructions, "keep warm and well fed," correspond to the two needs mentioned. The speaker thus shows that he is well aware of those needs.

The imperatives, "keep warm and well fed," may be either middle or passive. If middle, the advice is, "Keep yourselves warm, and have plenty to eat" (NEB). Then the meaning in effect is, "Let the shivering, hungry brothers or sisters pull themselves up by their own bootstraps."[28] So understood, there is an unavoidable tone of mockery in the advice, intended to shock the readers. There is also a subtle implication of blame: "If the poverty-stricken brothers or sisters would only exert themselves, they would have plenty to eat and sufficient clothing to wear."[29] Davids supports the middle voice here "since a middle sense appears to be the normal case in both verbs in biblical Greek."[30] But the passive here seems preferable[31] and has the support of Ropes and Adamson.[32] The passive implies, "Let someone else feed and warm you," but indicates that the speaker has no intention of doing that himself. Oesterley suggests that possibly the speaker was acting upon a mistaken application of the words of Jesus in Matthew 6:25-30, and that he was piously commending the needy individual to God with the assurance that God would supply his needs.[33] Such expressions of sympathy are valuable and can perform a refreshing and strengthening ministry in the soul of the needy, *if* that is all that one can give to the shivering and starving. Under either voice the speaker reveals an inactive faith that fails to meet the needs of needy members of the Christian community.

"But does nothing about his physical needs" makes clear that this is not a case of inability in the face of a sincere desire to meet the need. It is the case of a professed faith that produces no desire to act. This comfortable and pious "armchair philanthropist"[34] has no intention to supply the need personally. "But" (*de*) marks the inconsistency between the warm verbal expressions and the definite failure to act. "Does nothing" (*mē dōte*, literally "not you give") may be called a collective plural,[35] but it does imply that the readers, in condoning such a hollow mockery in their midst, in reality share in the guilt for the tragic scene.

The expression "his physical needs," literally "the needful things of the body," occurs only here in the New Testament, but it was common in secular Greek literature. While the direct reference is to the needed food and clothing, James apparently intended it to include all those things that are necessary for bodily existence and well-being.

His rhetorical conclusion to his hypothetical picture, "What good is it?" indicates what James thinks of such "faith." The repeated question (v.14) is a renewed demand that his readers acknowledge its uselessness. It brings no gain either to the speaker or to the needy brother or sister.

c. *The application to inoperative faith* (v. 17). "In the same way, faith by itself, if it is not accompanied by action, is dead." "In the same way" (*houtōs*), "in this manner, likewise," makes the application by drawing an analogy between the illustration and inoperative faith. The observed phenomena illuminate the principle. What was seen of the individual in the illustration in verses 15-16 is now applied to "the faith" (*hē pistis*) that the individual claims to have (v. 14).

James is not depreciating faith. Zerr rightly remarks, "Faith is a grand principle and no man can be a Christian without it."[36] But the analogy does apply *if* the faith that is professed "is not accompanied by action," more literally "not may be having works." The use of the third class conditional sentence here again leaves that point undetermined. It is assumed that faith can be rightly expected to have works, but each case must be tested on that point. The illustration pictures a case where that which calls itself faith is indeed without works. This is the fatal defect in the "faith" that James is condemning. "Because life is dynamic and productive, faith that lives will surely produce the fruit of good deeds."[37] The illustration demanded that faith must produce acts of social beneficence; but in the application James calls for "deeds," thus giving the demand a wider scope. Easton notes that James does not charge these proponents of an inoperative faith "with antinomianism but with lack of moral effort; they praise virtue (v. 16) but do not practice it."[38]

The inescapable verdict is that "faith by itself, if it is not accompanied by action, is dead." As Adamson observes, "having form, this faith lacks force —'outwardly inoperative, because inwardly dead'."[39] The phrase "by itself" (*kath' heautēn*) may mean that this "faith" is dead "in itself," in its very nature it is inwardly dead. Thus Ropes rightly emphasizes that the contrast here is not simply between faith and works but between a dead faith and a living faith.[40] Lenski interprets the phrase to mean "according to its own showing." It had a splendid opportunity to show its life, but its failure to act showed it was lifeless.[41] In view of the fact that the phrase in the original stands at the very end, after "is dead," it emphatically states "that a faith without works is not only dead in reference to something else, but dead in reference to itself."[42] True faith, like a living tree, will reveal its life by the deeds it produces. "Works are not an 'added extra' any more than breath is an 'added extra' to a living body."[43] See 2:26. James, like Paul, believes that in judging any profession of faith, "the only thing that counts is faith expressing itself through love" (Gal. 5:6).

2. The Barrenness of Orthodox Faith Without Works (vv. 18-20)

James further points out that a useless faith may indeed be an orthodox faith. The orthodoxy of the faith professed does not guarantee that it is a living faith. If it is unproductive, it also will fall under condemnation as useless.

Our interpretation of these verses will depend upon our understanding of verse 18. Usually James's statements are clear and pointed, but here problems arise as to the intended structure and meaning. Efforts to establish the precise force of the verse have taxed the ingenuity of the commentators. Blackman calls this verse "one of the most problematic in the New Testament."[44] Points of uncertainty are: (1) Who is the speaker in the words "someone will say"? (2) How much is to be included in what he says? and (3) Who are the "You" and "I" in the words "You have faith; I have deeds." The problems are interrelated. Varied solutions have been proposed, but it would require pages to delineate them.[45] Without assuming that other views are not possible, our own view is that the "someone" speaking is an objector to James's view and that his objection is contained in the first half of the verse. Thus we assume that in these verses James sets forth the words of an objector (v. 18*a*), gives his challenge in reply to the objection (vv. 18*b*-19), and concludes with a searching application to the objector (v. 20).

a. *The assertion of an objector* (v. 18*a*). "But someone will say, 'You have faith; I have deeds.'" "But" represents the common adversative particle *alla*, usually rendered "but"; it denotes a transition to something different or contrasting.[46] It may have an emphatic force, but its usual adversative force is in keeping with the opening formula *all' erei tis*, "but someone will say," which was a common device for introducing the words of an objector (Rom. 9:19; 11:19; 1 Cor. 15:35). The ordinary reader would assume that some counterargument was being introduced. The future "will say" implies that it is anticipated that objection to the teaching just given (vv. 14-17) will be raised. The indefinite pronoun (*tis*) puts the objector's identity aside; the concern is the objection raised. Because of the context, it has been suggested that the speaker is a modest substitute for James himself,[47] or an ally, either Christian or non-Christian, who agrees with James.[48] But it is difficult to feel assured that the ordinary reader would assume this interpretation of the scene without any further indication.

When the objector says, "You have faith; I have deeds," to whom is he speaking? The natural assumption is that the objection would be addressed directly to James. But then the pronouns, both of which are emphatic, produce difficulty. "You" would mean James and "I" the objector. But this just reverses the views,⁴⁹ since James is insisting on the need for works, while the objector stresses his faith. For this reason some see the speaker as an ally of James, or a professed arbitrator.

Lenski offers a solution with the suggestion that the speaker is a third party who does not address James but the troubled "faith only" church member.⁵⁰ As an opponent of James's view, he is seeking to reassure this troubled member, urging him to hold onto his faith, even though James is insisting strongly on works. Let this agitated member rest assured that, in spite of the claims of James, it is his Christian faith that saves him. Objection may be made to this view that the literary style of the diatribe requires that the quoted material come directly from the censured individual. While it is questionable that the problem must be settled on the basis of the Greek diatribe style, in reality this view does not directly violate that pattern, since this third party does in fact identify himself with the view censured by James. Thus we have two opponents seeking to win a third party. In this semidialogue James refers to himself quite naturally as "I."

Ropes proposes to solve the difficulty by depersonalizing the emphatic pronouns "you" and "I," making them equivalent to "one" and "another." He holds that James's words are "merely a more picturesque mode of indicating two imaginary persons."⁵¹ This view is followed in the *New English Bible*: "Here is one who claims to have faith and another who points to his deeds." Then any specific identity of the objector is dissolved in the generalized claim. Hodges objects that this suggested usage of the two emphatic pronouns "would be extremely obscure" and points out that the availability of varied Greek idioms "to express the idea of *one* and *another* reduces the probability of Ropes's suggestion to a near vanishing point."⁵² This meaning assigned to these two emphatic personal pronouns (*su* and *ego*) was obviously generated by the difficulty of the context. Under this view it is generally held that the objector contends that since there are diversities of gifts, it must be recognized that some Christians excel in works while others are strong in faith, and that there is room in the church for both sides. His claim that faith and works are two distinct virtues of equal worth is a direct attack upon James's position.

Another proposal toward a solution is to place some punctuation after the first verb in the expression "You have faith; I have deeds," thereby limiting the objector's words to only the first verb. Then the second verb begins James's reply. Then two interpretations are possible. One view is to have the objector challenge James's faith. Thus Westcott and Hort in the margin of their Greek text suggested a question mark after the first verb, "Do you have faith?" Moffatt prefers an exclamation point: "And you claim to have faith!" meaning, "You who talk so highly of deeds! What do you know of religious belief?"⁵³ Ward, however, suggests that the objector is minimizing the difference between himself and James. The objector "merely says, *You* (James) have faith. He means: 'You are in the same position as we are; you are one of us.'"[54] This attempt to limit the objector to the first verb alone has not generally commended itself. The two verbs seem best understood as coming from one speaker, who thus contrasts his position with that of James. *Kai* ("and"), omitted in NIV, coordinates the two verbs.

But how far do the words of the objector run? Here again there is no agreement among the interpreters. His words are variously taken as extending through verse 18, or verses 19, 20, 23, and even 26. But the latter part of verse 18 is clearly a challenge to the objector and is best taken as James's reply. We accept that the objector's words are contained in the remark "You have faith; I have deeds." By their use of quotation marks, a device not available to ancient writers, a number of our modern English versions support this view.[55] It also receives the support of such diverse interpreters as Ropes,[56] Winkler,[57] Lenski,[58] Dibelius,[59] Mitton,[60] Kistemaker,[61] and others.

b. *The challenge to the objector* (vv. 18b-19). James meets the objector with a sharp challenge. He is challenged to demonstrate that he has faith apart from works (v. 18b) and reminded of the true character of an orthodox faith without works (v. 19).

(1) The demonstration of faith by works (v. 18b). The challenge to the objector is precisely stated: "Show me your faith without deeds, and I will show you my faith by what I do." "Show" (*deixon*) demands that the objector as a definite act "demonstrate," or "exhibit," his faith directly (*moi*) before James. Since faith is invisible, "the faith" (*hē pistis*) that he claims to possess must be manifested by "deeds" (*tōn ergōn*), "the deeds" that James insists must accompany genuine faith. (Adamson notes a limitation by remarking that James "is contemplating a normal man, not, for example, a helpless paralytic, whose faith, if any, is perceptible only to God.")[62] The challenge implies that "without" (*chōris*, "apart from")[63] deeds, which his "faith" does not have, such a demonstration is impossible. And this inability to demonstrate his faith will prove that it is not true faith. Faith and works are inseparable.

James is willing and able to meet his own challenge: "And I unto thee will shew by my works my faith" (Rotherham). The forward position of "unto thee" stresses that James himself is eager to provide the demonstration that he has demanded of the objector. That demonstration will be provided "by" (*ek*), "out of," and will have its source in the works that his faith produces. James can start with his works and point to them as the proof of something beyond the works. The works prove that he has faith, for without that faith he could not do them. "In everything he does, faith is the main ingredient. Just as a motor produces power because an electrical current flows into it, so a Christian produces good deeds because true faith empowers him."[64] James has no quarrel with those who insist upon the centrality of faith in the Christian life, but he is controverting the validity of a professed "faith" that produces no outward results in conduct.

Attention may be called to the elegant stylistic structure of this reply. The order is chiastic and beautifully corresponds with the emphasis being made.

your faith ⟍ ⟋ apart from works

by my works ⟋ ⟍ my faith

(2) The character of faith without works (v. 19). The objector is further challenged to recognize the true nature of an orthodox faith that is inoperative. "You believe that there is one God." The second person singular pronoun (*su*) with the verb makes the addressee emphatic. James confronts the objector directly on his own ground, namely, his treasured orthodox faith. "You believe that there is one God" may be punctuated as a question,[65] but it is more impressive if read as a statement of fact. James is not questioning the contents of what the objector "believes." His professed faith is orthodox: "that there is one God," stressing monotheism. The verbal construction "you believe that" "indicates an intellectual commitment on his interlocutor's part to a creed (*pisteueis hoti*) rather than the distinctly Christian personal trust and commitment which would include obedience (*pisteueis* plus dative, *en* or *eis*)."[66] There is considerable manuscript variation as to the exact expression of the thing believed.[67] The NIV rendering, "there is one God," stresses the monotheistic nature of his faith, consistent with Jewish orthodoxy. The ASV reading, "God is one," agrees with the Christian doctrine of the unity of the Godhead. Textual critics differ as to which was the original reading.[68] But there is no crucial difference in the meaning of these readings. All the textual variants express the opening line of the Jewish confession of faith, the *Shema*, grounded in Deuteronomy 6:4-5, which every pious Jew recited both morning and evening. The Jewish Christians to whom James wrote probably used it regularly in their worship. This fundamental proposition of faith, common to both Judaism and Christianity, is mentioned here as being representative of an orthodox creed. James is not concerned with setting forth the whole of Christian faith, and he makes no mention of Christ in relation to monotheism (cf. 1 Cor. 8:4-6; Eph. 4:4-6; 1 Thess. 1:8-10). Both Jews and Christians treasured their monotheistic faith as distinguishing them from polytheistic heathenism.

"Good!" (*kalōs poieis*, "Well you are doing") expresses James's approval upon this confession. The words need not be taken as ironic; it is unlikely that James would speak slightingly of this basic doctrine. He is not belittling any sincere claim to orthodox faith. The confession is good as far as it goes. "Orthodoxy is better than heresy."[69] But James is painfully aware that such an intellectual confession alone is tragically inadequate, is worse than useless.

With one stunning remark James shatters the value of such an orthodox faith if it is inoperative: "Even the demons believe that—and shudder." With his use of "even" (*kai*) James places such an inoperative faith on the level of the demonic. They also believe in one transcendent God. No atheists or skeptics are among them.

In classical Greek "the demons" (*ta daimonia*) was commonly used of the pagan gods (cf. Acts 17:18), but here the reference is clearly to the unseen evil spirits so often mentioned in the gospels. In the story of the Gerasene demoniac (Mark 5:1-10; Luke 8:26-33; cf. also Mark 1:23-24) we have a clear illustration of such a faith on the part of the demons. These malicious supernatural spirits, engaged in seeking to possess and torment men, readily confessed God's existence and omnipotence; further, they know that as such He is totally and consistently their enemy. But their "faith" does not transform their character and conduct or change their prospects for the future. They establish the sad truth that "belief may be orthodox, while the character is evil."[70]

The only effect that their faith has upon the demons is an inner reaction—they "shudder" (*phrissousin*). The verb, occurring only here in the New Testament, means "to bristle," conveying the picture of a horror that causes the hair to stand on end. The present tense pictures this as their characteristic reaction whenever they face the reality of the eternal God. This term is not strictly applicable to spirits, yet it effectively conveys the intensity of the horror that seizes the demons when confronting God. They have an intense, unquestioned belief in God's existence and power, but their faith brings them no peace or salvation. They are fully aware that doom awaits them at the hands of the infinitely perfect God (Matt. 8:29; 25:41; Luke 8:31).

It is true that this "reference to demons reflects the first-century understanding of the existence of demons,"[71] but it would be an unwarranted assumption that James personally rejected the correctness of that understanding. We fully agree with Roberts's statement,

> We are not to attribute the statements of the Bible about demons to superstition or mental diseases. God's word affirms their existence. It is no more difficult to believe in demons than to believe in God, Christ, the Holy Spirit, angels, or the devil.[72]

The modern resurgence of the occult is again bringing the reality of the demonic world into tragic prominence.[73]

c. *The appeal to the objector* (v. 20). "You foolish man, do you want evidence that faith without deeds is useless?" The rendering of Rotherham retains the literal order of this penetrating appeal: "But art thou willing to learn, O empty man! That faith apart from works is idle?" The use of *de*, "but," not in the NIV, indicates some intended connection with what precedes. The particle may have an adversative force to introduce some contrasting matter, but it seems better here to accept a continuative force,[74] implying that something further must be said. The question directed to the objector naturally follows from the challenge to his inoperative faith just made (vv. 18-19). So confident is James of the truthfulness of his reasoning that he calls upon the objector to concede the error of his position.

"Do you want evidence" (*theleis gnōnai*), "are you willing to know," implies an unwillingness by the objector to face the issue. His unwillingness to agree with the truth set forth is not due to any obscurity of the subject but to his reluctance to acknowledge the truth. The aorist infinitive rendered "know" also can mean "recognize" or "acknowledge" and calls for a definite act of acknowledgment by the objector. His refusal to do so would imply inner perversity of will.

The insertion of the direct address within the appeal, "O foolish man" (*ō anthrōpe kene*), suggests a feeling of impatience with the objector. The Greek is sparing in its use of "O." Winkler notes that it "occurs in the New Testament only in addresses of adjuration and censure."[75] "Foolish" properly means "empty," or " hollow," indicating that the objector in adhering to his inoperative faith is devoid alike of good moral sense as well as living faith. Trench remarks that, whenever this adjective is used of persons, it implies "not merely an absence and emptiness of good, but, since the moral nature of man endures no vacuum, the presence of evil."[76] Dibelius notes that the term was at times used of one who boasts foolishly, and accordingly he suggests the rendering "You braggart!"[77] But that does not seem to be the objector's error; rather, he seems to be guilty of honestly refusing to acknowledge the error of his position. James's designation here seeks to be the linguistic equivalent of Jesus' expression *raka* in Matthew 5:22, "empty-head, numb-skull, fool."[78] Huther suggests that the term James employs here implies "the want [lack] of true intrinsic worth, in opposition to the imaginary wealth which the opponent fancies he possesses in his dead faith."[79]

James appeals to the objector to recognize "that faith without deeds is useless." "Faith" here has a definite article, "the faith," and points back to the nature of the faith under discussion. "Deeds" likewise has a definite article, "the deeds" that a living faith naturally produces. Such a faith in its very nature is "useless" (*argē*), "unproductive." The adjective was used of money that was yielding no interest or of a field lying fallow. It is unproductive for salvation. The Textus Receptus uses the word "dead" (cf. v. 17).[80] Although this reading has good manuscript support and has the advantage of preserving a subtle play on words, *ergōn—argē*, "works—workless," a scribe would be more probable to replace this less familiar term with the common word "dead" in view of verses 17 and 26.

Verse 20 admittedly has a transitional character. In view of the connective particles, we have included it with the preceding verses. Thus it calls upon the objector to acknowledge the conclusion just reached. Verse 20, as

Moo notes, "re-states the main point of the entire section; faith without works does not 'save' (v. 14), does not 'profit' (v. 16): it is 'dead' (vv. 17, 26) and useless."[81] As transitional, it also looks to what follows, challenging the objector to recognize the principle that is to be illustrated in the lives of Abraham and Rahab.

B. THE MANIFESTATION OF SAVING FAITH
THROUGH WORKS (vv. 21-25)

Having established the negative aspect of this test of faith, namely, that a faith without works is useless, James now turns to establish from Scripture the positive truth that a saving faith manifests itself in the production of works. As evidence he cites the Old Testament record concerning Abraham (vv. 21-24) and Rahab (v. 25). The reference to each is introduced with a rhetorical question inviting an affirmative response.

1. The Working of Abraham's Faith (v. 21)

"Was not our ancestor Abraham considered righteous for what he did when he offered his son Isaac on the altar?" The original makes prominent the identity of this supreme example of an active faith: "Abraham our father —was not he declared righteous out of works?" (R. Young).[82] Abraham's example would carry great weight for the readers. He was their most illustrious progenitor, a man of faith who enjoyed a close relationship with God. No position could be accepted that was contrary to Abraham's experience.

The expression "our ancestor Abraham" is fully consistent with the view that the readers were Jewish Christians,[83] but it does not prove that view.[84] While it was a "stereotyped phrase in Jewish literature,"[85] it also was freely used by Christians. Paul as a Jewish Christian (Rom. 4:1, 12) used it even when addressing believers of Gentile extraction (Rom. 4:16-17; Gal. 3:7, 29), and it even was used by Gentile believers (1 Clement 31:2), because Abraham was accepted as the spiritual father of all believers (Rom. 4:11). The New Testament writers view Abraham as the representative man of faith, and their citations of his example point to different aspects of his faith.[86]

The negative *ouk* in the rhetorical question[87] indicates that James expected his readers to confirm that Abraham was "considered righteous for what he did" (*ouk ex ergōn edikaiōthē*) when he offered his son Isaac upon the altar of sacrifice. "For what he did," more literally "out of works," stands emphatically before the verb, indicating the source or reason, not the means, of the justification. The plural "works" may be viewed as the plural of category, but apparently James is thinking of the offering up of Isaac as the culminating event in the story of the faith-prompted works that characterized the life of Abraham. Scripture records no further testings of Abraham after this supreme testing of Abraham's obedience to God, demonstrating that God was first in his life. His faith-prompted action was the supreme example of the kind of works that James insists must result from a living faith.

The aorist passive verb "was . . . considered righteous" is historical, recording the divine response to Abraham's faith-prompted action in Genesis 22. When in Genesis 22:12 God responded, "Now I know," it was His pronouncement upon the character of Abraham, confirming his faith as authentic. The verb (*edikaiōthē*), with which James expected his readers to be familiar, has two general meanings: (1) "to acquit, to pronounce and treat as righteous," the opposite of "to condemn" (Ex. 23:7; Deut. 25:1; Isa. 5:23; 53:11; Matt. 12:37; Luke 18:44; Rom. 3:24; 5:1); (2) "to vindicate or show" that a certain course is wise or just (Isa. 42:21; 43:9; Matt. 11:29; Luke 7:25, 35; Rom. 3:4; 1 Tim. 3:16). The former, commonly called the forensic usage, indicates the divine approval of the one thus declared righteous on the basis of Christ's atonement (Rom. 3:21-26). But the point of James's argument here clearly does not imply a forensic declaration of justification; rather, he is pointing to the divine vindication of the righteous nature of his character, manifested by the deeds flowing from his faith. Thus Schonfield renders, "Was not our father Abraham vindicated by his deeds?"[88] And interpreters such as Tasker[89] and Vaughan[90] hold that the verb here means "to be vindicated, shown to be righteous." Thus on this climactic occasion when Abraham was willing to offer even his son, God spoke to declare that Abraham "was considered righteous for what he did."

"When he offered his son Isaac on the altar" records the specific faith-prompted deed that called forth God's commendation. Hebrews 11:17-19 is the only other New Testament reference to the scene in Genesis 22:1-18. The aorist participle records an action antecedent to the announcement made; the verdict pronounced on Abraham arose "out of" (*ek*) the act of offering up his son. Although Genesis 22 describes how God halted the offering before it was consummated, the use here of the aorist presents it as a completed act in Abraham's intention.

"His son Isaac" indicates something of the heartrending cost of that act for Abraham. As the author of Hebrews indicates (11:17-18), the hardest part of the test for Abraham was the fact that the command to offer up Isaac appeared totally inconsistent with the revelation of God's purpose concerning Isaac, the promise-bearer. Only Abraham's active faith enabled him to find a reconciliation in Isaac's resurrection (Heb. 11:19; cf. Abraham's "we" in Genesis 22:5). That faith-prompted act called forth this further divine declaration. It was the divine seal upon Abraham's consciousness of his acceptableness with God, begun in simple faith years before.

An apparent verbal contradiction exists between James's statement that Abraham "was justified by works" (2:21, ASV) and Paul's teaching that Abraham "believed God, and it was reckoned unto him for righteousness" (Rom. 4:3; Gal. 3:6, ASV). But a comparison of their statements in context at once reveals that they refer to different events in Abraham's life. Paul refers to the initial justification of Abraham in Genesis 15, when he believed God's promise in the face of apparent impossibility; James refers to the divine pronouncement in connection with Abraham's act of faith in Genesis 22, thus sealing Abraham's consciousness of his approval before God. In both instances the justification was in response to Abraham's living faith. In the words of Cranfield,

> for James, no less than for Paul, the words of Gen. 15:6 quoted in verse 23 ("And Abraham believed God, and it was reckoned unto him for righteousness") are decisive. It was by his faith that Abraham was justified. His works (his readiness to offer up Isaac related in Gen. 22) did not earn his justification (about which we hear already in Gen. 15); they were simply the fruit and the outward evidence of his faith.[91]

James cites the event in Genesis 22 because it is a clear illustration of his position that true faith and resultant works are inseparable. "Had there been no works, Abraham would not have been justified; but that would have been because the absence of works would have meant that he had no real faith."[92] That Paul also believed that a faith that justifies must be working faith is clear from his demand for "faith working through love" (Gal. 5:6; cf. Eph. 2:8-10; Titus 2:14; 3:8).

b. *The results of Abraham's working faith* (vv. 22-23). James now calls attention to the results of the test that demonstrated that Abraham's faith had works. The singular "You see" marks that James is calling this evidence of his position (v. 18) to the objector's attention. Abraham's works supported his faith and took it to its proper goal (v. 22); they brought to ultimate fulfilment his initial justification (v. 23*a*); and they established his intimate friendship with God (v. 23*b*).

(1) The perfecting of his faith (v. 22). "You see that his faith and his actions were working together, and his faith was made complete by what he did." The punctuation for this verse is not certain. If it is taken as a question,[93] James is asking the objector if he recognizes that this conclusion follows from the example just cited. If it is a declarative statement, James formulates the logical deduction from the example. The latter is preferable. Dibelius holds that if it were intended as a reproachful question to the objector, some form of address would have been likely.[94] The present tense verb, "you see," implies that the double fact James advances from the example was so obvious that the objector could not fail to see these realities. This appeal to the individual suggests that each individual must see these spiritual realities for himself. "The Gospel," Zodhiates remarks, "is not something that is understood and appropriated collectively, but something that is seen personally and individually."[95]

"That his faith and his actions were working together" is the first aspect of the truth established by the example. "Faith" has the definite article (*hē pistis*) and refers to Abraham's faith, which, while left unmentioned in verse 21, was assumed as present and as explaining Abraham's deed. Without that faith the deed would not have been performed. It establishes the nature of his faith as living, dynamic, action-producing reality. "Working together" (*sunērgei*) asserts the close connection between Abraham's faith and his works. The compound verb may mean "to cooperate with," to work together as two quite independent forces. But James cannot mean that faith and works are two equal partners cooperating in the achievement of the stated result. Surely James did not teach such synergism. The preposition *sun* in the verb need not be so pressed. It seems better to accept that it has the force of working *with* in the sense of aiding and supporting; his works supported and sustained the fact that his faith was a living faith.

The imperfect tense suggests that this working union of faith and works was not limited to this occasion but was characteristic of Abraham's life of faith. "Faith is the motivating power of works and there can be no works of faith without faith, as there can be no fruit without the tree. We cannot say that the fruit of the tree cooperates with the tree, but we can say that the fruit helps us to know the nature of the tree."[96] This verse underlines the inseparability of a living faith and Christian deeds. Though Luther had trouble with the teaching of James, he himself, in his preface to the epistle to the Romans, speaks precisely as James does here.

> O it is a living, quick, mighty thing this faith; so that it is impossible but that it should do all good things without intermission. It does not ask whether good works are to be done, but before the question could be asked it does them, and is always doing them. He who does not these good works is a man without faith. . . . Yea, it is impossible to separate works from faith, as impossible to separate burning and shining from fire.[97]

Abraham's experience further revealed that "his faith was made complete by what he did." The statement implies the prior existence of his faith, but the meaning is not that his faith at first was defective and insufficient for God to declare him righteous. "There are in reality no degrees of justifying faith. Men either believe or they do not."[98] The verb "was made complete" (*eteleiōthē*) means basically "to bring to an end, to bring to its goal," whereas the passive voice indicates that it was God who brought Abraham's faith to its goal through this experience. God, who initially declared Abraham righteous in view of his faith (Gen. 15:6), had a great goal in view for that faith. That goal was that through faith Abraham should be brought into such intimate relations with God that he would voluntarily act to place God first in every area of his life. That goal was effectively attained through the events recorded in Genesis 22. And thus "by what he did," by his "works," "his faith was made complete," brought to its intended goal. The works demonstrated the vital nature of the faith that produced them. A fruit tree is made perfect, brought to its intended goal, by the fruit that it produces. So "wherever there is genuine faith it must blossom into works."[99]

(2) The fulfilment of the Scripture (v. 23*a*). "And" introduces a further result of Abraham's supreme act of faith: "The scripture was fulfilled that says, 'Abraham believed God, and it was credited to him as righteousness.'" For James the divine pronouncement upon Abraham in connection with the crucial event in Genesis 22 did not invalidate the scriptural assertion in Genesis 15 that Abraham was justified by faith; rather, it demonstrated what was latent in that earlier justification. Thirty years before,[100] when God told Abraham, as yet childless, that his descendants would be as numerous as the stars of heaven (Gen. 15:1-5), Abraham "believed God." The construction (the verb with the dative of personal relationship) means not merely that Abraham believed in what God said; rather, his faith centered upon God Himself, convinced that the character of God assured the fulfillment of the promise. His implicit trust in the divine promise "was credited[101] to him as righteousness" (see Gen. 15:6). The verb "credited" (*logizomai*) means "to count, calculate" and denotes that something is placed to one's credit as having equivalent force or weight with something else mentioned. God took Abraham's faith and regarded it as sufficient ground for receiving him into His favor, as having the value of "righteousness," which he did not yet have in the absolute sense, being a sinner. "Righteousness" denotes the characteristic of the "righteous man," one who fulfills all the duties required of men by God toward Himself as well as toward his fellow men. God accepted Abraham's attitude of complete trust in His word as the equivalent of the right actions that must follow from that faith. Abraham's faith could be counted for righteousness "because it had within it the principle, the seed, the potency of all righteousness."[102] The obedient action of Abraham in Genesis 22 revealed the true nature and potency of Abraham's faith.

In saying that the divine justification recorded in Genesis 15:6 "was fulfilled" in the offering up of Isaac, interpreters such as Ropes[103] and Mayor[104] understand James to declare that there was a prophetic element in that historical account of Abraham's initial justification. But others, like Moo, see no need for calling Genesis 15:6 "a prophecy that was 'fulfilled' later in Abraham's career. What he suggests, rather, is that this verse found its ultimate significance and meaning in Abraham's life of obedience."[105] Thus James starts with Genesis 22 and then indicates that the crucial event there recorded was the logical fulfillment of the statement in Genesis 15:6 that "Abraham believed God." James accepted the historical fact of Abraham's justification by faith as recorded in Genesis 15:6; but in view of later events, he saw that the divine acceptance of his faith contained in it an anticipation of the work of faith demonstrates in Genesis 22:1-14. Aware of the true nature of justifying faith, James saw that the state of mind that God accepted as righteousness in Genesis 15 must ultimately manifest itself in the unquestioning obedience described in Genesis 22. In thus testing Abraham's faith, God brought to explicit manifestation the implicit character of the faith that years before He had accepted as righteousness. Abraham's obedience drew forth the divine pronouncement recorded in Genesis 22:16-18, and James accepted that declaration as proof that a living faith must express itself in works. Cranfield remarks, "Had there been no works, Abraham would not have been justified; but that would have been because the absence of works would mean that he had no real faith."[106]

(3) The friendship with God (v. 23*b*). A further result was "and he was called God's friend." These words are not a part of the preceding scriptural quotation, and James adds no scriptural support for the statement. Nor does the Old Testament record that this honorable title was bestowed upon Abraham during his lifetime, although the intimate relationship indicated is clearly implied in God's words in Genesis 18:17-18 that He could not hide from Abraham what He was about to do. God regarded and treated Abraham as an intimate friend, one who understood and entered into the divine purposes. The passive "was called" makes clear that Abraham did not brashly apply this title to himself. In 2 Chronicles 20:7, King Jehoshaphat, in addressing God, spoke of "Abraham thy friend" ("thy beloved," LXX), and in Isaiah 41:8, God Himself speaks of "Abraham my friend" ("Abraham whom I loved," LXX). Although James may have used the title in view of Genesis 18, apparently it already was commonly applied to Abraham when he wrote.[107] It is the distinctive title for Abraham among the Arabs today.

The expression "friend of God" does not mean that Abraham initiated the friendship and made God his friend. Rather, the meaning is that Abraham had the great privilege of having God accept him as His friend, as the recipient of His love and intimacy. But it is obvious that God's love for Abraham called forth Abraham's love for God. The term "friend" (*philos*) denotes one who shares a love with another based on mutually held interests and concerns. The expression here is meant to call attention to the amazing privilege of intimacy with God that Abraham enjoyed. In the upper room, where our Lord shared with His disciples the divine truths that had been entrusted to Him, He applied this same title to His followers (John 15:14-15). But as Tasker observes, "both in the case of Abraham and of the apostles it was entirely due to divine grace that they were able to receive a title of such honour and dignity."[108]

c. *The conclusion from Abraham's example* (v. 24). "You see that a person is justified by what he does and not by faith alone." Assured that the objector's view (v. 18) has been effectively refuted, with his plural "you" (*horate*) James now pushed home his conclusion upon all of his readers. The verse is an answer to the question in verse 14, and the first part of this concluding statement is not to be pressed into isolation from the second part. Although based on Abraham's example, the thought is now general and not restricted to Abraham. Now the verb "is justified" is in the present tense as pointing to God's standing practice.

The formulation of the conclusion, both positively and negatively expressed, is startling if the negative addition is not given full recognition. Blackman maintains that James's conclusion "is a deliberate contradiction of Paul."[109] But that is an hypothesis that we need not accept. We agree with the view of Plumptre "that the teaching of St James was not meant . . . to be antagonistic to that of St Paul, nor even to correct mistaken inferences from it, but was altogether independent, and probably prior in time, moving in its own groove, and taking its own line of thought."[110]

James is not to be understood as teaching that a man is declared righteous as the result of his works, without faith. In view of his insistence upon the inseparableness of faith and works, the necessity of guarding himself against such a charge did not even occur to him. He would have rejected it as firmly as does Paul. James insists that any profession of being justified by faith must be proven by the works of the one making the profession. The second part of his statement proves that James holds to the primacy of faith in justification. The rendering of the ASV, "and not only by faith," places the emphasis on "faith" and does not adequately convey the force of "only," which stands emphatically at the end, "not by faith alone." "The accent falls not only on the necessity of works, but on the indissoluble union between faith and works."[111] James believes in justification by faith, a faith that produces works. But in refuting the position of his "faith only" opponent, James here accepts his opponent's way of speaking and denies that his inoperative faith alone saves. James believes that faith justifies but not a "faith" that remains alone and produces no works. James rejects it as not being true faith. He demands a working faith.

2. The Working of Rahab's Faith (v. 25)

"In the same way, was not even Rahab the prostitute considered righteous for what she did when she gave lodging to the spies and sent them off in a different direction?" "In the same way" (*homoiōs*) underlines that his second illustration teaches the same truth, while "even" (*de*) apparently is intended to suggest a contrast in the outward features. As Moo remarks, "if it might be objected that Abraham's works were no more than what might be expected from one who had so richly experienced God's grace, the same is certainly not true of Rahab."[112] The two examples cited form a striking contrast, suggesting that the truth concerning justification is of universal application. "He designedly put together two persons so different in their character," said Calvin, "in order more clearly to shew that no one, whatever may have been his or her condition, nation, or class in society, has ever been counted righteous without good works."[113]

This second illustration is presented in a parallel construction. As in verse 21, his use of a question challenges his readers to consider this further picture; the negative (*ouk*) with the question again implies that they must admit that it confirms his position. The identity of this individual is again placed emphatically forward: "also Rahab the harlot—was she not out of works declared righteous?" (Robert Young). James pointed concisely to her works by two added participles but felt it unnecessary to elaborate on the implications of this illustration.

"Rahab the prostitute," a designation also employed in Hebrews 11:31, makes prominent her immoral past. Robertson remarks, "Certainly, there is no desire in James nor in Hebrews to dignify her infamous trade which she renounced, but only to single her out as a brand snatched from the burning by the power of God."[114] The designation is drawn directly from the Old Testament record (Josh. 2:1; 6:17, 22, 25). Efforts have been made to tone down the term's moral implications with suggestions that it need denote no more than "innkeeper"[115] or "landlady," or perhaps "idolater," but the literal meaning of the term cannot be eliminated. As a Canaanite woman, she had succumbed to the prevailing immorality of her environment.

Rahab's story held the interest of the Jews, and various traditions concerning her subsequent life among the Hebrews developed. Ropes summarizes, "She was believed to have become a sincere proselyte, to have married Joshua, and to have been the ancestress of many priests and prophets, including Jeremiah and Ezekiel."[116] Her position of dignity among the Hebrews is evident from the fact that her name appears in Christ's genealogy in Matthew 1:5.

The author of Hebrews cites Rahab as a hero of faith (11:31), but James makes no mention of her faith. Since James and his readers were well acquainted with the Old Testament account of her expression of faith (Josh. 2:11-13), the fact of her faith is assumed. In keeping with his purpose, James insists that Rahab also was "considered righteous for what she did," deeds that were the evidence that Rahab had a living faith. Two participial phrases set forth the evidence. Both participles are in the aorist tense, summarily stating the historical facts.

Rahab "gave lodging to the spies" whom Joshua had sent to Jericho to spy out the city (Josh. 2:1-14). The participle rendered "gave lodging to" (*hupodexamenē*) denotes that she welcomed and entertained them as her guests. Apart from her faith in the God of Israel, her action could only have been viewed as an act of treason against her people.

James used a distinctive term to identify the two individuals who were the recipients of Rahab's hospitality. The Septuagint rendering of Joshua 2 called them "men" (*andres*) or "young men" (*neaniskoi*), whereas in Hebrews 11:31 they were called "spies" (*kataskopous*), but James uses the designation "the messengers" (*tous anggelous*), obscured by the NIV rendering "the spies." A few Greek manuscripts do use the term "spies,"[117] but the textual editors are agreed that the original reading is "the messengers." They were to be Joshua's messengers to bring back to him a report of the situation in Jericho, but James's assertion that Rahab received and protected the men as "the messengers" implies that she recognized them as God's messengers to her and her family. Rahab's testimony to her faith in the God of Israel in Joshua 2:8-12 indicates that her faith was based on second-hand testimony, but these two Hebrew men she recognized as authentic witnesses to the God of Israel were His "messengers" to her. Her faith revealed itself in her deeds.

James records concisely the outcome of her initial encounter with these two Hebrews with the remark that she "sent them off in a different direction" (cf. Josh. 2:15-22). The participle "sent off" (*ekbalousa*) indicates energetic action but not violence. She acted with urgency and personal concern for their safety. Her inventiveness to insure their safety is evident in the fact that she sent them forth "in a different direction" (*hetera hodō*, literally, "by another way"), not through her door but her window, not back to their camp but to the mountains (Josh. 2:15-16). Her works were entirely different than those of Abraham, but both alike prove that a living faith is a working faith.

C. THE UNION OF FAITH AND WORKS (v. 26)

James concludes his discussion of this test of faith with a striking analogy: "As the body without the spirit is dead, so faith without deeds is dead." The use of *gar* ("for"),[118] not in the NIV, binds this axiom to what has preceded and implies that the discussion is dependent upon the axiomatic truth stated here. If the inseparable connection affirmed here is false, then the test of faith propounded is futile and James's opponents are right.

The analogy is clearly drawn with "as" (*hōsper*), "just as," and "so" (*houtōs*) in precisely the same way. In both pairs, when the second member is missing, the inevitable result is death. It is not either/or but both/and. The article with the first member in each pair, "the body . . . the faith," is generic, making them representative of their class. But the second member in each pair is without an article, pointing to the crucial nature of the missing element.

Whenever we have the human "body" without that element that we characterize as "spirit," the inevitable result is that the body is "dead," the same decisive term as in verse 17. James's statement is popular, dividing man into two elements, the material and the nonmaterial; but it would be unwarranted to assume that James rejects the trichotomous (three-part) view implied in 1 Thessalonians 5:23. Some, like Lenski,[119] interpret "spirit" (*pneuma*) to mean "breath," a basic meaning of the term; but when opposed to the body, as here, it means that vital principle, divinely imparted (Gen.

2:7), that imparts life to the material body. The body has no independent life apart from the indwelling spirit. Without the spirit it is a useless corpse.

"So faith without deeds is dead" states the thrust of the analogy. "The faith" that a man may profess is surely "dead," lifeless and useless, "without deeds." The fact of death is as real here as in the former case. An inactive faith, entombed in an intellectually approved creed, is of no more value than a corpse. A saving faith is an active faith. As Epp notes, "Faith is first, but works must follow in order to demonstrate that faith is real. Although works will not bring one into right relationship with God, they are to be the natural result of salvation."[120]

The order in the analogy is remarkable: "faith" corresponds to "body," and "works" to "spirit." It may be felt that it would have been more appropriate to reverse the order, to compare works with the body and faith with the spirit. It may be replied that the one point in the analogy is the fact that the absence of the second member means sure death, and that it is the aim of James to establish that faith and works are inseparable. But in the light of the discussion, the order used is not inappropriate. Fausset observes, "He does not mean that faith in all cases answers to the body; but the FORM *of faith* without *the working reality* answers to the *body* without the *animating spirit.* It does not follow that *living faith* derives its life from works, as the body derives its life from the animating spirit."[121] In setting forth this test "James is concerned not that works be 'added' to faith, but that one possess the right kind of faith, 'faith that works.'"[122]

The relevance of this test of faith for our own age is inescapable. It offers "a greatly needed corrective to the unreal, verbalistic kind of religion that claims allegiance to high doctrine but issues in living on a low and selfish level."[123] James does not disparage the importance of correct doctrinal views, but he insists that such views are no substitute for practical holiness. Christian faith must manifest its existence in active obedience to God's Word.

NOTES FOR
James 2:14-26

1. Peter H. Davids, *The Epistle of James, A Commentary on the Greek Text*, p. 121.

2. Martin Luther, Preface to his 1522 edition of the New Testament. The reference to James as "a right strawy epistle" appeared only in the 1522 edition. See John Dillenberger, ed., *Martin Luther, Selections from His Writings*, pp. 18-19. Later Luther recognized James's contribution.

3. See William Barclay, *The Letters of James and Peter*, The Daily Study Bible, pp. 84-87; Martin Dibelius, "James. A Commentary on the Epistle of James," in *Hermeneia—A Critical and Historical Commentary on the Bible*, pp. 174-80; Doremus Almy Hayes, "James, Epistle of," in *The International Standard Bible Encyclopedia*, 3:1566-67; Robert Johnstone, *Lectures Exegetical and Practical on the Epistle of James*, pp. 214-18; C. Leslie Mitton, *The Epistle of James*, pp. 103-8; and Arthur E. Travis, "James and Paul, A Comparative Study," *Southwestern Journal of Theology* 12, 1 (Fall 1969): 57-70. For a listing of the variant views see Ralph P. Martin, *James*, Word Biblical Commentary, pp. 82-84.

4. Alexander Ross, *The Epistles of James and John*, The New International Commentary on the New Testament, p. 53.

5. John F. Macarthur, Jr., "Faith According to the Apostle James," in *Journal of the Evangelical Theological Society* 33, 1 (March 1990): 28.

6. Joseph B. Mayor, *The Epistle of St. James, The Greek Text with Introduction, Notes and Comments*, p. 92.

7. R. J. Knowling, *The Epistle of St. James*, Westminster Commentaries, p. 53.

8. Third class condition, *ean* and the subjunctive; it views the picture as undetermined but with expectation of its realization.

9. Robert Young, *THE HOLY BIBLE, Consisting of the Old and New Covenants, Translated According to the Letter and Idioms of the Original Languages.*

10. Johnstone, p. 203.

11. H. Maynard Smith, *The Epistle of S. James, Lectures*, p. 140.

12. Joh. Ed. Huther, *Critical and Exegetical Handbook to the General Epistles of James, Peter, John, and Jude*, p. 87.

13. Alexander Maclaren, "Hebrews Chaps. VII to End, Epistle of James," in *Expositions of Holy Scripture*, p. 416.

14. Johnstone, p. 205.

15. So the versions of Rotherham, Moffat, RSV, and MLB.

16. "That faith"—NASB, NEB, and TEV. "Such faith"—NIV, 20th Cent., Montgomery, Weymouth, and Williams.

17. Curtis Vaughan, *James, A Study Guide*, p. 57.

18. Spiros Zodhiates, *The Labor of Love*, p. 14.

19. Mayor, p. 93.

20. If the *de* is retained, then verses 15-16 are parallel to verse 14 and give a second statement of the difference between profession and reality.

21. James Hardy Ropes, *A Critical and Exegetical Commentary on the Epistle of St. James*, The International Critical Commentary on the Holy Scriptures of the Old and New Testaments, p. 206.

22. Zodhiates, p. 16.

23. M. F. Sadler, *The General Epistles of SS. James, Peter, John, and Jude, with Notes Critical and Practical*, p. 40.

24. Ross, p. 51, n. 10.

25. The plural is in accord with occasional usage in good classical writers. See F. Blass and A. Debrunner, *A Greek Grammar of the New Testament and Other Early Christian Literature*, pp. 74-75.

26. Marvin R. Vincent, *Word Studies in the New Testament*, 1:743.

27. Knowling, p. 54.

28. Simon Kistemaker, *New Testament Commentary, Exposition of the Epistle of James and the Epistles of John*, p. 89.

29. Kistemaker, p. 89.

30. Davids, p. 122.

31. Ropes holds that to make clear the middle voice "it would be necessary in the late usage of the NT to use the active with a reflexive pronoun" (p. 207).

32. Ropes, p. 207; James B. Adamson, *The Epistle of James*, p. 123.

33. W. E. Oesterley, "The General Epistle of James," in *The Expositor's Greek Testament*, 4:444.

34. J. A. Motyer, *The Tests of Faith*, p. 55.

35. Ropes, p. 207.

36. E. M. Zerr, *Bible Commentary*, 6:245.

37. Donald W. Burdick, "James," in *The Expositor's Bible Commentary*, 12:183.

38. Burton Scott Easton and Gordon Poteat, "The Epistle of James," in *The Interpreter's Bible*, 12:42.

39. James B. Adamson, *The Epistle of James*, p. 124.

40. Ropes, p. 208.

41. R. C. H. Lenski, *The Interpretation of the Epistle to the Hebrews and of the Epistle of James*, p. 589.

42. Huther, p. 89.

43. Davids, p. 122.

44. E. C. Blackman, *The Epistle of James*, Torch Bible Commentaries, p. 93.

45. See the summaries in Ropes, pp. 211-14; Dibelius, pp. 154-58; Sophie Laws, *A commentary on the Epistle of James*, pp. 122-24; Martin, pp. 77-79.

46. Arndt and Gingrich, p. 37.

47. Zodhiates, pp. 22-23.

48. J. Ronald Blue, "James," in *The Bible Knowledge Commentary, New Testament*, pp. 825-26.

49. The pronouns were reversed by the scribe of the Old Latin manuscript ff (Corbeiensis I); no other manuscripts reverse them.

50. Lenski, pp. 591-92.

51. Ropes, p. 209.

52. Zane C. Hodges, "Light on James Two from Textual Criticism," *Bibliotheca Sacra* 120, 480 (October-December 1963): 342.

53. James Moffatt, *The General Epistles, James, Peter, and Jude*, The Moffatt New Testament Commentary, p. 41.

54. Ronald A. Ward, "James," in *The New Bible Commentary, Revised*, p. 1228.

55. RSV, MLB, NEB, 20th Cent., Goodspeed, Montgomery, Kleist and Lilly, and Beck. See Bibliography.

56. Ropes, pp. 208-9.

57. Edwin T. Winkler, "Commentary on the Epistle of James," in *An American Commentary on the New Testament*, p. 40.

58. Lenski, p. 592.

59. Dibelius, p. 154.

60. Mitton, pp. 108-9.

61. Kistemaker, p. 91.

62. Adamson, p. 125.

63. The Textus Receptus reads, "Show me your faith out of (*ek*) your works," a reading that has not been adopted in any English version. Zane C. Hodges suggests that this reading may yet prove to be original and provide the key to the true understanding of this difficult passage. See his "Light on James Two from Textual Criticism," *Bibliotheca Sacra* 120, 480 (October-December): 341-50.

64. Kistemaker, p. 92.

65. So punctuated in the Greek texts of Westcott and Hort, Nestle, and the United Bible Societies. The modern English versions are divided between a question and an assertion.

66. Davids, p. 125.

67. For the evidence see United Bible Societies, *The Greek New Testament*, 3d ed.; Nestle-Aland, *NOVUM TESTAMENTUM GRAECE*, 26th ed.

68. Zane C. Hodges and Arthur L. Farstad, *The Greek New Testament According to the Majority Text* accept *ho theos heis estin*, "there is one God." On a scale of A to D the editors of the United Bible Societies text rate the reading *heis estin ho theos*, "God is one," as having a C probability as being original. See Bruce M. Metzger, *A Textual Commentary on the Greek New Testament*, p. 681.

69. A. T. Robertson, *Practical and Social Aspects of Christianity. The Wisdom of James*, p. 135.

70. W. Boyd Carpenter, *The Wisdom of James the Just*, p. 182.
71. Harold S. Songer, "James," in *The Broadman Bible Commentary*, 12:119.
72. J. W. Roberts, *A Commentary on the General Epistle of James*, p. 110.
73. See Merrill F. Unger, *Biblical Demonology. A Study of the Spiritual Forces Behind the Present World Unrest* and *Demons in the World Today*; Robert Peterson, *Are Demons for Real?*; John Warwick Montgomery, ed., *Demon Possession*; Johanna Michaelsen, *The Beautiful Side of Evil*; Randall N. Bear, *Inside the New Age Nightmare*; and R. K. Harrison, "Demon, Demoniac, Demonology," in *The Zondervan Pictorial Encyclopedia of the Bible*, 2:92-101.
74. H. E. Dana and Julius R. Mantey, *A Manual Grammar of the Greek New Testament*, p. 244.
75. Winkler, p. 41.
76. Richard Chenevix Trench, *Synonyms of the New Testament*, p. 181.
77. Dibelius, p. 161, n. 62.
78. Arndt and Gingrich, p. 741.
79. Huther, p. 93.
80. Papyrus 74 here stands alone in reading "empty" (*kenē*), a scribal change due to the preceding *kene.*
81. Douglas J. Moo, *The Letter of James*, pp. 107-8.
82. Robert Young, *THE HOLY BIBLE, Consisting of the Old and New Covenants, Translated According to the Letter and Idioms of the Original Languages.*
83. Knowling, p. 60; and Mayor, p. 99; Davids, p. 64; Kistemaker, p. 29.
84. Dibelius, p. 161.
85. Oesterley, p. 447.
86. See Mitton, p. 112, who notes that the New Testament references point to three aspects of Abraham's faith.
87. Contray to the common view, John Miller, *Commentary on Paul's Epistle to Romans; with an Excursus on the Famous Passage in James (Chap. II. 14-26)*, pp. 387-92, insists that James's words are not a question but a declarative statement. But the question is more in harmony with the structure of the sentence and the argument of the passage.
88. Hugh J. Schonfield, *The Authentic New Testament*, p. 375.
89. R. V. G. Tasker, *The General Epistle of James*, p. 68.
90. Curtis Vaughan, *James, A Study Guide*, p. 61.
91. C. E. B. Cranfield, "The message of James," *Scottish Journal of Theology* 18, 3 (September 1965): 340.
92. Ibid.
93. So in the KJV and the ASV margin. The punctuation in TEV is unique and not suggested by the Greek: "Can't you see? His faith and his actions worked together."
94. Dibelius, p. 163, n. 73.
95. Zodhiates, pp. 42-43.
96. Zodhiates, p. 44.
97. Quoted in Rudolf Stier, *The Epistle of St James*, pp. 351-52.
98. Tasker, *The General Epistle of James*, p. 69.
99. Mayor, p. 100.
100. The rabbis said fifty years before. See Mayor, p. 100.
101. In the Hebrew the verb is active, "He [God] reckoned it." But the quotations in the New Testament (Rom. 4:3-24; Gal. 3:6) use the passive of the LXX, thus stressing that justification is a gift.
102. Sadler, p. 43.
103. Ropes, p. 221.
104. Mayor, p. 104.
105. Moo, p. 113.

106. Cranfield, "The Message of Jesus," p. 140.

107. Mayor, pp. 101-2; Ropes, pp. 222-23; and Dibelius, pp. 172-73.

108. Tasker, p. 70.

109. Blackman, p. 96.

110. E. H. Plumptre, *The General Epistle of St James*, The Cambridge Bible for Schools and Colleges, pp. 669-70.

111. Richard Wolff, *General Epistles of James and Jude*, p. 54.

112. Moo, p. 116.

113. John Calvin, *Commentaries on the Catholic Epistles*, p. 316.

114. A. T. Robertson, *Practical and Social Aspects of Christianity: The Wisdom of James*, p. 141.

115. Josephus, *Antiquities of the Jews* (V.1.2) and the Palestinian targum on Joshua 2:1 make her "an innkeeper." William Whiston, translator of *Antiquities*, in a footnote says: "I will call this woman Rahab an *innkeeper*, not a *harlot*, the whole history, both in our copies, and especially in Josephus, implying no more. It was indeed so frequent a thing, that women who were innkeepers were also harlots, or maintainers of harlots, that the word commonly used for real harlots was usually given them." *The Life and Words of Flavius Josephus*, p. 142 n.

116. Ropes, p. 224. For sources see Hermann L. Strack and Paul Billerbeck, "Das Evangelium Nach Matthäus Erläutert Aus Talmud Und Midrach," in *Kommentar Zum Neuen Testament Aus Talmud Und Midrach*, pp. 20-23.

117. For the manuscript evidence see Nestle-Aland, *NOVUM TESTAMENTUM GRAECE*, 26th ed.

118. The conjunction is omitted in Codex B and the Peshitta, Armenian, and Ethioptic versions. Modern critical editors disagree. Tasker omits it; Westcott and Hort have it in the margin; Nestle, the United Bible Societies' text, and Souter agree with the Textus Receptus in retaining it. The manuscript evidence is strongly for it.

119. Lanski, pp. 607-8.

120. Theodore H. Epp, *James the Epistle of Applied Christianity*, p. 146.

121. Robert Jamieson, A. R. Fausset, and David Brown, *A commentary, Critical and Explanatory, on the Old and New Testaments*, 2:489. Author's italics.

122. Moo, p. 117.

123. Frank E. Gaebelsin, *The Practical Epistle of James*, p. 73.

9

VIII. FAITH TESTED BY
ITS PRODUCTION OF SELF-CONTROL

3:1-18 Not many of you should presume to be teachers, my brothers, because you know that we who teach will be judged more strictly. ²We all stumble in many ways. If anyone is never at fault in what he says, he is a perfect man, able to keep his whole body in check.

³When we put bits into the mouths of horses to make them obey us, we can turn the whole animal. ⁴Or take ships as an example. Although they are so large and are driven by strong winds, they are steered by a very small rudder wherever the pilot wants to go. ⁵Likewise the tongue is a small part of the body, but it makes great boasts. Consider what a great forest is set on fire by a small spark. ⁶The tongue also is a fire, a world of evil among the parts of the body. It corrupts the whole person, sets the whole course of his life on fire, and is itself set on fire by hell.

⁷All kinds of animals, birds, reptiles and creatures of the sea are being tamed and have been tamed by man, ⁸but no man can tame the tongue. It is a restless evil, full of deadly poison.

⁹With the tongue we praise our Lord and Father, and with it we curse men, who have been made in God's likeness. ¹⁰Out of the same mouth come praise and cursing. My brothers, this should not be. ¹¹Can both fresh water and salt water flow from the same spring? ¹²My brothers, can a fig tree bear olives, or a grapevine bear figs? Neither can a salt spring produce fresh water.

¹³Who is wise and understanding among you? Let him show it by his good life, by deeds done in the humility that comes from wisdom. ¹⁴But if you harbor bitter envy and selfish ambition in your hearts, do not boast about it or deny the truth. ¹⁵Such "wisdom" does not come down from heaven but is earthly, unspiritual, of the devil. ¹⁶For where you have envy and selfish ambition, there you find disorder and every evil practice.

¹⁷But the wisdom that comes from heaven is first of all pure, then peace-loving, considerate, submissive, full of mercy and good fruit, impartial and sincere. ¹⁸Peacemakers who sow in peace raise a harvest of righteousness.

Chapter 3 constitutes a self-contained section, dealing with the power of the tongue and its control. The statement in verse 2, that the power to control the tongue is the mark of "a perfect man," conveys the essence of this further test of a living faith. This test deals with an important matter that has only been touched on previously (1:19, 26; 2:12). The Bible has much to say concerning the power of speech for good or evil, and this chapter by James is the classic exposition of the problem of controlling the human tongue. James insists that a living faith must demonstrate its vitality by exercising control over the tongue. "The mouth," Blue remarks, "is, after all, connected to the mind. Winsome speech demands a wise source. Both controlled talk and cultivated thought are necessary."[1]

James points out the significance of a controlled tongue (vv. 1-2), graphically portrays the importance of controlling the tongue (vv. 3-6), asserts man's inability to control the tongue (vv. 7-8), rebukes the inconsistencies of an uncontrolled tongue (vv. 9-12), and concludes with a discussion of the wisdom controlling the tongue (vv. 13-18).

A. THE SIGNIFICANCE OF A CONTROLLED TONGUE (vv. 1-2)

In the previous test (2:14-26), James insisted that a living faith must reveal itself in the production of works. In chapter 3 this demand for a productive faith is continued but with a difference. James insists that a living faith also must produce an inward result, the development of self-control. And this power of self-control is tested most readily in the matter of controlling the tongue. James agreed with Jesus (Matt. 12:34-37) that a man's words are the revelation of his character. As the organ of speech, a man's use of his tongue provides a ready revelation of his inner nature, for "out of the overflow of the heart the mouth speaks" (Matt. 12:34). The power of speech is one of God's greatest gifts to men, and believers must be on constant guard against the perverted use of this mighty gift. James relates the control of the tongue to the Christian teacher (v. 1) and then to the believer generally (v. 2).

1. The Responsibility of the Teacher (v. 1)

Since the teacher's work is performed primarily through his use of the tongue, the controlled use of the tongue is of central importance for the Christian teacher. Fully aware of the teacher's responsibility, James issues a solemn warning: "Not many of you should presume to be teachers, my brothers, because you know that we who teach will be judged more strictly." This "somewhat interpretative translation" avoids "the impression that James is discouraging people from becoming teachers."[2] This is not an attack upon the office of the teacher or the teaching function, for James at once identifies himself as a teacher. Rather, he is seeking to restrain the rush to teach on the part of those not qualified.

In formulating his warning, James places the negative (*mē*) before "many" (*polloi*) and puts them both at the beginning of the sentence, thus indicating that of necessity some must assume the work of being teachers, but many others should not. The verb rendered "presume to be" (*ginesthe*) basically means "to become," while the present tense pictures continuing action. The negative with the imperative implies that there was a movement on the part of many to pose as teachers, but this movement had to be halted. Lilly seeks to convey the force of the prohibition by rendering it "Not many of you should set yourselves up as teachers."[3] The term "teachers,"[4] occurring only here in this epistle, is not to be restricted to officially appointed teachers but includes all who arise to instruct their fellow members. In these Jewish Diaspora congregations, there were recognized "teachers" whose ministry was concerned with the doctrinal and moral training of the members. But obviously it was not an officially limited group, and this ministry was actively shared by various members of the congregations.

This prohibition clearly reflects the democratic nature of the early Christian assemblies. As seen from 1 Corinthians 14:26-34, almost any believer was permitted to contribute something to the meeting. This freedom to offer instruction was in harmony with the liberty that the readers of this letter had known in the Jewish synagogues, where nearly anyone aspiring to teach could get a hearing (cf. Acts 13:5, 15). Further, the teaching ministry was highly esteemed in the early church. By its very nature, Christianity gave a prominent place to teaching (Matt. 28:19-20; Acts 13:1; Eph. 4:11) and encouraged believers to be teachers (Heb. 5:12). That freedom to teach obviously prompted certain members conceitedly to seize the opportunity to become teachers without being adequately qualified or realizing the responsibility involved. They desired the esteem of being acknowledged teachers without paying the price demanded by the position (cf. 1 Tim. 1:7). As Laws observes, "This is no doubt a perennial temptation in a community where teaching and hence the teacher is given an important place, enough for it to be the object of ambition."[5] James is censuring this false mania for teaching. He has no desire to restrain those who were conscious of God's call upon their lives to carry on the work of an accredited teacher in the assembly.

The direct address "my brothers," marking a new section in the letter,[6] assures the recipients of his warning that James accepts and acknowledges them as fellow members of God's family. The address, standing in apposition to the second person plural subject of the verb, makes clear that "the issue is not heretical teachers who need to be removed from office"[7] or the rejection of false teachers seeking opportunity to promulgate their views. James is seeking to curb "the danger of talkativeness, of reckless statements, of frothy rhetoric, of abusive language, of misleading assertions"[8] on the part of some aggressive members who were vocal in their opinions.

"Because you know that we who teach will be judged more strictly" states the reason for the warning. "Because you know" (*eidotes*[9]) renders a causative participle with a linear force, implying that those being warned did know that in assuming to be teachers they did thereby place themselves under the fact of stricter accountability. Joined to the hortatory verb, the participle also has a hortatory force; let them not forget that as teachers they "will be judged more strictly." The change from the second person imperative to the first person plural "we" who teach is conciliatory and a mark of the author's humility. Being himself a teacher, "he will not give others a warning without at the same time applying it to himself."[10] "This is the only piece of information he lets fall about himself."[11]

"Will be judged more strictly," more literally "greater judgment we will receive," clearly states what is involved. The noun "judgment" (*krima*) denotes the verdict pronounced by the judge. The term in itself is neutral, but in the New Testament it generally expresses an adverse judgment (Mark 12:40; Luke 20:47; 1 Tim. 5:24). The future tense looks forward to the time when as teachers they will stand before the judgment seat of Christ (Rom. 14:10-12; 1 Cor. 3:10-15; 2 Cor. 5:10) and be judged according to the impact of their lives. "The test of all ministry must come at last in the day of trial and fiery inquisition of God; this and not the world's opinion will be the real approval."[12] "More strictly" (*meizon krima*, "greater judgment") implies that they have not faithfully fulfilled the duties of the work that they rashly assumed. Judgment will be according to the principle that increased influence means increased responsibility; the greater the impact upon others, the greater the accountability. The comparative adjective "greater" implies degrees of treatment at the judgment seat. Those who undertake to speak as God's messengers will be held strictly accountable for the way they use their position. James is keenly conscious of the seriousness of the Christian teacher's task. As Zodhiates remarks,

> If we teach because of the desire to show off, without living Christ before we preach Him, the judgment of God will be a severe condemnation; but if our teaching is motivated by a sincere and honest love for the Lord and the edification of those who hear us, then we can welcome this judgment, for it will mean a great reward.[13]

2. The Evidence of the Perfect Man (v. 2)

"We all stumble in many ways" states the universal fact underlying the preceding warning. Teachers are no exception to the truth that "we all stumble."[14] "All" (*hapantes*), "everybody," is the strong form of the adjective, and James places it last with great emphasis. The statement is not to be limited to teachers; it is true of all humans (1 Kings 8:46; Prov. 20:9; Eccles. 7:20; Rom. 3:9, 23; 1 John 1:8). The word "stumble," as in 2:10, denotes a moral lapse. In its literal sense the term conveys the picture of the foot striking against some obstacle so as to cause the individual to trip or stumble; metaphorically it denotes the fact of a failure in duty, a mistake that is blameworthy, or a sin.

Lenski notes that to "stumble" does not necessarily suggest a fatal fall; it denotes a failure that arrests our progress along the road.[15] The present tense here denotes iterative action, indicating that such experiences of stumbling occur repeatedly in life. This sober reality is made prominent by the opening word *polla*, here rendered "in many ways." It may be taken as an adverb modifying the verb, "for oft are we stumbling one and all" (Rotherham).[16] But more probably it is an adjective. It could mean the number of sins, as the RSV "many mistakes" suggests, but more probably it denotes the variety of sins as the NIV suggests. So understood it denotes the wide variety of ways in which the stumbling occurs. As Epp notes, "The tongue can be used in so many ways that dishonor the Lord. It can be used to tell an off-color story; it can be used to utter profanity in a time of anger; it can be used to pass on idle gossip; and it can be used to report dishonest half-truths."[17] Thus the misuse of the tongue can result in a stumbling that goes vastly beyond the danger of the teacher's stumbling in his teaching ministry.

In saying "we stumble," James again frankly includes himself. His own experience confirmed the fact of human fallibility. Lenski remarks, "This is James's great confession of sin."[18] But in making this honest confession, he establishes his right to be heard. He insists that such stumbling cannot be condoned as a matter of indifference. But Stier points out a necessary limitation to James's confession: "Not as if he submitted any errors in his Epistle, written as it was through the Holy Ghost, to their criticism or ours; but he only maintains that, in ordinary life and independently of his office, the perfect man, who no longer offends in any word, is nowhere to be found."[19]

The ability to control his tongue is a matter of great significance for the believer. It is a test of Christian character, the proof of maturity and self-control. "If anyone is never at fault in what he says, he is a perfect man, able to keep his whole body in check." The conditional statement, "If anyone is never at fault" (literally, "stumbles not"), assumes the reality; the present tense indicates that his life is no longer marred by those repeated failures that characterize the ordinary individual. "In what he says" (literally, "in word") is not to be confined to teaching; it also includes speech in general. The reference is not to unintentional errors in articulation, but to spoken words that are the result of thought. In view of the preceding statement, the individual is not to be thought of as having attained absolute sinlessness.

"He is a perfect man" concisely states the character evaluation of the person just described. "He," the demonstrative pronoun (*houtous*, "this one"), summarizes and categorically identifies this individual as fulfilling the condition. Only such an individual will James acknowledge as "a perfect man" (*teleios anēr*). "Man" (*anēr*) need not be taken to limit the picture to the male (cf. 1:8, 12, 20). But Gaebelein aptly remarks that the term used shows that "James does not share the common male belief that women are chief offenders in the misuse of the tongue."[20]

"Perfect" does not mean that this individual is sinless, a goal not reached in this life (cf. 3:2*a*). As in 1:4, the adjective rather describes him as having attained the goal of spiritual maturity in the achievement of full self-control. He possesses "a maturity of religious life, a ripeness and richness of knowledge and character, such as may be supposed to mark the full-grown man, as contrasted with the babe in Christ."[21]

"Able to keep his whole body in check" amplifies his maturity at the point of interest in this test of faith. *Kai*, not in the NIV, with the "whole body," unfolds what is involved in his ability to control his tongue. Since the tongue is the most difficult to keep under control, victory at this point assures that he also is able to check and to control the activities of the "whole body." He is able to control all his members and capacities that sin seeks to use to express itself. The picturesque term "to keep . . . in check" (*chalinagōgēsai*) denotes that he is able to restrain his whole body effectively to prevent its use by sin, as well as to guide and direct its activities in desirable ways. He exercises self-mastery over his whole body, so that, like a horse under a stiff rein, it does his bidding. In Luke 11:53-54, Jesus is the perfect illustration of such a perfect man. See also 1 Peter 2:21-23. Laws well remarks that this perfection "relates not to a higher standard of virtue for some only to attain, but to the completeness and wholeness that is the ideal for anyone."[22]

Barclay notes that "James is not for a moment saying that silence is better than speech. He is not pleading for . . . a cowardly silence, but for a wise use of speech."[23] Nor does James hint that men must subject themselves to prolonged periods of enforced silence in order to gain mastery over their tongues. The ability to check and guide the tongue effectively only comes through the power of the indwelling Holy Spirit.

B. THE NEED FOR CONTROL OVER THE TONGUE (vv. 3-6)

The significance of a controlled tongue underscores the need for its effective control. James vividly illustrates the importance of controlling the tongue (vv. 3-5*a*) and portrays the damage caused by an uncontrolled tongue (vv. 5*b*-6).

1. The effects of a controlled tongue (vv. 3-5*a*)

James cites two familiar illustrations to establish the results of the application of proper control (vv. 3-4) and applies the pictures to the tongue (v. 5*a*).

a. *The illustrations of proper control* (vv. 3-4). James cites two common examples from daily life as a legal witness to the need for proper control in human experience.

(1) The horse and the bridle (v. 3). The reference to bridling the tongue in verse 2 naturally leads to the picture of the bridling of horses. "When[24] we put bits into the mouths of horses to make them obey us, we can turn the whole animal." "When" (*ei de*, literally, "if now"), introducing a first

class conditional sentence, does not imply doubt but is argumentative: since common experience shows that the application of control at the proper point is effective in dealing with horses, effective control also can be applied to the human tongue. The *de* ("now"), not in the NIV, is transitional, introducing further development of the discussion.

The genitive "the horses" stands emphatically forward as calling attention to the parallel between controlling the mouth of a horse and of a man. The articles used with both "horses" and "bridles" in the original are generic, denoting that each is simply representative of its class. The plural "horses" implies that the results obtained in bridling a particular horse are true of all horses. Zodhiates, indeed, suggests that this plural may indicate "a recognition of individual differences in horses" and that "for various kinds of horses there are corresponding bridles." He makes the application "Let no man complain if the kind of bridle God puts into his mouth is different from the one He puts into another's and if it hurts a little more than another's."[25]

The word rendered "bits" may be used to denote either the whole bridle or the bit that is placed into the horse's mouth. In view of verse 2, it is better to retain the rendering "bridle" here, since the whole bridle is needed to give effect to the bit in the horse's mouth. The verb "put" (*ballomen*), "to throw," has a mild force and need not imply violence. The present tense is iterative, indicating that this is a regular practice leading to an assured result. Stier remarks that the resultant control of "the strong and noble horse" is "the symbol of all animal nature which man has subjected to his service, since it is not our greater power which reduces him, but our understanding how to apply the instrument of our domination *in the right place*."[26]

"To make them obey us" indicates that the aim in bridling the horse is to secure the obedience of the whole horse, not just its mouth. But this is not achieved by accident. The application of control, represented by the bridle, must be applied at the proper place. (Who would ever think of controlling the horse by placing the bridle under its tail?) So James is not interested merely in a "tamed tongue" but in a properly controlled tongue manifesting itself in all areas of human life.

"We can turn the whole animal" states the result already implied. The verb "turn" (*metagomen*), to change the direction of, occurs only here and in verse 4 in the New Testament. The present tense is iterative, setting forth the customary result. The use of *kai*, "and" or "also" (not in NIV), adds the fact that control of the horse's mouth results in directing the movement of its whole body. The first personal plural "we," used with both verbs, indicates that this is an illustration with which both writer and readers were familiar from everyday experience. James, like Jesus, knew how to draw vital spiritual lessons from the events of everyday life.

(2) The ship and the rudder (v. 4). "Or take ships as an example. Although they are so large and are driven by strong winds, they are steered by

a very small rudder wherever the pilot wants to go." "Or take ships as an example" (*idou kai*, literally, "Behold also") directs attention to a further example. The exclamatory particle "Behold" (*idou*), which occurs six times in this epistle (3:4, 5; 5:4, 7, 9, 11), gives vividness to the style by calling the reader's special attention to what follows. "Also" (*kai*), standing next to the exclamation "Behold also the ships," connects this illustration with the first as further evidence of the tremendous power of little things. Stier suggests that it "is an example of man's art in machinery for reducing to subjection inanimate nature, and the very elements."[27]

The size of "the ships" and their movements were apparently a matter of deep personal interest to James. The two participial phrases describing the ships suggest that he had some acquaintance with the oceangoing vessels of that day. Although the correlative pronoun "so large" has in view the contrasting smallness of the rudder, the expression suggests that James felt amazement at the size of the ships he had observed. Some of the ancient ships were of impressive proportions. The merchant ship in which Paul was wrecked on his way to Rome accommodated 276 passengers, besides carrying a load of wheat (Acts 27:37-38). Blaiklock notes the mention of an ancient ship that "was said to carry corn enough to feed all Attica for a year."[28]

James further pictures these ships as being "driven by strong winds." Though these great ships, unlike the horses, had no will of their own, they were, however, subject to fierce forces beating against them from without. James characterizes these winds as "strong" (*sklērōn*), or "stiff," suggesting that these strong winds cannot be made to swerve from their course. Whereas these strong winds move the ships, they also, in the absence of effective control, could cause their ruin.

The point of present interest for James is that these ships "are steered by a very small rudder," in spite of their bulk and the force of the winds. The rudder of ancient ships was an oarlike projection fastened to the ship's stern. In Acts 27:40, the only other New Testament occurrence of the term, the plural indicates that the ship had two rudders fixed to both sides of the stern. Compared to the size of the ship, this rudder was indeed "very small" (*elachistou*), the superlative heightening the contrast.[29] How important to retain control over that small rudder! When the storms of life beat down on our lives, how important it is to ask God to place His hands on the rudder. He best knows how to guide our ship of life in a straight course, though narrow it may be.

This tiny rudder sends the big ship "wherever the pilot wants to go." The direction of the ship is not determined by the strong wind but by "the impulse of the steerman" (ASV). The noun rendered "impulse" (*hormē*) may refer to the physical pressure exerted on the tiller by the pilot, or it may indicate his personal inclination or desire. In Acts 14:15, the only other occurrence of the term in the New Testament, it refers to the inner eagerness of the opponents of the missionaries to use violence against them. But the fact that the ship moves in the direction that the pilot desires to go implies that he aggressively applies pressure to the tiller to accomplish his purpose. His inner desire must find expression in positive action to achieve the necessary control. The participial substantive rendered "the pilot" (*tou euthunontos*) means "the one guiding straight." The present tense points to the characteristic function and indicates that anyone who commands control of the rudder determines the course of the whole ship.

The two illustrations clearly establish the need in life for the exercise of control at the crucial point. But some scholars further propose to find a parabolic meaning in the illustrations. Thus Reicke suggests that the first illustration pictures "a church leader who regulates the preaching" and thereby controls "the whole group of believers"; for the second illustration, he holds that "the ship represents the church, and the rudder, which actually resembles a tongue, corresponds to the proclamation of the message within the congregation."[30] Johnstone thinks the horse pictures "the power of natural perversity" in human nature that must be kept in check, and the ship pictures "the power of temptation, the evil influences of the world and the world's prince."[31] But we must agree with Plummer that "such symbolism is read into the text, not extracted from it."[32]

b. *The application to the boasting tongue* (v. 5a). "Likewise the tongue is a small part of the body, but it makes great boasts." "Likewise" (*houtōs*), "so, in this manner," asserts the comparison. The horse's mouth is small compared to the size of its body; the ship's rudder is small compared to the whole ship; but though small, each controls the whole. In the same way the little tongue exerts a tremendous effect over the whole life. Zodhiates comments, "There is no independence in the tongue, either in its existence or its actions. Its activities will benefit or will harm the body, every member of the body. The tongue cannot absolve itself of the responsibility that it has and the effects it causes."[33]

The tongue, as the organ of speech, is viewed as having personality and great power in its action. It "makes great boasts" (*megala auchei*, "great things it boasts"). "Great things" is placed before the verb to stress the contrast between its small size and the great things it boasts of. It is not an empty boast, for "the whole argument turns upon the reality of the power which the tongue possesses."[34] Conscious of its tremendous power, the tongue arrogantly proclaims its own exploits. The results are out of all proportion to the size of the agent producing them. The expression occurs only here in the New Testament. The Textus Receptus reads the expression as one word (*megalauchei*), meaning "to be proud, to talk big." Then the thought is of the arrogant spirit displayed. The reading as two words is better attested and more suitable to the context. The expression marks the transition to the thought of the deplorable results of an uncontrolled tongue.

2. The Damage of an Uncontrolled Tongue (vv. 5b-6)

The contrast between the small and the great continues, but now the stress is on the often disastrous results produced by the tongue. James gives a concise illustration of those results (v. 5b) and then unfolds the nature and actions of an uncontrolled tongue (v. 6).

a. *The illustration of the vast damage* (v. 5b). "Consider what a great forest is set on fire by a small spark." "Consider" (*idou*, "behold") again calls special attention to the illustration. It would have been better to start a new verse here.

The tongue, like fire, when under control is a very useful agent, but when uncontrolled, how great the havoc! "What a great forest is set on fire by a small spark" embodies a wordplay that is difficult to reproduce in English. The Greek adjective *hēlikos* calls attention to the size of a thing and can mean "very large" or "very small"—"immensity or minuteness."[35] The context must make clear the distinction. Literally rendered, the exclamation is, "Behold, what sized fire what sized forest kindles!" The statement gets its dramatic effect from the common knowledge of the size of the two elements. The subject, "what sized fire,"[36] and the object, "what sized forest," are effectively placed in juxtaposition before the verb. The word for "forest" (*hulēn*) may mean a standing forest or a stack of lumber. The NEB represents the latter view: "What an immense stack of timber can be set ablaze by the tiniest spark!" But the picture of a forest is generally preferred as "far livelier and more graphic."[37] But Elliott-Binns maintains that in view of the Palestinian origin of this book, it would be more accurate to think not of a forest of towering trees but of the uncultivated brushwood or scrub characteristic of much of the country.[38] "With the setting of a hillside covered with dry brush or wood, such an environment is literally a tinderbox just waiting to explode at the slightest spark."[39] Bishop points to how quickly brush fires spread in the Palestinian dry season.[40] The verb "set on fire," rather than "consumed," points to the setting of the fire; it is so devastating because it is not controlled. An uncontrolled tongue can initiate forces and movements that are just as destructive. "The inflammable wood is always and everywhere, in natural humanity, prepared for the sparks of falsehood and sin."[41]

b. *The nature of an uncontrolled tongue* (v. 6). "Also" (*kai*) closely links the foregoing illustration with this portrait of an uncontrolled tongue. James unfolds a devastating picture: "The tongue also is a fire, a world of evil among the parts of the body. It corrupts the whole person, sets the whole course of his life on fire, and is itself set on fire by hell." Lenski well comments, "Nothing stronger was ever said about the tongue."[42]

"The tongue is a fire" is an apt metaphor of the tongue's destructive nature (Pss. 57:4; 120:3-4; Prov. 16:27; 26:18-21). It is an active, aggressive force; because of its very nature, the tongue is potentially so dangerous if left uncontrolled.

The structure and intended meaning of the remainder of verse 6 is beset with difficulty. There are five expressions in the nominative case with only one verb in the indicative. Different punctuations are possible. The presence of corruption and glosses has been suggested.[43] The intended connection of the expression "a world of evil" is not certain. Some editors and translators regard it as standing in apposition with what precedes; thus the NASB places a semicolon after it, whereas the NIV uses a period. But some interpreters believe that the expression does not fit well as an apposition to "fire." The alternative is to connect it with what follows, regarded as the predicate nominative of the following verb (*kathistatai*).[44] Then the predicate nominative stands emphatically before the subject and verb as stressing that the tongue is indeed "a world of evil." There is also uncertainty concerning the intended relationship of the following three participles to each other. This piling up of the pictures, with the resultant difficulty of determining the intended structure, indicates that James spoke "in accents broken by indignation, in representing the terrible mischiefs of the tongue."[45]

The NIV rendering, "a world of evil among the parts of the body," presents this expression as a further picture of the nature of the tongue. This view explains the second use of "the tongue" (*hē glōssa*), omitted in the NIV as redundant. Thus James further pictures the tongue as "a world of evil" (*ho kosmos tēs adikias*). The use of the article with both nouns stresses its distinctive character as such. The term "world" has a root meaning of adorning or adornment; it is used of a woman's attire in 1 Peter 3:3. It is commonly used to denote the world or universe, viewed as an orderly system. Thus James stamps the tongue as a vast system or organism connected with "evil," that which is unjust and unrighteous in character. The genitive "of evil" may mean a world "composed of evil" (genitive of substance) or "characterized by evil" (genitive of quality). In this epistle the term "world" always has a bad sense; James connects it here with "*the* evil," "*the* unrighteousness," that well-known force of unrighteousness and evil against which believers must stand in constant conflict. Dibelius holds that the genitive in this picturesque phrase is simply the Hebrew substitute for the adjective, "the evil world."[46] Under either view, James paints a dark picture of the tongue's nature.

Others see the expression "the world of evil" as intended to convey quite a different meaning. Accepting the meaning of "adornment" for "world," it is suggested that James means that the tongue adorns iniquity and makes it appear attractive. Thus Lilly renders, "it [the tongue] makes wickedness attractive."[47] Accepting the meaning of "ornament, decoration," Zodhiates comments: "The good and sanctified tongue will condemn unrighteousness, but the evil tongue will compliment it, will flatter it, will make it appear as if it were righteousness."[48] But this view has found little acceptance, and Blackman stamps it as "fanciful in this context."[49]

From the context it seems best to accept that James thinks of the tongue as a vast system of iniquity. The use of the definite article with both nouns in this expression makes it specific; the tongue is verily "*the* world of evil," for it embodies in itself the essence of all wickedness. Since the tongue can play a part in all the sins in the world, it incorporates in itself the whole story of evil in this world.

Although omitted in the NIV, "the tongue" is repeated in this second statement, giving it prominence, for the tongue has a unique place "among the parts of the body." No other member of our physical body has comparable power and range of influence for evil. It can give utterance to every evil thought and motive and put every evil deed into words. It is a microcosm of evil among our members. In rendering "the tongue *is* a fire" the NIV supplied the unexpressed verb in the first statement; then, assuming the use of the same verb here, it does not translate the expressed verb of the original (*kathistatai*) in this second expression. "Is" would be a somewhat weak rendering of this verb, which basically means "to place, appoint, make, constitute." Mayor suggests that its use here "implies a sort of adaptation or development as contrasted with the natural or original state."[50] The verb often is taken as in the passive voice: "is set" or "is constituted." But it seems better to take it as middle, "makes itself," implying that "it was not so 'made' by God."[51] It is the same form used in 4:4, where it is well rendered "maketh himself" (ASV). As a God-given means of human self-expression, the tongue is a wonderful gift. "It is by its own undisciplined and lawless career that it makes itself 'the world of iniquity.'"[52]

The remainder of the verse has no finite verb and is structurally in apposition to the statement that the tongue is a world of iniquity. It consists of three participles, only the first of which has the definite article. Grammatically, two constructions are possible. All three participles may be viewed as being under the government of the one article and forming one compound appositional designation. Or the first participle alone, having the article, may be viewed as appositional, with the other two participles expanding the picture in the first participle. We accept the latter view as more probable. The NIV makes this part a new sentence, rendering the participles as finite verbs.

"It corrupts the whole person" declares the defiling impact of an uncontrolled tongue. As itself morally evil, it has a corrupting and defiling impact. The present active articular participle, "the defiler of the whole body,"[53] depicts the progressive moral impact that it produces. The verb "corrupts" (*spiloō*), occurring only here and in Jude 23, pictures its moral effect. The verb, which means "to stain, defile," here has a symbolic force, denoting the moral corruption that it imparts. In 1:27 the correlative adjective in its negative form was used of the truly religious man who keeps himself from being "polluted by the world." But the impure and vicious utterances of an uncontrolled tongue are "infections to the blood of the utterer—a moral leprosy, influencing all the members and defiling all the actions."[54] It imparts its moral stain and corruption to "the whole person" (*holon ton soma*). In verse 3 the same expression was used of the horse and rendered "the whole animal." Here the word "body" properly denotes the whole personality, since the person resides in the body and uses his body as his instrument.

Since we do not ordinarily think of fire as defiling, it has been held that James was not consistent with his picture in now speaking of the tongue as "corrupting" the whole man. But the remainder of the verse, which continues the picture of fire, indicates how this morally defiling impact is imparted.

The remaining double statement, "sets the whole course of his life on fire, and is itself set on fire by hell," consists of two participial clauses. The participles match: both are from the same verb, "to set on fire," and have the same tense; the active voice of the first is balanced by the passive voice of the second; the use of *kai* with both statements suggests the translation "both . . . and." We accept these two participles as modifying the previous articular participle, "the one defiling the whole body" (ASV). They expound the vicious, defiling function of the uncontrolled tongue.

The meaning of the phrase "sets the whole course of his life on fire" is not certain. Varied renderings have been offered: "setting on fire the cycle of nature" (RSV); "setting fire to the round circle of existence" (Moffatt); "it keeps the wheel of our existence red-hot" (NEB); "sets the whole course of our lives on fire" (Weymouth); and "is the inflamer of the process of generation" (Schonfield).

Both nouns in the expression "the whole course of his life" (*ton trochon tēs geneseōs*) may have more than one meaning. The second noun in the Greek, which is our word *genesis*, may mean "birth" (as in the ASV margin here) or "origin" (Matt. 1:18, history of the "origin"), or it may mean "existence," as in James 1:23 ("his natural face," ASV), that is, the face of his existence. The former noun, depending on the position of the accent in the Greek, may mean either "wheel" or "course," "a running" with a circular idea. Papyrus usage seems to favor the rendering "wheel." Some kind of cyclical action or existence seems implied.

The suggestion that James derived the expression from the Orphic Mysteries, which taught the reincarnation of souls and thought of life as a dreary round of reincarnations,[55] is improbable. Whatever the origin of the expression, it is certain that such a concept was foreign to James's thinking. Nor could he have expected his readers to draw that concept from the statement. As a practical man, James expected his readers to understand the expression as a common-sense description of life.

Some suggest that James is thinking of life as represented by a wheel that is set in motion at birth and continues rolling until death. Or it is thought to picture daily life as a wheel, life with its continuous recurrence of daily affairs. Some would elaborate the picture to mean that the tongue is the axle of this wheel and that as a fire it set the whole wheel aflame (cf. the NEB rendering above).

From the context it seems that James, in speaking about "the whole course of his life," did not intend to limit this picture to the life of the individual. The pronoun "his" in the NIV is not in the Greek text, and it seems best to omit it here. Since the preceding phrase spoke of the impact of the tongue on "the whole person" of the individual, this expression seems intended to set forth the wider social impact of the uncontrolled tongue. James seems to be thinking of the whole wheel of human existence, of which we are individually a part. Thus this expression serves to convey the thought of life's varied relationships being set ablaze by an uncontrolled tongue. It is a common observation that an unconsidered, slanderous report can set a whole community on fire; a whole nation can be aroused by some vicious propaganda, setting different classes of men into ruinous conflict; and wild, passionate words of national hatred can stir international conflicts whose flames may need to be quenched with rivers of blood. Likewise, "vicious moral teaching, popular religious and doctrinal errors, rage like vast conflagrations, leaving countless victims in their wake."[56] Truly an uncontrolled tongue can produce the same destructive effect among men that an uncontrolled spark has on a vast forest.

"And is itself set on fire by hell" reveals the origin of the tongue's destructive fire. It adds a deep spiritual dimension to the picture. As Blue remarks, "The tongue is only the fuse; the source of the deadly fire is hell itself."[57] The evils of an uncontrolled tongue have a connection with the unseen spiritual world of evil. "Only fire such as that pictured in the lake of fire, the second death, could light such a destructive fire as that spread by the tongue."[58] The present passive participle implies that the uncontrolled tongue is habitually set on fire by hell. It permits itself to be used by satanic evil.

"Hell" (*geennēs*) is Gehenna and occurs only here outside the Synoptic Gospels. It is the Greek form of the Hebrew *ge-henom*, "the valley of Hinnom" or, more fully, "the valley of the sons of Hinnom," that lay south-southwest of the Jerusalem walls. During the days of Ahaz and Manasseh, human sacrifices were offered there to the pagan god Moloch (2 Chron. 28:3; 33:6). When Josiah came to the throne, he "defiled" the place (2 Kings 23:10), thus preventing further human sacrifices there. Later the place was used as the dumping ground for the city of Jerusalem, and fires were kept burning continually to destroy the rubbish and filth. It was a place of defilement and continual fire. The scene came to be regarded as an apt picture of the place of final punishment of the wicked.[59] Jesus used the term *gehenna*[60] in speaking of the punishment of the wicked as a place "where their worm dieth not, and the fire is not quenched" (Mark 9:48, ASV). Gehenna is to be identified with the "lake of fire" (Rev. 19:20; 20:10, 14, 15).

But in connecting the tongue with gehenna, James does not speak of it as the fit place of punishment for the sins of the tongue. To his mind it calls up the satanic hosts of evil who will yet be consigned to Gehenna but are now habitually active in motivating human wickedness (cf. 3:15). All too readily an uncontrolled tongue can become the tool of Satan and his hosts in spreading the fire of hell. It is not in keeping with James's purpose to elaborate the opposite truth, that a yielded tongue also can be touched by fire from God's altar to be used in His service (Isa. 6:6-9).

C. THE UNTAMABLE NATURE OF THE TONGUE (vv. 7-8)

The opening "for" (*gar*) of verse 7 (not in NIV), substantiates that man's tongue is so mischievous because it is humanly untamable. Lange holds that the intended connection is with the immediately preceding statement that the tongue is inflamed by hell.[61] But it seems better to view it as substantiating the whole devastating picture in verses 5 and 6. The proof is presented in the form of a contrast. Man displays amazing ability to dominate the animal world (v. 7), but he cannot tame his own vicious tongue (v. 8).

1. The Ability to Tame Animals (v. 7)

"All kinds of animals, birds, reptiles and creatures of the sea are being tamed and have been tamed by man." The ancient world took pride in mankind's ability to subdue, tame, and control the animal kingdom. Psalm 6:6-8 celebrates man's God-given domination over the animal creation. James's assertion is not that every creature has been tamed by man's art and ingenuity; nor is it necessary to insist that every species of animal has been tamed by man. The noun "kind" (*phusis*) means "nature" and points to the distinctive natural characteristics that divide the entire animal world into distinct groups. By his twofold use of the term in this verse, James marks the contrast between animal nature and human nature; the latter dominates the former. "Every nature" (*pasa phusis*) of creatures composing the animal world is open to control by "the human nature" (*tē phusei tē anthrōpinē*), "the nature, the human."

The classification of the animal world given by James resembles that found in Genesis 9:2 and 1 Kings 4:33 (cf. Gen. 1:26). They are grouped in two pairs: those that walk and fly, apparently viewed as the nobler creatures; and those that crawl and swim. It is not a scientific classification, but it is fully sufficient for the purpose. "Animals" denotes quadrupeds, but apparently the intended meaning here is "wild beasts," since there would be no need to insist upon the taming of domestic animals. The word "reptiles" was used especially of snakes, but here the term is broader. "Creatures of the sea" (*enalion*), used only here in the New Testament but common in secular Greek, denotes fish as well as other creatures living in the sea.

"Tamed" need not imply domestication. The verb here used is stronger than "tamed" and means "to subdue, curb, subjugate," to bring under control for one's purpose. Elsewhere in the New Testament it occurs only in Mark 5:4, of the Gerasene demoniac who could not be controlled. Many wild creatures have been subdued by man without being domesticated to the extent that the restraining leash imposed upon them might be safely removed.

The double use of the term "tamed," in the present and the perfect tenses, calls forth the evidence from observation and history. The present tense pictures human nature's domination of animal nature as a fact repeatedly being observed. As Kistemaker remarks, "We see this displayed in a circus performance where wild animals obey their trainer who merely cracks a whip, snaps his fingers, or claps his hands."[62] The use of the perfect tense "have been tamed" adds that history is replete with such examples. This amazing ability of man is nothing new; it is part of God's original purpose for man (Gen. 1:26; 9:2; Ps. 8:6-8). It is standing proof of the inherent superiority of human nature over animal nature.

2. The Inability to Tame the Tongue (v. 8)

"But" introduces the sad contrast "but no man can tame the tongue." The present tense "can" (*dunatai*), "is able," declares man's standing inability "to tame" (aorist tense) his tongue as an effective achievement. "Because of the fall," Tasker remarks, "man has lost dominion over himself."[63] "The tongue," placed emphatically forward, marks the human tongue as "the one-of-a-kind creature; namely, *untamable*!"[64] "No one" (*oudeis*), which leaves no exceptions, is limited by the genitive "of men" (*anthrōpōn*), which stands emphatically at the end of the statement. "This inability is purely moral, due simply to a weakness of will."[65] But what is hopeless for fallen man can become a reality by God's grace and power.

Some interpreters suggest that James means that, although man can control the animals, he cannot control the tongue of his fellowman. But the entire discussion points, rather, to man's inability to control his own tongue.

James adds a double picture of this tongue that man cannot control: "It is a restless evil, full of deadly poison." No finite verb is expressed in these phrases. The two phrases might be viewed as forming an apposition to "the tongue" (*tēn glōssan*), but this would require the grammatical irregularity of having the nominative *mestē* ("full") standing in apposition with an accusative. Generally both phrases are regarded as predicate nominatives, with "is" understood, as in the NIV above. But it seems more forceful to regard them as exclamations of moral indignation, so needing no copula: "A restless evil! Full of deadly poison!"[66]

The adjective "restless" (*akatastaton*), which was rendered "unstable" in 1:8, characterizes the tongue as being fickle and inconstant; it cannot be trusted to stay submissively in its proper place. It is notoriously unreliable, constantly prone to break out in vicious words. The adjective suggests the picture of "some caged but unsubdued wild animal, ever pacing uneasily up and down its den."[67] The nature of this restless tongue is "evil" (*kakos*), base, and degraded in character, and prone to be injurious.

The rendering "an unruly evil" (KJV) is based on a variant reading (*akatascheton*), "uncontrollable, that cannot be restrained." But this reading is not strongly attested and adds nothing to the total picture.

The impact of the tongue is deadly: "full of deadly poison." "Deadly," more literally, "death-bearing," is probably an allusion to the poison of the serpent's tongue (Pss. 58:4; 140:3). The adjective occurs only here in the New Testament. "Poison" is an apt term for the deadly work of a vicious tongue. "A word of evil from the old Serpent consigned our race to death, and, like Satan's tongue, are in a degree the tongues of all his children."[68]

D. THE INCONSISTENCY OF THE TONGUE (vv. 9-12)

James recognizes that the tongue can be used in the noble activity of praising God; but it also is readily used to curse men. This double-dealing establishes the depth of its moral perversity and makes its good all the more reprehensible. James sets forth this gross inconsistency (vv. 9-10*a*), expresses his rebuke (v. 10*b*), and illustrates the perversion from nature (vv. 11-12).

1. The Statement of the Inconsistency (vv. 9-10*a*)

The absence of any connecting particle marks this section as a new aspect of the discussion. "With the tongue we praise our Lord and Father, and with it we curse men, who have been made in God's likeness." "With the tongue" (*en autē*, "with it") gives recognition to the fact that the tongue is only the instrument that the speaker uses to express himself. This fact is underlined by the repetition of the expression in the following clause. While James has practically personified the tongue, he is fully aware of the person behind the tongue. "We" indicates that this perverted use of the tongue is characteristic of mankind in general, and James acknowledges that Christians still have this nature. Even believers may be guilty of duplicity. "Praise" and "curse" are in the present tense and indicate that the tongue's ability to play the part of Dr. Jekyll and Mr. Hyde is not an isolated occurrence. It is "used for incompatible activities: on the one hand it is very religious, but, on the other, it can be most profane in daily life."[69]

"With the tongue we praise our Lord and Father" states the highest and noblest employment of the human tongue. "Praise" (*eulogoumen*) means "to speak well of, to extol," and when God is the object it means to celebrate His name and acts with praise. Our praise is directed to "our[70] Lord and Father,"[71] a phrase unique in the New Testament. The two titles, combined under one article, point to God's authority and sovereign power and also His love and compassion. Both aspects are part of the biblical revelation of the nature of God. "The word Father," Wolff notes, "introduces the idea of the divine likeness of man and stresses His love in sharp contrast with the mutual hatred of men cursing each other."[72]

It was the pious practice among the Jews, both in speaking and in writing, to add "Blessed [be] He" after each utterance of the name of God. No doubt, the readers of this epistle still continued this practice whenever God was mentioned. Such a practice of praising God is worthy of every Christian tongue.

"And with it we curse men" places this evil use of the tongue alongside its prior noble use. "With it" denotes that here again the tongue is but the instrument giving expression to the feelings in the speaker's heart. The verb "curse" (*katarōmetha*) quite literally means "to call down curses upon." Zodhiates remarks, "In order to call down curses, a person must think himself high up, over and above those whom he showers with uncomplimentary remarks."[73] Oesterly points out that the term denotes "personal abuse, such as results from loss of temper in heated controversy."[74] The reference is not to the use of profanity in vulgar speech but apparently seems to envision angry disputes and slanderous remarks in inner-church party strife (cf. 4:1-2, 11-12) that resulted in loss of self-control and elicited vicious invectives. "We" does not imply that James himself was guilty, but it does indicate that even Christians, with whom James identifies himself, were at times guilty of this evil.

The depth of this evil of cursing "men" (*tous anthrōpous*), distinctively, fellow "human beings," is underlined by the appositional addition "who have been made in God's image." The perfect tense "have been made" indicates that the divine likeness imparted at creation has not been totally obliterated. The reference is to man as he now is. Sin has marred this likeness in fallen man; yet, as God's noblest creature, every human being retains "an indestructible nobility"[75] that declares his divine origin and his dignity as the crown of creation. Fallen man is indeed "the scandal," but also, as God's appointed representative over creation (Gen. 1:26; Ps. 8:4-8), he is "the glory of the universe" (Pascal). "The likeness of God" consists chiefly in the fact that man is a personal, rational, moral being. Beyond all God's other creatures, he possesses the attributes of reason, will, and conscience, as well as the ability to know and serve God, and the capacity to be conformed to God's moral and spiritual likeness. Therefore, to curse a man is to insult the God whose likeness man still bears. Stier comments, "Because St. James is speaking to *brethren*, he does not expressly *mention* the direct and open blasphemy against God; nevertheless, he gives it to be understood that he who injures and dishonours man, similarly sins against the image of *God*."[76] Rather, the fact of man's innate nobility should inspire respect and goodwill, even when they cause irritation and possible injury.

The added comment, "Out of the same mouth come praise and cursing" (v. 10*a*), drives home the fatal inconsistency. The emphasis is upon "the same mouth." That both blessings and curses flow readily from the same mouth establishes the moral perversity of their source. Martin remarks that "this switch from tongue to mouth (*stoma*) is noteworthy," stressing that "what comes out of a person is what defiles that person (Matt. 15:11, 20)."[77] James agrees with the teaching of Jesus concerning the defiling power of speech. The praise to God loses its noble character and becomes tainted with the bitterness of the cursing. No man can acceptably praise and bless God while feeling bitter hatred toward his fellowman who bears God's image (cf. 1 John 4:20). James, without doubt, had witnessed manifestations of this spirit in the Pharisees, who paraded as the pious leaders of the people yet pronounced their curses upon the multitude (John 7:47-49). James likewise must have detected this spirit among those who "broke out in tones of bitter contempt against those whom Peter had evangelised, Acts xi. 2, 3; the spirit which not only refused to tolerate, but which even excluded from the pale of salvation those who were uncircumcised, Acts xv.1."[78]

2. The Rebuke for the Inconsistency (v. 10*b*)

"My brothers, this should not be." The rebuke is delivered with gentleness and fullness of affection. James is grieved that there is such inconsistency among those he accepts as "my brothers." "Moral indignation ends when he is no longer denouncing sin in its hatefulness, but is dealing with the sinner in his shame."[79]

The verb "should" (*chrē*) occurs only here in the New Testament; it carries the thought of fitness or congruity. The presence among them of "this" (*tauta*, "these things"), praising God and cursing members of God's family, constitutes a moral abnormality that nature and grace repudiate. James added an adverb, *houtōs* ("thusly, in this manner"), not translated in the NIV, to sum up the incongruous situation. The strengthened expression makes clear that this palpable evil must not be tolerated among them. It is entirely inappropriate and unbecoming among brethren.

3. The Condemnation from Nature's Consistency (vv. 11-12)

James again resorts to illustrations from nature to drive home this inconsistent use of speech. "Can both fresh water and salt water flow from the same spring? My brothers, can a fig tree bear olives, or a grapevine bear figs?" (vv. 11-12*a*). The questions call for a strong negative reply. The interrogative particle *mēti*, not translated, has the force of "surely they do not, do they?" implying that the universally known facts leave no doubt what the answer must be. "The same spring" marks that the consistency of the material creation condemns man's glaring inconsistency. The more literal rendering of Rotherham, "Doth the fountain out of the same opening teem forth the sweet and the bitter?" marks that "the spring" (*hē pēgē*), a specific spring as representative of its class, does not display the inconsistency revealed by the human mouth in giving utterance to blessing and cursing.

The importance of a spring of water would be assumed by all the readers familiar with conditions in dry Palestine. The existence of many of its villages depended on the availability of such a source for its water. It was important that the water from it continued to be fresh and usable. The verb "flow from" (*bruei*), used only here in the New Testament, denotes something that is full to bursting; it indicates that the spring copiously gushes forth its water. But a traveler, or a resident of the village dependent upon its water, in coming for water does not expect that it will alternate in providing "fresh water" (*to gluku*), clear, drinkable water, and "salt water" (*to pikron*), brackish, salty, undrinkable water, from the same opening in the cliff. The original omits the word "water," although it is clearly implied, thus setting the two adjectives "fresh" and "salt" in sharper contrast. No spring is so inconsistent.

Orchard and vineyard likewise cannot be so inconsistent (v. 12). "Can" (*mē dunatai*) calls for a ringing no answer; it is a standing impossibility for a fig tree to produce olives or a vine figs. Each produces in harmony with its own nature. James is recalling the teaching of Jesus (Matt. 7:16-20). The insertion of the direct address "my brothers" marks James's affectionate concern to drive home this point for fellow believers.

The fig, the olive, and the vine were the three chief natural products of Palestine. James's appeal to these familiar objects is another instance of his ability to draw needed spiritual lessons from the material world around him. "As the fig tree cannot produce olives or the grapevine figs, so the pure heart cannot produce false, bitter, harmful speech."[80]

James concludes the lesson with a categorical assertion: "Neither can a salt spring produce fresh water."[81] It is another allusion to the Palestinian scene. No one visiting the Dead Sea area, where salt springs abounded, would expect such an inconsistency to take place. "Salt spring" (*halukon*) is simply the adjective "salty" and occurs only here in the New Testament. In this verse it is commonly understood to mean "a salt spring." In the Septuagint the adjective is used of the "Salt Sea" (Num. 34:3, 12; Deut. 3:17; Josh. 15:2, 5). Neither a salt spring nor the Sea of Salt could be expected to produce sweet water. Nature is consistent with itself. "Everything in nature continues this day according to God's ordinance, and all things serve Him; man alone would pervert that order in the endeavour to unite what God and nature had put asunder."[82] James insists that "the mouth that speaks for the Christian heart must be consistent in its behavior toward God and toward His creatures."[83]

James draws no stated conclusion from these illustrations. But the examples cited so obviously condemn man's inconsistency that no application is needed.

E. THE WISDOM CONTROLLING THE TONGUE (vv. 13-18)

James used no connecting particle to posit a close connection between this paragraph and what has preceded. Some scholars, like Dibelius, assert that there is in fact "no connection in thought."[84] But a "loose connection" is

generally accepted. The common view is that this paragraph "resumes directly the opening warning in vss. 1-2a."[85] Then these verses are understood as
addressed directly to the teachers in the churches. Though this paragraph
does have special relevance to the Christian teacher, we fully agree with Mitton that "there is nothing in the paragraph which may not apply equally to
Christians other than teachers."[86] It seems better to accept that this paragraph,
setting forth two kinds of wisdom, relates to the entire picture just given
concerning the tongue. These verses elaborate the basic truth, already indicated in verse 9, that the tongue is the instrument whereby the spirit of the
inner man is revealed. The use of the tongue manifests the nature of the
spirit dominating a man, whether or not it is wisdom coming from above.
These significant verses justify the assertion that the book of James is the
"Wisdom Literature" of the New Testament.

In verse 13, James challenges the man who is truly wise to reveal that
fact through his good life. The test may reveal two kinds of wisdom: James
first portrays the evidence when a false wisdom is in control (vv. 14-16) and
then sets forth the evidence when true wisdom is in control (vv. 17-18).

1. The Challenge to the Wise to Show His Wisdom (v. 13)

James begins his challenge with a probing question: "Who is wise and
understanding among you?" The interrogative approach, with its personal
appeal, aims at the conscience of each of his readers. His question does not
imply that none is wise but challenges to self-examination those who rashly
assume that they are.

The use of such rhetorical questions was a characteristic of Hellenistic
diatribe. But that need not imply that James drew the practice from Hellenistic writers, for they did not have a monopoly on this well-known literary
device. It is a practice often used by Jesus (e.g., Matt. 11:16; Mark 4:21, 30) as
well as various Old Testament writers (Ps. 15:1; Prov. 6:27-28; 8:1; Isa. 50:1;
Mic. 4:9). As an experienced speaker, James well knew the value of the method. Blackman notes that this feature "is also characteristic of the style of our
author, and we may well think with reference to him that 'the style is the
man.'"[87] James might have formulated this part of his challenge as a conditional sentence, but that would have weakened the force of the challenge.

The two adjectives "wise and understanding" are used together only
here in the New Testament. They appear in Deuteronomy 1:13 (LXX) as the
needed qualifications of tribal judges in Israel; but in Deuteronomy 4:6 and
Hosea 14:9 they are united as desired qualities in all God's people. Obviously
James expected these qualities to characterize the teachers in their midst to
an eminent degree, but their possession should mark all true believers. Their
union stresses the essential moral quality demanded.

In Jewish usage, "wise" (*sophos*) described the individual who possessed moral insight and skill in deciding practical issues of conduct, a wis-

dom derived from his personal knowledge of God (cf. under 1:5). "Understanding" (*epistēmōn*), which occurs only here in the New Testament, was used of one having the knowledge of an expert, a specialist able to apply his fuller knowledge to practical situations. The two terms are synonymous, and suggested precise distinctions are not certain. Probably the first denotes a moral quality and the second an intellectual. The call is for an individual who possesses not merely academic learning but also practical moral and spiritual insight.

Did James expect such a man to identify himself or to be identified by others? The former seems implied by the charge given the one so identified: "let him show it by his good life, by deeds done in the humility that comes from wisdom." James demands that the possession of wisdom, like faith (2:14-26), must be proved by conduct. The aorist imperative "let him show" (*deixatō*) calls for an effective demonstration. The proof must be given, not through victory by a clever argument, but "by his good life." "By" (*ek*), better "out of," points to the general source whence the proof is to be drawn. (Compare the exact parallel in 2:18, "by my works.") The proof must appear from "his good life." The noun "life" (*anastrophēs*) denotes "the life of movement and action,"[88] a turning here and there in the daily affairs of life.[89] His social behavior must be recognized as "good" (*kalōs*), "noble, beautiful, attractive." His winsome daily conduct should demonstrate his possession of the needed practical insight and understanding to deal with the daily problems of life. "Not one's orthodoxy (right preaching) but one's orthopraxis (right living) is the mark of true wisdom."[90]

The attractiveness of his life must be established "by deeds done in the humility that comes from wisdom." His deeds, which are the acid test of his wisdom, must be wrought by his personal faith, providing external evidence of God's transforming power within.

His deeds must be "done in the humility that comes from wisdom." The emphasis is on "humility" (*prautēti*), more commonly translated "meekness" or "gentleness." Such "meekness" is a characteristic of true wisdom and is the opposite of arrogant self-assertiveness (cf. 1:21*b*). It is that attitude of heart that produces gentleness and mildness in dealing with others—not weakness (Matt. 11:29) but power under control. The meek man does not feel a need to contend for the recognition of his rights or acceptance of his personal views. His life will be characterized by modesty and unobtrusiveness. "This Christian meekness," Moo notes, "involves a healthy understanding of our own unworthiness before God and a corresponding humility and lack of pride in our dealings with our fellowmen."[91] Understandably, such an attitude of meekness was not prized or appreciated in the non-Christian world.

2. The Evidence of False Wisdom in Control (vv. 14-16)

The initial "but" (*de*) points to the sure consequences when "the humility that comes from wisdom" is lacking in their midst. James does not identify the exact opposite of such wisdom-produced meekness; rather, he proceeds to picture the alternative results when two different kinds of wisdom are in control. If they are controlled by a spirit of "bitter envy and selfish ambition" (v. 14), it proves the presence of a false wisdom (v. 15), a fact confirmed by the sure evil results of its sway (v. 16).

a. *The manifestation of this wisdom* (v. 14). "But if you harbor bitter envy and selfish ambition in your hearts, do not boast about it or deny the truth." The conditional form "if you harbor" softens the statement of the sad picture, but it assumes the reality of such a state of affairs.[92] "Harbor" (*echete*, "have" or "hold") seems to imply that the situation is not only present but is being fostered.[93]

"Bitter envy," the first of two evil elements in their attitude, is placed emphatically before the verb. The noun "envy" (*zēlon*), the Greek term from which we derive our English "zealous," is a neuter term and may have either a good sense (John 2:17; 2 Cor. 7:7; 11:2) or a bad sense, which is its predominant use in the New Testament. The bad sense here is strengthened by the adjective "bitter" (*pikron*). In verse 11 the adjective was used literally of "salt" or bitter water; here the usage is figurative, to denote a bitter or harsh attitude. In a bad sense, the noun denotes "jealousy" or "envy." Modern versions variously render the expression "bitter jealousy,"[94] "bitter envy" (NIV; Lattey; Weymouth), "bitter emulation" (Darby), or "bitter zeal" (Robert Young). Since the reference seems to be to a religiously motivated feeling, "bitter zeal" or "harsh zeal" seems the best rendering. Religious zeal or "enthusiasm" for God and truth is a commendable attitude, but the subtleties of sinful human nature can readily pervert it into bitter antagonism against those who do not express their adherence to God and His truth in the same way we do. If the picture is restricted to the teachers in the Christian community, then the reference is to a jealous rivalry between religious leaders competing for a following. But the same spirit can readily manifest itself in their followers.

This connotation of religious zeal is consistent with the second element in their evil attitude: their "selfish ambition" (*eritheian*). No adjective is added to the noun, but its evil import is obvious, although the term's precise significance is not certain. It is only known to occur in Aristotle prior to New Testament times; he used it to denote "a self-seeking pursuit of political office by unfair means."[95] It now is generally accepted that the word is not derived from *eris*, "strife," but from *erithos*, "a hired servant, one working for a cause for pay," since both of these terms occur in Paul's lists of vices in 2 Corinthians 12:20 and Galatians 5:20. The basic thought of the term seems to be that of one who, for personal advantage, works to promote a definite cause in an unethical manner. It thus denotes a party spirit, or factiousness. This meaning makes good sense in all its New Testament occurrences (Rom. 2:8; 2 Cor. 12:20; Gal 5:20; Phil. 1:17; 2:3; James 3:14, 16).[96] Thus it denotes a willingness "to use unworthy and divisive means" to promote one's own views or interest.[97] It is a temper tragically injurious to Christian fellowship.

By adding "in your hearts" James reminds his readers that the problem is not external but internal. The phrase goes with both nouns. Both "bitter envy" and "selfish ambition" are present within them as strong motivating forces. The evil impulses within, not the Holy Spirit, are the true source of these evils. James portrays them from God's standpoint. In Hebrew thought, the heart was the source of moral action (Prov. 4:23). James reminds his readers that "no loud and pretentious claim to the possession of 'wisdom' could avail while 'out of the heart proceeded evil things.'"[98] (cf. Matt. 15:19-20).

James censures their inner evil attitude with a double demand: "do not boast about it or deny the truth." His singular negative (*mē*) must be taken with both verbs; the negative with the present imperative verbs demands that these actions, expressive of their attitude, must cease.

The compound verb "boast about" (*katakauchasthe*) means "to boast against, exult over" and conveys the picture of gloating over another on the ground of assumed superiority. It thus denotes "the malicious triumphing at the least point of vantage gained by one party" over its opponents in their disputes.[99] It was the natural fruit of their bitter zeal and party spirit. In 2:13, James used the verb of the triumph of mercy over strict justice in the coming judgment; here the picture relates to the triumph of arrogant pride over others in the interactions of daily life. The "it," not in the Greek, may denote either "the truth" they professed to advance or the "wisdom" they claimed to possess. Bultmann notes that this compound verb appears only once outside of biblical and Christian writings.[100] Apparently Christianity brought this evil into open consciousness.

James further demands that they do not "deny the truth" (*kai pseudesthe kata tēs alētheias*, literally "nor be lying against the truth"). "The truth" here has been differently understood. It may denote the facts in the case, as in Mark 5:13; Zodhiates holds that "it just means uprightness, honesty, verity, the opposite of lying,"[101] or it may denote the truth of the gospel (1:18; 5:19). The last seems preferable here as bringing out the full seriousness of their guilt. By their attitude and acts they were repudiating "the truth" of the gospel, which as Christians they professed to accept and promote.

The phrase "against the truth" may be taken with both verbs or with the latter only. Dibelius accepts the former view but observes that "the formulation suffers from redundancy," since James simply means, "Do not boast and lie against the truth."[102] But others, like Mayor,[103] prefer to take "against the truth" only with the second verb. This is more forceful and avoids a measure of tautology. Then the two verbs may be viewed as having a cause and effect sequence: "do not be arrogant and *so* lie against the truth" (NASB).[104] Davids remarks, "The sense in any case is clear: those full of party spirit and bitter zeal ought at least to be honest and stop claiming to be inspired by God's heavenly wisdom."[105]

b. *The character of this wisdom* (v. 15). "Such 'wisdom' does not come down from heaven but is earthly, unspiritual, of the devil." "Such 'wisdom'" (*hautē hē sophia*) summarizes the picture of verse 14. A wisdom devoid of meekness and producing jealousy, selfish ambition, and bitter conflict may claim to be wisdom of a kind, but it cannot be one of those "perfect gifts" that come down from the Father of lights (1:17). Had James possessed the modern literary device of quotation marks, he doubtless would have used them with the term here, as the NIV effectively does.

Negatively, the truth is that such professed "wisdom" "does not come down from heaven," does not have the character of the wisdom that has a heavenly source. It does not qualify to be classified as true wisdom.

Positively, "such 'wisdom'" must be characterized as being "earthly, unspiritual, of the devil." These three adjectives form a climax, indicating a "mounting sense of distance and alienation from God."[106] The import of each term is heightened by its implied opposite.

"Earthly" (*epigeios*) stamps it as "earth-bound" (NEB), marking a sharp contrast to the wisdom "coming down from above" (Greek). "On the surface," Davids remarks, "to say that something belongs to the earth is not bad, but it is bad if the something is claimed to come from God (1 Cor. 15:40)."[107] As "earthly" it springs out of and is limited to the frail and finite life of unregenerated humanity and associated with its turbulent affairs. In 1 Corinthians 1-2, Paul, in rebuking the quarreling Corinthians, makes a clear distinction between two kinds of wisdom: "the wisdom of the world" (1:20; 2:5-6) and "the wisdom of God" (1:24; 2:7).

"Unspiritual" (*psuchikē*), the adjective form of the noun "soul" (*psuchē*), means "pertaining to the life of the soul." In biblical usage this adjective relates to "the life of the natural world and whatever belongs to it, in contrast to the supernatural world."[108] The term does not refer to the gross lusts of the flesh but rather denotes that which is essentially human, life apart from God as contrasted to life imparted by God, devoid of the Spirit of God, hence "unspiritual." In terms of the trichotomy of 1 Thessalonians 5:23, the adjective describes that part of man's nonmaterial being that he has in common with the animal world around him. It refers to the forces and endowments of unregenerate human nature, man as he is in Adam. Paul's use of the term in 1 Corinthians 2:14 gives the force here: "The natural [*psuchikos*] man receiveth not the things of the Spirit of God: for they are foolishness unto him; and he cannot know them, because they are spiritually judged" (ASV). Thus the term here describes a wisdom that springs from the mental and emotional impulses of fallen humanity and is marked by its depraved concepts, desires, and aspirations.

"Of the devil" (*daimoniōdēs*), literally "demoniacal," stamps this "wisdom" as demonic in character. The adjective, used only here in the New Testament, is derived from the common noun *daimonion* (demon or evil spirit), denoting that which is characteristic of or proceeding from an evil spirit. The term does not relate to the devil personally; in Scripture, Satan is never called a demon, and the great host of his ministers are never spoken of as devils.[109] There is only one devil, Satan, but there are vast numbers of demons who further Satan's work. James is referring to those unclean spirits whose unhappy victims he had often seen (cf. 2:19). In 1 Timothy 4:1, false doctrine is ascribed to the influence of demons. Behind this "wisdom," marked by jealousy, crafty party factions, and egotistical boasting, James detects the work of the demons in seeking to corrupt the harmony and very life of the Body of Christ.

In later years the Christian church, in battling with the heretical views of gnosticism, stamped its professed superior spiritual insights as demonic. But there is no evidence that the exponents of the "wisdom" that James castigates were early exponents of gnosticism. Dibelius concludes his investigation with the remark "There is no reason to assume that James is related to, or directed against Gnostics."[110]

c. *The outcome of this wisdom* (v. 16). With the word "for," James introduces the justification for his strong condemnation of this "wisdom." "For where you have envy and selfish ambition, there you find disorder and every evil practice." It is condemned by its disastrous results. "Where . . . there" marks the correlation between the manifestations of this wisdom (v. 14) and the social consequences. There is an inevitable cause and effect relation.

James declares that the sure result of "bitter envy" (v. 14) is "disorder" (*akatastasia*), pointing out the chaotic effects of this "wisdom." In 1:8, James used the adjective to describe the impact of double-mindedness upon the individual, and in 3:8 it is descriptive of the uncontrolled tongue. Here the noun points to the resultant public confusion, disorder, and chaotic turbulence in the assembly. Ropes notes that "the word seems to have something of the bad associations of our word 'anarchy.'"[111] In Luke 21:9 it is used to describe the tumults, uprisings, and revolutions that will mark the period preceding the *parousia*. Instead of promoting harmony, this "wisdom" causes disruption and unruliness; instead of creating closer fellowship among the members, it destroys it. Such a "wisdom" cannot be from God.

It is ultimately the root of "every evil practice." "Practice" (*pragma*) may denote a deed or event that has occurred without any indication as to its moral quality; more generally it may mean "thing, matter, affair." Here the adjective "evil" (*phaulon*) marks the moral character of the event or situation. It contemplates evil, not from the aspect of its "active or passive malignity" but rather from "its good-for-nothingness, the impossibility of any true gain ever coming forth from it."[112] But in the New Testament it is commonly used with a moral connotation as the opposite of the good. "In the realm of morals," Robertson observes, "what is merely indifferent soon gets to be bad."[113] The noun and adjective may well be rendered "every vile thing" (NASB), as comprehending all forms of evil. Since this "wisdom" is totally without ethical or spiritual value, it cannot be one of God's beneficent gifts (1:17).

3. The Evidence of the True Wisdom in Control (vv. 17-18)

With an adversative "But" (*de*), James now skillfully portrays the characteristics (v. 17) and fruit (v. 18) of God-given wisdom.[114]

a. *The characteristics of this wisdom* (v. 17). Unlike the spurious "wisdom" just exposed, this wisdom has a divine origin. In verse 15, James asserted that there is a wisdom that comes down from above, but the false wisdom did not qualify. Now he does not use the full expression "come down from heaven" (*anōthen katerchomenē*) but simply uses the adverb *anōthen*, literally, "from above," to stress the basic nature of this wisdom. The characteristics to be enumerated belong to "the from above wisdom" (*hē anōthen sophia*).

James enumerates seven characteristics, one of them with a double element. This wisdom "is first of all pure, then peace loving, considerate, submissive, full of mercy and good fruit, impartial and sincere." Zodhiates points out that "James uses these adjectives to describe the wisdom from above instead of the man who possesses it."[115]

This heavenly wisdom "is first of all pure," making prominent the intrinsic quality of this heavenly wisdom. In its very nature it is "pure," clean and undefiled, free from all vices, such as jealousy and party factions. It involves the thought "of shrinking from contamination, of a delicate sensibility to pollution of any kind."[116] Adamson notes that this term, "infrequent in both LXX and NT, which here describes not only freedom from ceremonial or corporal defilement but sincere moral and spiritual integrity," is "associated especially with Christ, as in 1 John 3:3."[117] In His character, Christ is the moral pattern for all believers. This virtue stands first, not in the matter of time but in importance. It is the source and key to all the following qualities.

"Then peace-loving" names the first of the external qualities flowing from the inner purity of this wisdom. This heavenly wisdom is "ready for peace,"[118] desiring and fostering peace by restraining discord and pacifying the turbulent elements around it. It promotes "right relationships between man and man, and between man and God."[119] But it does not pursue peace at the expense of purity. It will not compromise with sin to maintain peace. But even when fighting against sin, it hungers for peace, yearning to heal all divisions by its wise counsel.

"Considerate" (*epiekēs*) is an adjective not easily translated into English. Barclay calls it "the most untranslatable" term in this list.[120] Besides the commonly used "gentle," our English versions employ a variety of terms: "considerate" (NEB; NIV; Goodspeed), "forbearing" (Moffatt), "courteous" (MLB; Weymouth), "reasonable" (Rotherham; Schonfield), and "kindly" (JB). It conveys the thought of respect for the feelings of others, being willing to waive all rigor and severity in one's dealings with others. Burdick notes that in the Septuagint this adjective "is used mostly of God's disposition as King. He is gentle and kind, although in reality He has every reason to be stern and punitive toward men in their sin. God's people are also to be marked by this godlike quality."[121] The opposite characteristic is pictured by Jesus in Matthew 18:24-30 in speaking of the servant who had much forgiven but acted with implacable harshness in dealing with his fellow servant. Knowling suggests the rendering "gently-reasonable" as combining the thoughts of gentleness and fairness.[122]

"Submissive" (*eupeithēs*), found only here in the New Testament, etymologically suggests the meaning "easily persuaded, with the implication of being open to reason or willing to listen."[123] It has a conciliatory attitude and is ready to cooperate when a better way is shown; it is the opposite of being stubborn and unyielding. As Moo notes, this wisdom is "'easily persuaded' —not in the sense of a weak, credulous gullibility, but in the sense of a willing deference to others when unalterable theological or moral principles are not involved."[124]

"Full of mercy and good fruit," the only double characteristic in the list, stands in direct contrast to "every vile deed" in verse 16. "Mercy" is more than a feeling of pity; it is an attitude of compassion toward those in distress that leads to practical help. Mercy prefers to deal with the needy in terms of what is needed rather than what is deserved. It is one of the attributes of God Himself (Pss. 86:5; 100:5; 103:8; Eph. 2:4), for He prefers mercy to judgment (James 2:13). God desires and approves the practice of mercy in human relations (Isa. 58:6; Hos. 6:6; Mic. 6:8; Matt. 23:23; Luke 10:37). The adjective "full" underlines that this heavenly wisdom is characterized by an abundant measure of mercy. Such a life also will be full of "good fruit" (*karpōn agathōn*). Zodhiates notes that "the very word 'fruits' used here by James indicates the desirability and expectancy of results through our words and works of mercy."[125] The adjective "good" indicates the beneficial nature of these results, whereas the plural noun indicates the variety of the fruit produced. The many acts of practical mercy mature in a rich harvest of variegated fruit.

Two negative characteristics conclude the picture of this heavenly wisdom. "Impartial" (*adiakritos*) translates an adjective whose meaning is somewhat uncertain. It occurs only here in the New Testament. It is formed from the common verb *diakrinō*, basically meaning "to divide," with the letter *alpha* prefixed, giving it a negative quality. If used with the passive sense, the adjective means "undivided" to denote that it is without division or discord, hence unwavering, without vacillation. James used the positive form of the verb in this sense in 1:6. Then the meaning is that this wisdom acts consistently; it does not take one position in one circumstance and another in a different one. It is the direct opposite of the duplicity of an uncontrolled tongue as described in verses 9-12. This seems the intended meaning in the rendering "without variance." (ASV). Other modern versions employ varied expressions such as "unwavering" (NASB), "without uncertainty" (RSV), "free from vacillation" (Weymouth), and "straight-forward" (NEB). If, however, this verbal adjective is taken with an active meaning, "to make a distinction," then it has the force of "impartial" (NIV; MLB), or "without partiality" (KJV; Montgomery; Rotherham). The verb probably has this meaning in 2:4. Then the teaching is that this heavenly wisdom is not guilty of the partiality that James already has condemned. Mitton supports this view because it "suits what we know of James."[126] Either meaning is possible. Clearly this wisdom is "undivided in mind"[127] and as such does not cause division or disunity.

"Sincere" (*anupokritos*), literally "unhypocritical," denotes that this wisdom is free from all pretense; it does not need to work under a mask since it has nothing to hide. Where the stand taken is always straightforward, there is no risk of pretense. Positively stated, the meaning is that this wisdom is "sincere," wholly genuine.

b. *The fruit of this wisdom* (v. 18). "Peacemakers who sow in peace raise a harvest of righteousness." James added this concluding statement with *de*, not translated in the NIV, indicating that something further was to be said; it does not add a further description of true wisdom but adds the thought of its results to complete the picture. James concludes his argument "with a statement of peacemaking, rather than simply leaving 'peaceable' as one among the many qualities of wisdom."[128]

The NIV rendering reverses the order of the original, which is somewhat redundant, in order to present a clear translation. Very literally translated the verse reads, "Now [the] fruit of righteousness in peace is sown by those that make peace." The express subject of the assertion is "fruit of righteousness" (*karpos dikaiosunēs*). The absence of an article with either noun makes clear the quality of this fruit. The expression may be understood in two ways. The genitive "of righteousness" may be appositional, the fruit that consists of righteousness; or it may be subjective, the fruit that righteousness produces. In support of the former view, Knowling points to Amos 5:7 where "the fruit of righteousness" is opposed to "wormwood" (bitterness).[129] Mitton feels that the context here also favors this view.[130] But others see clear support for the subjective meaning from the obvious relationship between righteousness and peace set forth in Isaiah 32:17,[131] as well as the analogous structure in Luke 3:8 ("fruits worthy of repentance"); Ephesians 5:9 ("the fruit of the light," ASV); and Galatians 5:22 ("the fruit of the Spirit"). Under the former view, the righteousness that characterizes the godly life is itself the fruit that is sown. Under the latter view, the fruit that righteousness produces contains in itself seed that, when planted, produces a harvest of a similar kind. The resultant meaning is practically the same, but the latter interpretation seems preferable.

The statement that this fruit "in peace is sown" is unusual; we think of sowing seed, not fruit. But the statement implies a lively anticipation of the resultant harvest when the seed is sown. People still speak of sowing a crop. The present tense marks the customary practice; the passive voice leaves the sower unnamed, but obviously he is the peacemaker as a righteous man. As Davids notes, "James himself is portrayed as a peacemaker in Acts 15 and 21, but his teaching comes not from his personal preference but from Jesus, who said, 'Blessed are the peacemakers' (Matt. 5:9)."[132] "In peace," which stands before the verb, stresses the circumstances needed for the crop. "Peace" here is viewed in its manward aspects and points to the harmonious relations that this true wisdom produces. Righteousness cannot effectively be cultivated amid strife and turbulence.

"By those that make peace" (*tois poiousin eirēnēn*) can mean "for them" (the dative case) or "by them" (the instrumental case). Perhaps James deliberately left the construction unlimited by a preposition in order to leave room for both meanings. The fruit of righteousness is not only sown by the peacemakers, but they also enjoy the results of their work. "The whole process begins, progresses, and ends in peace."[133]

"Those that make peace" identifies the sowers by their characteristic activity; no official status is required to engage in this activity. They are peaceful themselves, but they also practice promoting peaceful relations between others. Motivated by this heavenly wisdom, they aim at reconciling quarrels and bringing men into peaceful relations with each other as brothers. In so doing, they themselves share in the blessings of the peace and fellowship that they promote.

NOTES FOR
James 3:1-18

1. J. Ronald Blue, "James," in *The Bible Knowledge Commentary, New Testament*, p. 827.
2. Simon J. Kistemaker, *New Testament Commentary, Exposition of the Epistle of James and the Epistles of John*, p. 106.
3. James A. Kleist and Joseph L. Lilly, *The New Testament Rendered from the Original Greek with Explanatory Notes*.
4. The Old English rendering "masters" (KJV), in the sense of "schoolmaster," may be misunderstood. The term denotes the teacher-student relationship, not a master-slave relationship.
5. Sophie Laws, *A Commentary on The Epistle of James*, p. 141.
6. James Hardy Ropes, *A Critical and Exegetical Commentary on the Epistle of St. James*, The International Critical Commentary on the Holy Scriptures of the Old and New Testaments, p. 227.

7. Harold S. Songer, "James," in *The Broadman Bible Commentary*, 12:120.

8. James Moffatt, *The General Epistles, James, Peter, and Judas*, The Moffatt New Testament Commentary, p. 47.

9. *Eidotes* is an old perfect form but used as a present.

10. E. H. Plumptre, *The General Epistle of St. James*, The Cambridge Bible for Schools and Colleges, p. 78.

11. E. C. Blackman, *The Epistle of James*, Torch Bible Commentaries, p. 108.

12. E. G. Punchard, "The General Epistle of James," in *Ellicott's Commentary on the Whole Bible*, 8:368.

13. Spiros Zodhiates, *The Labor of Love*, p. 78.

14. The rendering in the KJV, "in many things we offend all," should not be misinterpreted to mean "we are an offense to all."

15. R. C. H. Lenski, *The Interpretation of the Epistle to the Hebrews and of the Epistle of James*, p. 610.

16. Jospch Bryant Rotherham, *The Emphasized New Testament*.

17. Theordore H. Epp, *James, the Epistle of Applied Christianity*, p. 155.

18. Lenski, p. 610.

19. Rudolf Stier, *The Epistle of St. James*, p. 367.

20. Frank E. Gaebelein, *The Practical Epistle of James*, p. 77.

21. Robert Johnstone, *Lectures Exegetical and Practical on the Epistle of James*, p. 238.

22. Laws, p. 145.

23. William Barclay, *The Letters of James and Peter*, The Daily Study Bible, p. 99.

24. "Behold" in the KJV follows the reading *idou* of the Textus Receptus, a reading found only in a few late manuscripts. The manuscripts vary between *ei de* ("now if") and *ide* ("behold"). In view of the common confusion in the manuscripts between *ei* and *i*, the copyists probably wrote *ide* but meant *ei de*. Modern critical editors agree in accepting *ei de* as most probably original; it best explains the origin of the variants and is the more difficult reading. The Textus Receptus changed *ide* to the more familiar *idou*. See the evidence in United Bible Societies, *The Greek New Testament*, 3d ed., or Nestle-Aland, *Novum Testamentum Graece*, 26th ed.

25. Zodhiates, pp. 94-95.

26. Stier, p. 370.

27. Ibid.

28. E. M. Blaiklock, "Ships," in *The Zondervan Pictorial Encyclopedia of the Bible*, 5:414.

29. As usual in the New Testament, the superlative adjective here has an elative force, "very" or "exceedingly." See H. E. Dana and Julius R. Mantey, *A Manual Grammar of the Greek New Testament*, p. 121.

30. Bo Reicke, "The Epistle of James, Peter, and Jude," in The Anchor Bible, 37:37-38.

31. Johnstone, p. 249.

32. Alfred Plummer, "The General Epistles of St. James and St. Jude," in *An Exposition of the Bible*, 6:597.

33. Zodhiates, p. 104.

34. Joseph B. Mayor, *The Epistle of St. James. The Greek Text with Introduction, Notes and Comments*, p. 108.

35. Douglas J. Moo, *The Letter of James*, p. 123.

36. The Textus Receptus here reads "small" (*oligon*), but that reading has inadequate manuscript support.

37. Henry Alford, *The Greek Testament*, vol. 4, pt. 1, p. 304.

38. L. E. Elliott-Binns, "The Meaning of *Hulē* in Jas. III.5," *New Testament Studies* 2, no. 1 (September 1955): 48-50.

39. Ralph P. Martin, *James*, Word Biblical Commentary, p. 113.

40. Eric F. F. Bishop, *Apostles of Palestine*, p. 186.

41. Stier, p. 372.

42. Lenski, p. 615.

43. See Ropes, p. 234; Burton Scott Easton and Gordon Poteat, "The Epistle of James," in *The Interpreter's Bible*, 12:47; Martin Dibelius, "James. A Commentary on the Epistle of James," in *Hermeneia—A Critical and Historical Commentary on the Bible*, pp. 194-95 and n. 69; Martin, pp. 113-15; James B. Adamson, *The Epistle of James*, pp. 158-64.

44. F. Blass and A. Debrunner, *A Greek Grammar of the New Testament and Other Early Christian Literature*, p. 143.

45. Edwin T. Winkler, "Commentary on the Epistle of James," in *An American Commentary on the New Testament*, p. 47.

46. Dibelius, pp. 193-94 and n. 65.

47. Kleist and Lilly.

48. Zodhiates, p. 109.

49. Blackman, p. 110.

50. Mayor, p. 111.

51. R. J. Knowling, *The Epistle of St. James*, Westminster Commentaries, p. 75.

52. Plummer, 6:598.

53. J. N. Darby, *The "Holy Scriptures," A New Translation from the Original Languages*.

54. Winkler, p. 47.

55. Dibelius, pp. 196-98.

56. Lenski, p. 618.

57. Blue, p. 828.

58. J. W. Roberts, *A Commentary on the General Epistle of James*, p. 131.

59. R. E. Davies, "Gehenna," in *The Zondervan Pictorial Encyclopedia of the Bible*, 2:670-72.

60. Matthew 5:22, 29, 30; 10:28; 18:9; 23:15, 33; Mark 9:43, 45, 47; Luke 12:5.

61. John Peter Lange and J. J. Van Oosterzee, "The Epistle General of James," in *Langes's Commentary on the Holy Scriptures*, 23:97.

62. Kistemaker, p. 112.

63. R. V. G. Tasker, *The General Epistle of James*, p. 77.

64. Roy R. Roberts, *The Game of Life, Studies in James*, p. 92 (italics original).

65. Johnstone, p. 260.

66. So the RSV, the versions of Beck, Rotherham, and Weymouth, and similarly the MLB.

67. Alexander Maclaren, "Hebrews Chaps. VII to End, Epistle of James," in *Expositions of Holy Scripture*, p. 435.

68. Quoted in Winkler, p. 48.

69. Peter H. Davids, *The Epistle of James*, p. 145.

70. The Greek uses the definite article "the" as pointing specifically to God in His indicated character. The NIV "our" adds the thought of our personal relationship to Him.

71. The reading "God, even the Father" (KJV) follows the Textus Receptus. It has less textual support and is probably a scribal alternation of this unusual designation.

72. Richard Wolff, *General Epistles of James and Jude*, Contemporary Commentaries, p. 60.

73. Zodhiates, p. 120.

74. W. E. Oesterley, "The General Epistle of James," in *The Expositor's Greek Testament*, 4:454.

75. John Albert Bengel, *New Testament Word Studies*, 2:454.

76. Stier, p. 377 (italics in original).

77. Martin, pp. 119-20.

78. Knowling, p. 81.

79. H. Maynard Smith, *The Epistle of S. James. Lectures*, p. 188.

80. Moo, p. 130.

81. The manuscripts here reveal variant readings. The Textus Receptus reads "so no salt spring also" (*houtōs oudemia pēgē halukon kai*). *Houtōs* ("so") is absent from early and important manuscripts but is found in many others. Textual critics generally agree that it is more probable that a scribe added it than omitted it; it seems a natural addition to round out the picture. Whereas the text is uncertain, the sense of the statement is not materially affected. For the data, see United Bible Societies, *The Greek New Testament*, 3d ed.

82. Knowling, p. 83.

83. Zodhiates, p. 132.

84. Dibelius, p. 207.

85. Easton and Poteat, p. 50; Joh. Ed. Huther, *Critical and Exegetical Handbook on the General Epistles of James, Peter, John, and Jude*, p. 119.

86. C. Leslie Mitton, *The Epistle of James*, p. 134.

87. Blackman, p. 120.

88. Arthur Carr, "The General Epistle of St. James," in *Cambridge Greek Testament*, p. 47.

89. When the KJV was made, the rendering "conversation" accurately represented the Greek, since the word then meant the manner in which one conducted himself in society. It is now misleading since the term has come to mean simply "to talk." See *The Oxford English Dictionary*, 2:546.

90. Peter H. Davids, *James*, New International Biblical Commentary, p. 88.

91. Moo, p. 132.

92. First class condition, assuming the reality of the condition. See A. T. Robertson and W. Hersey Davis, *A New Short Grammar of the Greek Testament*, p. 350.

93. Lange and Van Oosterzee, p. 100.

94. So RSV, NASB, MLB, NEB, Beck, Kleist and Lilly, Moffatt, Montgomery, Rotherham, and Williams. See Bibliography.

95. William F. Arndt and F. Wilbur Gingrich, *A Greek-English Lexicon of the New Testament and Other Early Christian Literature*, p. 309.

96. The plural forms in 2 Corinthians 12:20 and Galatians 5:20 denote "outbreaks of selfishness" or "disputes."

97. Ropes, p. 246.

98. Knowling, p. 86.

99. Oesterley, p. 455.

100. Rudolf Bultmann, "Katakauchaomai," in *Theological Dictionary of the New Testament*, 3:653.

101. Zodhiates, p. 160.

102. Dibelius, p. 210.

103. Mayor, p. 123.

104. So in effect also the translations of Goodspeed and Lilly.

105. Davids, *The Epistle of James*, p. 151.

106. Harold S. Songer, "James," in *The Broadman Bible Commentary*, 12:125.

107. Davids, *James*, New International Biblical Commentary, p. 89.

108. Arndt and Gingrich, p. 902.

109. The KJV rendering "devils," retained in the *Revised Version* of 1881, is an unfortunate mistranslation.

110. Dibelius, p. 212.

111. Ropes, p. 248.

112. Richard Chenevix Trench, *Synonyms of the New Testament*, p. 317.

113. A. T. Robertson, *Practical and Social Aspects of Christianity. The Wisdom of James*, p. 182.

114. Scholars have commented on the skill revealed in the Greek formulation of this list. See Adamson, *The Epistle of James*, p. 154; Martin, p. 133.

115. Zodhiates, p. 174.

116. Brooke Foss Westcott, *The Epistles of St. John, The Greek Text*, p. 101.

117. Adamson, p. 154.

118. Werner Forester, "Eipenikos," in *Theological Dictionary of the New Testament*, 2:419.

119. William Barclay, *The Letters of James and Peter*, The Daily Study Bible, p. 111.

120. Ibid., p. 112.

121. Donald W. Burdick, "James," in *The Expositor's Bible Commentary*, 12:191.

122. Knowling, p. 89.

123. Johannes P. Louw and Eugene A. Nida, *Greek-English Lexicon of the New Testament Based on Semantic Domains*, 1:423.

124. Moo, p. 136.

125. Zodhiates, p. 201.

126. Mitton, p. 141.

127. Adamson, p. 156.

128. Laws, p. 165.

129. Knowling, p. 91.

130. Mitton, p. 143.

131. Ropes, pp. 250-51.

132. Davids, *James*, New International Biblical Commentary, p. 91.

133. Plummer, 6:607.

PART 3 (4:1–5:12)

THE REACTIONS OF
LIVING FAITH TO WORLDLINESS

James introduces his lengthy discussion of faith's reactions to worldliness (4:1–5:12) without a connecting particle or the usual direct address "my brothers" (1:19; 2:1, 14; 3:1), both of which suggest a new beginning. The sudden transition from the beautiful picture in 3:17-18 of a life governed by heavenly wisdom to the appalling picture in the opening verses of chapter 4 is startling, but it demonstrates effectively the need for this vigorous rebuke now administered to the spirit of worldliness. The readers' turbulent relations, marked by "fights" and "quarrels," are due to their selfish attempts to gratify their base inner cravings. It is evidence that they are being governed by the spirit of worldliness. As "brothers" (v. 11) they belong to the family of God, but their efforts to satisfy their self-centered cravings, even when the results lead to quarrels and disputes, demonstrate that they are "double-minded" (4:8) and are guilty of an adulterous love for the world (4:4). Their selfish desires and self-centered cravings are manifestations of the fundamental nature of the world in its alienation from God.

Their circumstances reveal that as believers they are not dealing effectively with the conflicting tendencies of their inner nature. This conflict between the believer's lower and higher nature is depicted in Galatians 5:17-24. James already touched on the problem in 3:10 when rebuking their inconsistent use of their tongues. By faith, true believers have enthroned God as supreme in their lives, but in yielding to these self-centered demands of their old nature, they are allowing self to act as the governing force in their aspirations and activities. Acting in disregard of God's sovereign claims upon their lives, they are motivated by the spirit of worldliness. "The worldly person is the self-centered person."[1]

The spirit of worldliness has always been a problem for the church; it manifests itself in varied and often subtle ways. James discusses its manifestation in the lives of believers in four different areas. Worldliness reveals itself in their selfish strife (4:1-12), in an attitude of presumptuous self-sufficiency in business planning (4:13-17), in wrong reactions to experiences of injustice (5:1-11), and in the use of self-serving oaths (5:12).

NOTE FOR
Part 3

1. J. A. Motyer, *The Tests of Faith*, p. 82.

10

IX. THE REACTION OF
LIVING FAITH TO SELFISH STRIFE

4:1-12 What causes fights and quarrels among you? Don't they come from your desires that battle within you? ²You want something but you don't get it. You kill and covet, but you cannot have what you want. You quarrel and fight. You do not have, because you do not ask. ³When you ask, you do not receive, because you ask with wrong motives, that you may spend what you get on your pleasures.

⁴You adulterous people, don't you know that friendship with the world is hatred toward God? Anyone who chooses to be a friend of the world becomes an enemy of God. ⁵Or do you think Scripture says without reason that the spirit he causes to live in us tends toward envy, ⁶but he gives us more grace? That is why Scripture says:

> "God opposes the proud
> but gives grace to the humble."

⁷Submit yourselves, then, to God. Resist the devil, and he will flee from you. ⁸Come near to God, and he will come near to you. Wash your hands, you sinners, and purify your hearts, you double-minded. ⁹Grieve, mourn and wail. Change your laughter to mourning and your joy to gloom. ¹⁰Humble yourselves before the Lord, and he will lift you up.

¹¹Brothers, do not slander one another. Anyone who speaks against his brother or judges him, speaks against the law and judges it. When you judge the law, you are not keeping it, but sitting in judgment on it.¹² There is only one Lawgiver and Judge, the one who is able to save and destroy. But you— who are you to judge your neighbor?

James describes and rebukes their turbulent conditions that manifest the operation of worldliness in their midst (vv. 1-6), and then he exhorts his worldly-minded readers concerning their Godward and manward relations (vv. 7-12).

221

A. THE CONDITION MANIFESTING WORLDLINESS (vv. 1-6)

James first describes their turbulent manifestations of worldliness (vv. 1-3) and then severely rebukes their adulterous friendship with the world (vv. 4-6).

1. The Description of the Condition (vv. 1-3)

Two sharp questions identify the source of their turbulence (v. 1); two parallel sets of sequences delineate the outcome of their worldliness (v. 2*a*); and two incriminating reasons are pointed out for their condition (vv. 2*b*-3).

a. *The questions exposing the source* (v. 1). The opening question is frankly diagnostic: "What causes fights and quarrels among you?" (*pothen polemoi kai pothen machai en humin*). The absence of a finite verb and the repetition of the interrogative adverb *pothen*[1] add pungency to the question. Fully aware that all their conflicts are only symptomatic of something deeper, James goes right to the heart of their trouble. They are challenged to identify the true source of their "fights and quarrels." The plurals indicate that the reference is not to an isolated occurrence in their midst but to a chronic condition.

When used in combination, the first of these strong terms denotes the protracted state of hostility, while the latter points to the specific outbursts of hostility in active conflict.

This combination was used of literal political or national conflicts, but it also was used figuratively to denote feuds, conflicts, and open hostility among individuals and local groups. Those who take the terms to denote literal warfare point to the chaotic state of affairs in Palestine that surrounded James during the closing years of his life.[2] But since James is addressing Jewish Christians in the Dispersion, it is highly improbable that they were directly caught up in that turbulence. Nor does an early date for the letter fit into that scene. Certainly James is not dealing with the academic question of war, and it is most natural to see a reference to "the factional bickerings in the churches, the personal wrangles that embitter church life."[3] We have no explicit indication as to what these disputes were about. But, as Moo remarks, "James seems to be bothered more by the selfish spirit and bitterness of the quarrels than by the rights and wrongs of the various viewpoints."[4] This picture of open quarrels and bitter disputes among the readers of this letter at once dissipates any view that apostolic churches were ideal churches. Compare the conditions in the Corinthian church.

"Among you" (*en humin*) may be rendered "in you" and taken to refer to the old nature in the believer causing inner feelings of tension and frustration.[5] But the context makes clear that agitated community relations are in view. Some, such as Easton, hold that this picture is "grotesquely unsuited to members of the early Christian churches,"[6] and that the reference is to be taken of the communities as a whole.[7] But the use of "you" is best taken as restricting the reference to the readers of the epistle. Zodhiates suggests that by saying "among *you*" James "speaks as if he were outside that circle of fighters and disturbers."[8]

The second question challenges the readers to acknowledge the correctness of the diagnosis James is making: "Don't they come from your desires that battle within you?" The negative "don't they come from" (*ouk enteuthen*) not only calls for an affirmative answer but the added adverb *enteuthen*, not directly represented in the NIV rendering, catches up the thought of the previous *pothen*, "whence," and like a finger points to the true source. The unpleasant fact is that their turbulence comes "from" (*ek*, "out of") "your desires that battle within you." It derives not from "a noble fighting for the truth," nor an evil environment beyond their control, but from their own self-seeking desires.

"Desires" (*hēdonōn*), the term from which we derive our English term "hedonism," denotes the enjoyment derived from the fulfillment of one's desires or, as here, the craving for the pleasure itself. This hedonism, "the playboy philosophy that makes pleasure mankind's chief end, still wages battles in people's hearts."[9] The Greek term is rare in the New Testament,[10] always with a bad connotation, being "one of the many forces which belong to the world of unsanctified carnality, which strive against the work of God and His Spirit."[11] The cause of their widespread bellicosity lay in their strong desires to please themselves, the yearnings of self-love.

James continues his battle imagery in describing these pleasures as engaged in constant warfare. The appositional present participle *tōn strateuomenōn*, "that battle," depicts these pleasures as soldiers carrying on a military campaign aimed at securing the satisfaction of their cravings. This self-centered, pleasure seeking activity stands over against their proper submission to God (cf. v. 7). "The ultimate choice in life lies between pleasing oneself and pleasing God."[12]

"Within you" (*en tois melesin humōn*, literally "in your members") indicates that the thought now passes from their external conflicts to the inner basis of those conflicts. The noun "members," which James has already used for a part of the human body, denotes that their "desires" or cravings have their seat in the readers' bodily members. Their pleasures have their camp in the sensuous part of human anatomy. James recognizes the "human personality has, as it were, been invaded by an alien army which is always campaigning within it."[13] These conflicting cravings, which throw the individual into inner turmoil, are the expressions of the believer's old nature seeking self-satisfaction (Rom. 7:14-25; 8:6-7). But these cravings, rooted in their sensuous nature, in demanding gratification, actively enter into conflict with fellow believers who thwart the fulfillment of those desires. These outer conflicts reveal their inner tensions.

b. *The outcome of the condition* (v. 2*a*). The tragic result is graphically portrayed: "You want something but don't get it. You kill and covet, but you cannot have what you want. You quarrel and fight." This accumulation of verbs illustrates James's abrupt style. But the intended grouping of this series of finite verbs is not certain. The punctuation commonly used, as in NIV, draws "you kill and covet" closely together. But it is generally believed that to join "you covet" with the preceding strong "you kill" seems "intolerably harsh" and creates "an impossible anticlimax."[14] Smith thinks that the combination was deliberate because James "wanted to bring out the illogical sequences in the life devoted to pleasure."[15] Lenski holds that the incongruity is removed in recognizing a sigurative meaning for "kill";[16] but even then the verb "covet" seems extraordinarily tame after the strong imagery in "kill." Erasmus felt the inconsistency and conjectured that instead of *phoneuete* ("ye kill") we should read *phthoneite* ("ye envy").[17] This conjecture was accepted by Calvin[18] and appears in the KJV (ye "desire to have") as well as in the translations of Moffatt and of Schonfield.[19] It is supported by various commentators.[20] But this ingenious conjecture is devoid of all manuscript support. It is unwarranted to accept such an unfounded textual conjecture when an acceptable solution is available.

The fundamental problem is to determine the relationship of the series of verbs in the first half of verse 2. The NIV punctuates them as three separate sentences:

> You want something but don't get it.
> You kill and covet, but you cannot have what you want.
> You quarrel and fight.

But the simplest solution to this difficulty seems to be to place a strong punctuation after "you kill." Then the verbs naturally constitute two parallel series, resembling a couplet of Hebrew poetry. This view, accepted in the ASV, is made clearer by putting a period after "kill":

> Ye lust, and have not: ye kill.
> And ye covet and cannot obtain: ye fight and war.

The last element indicates the result of the previous verbs. This view has the support of various commentators.[21] It was adopted in the Greek text edited by Tasker,[22] is recognized in the margin of the Greek texts of Westcott and Hort, United Bible Societies, and Nestle-Aland, [23] and is used in numerous modern English versions.[24] We accept this punctuation as definitely preferable.

The first sequence, "You want something but don't get it: you kill," starts from the picture of their "desires" in verse 1. The present tenses are iterative, describing the repeated situation. "You want something" (*epithumeite*) is the verbal form of the noun used in 1:14; it means "to long for, strongly desire, crave for." The craving in itself may be either good or bad, but here it clearly has an evil connotation and so may be rendered "you crave or lust." What they lusted for is not stated, but verse 1 indicates that they were things that would minister to their own gratification. They sought satisfaction and self-advancement in preference to God's will and work.

"But don't get it" records that their self-seeking was often frustrated. This thought, mentioned thrice in this verse, underlines the fact that the methods they used did not bring the desired satisfactions. And when they did attain the thing fought for, they found that it did not yield the satisfaction anticipated. Roberts summarizes, "These people were hotly desiring but were unrequited and unsatisfied."[25] The aim to find true satisfaction through self-gratification is an ever eluding goal.

The failure to attain stirred a vicious reaction: "you kill." Some modern translations seek to soften the startling force of the term: "and so you are bent on murder" (NEB); "so you are ready to kill" (TEV). Some interpreters understand James to mean literal murder.[26] Moo concludes, "It is simplest to take 'murder' straightforwardly and to regard it as that extreme to which frustrated desire, if not checked, may lead."[27] But if James is addressing Christians, such a literal meaning is difficult to accept. Lenski discounts the view with the remark "For such murders the criminals would have been executed by the secular government."[28] Plummer proposed a semiliteral meaning for the term with the suggestion that defrauding the poor was the equivalent of destroying him, and cited Deuteronomy 24:6 and Ecclesiasticus 34:21-22 as support.[29] But such a means of destroying an opponent would be available only to the rich (cf. 5:4). It seems best to hold that James, like John (1 John 3:15), used the term figuratively; in Matthew 5:21-22, Jesus transferred the guilt from the outward act to the inner spirit. "Hate is potential murder."[30] This is consistent with the figurative usage of "wars" and "fightings" (ASV) in verse 1. The word "kill" is startling and was meant to startle; James sought to force his readers to realize the depth of the evil in their bitter hatred toward others.

The "and" (*kai*), connecting the second series of sequences with the first, seems somewhat awkward, but as a paratactic conjunction it may be rendered "also" or "indeed."[31]

You "covet, but you cannot have what you want." The finite verbs are again in the present tense and picture the repeated process. "Covet" (*zē-loute*) is the verbal form of the noun rendered "envy" in 3:14, 16. The essential significance of the term is a hot or intense feeling either for or against. Like the noun, the verb can have either a good or a bad connotation. As in Acts 7:9 and 1 Corinthians 13:4, it here has a bad force, "to be filled with jealousy, to envy" or "to covet" what someone has. In view of the following verb, the meaning is a hot desire to possess something for self-gratification.

"You cannot have what you want" pictures their repeated inability actually to possess that which they so ardently sought. Failure and frustration harass the self-centered life.

In reaction to this repeated frustration, "you quarrel and fight." These verbs, in reverse order, return to the picture in verse 1: "fights and quarrels among you." Here again the usage is metaphorical, pointing to the bitter quarrels and disputes that ensue. Winkler remarks, "This is the condition to which lust consigns its votaries; it disappoints them, and makes them mutual tormentors."[32]

c. *The reasons for the condition* (vv. 2b-3). Two reasons for their turbulent relations are named; they stand side by side as alternative explanations.

"You do not have, because you do not ask" (v. 2b). This third reference to their lack serves to hold before them their tragic spiritual condition. Instead of turning to God as the Giver of every good and perfect gift (1:17), they attempt to satisfy their gnawing wants through their own efforts. Their approach is self-centered and worldly. Instead of wrestling with God in prayer, they wrangle bitterly with men.

"Because you do not ask" need not mean that they were utterly prayerless, but apparently they felt it inappropriate to ask God for the things they had their heart set on. They devised carefully laid plans to attain their desires, but their ruthless efforts to achieve them in disregard of the rights of others resulted in failure and frustration. "Ask" (*aiteisthai*) is in the present tense and points to their repeated failure to ask; the middle voice implies an asking that involved their personal interests.[33] They failed to put into practice Jesus' teaching "Ask, and it shall be given you" (Matt. 7:7).

The second reason for their failure to gain their desires applies to a different group, those who have abandoned their failure to ask. "When you ask, you do not receive, because you ask with wrong motives" (v. 3a). James knew some did pray about the things they desired. They could honestly say that they did "ask" (*aiteite*) as a deliberate act. Although they made it a practice to ask, answers to their prayers were not forthcoming.

God does not answer all "prayers" directed to Him, for true prayer must meet His conditions. True prayer is always answered according to God's wisdom. Davids well notes,

> If prayer is no more than a formula (saying the right words, believe hard enough, confess; it will happen), then Christians are back to a type of magic: They can manipulate God or impose their will on God, for he *has* to answer. In contrast, New Testament prayer grows out of a trusting relationship with a father whose will is supreme.[34]

James 1:6 says effective prayer must be in faith, without doubting. Here James points to the need for proper motives in offering petitions to God. Their prayer was not wrong because it involved their personal concerns but because their motives were wrong, "because you ask with wrong motives." "With wrong motives" (*kakōs*) renders an adverb, standing emphatically before the verb, and means "in an evil manner, badly." Their petitions were motivated by a mean and unacceptable desire.

The nature of the evil is exposed in the added purpose clause, "that you may spend what you get on your pleasures." "On your pleasures" stands emphatically forward: "in order that in your pleasures you may spend (it)."[35] "In" (*en*) marks their "pleasures" (cf. v. 1) as the sphere where they intended to use the gift being asked of God. They are not accused of praying for sinful things, but their basic purpose in making their requests is to further their personal pleasures. It is possible to ask for good things for a bad reason. "To use what is requested from God in accordance with ungodly principles is a complete perversion of the relationship to God."[36] Their worldly, self-centered desires have invaded their prayer life and perverted their relation to God.

The gifts they are asking for they intend to "spend," (*dapanēsēte*, "spend freely,") on themselves. The verb, which in Luke 15:14 is used of the prodigal son, may here have the added connotation of wastefulness.[37] The aorist tense suggests that their intention to indulge in selfish pleasure was the unifying urge behind all their asking.

2. The Rebuke for the Condition (vv. 4-6)

The exposure of their worldliness is now followed by a sharp rebuke to the worldly-minded. The rebuke is administered in three areas. Their friendship with the world is spiritual adultery (v. 4), it disregards the warning of Scripture (v. 5a), and it evokes divine displeasure (vv. 5b-6).

a. *The adulterous character of worldliness* (v. 4). The writer's vigorous objection to their worldliness is immediately made clear by his stinging characterization of his readers: "You adulterous people." It makes clear that "he has broken off analysis and is now preaching repentance."[38] This startling designation reflects the readers' Jewish background; they would immediately see the import of the terminology.

The reading of the Textus Receptus, "Ye adulterers and adulteresses," is best understood as being a well-intentioned scribal addition because the term was understood literally; puzzled that only the women should be rebuked as guilty, the scribe added a reference to the men. The shorter reading is well supported by the textual witnesses, and all modern editors of the Greek text agree in accepting it as the original, "Adulteresses!"

Few modern commentators understand the term literally. Caton admits that the term may be used with a figurative meaning to denote idolatry, but he rejects a reference to idolatry since Israel no longer was guilty of idol worship and actively crusaded against idolatry.[39] But this fails to recognize the figurative import of the language here. The readers' worldly-mindedness was indeed spiritual idolatry. Oesterley accepts the shorter reading but holds that the women are singled out because they were so prominently connected with the moral depravity of the time.[40] Most naturally the term is here used in its deeper ethical or, more precisely, spiritual sense. This is in accord with the figurative use of "you kill" in verse 2.

The feminine form was used because of the very nature of this Old Testament figure. The nation of Israel was viewed as bound to Jehovah by the marriage tie, and any turning to idols by Israelites was stamped as spiritual adultery (Ps. 73:27; Isa. 54:5; 57:3-13; Jer. 3:20; Ezek. 16:6-29; 23:1-49; Hos. 9:1). Jesus Himself used the figure in Matthew 12:39; 16:4; and Mark 8:38. It also appears in Revelation 2:22. Thus the feminine was appropriate in view of Christ's relationship to His church (Eph. 5:22-32). But the plural here implies that James is directing his rebuke at those individuals who were unfaithful to their covenant with Christ as the Bridegroom of the church (cf. 2 Cor. 11:2). The figure aptly summarizes the condition rebuked in the remainder of verse 4. James lays upon their conscience the enormity of their sin with a question of rebuke and a ringing declaration of the significance of their attitude.

(1) The question of the rebuke (v. 4*a*). "Don't you know that friendship with the world is hatred toward God?" "Don't you know?" calls for an affirmative answer and implies that they have received instruction concerning the demands of Christian discipleship (Matt. 6:23-24; Luke 16:13). Their conscience will confirm that in their self-indulgence and love for the pleasures of the world they are unfaithful to the Lord to whom they have pledged their full allegiance (1 John 2:15). James's question to them implies that their friendship with the world was so pleasurable and acceptable that they had lost their consciousness of its sinfulness.

"Friendship with the world" points out the true nature of their pleasure-seeking activity. The noun "friendship" (*philia*) occurs only here in the New Testament, but the kindred word "friend" (*philos*) is common; both come from the common verb *phileō*, which means "to love, to have affection for"; it also means "to kiss" as an indication of affection. "Friendship" thus denotes an attitude that is marked by kindly regard and affection. "With the world" (*tou kosmou*, an objective genitive) marks the "world" as the object of this affection. Although the expression may involve a mutual relationship of affection, here the meaning is clearly that those being rebuked are entertaining a feeling of friendliness and affection for the world. "The world" here does not refer to the material creation but rather to the mass of unredeemed humanity as an egocentric world-system that is hostile to God. It is "a mighty flood of thoughts, feelings, principles of action, conventional prejudices, dislikes, attachments, which have been gathering around human life for ages, impregnating it, impelling it, moulding it, degrading it" (Liddon).[41] Its central aim is self-enjoyment and self-aggrandizement in disregard of or in open hostility toward God. To cultivate the world's friendship implies conformity to its principles and aims. To be controlled by the spirit of worldliness is wholly incompatible with loyalty to God; it makes them guilty of spiritual adultery.

Have they not realized that such an attitude on their part "is hatred toward God?" "Hatred" (*echthra*) denotes an attitude of personal hostility, the opposite of "friendship." "Toward God" (*tou theou*) is again the objective genitive, "enmity toward God." "The enmity is not on God's side but on that of the man who makes himself 'a friend of the world.'"[42] The definite article with "God" points to the God whom Christians openly acknowledge and to whom they have pledged their total allegiance. They cannot embrace both God and the world. As objects of fellowship and love, they are mutually exclusive (Rom. 8:5-8). In yielding to the spirit of the world, they are in fact taking up a position of opposition to God.

(2) The significance of their attitude (v. 4*b*). "Anyone who chooses to be a friend of the world becomes an enemy of God." The use of *oun*, "therefore," not in NIV, indicates that this solemn fact is the logical consequence of their attitude. The truth that the preceding question pressed upon their conscience is now stated as a general principle. "Anyone who chooses to be" (*hos ean boulēthē*)[43] leaves the statement general but makes it a matter that must be individually decided. The subjunctive mode leaves the decision open. The verb indicates that the decision to be made is a matter of the will after previous deliberation. The aorist subjunctive looks to the time of his decision whether he wishes or intends to be a friend of the world. Whenever the world's allurements lead a man to resolve deliberately to foster friendship with the world, he becomes guilty of unfaithfulness to God.

Whoever makes such a decision thereby "becomes an enemy of God." "An enemy of God," placed emphatically before the verb, states in concrete terms the implication of the previous abstract "hatred" or "enmity." The articular construction (*tou theou*) again points to personal identity, the God whom Christians know and acknowledge. By his decision he assumed a relationship to God that is the exact opposite of that recorded of Abraham, who was acknowledged as the "friend of God" (2:23).

"Becomes" (*kathistatai*), the very term used in 3:6, asserts that by his decision to foster friendship with the world the individual "becomes," "constitutes himself," or takes his stand as, God's enemy. The present tense points to the continuing condition, whereas the middle voice marks it as a self-chosen position. It is not a matter of a Christian quite unintentionally finding himself in an atmosphere pervaded by worldliness. He has made his deliberate choice to be a friend of the world. Neutrality Godward is impossible. His decision to love the world defies God's rightful claim to his total allegiance. As Moo remarks, "God will brook no rival, and when the believer behaves in a way that is characteristic of the world, he demonstrates that, at that point, his allegiance is to the world rather than to God."[44] The startling result of their attitude is a serious call to repentance.

b. *The authoritative message of Scripture* (v. 5a). "Or do you think Scripture says without reason . . . ?" "Or" introduces a question to prove that their reprehensible pursuit of friendship with the world may be looked at from another angle. The question probes their personal attitude toward the authoritative message of Scripture. "Do you think" (*dokeite*), do they hold it as their subjective opinion, that Scripture speaks "without reason?" "Without reason" (*kenōs*) stands emphatically forward, stressing that this is the point of concern. Is the message that Scripture declares "without reason," spoken in a hollow way to no purpose, so that it has no authoritative claim on our conduct? Gaebelein remarks, "While most Christians would answer with an emphatic 'No,' the honest reply, according to the practice of many a life, must be 'Yes.'"[45] James is probing an area that the Christian cannot disregard in daily life.

But what is the intended reference in "Scripture says" (*hē graphē legei*)? It is commonly assumed that the first part of verse 5 is a formula of quotation and that the latter half constitutes the quotation. This is in accord with Lightfoot's assertion "that the singular *graphē* ['scripture'] in the NT always means a *particular passage* of Scripture."[46] The NASB is representative of this view: "Or do you think that the Scripture speaks to no purpose: 'He jealously desires the Spirit which He has made to dwell in us'?" But the difficulty is that there is no scriptural passage, either Old or New Testament, that contains the words of the assumed quotation. Varied views have been advanced.

Improbable is the suggestion of some that the quotation that James has in mind is found in verse 6 and that the intervening matter is to be regarded as parenthetical.[47] But such a long parenthesis is not indicated in the text, and in the New Testament the quotation at once follows the introductory formula. This view also does not account for the introductory formula in verse 6.

Others, such as Dibelius,[48] hold that the quotation is from some unknown apocryphal work that James accepted as holy. He points to some close resemblances in the Shepherd of Hermas (c. A.D. 90-140) to support the existence of such an unknown work. Others have conjectured that James was referring to an unrecorded saying of Jesus. Guesses that the reference is to some New Testament passages have brought no agreement.[49] Blackman believes that any New Testament reference is improbable because of the clear quotation from the Old Testament in verse 6.[50]

Common is the view that James is paraphrasing some particular Old Testament passage. Various passages have been suggested: Genesis 6:3-5; 8:21; Numbers 11:29; Deuteronomy 5:9; 32:21; Psalm 119:20; Proverbs 21:10; Song of Solomon 8:6; Isaiah 63:8-16; Ezekiel 36:17; Zechariah 1:14; 8:2.[51] A recent nomination as to the source is Psalm 83.[52] Most probable is the view that James was not citing a particular passage but summarizing the truth expressed in several Old Testament passages.[53]

This bewildering array of views suggests that a different approach is called for. A simple solution is to hold that verse 5 consists of two independent sentences.[54] This solution is adopted in the ASV,[55] the MLB, and the versions by Darby, Phillips, and Rotherham.[56] This view relieves us of the apparently futile attempt to identify the source of the assumed quotation in the latter part of the verse. Nor is it necessary to hold that the singular "the scripture" demands a citation of some specific passage, as the dictum of Lightfoot asserts. It is true that in the singular some particular passage is generally in view; but as Arndt and Gingrich point out, in some passages the singular has the sense of a "designation of Scripture as a whole."[57] They refer to John 7:38, 42; Acts 8:32; Romans 4:3; 9:17; 10:11; Galatians 4:30; 1 Timothy 5:18, and the present passage as instances of this collective use of the singular. Lenski supports the view that verse 5 consists of two sentences by pointing out that the wording of the first part of the verse never occurs elsewhere as a formula of quotation; he insists, "If a quotation were to follow, we should certainly expect the addition, 'saying that.'"[58]

When the first part of verse 5 is accepted as a separate question, by "the scripture" James is seen to refer to the teaching of the Scriptures as a whole, which supports the truth already declared in verse 4, that man cannot love both God and the world at the same time. If the readers are prone to question the truth of what James had just said, as might be implied from their conduct, does that mean that they regard the teaching of Scripture—that worldliness and godliness cannot exist together—as without abiding authority? We accept the rendering of the ASV, which makes two sentences of verse 5, as the most probable solution.[59]

a. *The divine response to the worldly* (vv. 5b-6). Having rebuked their worldliness as spiritual adultery (v. 4) and a disregard for the teaching of Scripture (v. 5a), James adds a third rebuke; it evokes God's adverse response (vv. 5b-6). He speaks of the reaction of the indwelling Spirit (vv. 5b-6a) and quotes the Old Testament as confirming that God's response to man is in accord with man's inner attitude (v. 6b).

(1) The yearning of the Spirit (vv. 5b-6a). "That the spirit he causes to live in us tends toward envy?" The interpretation of this sentence is beset with great difficulty. The interpreters agree with Plummer that the passage in verses 5-6 is "the most difficult in this Epistle, and one of the most difficult in the whole New Testament."[60]

The word order in the original, not obvious from the NIV, is clearly reproduced in R. Young's rendering, "To envy earnestly desireth the spirit that did dwell in us."[61] The main verb, "earnestly desires" (*epipothei*), is a strong term. The preposition (*epi*), according to Vincent, gives it a directive force, "to long for, yearn after"; but others, like Zodhiates, hold the more probable view that its force is intensive, "to long for greatly, to crave," as expressing "the greatest possible desire and yearning."[62] The verb occurs only here in James, but, as Knowling notes, it "is frequently used elsewhere in the NT and always in a good sense, as also its cognate substantive and adjective."[63] Ropes remarks that the term denotes "the longing affection of the lover."[64]

This longing is limited by a prepositional phrase, "toward envy" (*pros phthonon*), which stands emphatically before the verb as the first part of the sentence. This prepositional phrase, which does not occur elsewhere in the New Testament, may be viewed in two different ways. Interpreted strictly as a prepositional phrase, the preposition *pros* with the accusative indicates the direction toward which the envying looks or moves: "tends toward envy" (NIV); or "turns towards envious desires" (NEB). The expression also can be taken as adverbial in force, "jealously" or "enviously." But does this expression denote an evil or a justifiable feeling? Trench concluded that the noun used by James (*phthonon*) "is used always and only in an evil signification."[65] So understood, the yearning depicts an undesirable human disposition and could not be ascribed to God or the Holy Spirit. Ropes notes that the noun primarily means "ill will, malice," but he concludes that the expression here means "begrudgingly," as describing a begrudging spirit as shown in a refusal to share with another.[66] (This was a recognized meaning of the cognate verb in classical Greek.) Carson notes that the term "was used of the jealous feeling of a lover towards a rival."[67] Further, the nouns *phthonos* [envy] and *zēlos* [zeal, jealousy] were sometimes used interchangeably. "*Phthonos* was occasionally used in Greek writers of the jealousy of the Olympian gods,"[68] and both terms were "often used for the 'jealousy' of God (1 Mac. 8:16; *T. Sim.* 4.5; *T. Gad.* 7.2; *1 Clem.* 3.2; 4.7; 5.2)."[69] So understood, the expression could be used to describe God's unwillingness to share man's affections with the world. (See the second marginal reading in NIV.)

The fact that "the spirit" (*to pneuma*) may grammatically be either the subject or object of the verb, and may mean either the human spirit or the divine Spirit, further complicates the interpretation. The noun is modified by the relative clause "[which] he causes to live in us" (*ho katōkisen en hēmin*). The subject of this verb is not stated, but obviously it is God. A textual problem is connected with this verb. "Causes to live" (*katōkisen*) is accepted as the original reading by all modern editors of the Greek text, whereas the Textus Receptus has a cognate form (*katōkēsen*) meaning "to live, dwell, inhabit." The latter merely records the fact of the spirit's indwelling; the aorist tense looks back to the time of its commencement. Manuscript evidence is divided, but the former verb has somewhat better support. Since the former verb occurs only here in the New Testament, it is transcriptionally more probable that the copyists would replace the less common verb with the more familiar form. The reading "causes to live" rules out any thought that the spirit is satanic. "In us" may denote "us" as believers or as human beings.

When the second half of verse 5 is accepted as a separate sentence, is it to be punctuated as a question or as a declarative statement? The ASV makes it a question, but its contents may equally be regarded as a declarative statement.[70] Its close connection with the statement in the first part of verse 6 supports the view that this is also a statement of fact. We accept it as a statement of fact made by James.

In view of the grammatical structure, there are four possibilities as to the intended meaning:

1. The human spirit as the object of the main verb: "He [God] yearns enviously for the spirit which He caused to dwell in us." Then the meaning is that God, who placed man's spirit in him at creation, longs for its total loyalty and devotion to Him.

2. The divine Spirit as the object of the verb: "He [God] yearns enviously for the Spirit which He caused to dwell in us." But it is difficult to see how one member of the Trinity should be pictured as enviously longing for another. This alternative is highly improbable.

3. The human spirit as the subject of the main verb: "The spirit which He made to dwell in us longs enviously." Then the meaning is that the human spirit, imparted at creation, longs perversely for enjoyment of the world's pleasures, even to the point of envy. Then James charges his readers with perverseness in being cool toward God while yearning for the world's pleasures.

4. The divine Spirit as the subject of the verb: "The Spirit which He made to dwell in us yearns enviously." Then the meaning is that the Holy Spirit, imparted to us by God at conversion, yearns enviously for our total loyalty and devotion to Him. The incoming Holy Spirit, who sealed our redemption, justly claims our undivided love. He can brook no rival for our affection. The only reference to the Holy Spirit in this epistle is under the second and fourth views.

In view of the rebuke to worldliness that James is administering to his Christian readers, the last view seems most probable. Then this reference to the Holy Spirit's reaction to their worldliness fittingly expresses a further ground for censure. This view harmonizes with the natural force of the relative clause. The assertion that God caused the Spirit to dwell in believers is a central teaching of the New Testament (Acts 5:32; Rom. 8:11; Gal. 4:6; 2 Tim. 1:14). The better-attested verb "causes to live" (*katōkisen*) most naturally points to a distinctive experience that is not true of all men and is best taken as referring directly to the Spirit's impartation at regeneration. This view also gives the most natural meaning to "us" as restricted to Christians. This picture of the Holy Spirit's yearning for the undivided love of His people, and grudgingly refusing to yield to a rival, is consistent with the statement in Galatians 5:17 concerning the Spirit's opposition to the lusts of the flesh. This view also is supported by the assertion in the first part of verse 6, which stands in close connection with verse 5*b*.

"But he gives us more grace" (v. 6*a*) adds an assuring note. The NIV makes these words part of the question of verse 5. But with most other mod-

ern translations it is better to accept these words as a definite assertion. "But" (*de*) suggests a contrast; if a contest is intended, it is between the yearning of the Spirit and the unmerited grace He continues to give to the worldly-minded. But the conjunction seems rather to have a continuative force, indicating that something further must be said to complete the picture. Lenski renders it "moreover."[71] The subject of the verb "he gives" is left unexpressed, but it is so obviously God that James did not feel the necessity of mentioning it. The reference can be either to the Father or to the Spirit, probably the former; but in this statement of Christian experience, no sharp distinction need be sought. When the world competes for our love for God, resulting in our divided loyalty, God does not immediately cast us off but continues to give "more grace."

"More grace" (*meizona charis*) is literally "greater grace," but the point of the comparative form is not indicated. Greater than what? Johnstone thinks the comparative indicates that God's grace is "greater than the strength of depravity, greater than the power of the spirit of darkness, from whom temptations to envy and all forms of worldliness come."[72] Mitton suggests that the comparative may be loosely used to mean "more and more grace" or "abundant grace."[73] But the expression seems to point to a comparison with some other measure of grace. Perhaps the thought is that because of their worldliness, God graciously works in their lives so that they actually experience a greater measure of His grace than they would otherwise have been conscious of. "Where sin abounded, grace did abound more exceedingly" (Rom. 5:20*b*). "God's desire to forgive is a precept upon which his [James's] whole book is based (5:19-20)."[74] "Grace" here seems to suggest the thought of God's "gracious gift" of help (cf. Heb. 4:16). It may be understood in a very concrete sense as the practical equivalent of His power; His grace works in them the desire and ability to surrender completely to God's love and to serve Him with their whole heart. This brief statement has been called "one of the mostly comforting verses in Scripture."[75]

(2) The verification from Scripture (v. 6*b*). "That is why Scripture says: 'God opposes the proud but gives grace to the humble.'"

"That is why" (*dio*), "because of this, for this reason," introduces scriptural verification of the truth just presented (vv. 5*b*-6*a*). God's attitude toward an individual is determined by the person's inner attitude. This involves both a threat and a promise.

The formula of the quotation "Scripture says" (*legei*) leaves the subject unexpressed. The intended subject is either "the scripture"[76] or "he," that is, God through His Spirit.[77] Alford holds that "he says" is preferable as bringing out the thought that "the same Spirit who is implanted in us speaks in Scripture."[78] (Compare the identical form in Eph. 4:8; 5:14.) But others prefer the impersonal "it."[79]

The quotation is taken from Proverbs 3:34 in the Septuagint, except that James changes "Lord" to "God." (The same variation occurs in 1 Peter 5:5.) The Septuagint rendering of the first part is an interpretation of the Hebrew. The quotation aptly continues the previous warning but also clearly states the good news of God's grace to those with a humble attitude. In now quoting this double scriptural assertion immediately after the blessed assurance "but he gives us more grace," James reminds his readers, "Here is grace abundant, but in order that you make it yours you need a certain kind of receptacle."[80] The experience of God's grace is conditioned by the attitude of the human heart.

"God opposes the proud" is a solemn warning. The definite article with "God" (*ho theos*) makes it specific, the God to whom as believers they have pledged their allegiance and who is now confronting them in their worldliness.

"The proud" (*huperēphanois*) is placed next to the subject and without an article stresses the character rather than the identity of those whom God resists. The adjective designates individuals who are "proud, haughty, and arrogant" in their attitude. Formed from the preposition *huper*, "over, beyond," and the verb *phainomai*, "to appear, to show oneself," it denotes "one who shows himself above his fellows."[81] Feeling himself conspicuously above others, he assumes an attitude of haughty superiority and pride. As Wolff notes, "The word reflects a false self-estimate which manifests itself in arrogance. The emphasis of the Greek word falls on thought, not speech, as an attitude cherished in the secrecy of the heart."[82] Gripped with a false sense of self-sufficiency, he regards himself as the standard of excellence and disdains those who fall short of the standard. It is an attitude of self-glorification, an attempt to disown his dependence on God. "The proud man cuts himself off from all the salutary effects of rebuke, criticism, and counsel."[83]

Such an attitude God "opposes" (*antitassetai*). Composed of the preposition *anti*, "opposite, over against," and the middle voice of the verb *tassō*, "to station, order, arrange," the verb vividly pictures God as placing Himself in battle array against such an individual. God is the active antagonist of the proud and self-sufficient.

"But" (*de*) introduces the contrasting message of encouragement: God "gives grace to the humble." He continually imparts His grace to those who take a lowly position and have a humble attitude. This quality of humility is stressed by the absence of an article (*tapeinois*) as well as its forward position in the sentence "to lowly ones He gives grace." The humble, deeply conscious of their sinfulness and need, gladly acknowledge their dependence on God and rest in His all-sufficiency. Like empty vessels, they are ready to receive His grace, and His help goes far beyond anything they deserve or can rightly expect.

God's free grace is never intended to make men think lightly of sin. The promise of grace is the basis for the injunctions that follow (vv. 7-12).

B. THE EXHORTATIONS TO THE WORLDLY (vv. 7-12)

Having diagnosed their selfish strife as a manifestation of worldliness and shown the seriousness of their condition, James at once calls for rectification. "Then" (*oun*, "therefore, consequently") indicates that his injunctions are prompted by the condition just exposed. Having yielded to the world's allurements, they had to be restored to the pathway of separation. They had to resume a right relation to God (vv. 7-10) and cease their censoriousness of their brethren (vv. 11-12).

1. The Call to Return to God (vv. 7-10)

The ten aorist imperatives in these verses constitute an urgent call to repentance to correct their blameworthy position before God. These imperatives, like curt military commands, demand incisive action. They reflect the seriousness with which James viewed their double-mindedness. Verse 7 sets forth the basic requirement, while verses 8-10 identify specific elements required for a renewed attitude Godward.

a. *The statement of the basic demand* (v. 7). The demand is twosided: "Submit yourselves, then, to God. Resist the devil." "Submit yourselves to God" as an aorist imperative conveys a sense of urgency, demanding immediate compliance. The compound verb (*hupotagēte*), consisting of the preposition *hupo*, "under," and *tassō*, "to order, place, station," demands that they accept their proper station under God as their captain. The passive is to be understood in the sense of the middle, calling for an action that centers on ourselves. "It is an action that we must bring about ourselves as the Holy Spirit operates in us."[84] It is a call for their voluntary subordination to God and His will. God does not want forced obedience. Thus they must express their recognition of God as supreme in their lives. This subordination, so hard for the proud and self-reliant, is essential to cure their worldliness. "Submission to God is the beginning, middle, and end of the prodigal's return from disastrous familiarity with the world to the security of the Father's home."[85] The kindred compound verb in verse 6 warned that because of their friendship with the world, God was arraying Himself against them as their antagonist; that situation had to be rectified by their act of submitting themselves to God in total loyalty to Him.

"Resist the devil" states the other side of the basic demand. By his use of *de*, not represented in the NIV rendering, James reminds that this is a further matter required of them. Wholehearted submission to God is only possible as they resist God's archenemy. "Resist" (*antistēte*), composed of *anti*, "against," and the verb *histēmi*, "to stand," continues the military metaphor; as a definite act, they must take their stand in opposition to "the devil" as their true enemy. There is no middle ground. Instead of their conflicts with each other, here is "the true field for the exercise of the combative element which enters into man's nature."[86] Let them wholeheartedly participate in this "perpetual resistance movement."[87]

The Greek term rendered "the devil" (*tō diabolō*) means "the slanderer" and gives a description of his principal activity. But James here simply thinks of him as God's enemy and does not stress that activity. In the Septuagint, this Greek term is used almost uniformly to render the Hebrew term *Satan*.[88] But the articular designation, in the context, makes it unmistakable that James thinks of the devil, the chief power of evil, as a person.[89] As God's inveterate enemy, he is constantly engaged in seeking to subvert the allegiance of God's people by leading them to self-centered and world-centered attitudes and activities. "Satan is the prime and most perfect *enemy of God*, the beginner and finisher of all *pride* leading to apostasy from the Supreme, to whom all things should be *submissive*."[90]

The added promise "and he will flee from you" assures them that successful resistance to this mighty enemy is possible. "And" indicates that the promised victory is based upon active resistance to the devil. An attitude of indecision and doubt when facing the devil makes him bold and aggressive in his attacks, but confronting him with a resolute will and firm confidence in God's promise unmasks him as a coward. Our Lord's victory over the devil (Matt. 4:1-11; Mark 3:22-27), reaching its culmination in the cross (John 12:31-33), has left Satan a defeated foe. When confronted with the whole armor of God and the sword of the Spirit (Eph. 6:12-17), the devil acknowledges his defeat in abrupt flight. He cannot lead a man into sin without the consent of the man's will. As long as a man's will is submissive to the control and guidance of the Holy Spirit, he can stand victorious against all the seductive arts of the devil. As a defeated foe Satan now has no power over the Christian except the power of seduction. But he is a persistent foe. When confronted with the sword of the Spirit he surely flees, but "he returns again and again, sometimes, immediately after the most shameful defeat."[91]

b. *The elaboration of specific requirements* (vv. 8-10). Involved in the basic demand of verse 7 are various injunctions to be obeyed. Involved are a wholehearted return to God (v. 8*a*), personal cleansing (v. 8*b*), open repentance (v. 9), and humility (v. 10).

(1) Nearness to God (v. 8*a*). "Come near to God" indicates that their worldliness has resulted in a distance separating them from God. They must return to an intimate relationship with Him. The aorist imperative calls for a decisive, complete return on their part. This does not mean that the initiative for restored relations lies with man, but the imperative is a call to man's will to respond to the divine call. "Come near" (*enggisate*, "approach, draw near") was used in the Septuagint of the priests in the Tabernacle, duly qualified to approach God with their sacrifices (Lev. 10:3; 21:21-23); it also was used in a wider sense of man's approach to God in worship (Isa. 29:13; Hos.

12:6). Thus the term conveys the thought of entering into communion with God as acceptable worshipers. Such drawing near to God marks "those who long to come into the closest possible relation to Him, in contrast to those who are His enemies and who keep at a distance from Him.[92]

Their sincere approach is assured of God's favorable response: "and he will come near to you." Like the returning prodigal (Luke 15:20), they will find God waiting to welcome and restore them.

(2) Personal cleansing (v. 8*b*). Their worldliness has left them polluted; personal cleaning is needed. This demand for cleansing is stated in the form of a poetic parallelism: "Wash your hands, you sinners, and purify your hearts, you double-minded." As Moo notes, "Blunt vividness is given the two clauses in the Greek by the lack of any articles or possessive pronouns."[93] Only the pure in hand and heart can enter into communion with God in His holiness.

The injunction "wash your hands" employs the language of ceremonial cleansing for the priestly approach to God (Ex. 30:19-21; Lev. 16:4), but it is now employed with a moral connotation to denote a definite cleansing from the defilement of sin (2 Cor. 7:1). This figurative usage appears in the Old Testament (Ps. 24:4; Isa. 1:15-16). As the instruments of ethical conduct, their "hands" are symbolic of their defiling deeds. The aorist active imperative presents this as their personal duty. They must act to cleanse their hands by withdrawing them from every evil deed and from reaching after the world's contaminating pleasures. Perhaps James is thinking of the Jewish custom of praying with uplifted hands (Pss. 28:2; 134:2; 1 Tim. 2:8).

The sharp address "you sinners" (*hamartōloi*) seems to be used deliberately to pierce the readers' conscience. Although commonly used of the unsaved, the parallel with "double-minded" makes clear that James is applying the term to Christians. They are manifestly guilty of sin in failing to maintain God's standard for His saints. In his use of the term here, James clearly indicates that their return to close communion with God demands a change in their worldly conduct.

"Purify your hearts" again employs familiar Jewish ceremonial language (cf. John 11:55), but here, as in 1 Peter 1:22 and 1 John 3:3, it has a moral meaning, calling for inner purification. The term basically denotes a removal of that which disqualifies one for acceptable worship, resulting in a condition of purity and chastity. The "heart" again denotes their whole inner life (cf. 1:26; 3:14). As those who foster friendship with the world and are guilty of spiritual adultery, they need an inner purification, renewing total dedication to God. A similar purity of hand and heart is called for in Psalm 24:4 for those approaching God.

"You double-minded," literally "two-souled" (cf. 1:8), reproves them sharply for their divided affections: hankering for the world while trying to hold to God. They are guilty of trying to serve two masters (Matt. 6:24). God demands undivided affection as well as undefiled conduct.

(3) Open repentance (v. 9). Three further aorist imperatives without any modifiers, "grieve, mourn and wail," unite to form an urgent demand for open and thorough repentance. The intensity of the demand is startling, intended to shake these double-minded believers.

"Grieve" (*talaipōrēsate*), "be wretched, be afflicted," calls for a recognition of their wretchedness and shame because of their sins. The verb, which occurs only here in the New Testament, primarily denotes going through hardship and distressing circumstances; then it came to be used of the feeling of misery and wretchedness because of the outward circumstances. Ropes renders it "Make yourselves wretched,"[94] but there is no indication that James is calling for ascetic practices, such as fasting in sackcloth and ashes, to induce this feeling. Mayor holds that, since James was known for his asceticism, this imperative "is best understood of voluntary abstinence from comforts and luxuries."[95] Well aware that such practices were no satisfactory substitute for inner penitence, James is best understood as calling for a deeper inner feeling of wretchedness and shame because of their sins. The aorist imperative is probably ingressive: "become wretched." When a true realization of their sinfulness strikes home, the feeling of wretchedness and grief will follow.

"Mourn and wail" denote the natural outward manifestations of their sense of wretchedness. The verbs often are used together to portray the intensity of such a feeling (Mark 16:10; Luke 6:25; Rev. 18:15). "Mourn" relates to the general outward demeanor of those gripped by deep grief. Trapp remarks that it "imports a funeral-grief."[96] It indicates a grief of such intensity that it cannot be concealed.[97] "Wail" points to the resultant overflow of tears. The verb was used of wailing for the dead, but here it means crying or sobbing because of sin and shame. Such tears are "a sign that a man is broken to pieces because of sin."[98] The two verbs picture the emotional expressions of penitence, as Peter sobbing in shame when seized with a realization of his sin in denying Jesus (Mark 14:72).

"Change your laughter to mourning" calls for a striking reversal in their emotional expressions. "Laughter" (*gelōs*), occurring only here in the New Testament,[99] looks to their loud, unseemly gaiety as pleasure-loving friends of the world. Their hilarity will become mourning when the realization of their folly seizes them (Prov. 10:23; Eccles. 7:6). The verb "change" (*metatrapetō*), "turn back, turn around," occurs only here in the New Testament.[100] The aorist passive third person singular points to a force outside of themselves producing the reversal, whereas the imperative calls upon their will to let it work. The change will occur as Spirit-wrought conviction seizes them. The demanded reversal relates to their past sinful pleasures. This does not mean that laughter in itself is evil (cf. Ps. 126:2), nor is James prohibiting future laughter for his readers. "James is no killjoy," Moo asserts and then points out, "But 'laughter' in the Old Testament and Judaism is often the scornful laughter of the fool (Ec. 7:6; Ecclus. 27:13) who blithely refuses to take sin seriously."[101]

"And your joy to gloom" indicates a parallel reversal. "Joy" looks back to their inner feeling that expressed itself in laughter. This "joy" (*hē chara*)[102] must become "gloom" (*katēpheian*), "gloominess, dejection." The noun, used only here in the New Testament, denotes the downcast expression caused by a heavy heart. It is the picture of the publican in Luke 18:13 who acknowledged himself as "the sinner" (*ho hamartōlos*) and in shame would not lift his eyes heavenward.

(4) Godly humility (v. 10). "Humble yourselves before the Lord" calls for their acceptance of this attitude. The aorist passive may be understood in the sense of the middle "humble yourselves," but it could mean "allow yourselves to be humbled." It is not to be a forced humiliation, but a voluntary self-abasement. The preposition "before" (*enōpion*, "in the sight of") suggests the thought of being under the eye of "the lord" (*kuriou*), their heavenly Master in all His ineffable majesty. The sense of their own utter unworthiness in His presence can only induce humility. In speaking of "the Lord" without the article, James is simply thinking of the living God who has revealed Himself in Christ Jesus our "Lord."

"And he will lift you up" adds a precious promise. "The picture," Davids points out, "is that of someone prostrate before an oriental monarch, begging mercy. The monarch leans down from the throne and lifts the petitioner's face from the dust. The person rises with grateful joy, knowing he or she is forgiven."[103] This divine lifting up of the humble constituted a searching challenge to James's self-seeking readers. The true way to exaltation leads through the valley of humility. It reflects Jesus' teaching in Matthew 23:12 and Luke 14:11 and would be familiar to the Jewish readers from their Old Testament (Job 5:11; Pss. 147:6; 149:4; Ezek. 21:26). The promised exaltation begins with the experience of pardoning grace restoring the penitent sinner to a position of favor with God and producing an inner consciousness of liberty and exaltation; it will come to its outward future consummation when our Lord returns and His saints are manifested with Him in glory (Col. 3:4; 2 Thess. 1:10).

2. The Injunction Against Censoriousness (vv. 11-12)

Although no connecting particle is used, there is no need to assume that these verses begin a new section of the epistle.[104] That there is a connection with what has gone before is generally recognized. If these verses are regarded as closely connected with verse 10, they may be seen as showing the result when humility is lacking.[105] Ropes thinks of them as a loosely con-nected "sort of appendix,"[106] and Robertson stamps them as "a sort of post-script on the tongue."[107] It seems simplest to regard these verses as a continuation of the exhortations to the worldly begun with verse 7. Verses 7-10 looked Godward, these verses manward. The people's rectification of their relationship upward involves the need to terminate their censorious-ness manward. James states bluntly the prohibition against censoriousness (v. 11*a*) and justifies the prohibition (vv. 11*b*-12).

a. *The statement of the prohibition* (v. 11*a*). The prohibition beginning this verse may more literally be rendered "Do not be speaking evil of one another, brothers." The prohibition (*mē katalaleite*), the only imperative in these verses, stands in marked contrast to the ten aorist imperatives of verses 7-10. The present tense denotes that this evil is an habitual practice among them, whereas the *mē* demands that it be terminated. Apparently the refer-ence is to the major way in which their "fights and quarrels" (v. 1) expressed themselves. The compound verb literally means to "speak down on" (com-pare the common expression "running each other down") and is broader than "slander" in the NIV rendering. Basically meaning to "speak evil of," Wolff notes that such evil speaking "includes (1) willful false accusations, (2) exaggerations of faults that are real, (3) needless repetition of real faults, (4) slander."[108] It thus denotes critical, derogatory speech that is maliciously in-tended to influence others against the person being spoken against. It is gen-erally assumed that the harsh, critical remarks are about someone absent. It is the temper that deliberately calls attention to the faults of others while minimizing their virtues. Kittel notes that the essence of the evil lies in the preposition *kata*, "down, against," and that the point is not the falsity of what is said but rather its uncharitableness.[109] The evil lies in the speaker's hostile intention, aimed at eroding the position or character of the one spoken against. It is an activity related closely to the work of the devil, the slanderer (cf. v. 7).

This term is used in 1 Peter 2:12 and 3:16 to describe the persecution of Christians by non-Christians. That the Christian readers addressed by James were guilty of this malicious evil of speaking against "one another" (*allē-lōn*)[110] indicates how strained their mutual relations were. The reciprocal pronoun declares that the practice was not one-sided; those who have thus suffered from opponents are using it against them. This picture should help us understand the strong language in verses 1-3. The address "brothers," placed after the verb, forms a rebuke of their unbrotherly practice and pre-pares the way for the pathetic repetition of the term in this paragraph.

Kittel notes that this evil was not stressed "in the ethical exhortations of the non-biblical world" and that "even the lists of vices in the Stoics and Philo do not contain it." In contrast, he notes that the unusual frequency with which the subapostolic Fathers referred to this sin shows that it was emerging in these churches but also indicates "how seriously the command against evil-speaking was still taken."[111]

b. *The justification for the prohibition* (vv. 11*b*-12). James first states objectively the significance of this evil practice: "Anyone who speaks against his brother or judges him, speaks against the law and judges it." "Anyone who speaks" (*ho katalalōn*), an articular present participle, denotes that his derogatory speech is characteristic or habitual. It "does not refer to an occasional slip of the tongue, but to habitual slipping, to constant criticizing and judging."[112] The object of his censorious words is "his brother" (*adelphou*), a fellow Christian. The absence of the article does not necessarily make the term indefinite but rather marks the qualitative relation; he is one who also is a member of the Christian brotherhood. The speaker habitually watches another who is a "brother" in order to criticize him.

"Or judges him" (*ē krinōn ton adelphon autou*, more literally, "or judging his brother") continues the picture of his censoriousness. The conjunction "or" may be disjunctive to denote a separate and distinct activity, but it is better to take it as conjunctive to denote that it is the same activity viewed from a different angle.[113] This is in accord with the fact that both participles are under the government of one article. With "judges" the thought shifts from his malicious activity against a brother to his condemnation of "his brother." This repeated use of "brother," omitted in the NIV, strengthens the fact of the brotherhood of believers. "His" (*autou*) stresses their oneness as brothers and intensifies the evil of his practice. This condemnation "does not imply flabby indifference to the moral condition of others nor the blind renunciation of attempts at a true and serious appraisal of those with whom we have to live."[114] James condemns the critical evaluation because of the evil intention of the critic.

"Speaks against the law and judges it" (*katalalei nomou kai krinei nomon*, "speaks against [the] law and judges [the] law") unveils the deep meaning of the reprehensible practice. James might have condemned it as a revelation of personal lovelessness; instead, he related it to "the law" and, beyond that, to God. Both occurrences of "the law" are without the article here, thus keeping the thought purely qualitative. The reference is not to the Mosaic law but rather to the law governing the Christian life that James has already spoken of as "the perfect law, the law of liberty" (1:25) and "the royal law," that is, the law of Christian love (2:8). Now he thinks of it simply as having the force of "law" for believers. Its characteristic quality is that they must love their neighbor as themselves (Lev. 19:18; Matt. 22:39; Rom. 13:8-10; Gal. 5:14). The vicious speaking against a brother is a violation of this law of love. "All law demands obedience and deliberate transgression says in effect that the law is bad, too strict perhaps, and that our standard is superior."[115] In his practice this critic opposes the God-given law governing relations among the brethren. In thus violating this law of brotherhood, he in effect criticizes the law, implying that it is not good and should be abrogated. His practice as a Christian suggests that presumably he claims to be acting according to higher principles. "However high and orthodox our view of God's law might be," Moo remarks, "a failure actually to do it says to the world that we do not *in fact* put much store by it."[116] For James, a living faith is an obedient faith.

Another line of exposition, followed by Oesterley[117] and Carr,[118] holds that the reference is to the Mosaic law and the problem of its observance by Christians. Carr thinks some of the Jewish Christians, foreseeing the law's transitory character, were with inappropriate zeal condemning the continued observance of the Mosaic law and were speaking against those brethren whose conscience led them to observe it. He holds that James believes its observance is still binding on believers and regards those who speak against its observance as judging the law. He holds that the law, given by God, is binding until God Himself changes it. Oesterley thinks the problem is concerning what is involved in the keeping of the law; those who follow one school of interpretation condemn others, whose understanding of the law leads them to act contrary to what they hold is demanded. These issues might have arisen among the Jewish Christians addressed, but nothing is in the context to suggest either view. It does not agree with the use of the word "law" by James elsewhere or with the meaning of "speak against" as malicious criticism of others.

James restates the significance of their censoriousness in personal terms: "When you judge the law, you are not keeping it, but sitting in judgment on it." The opening *de*, not in the NIV, apparently suggests a contrast, but these words are rather a restatement; it is better to take the conjunction simply as transitional in force and render "now" or "and." "When you judge" (*ei*, "if" with the indicative) introduces a first class conditional construction that assumes the condition is true to fact. But in now using the second person singular verb, "you," James confronts his readers individually. He calls upon the guilty readers individually to judge themselves in light of the statement being made.

His censorious evaluation of his brother indicates that in attitude he is opposed to the royal law of love and implies that he is exempt from obeying it. When in actual practice he is not keeping it, "but sitting in judgment on it" (*krinei nomon*, "judges [the] law"), he reveals his true character. "Law," again without the article, is qualitative, marking him in practice as a "lawless" individual. In thus setting himself above the law, he usurps the office of the judge whose function is to determine whether a man's actions come under the authority of a certain law. In effect, he proposes that he is qualified to enact a better law. He is usurping the prerogatives of the divine Lawgiver.

Let such arrogance face the solemn reality: "There is only one Lawgiver and Judge, the one who is able to save and destroy" (v. 12*a*). God alone is the ultimate source of all law and authority.

In the assertion "there is only on Lawgiver and Judge," the numeral "one" (*heis*) may be taken as the subject of the verb "is" or as a numeral describing the predicate nominative "Lawgiver and Judge." Huther holds that "the chief accent lies on *heis*, in opposition to men who presume to be judges"[119] and supports the rendering "one is the lawgiver and judge." This rendering strongly underlines the truth of monotheism. This sets God in contrast to those of His creatures who through their evil-speaking of their fellow brothers usurp the divine prerogative. It is utter folly for finite human beings to attempt to assume His distinctiveness as "Lawgiver and Judge."[120] The NIV rendering, "there is only one Lawgiver and Judge," accepts the numeral *heis* as descriptive of the predicate nominative and stresses that as the only Lawgiver and Judge all of His laws are harmonious and all judgment is in perfect accord with His nature and actions. His uniqueness as Lawgiver and Judge belong together; God gives the law and God enforces the law.

This unique and sovereign God is further identified as "the one who is able to save and destroy." "The one who is able" (*ho dunamenos*), an articular present participle, stands in apposition to "One" as further establishing His uniqueness. He unfailingly possesses the ability to carry out His purposes, thus confirming His exclusive prerogatives as "Lawgiver and Judge." As Lawgiver He declares His will for His creatures, and as Judge He upholds and enforces His revealed will.

"To save and destroy" summarizes God's exercises of His sovereign power. The two aorist infinitives indicate that God's decisions are effectively executed in any given situation. This ability belongs to God alone. The statement is general, and the two activities need not be limited as to their nature or time. They have a present application, but the eschatological verdict of God as Judge seems primarily in view.

James concludes with a withering question: "But you—who are you to judge your neighbor?" This rendering conveys the stinging force of the Greek construction. "But" sharpens the contrast between the sovereign God and this foolish individual who is usurping God's right as the Judge. The use of the emphatic personal pronoun (*su*) underlines the contrast and increases the note of scorn. Burdick well remarks that James's shattering bluntness is not intended "to rule out civil courts and judges. Instead, it is to root out the harsh, unkind, critical spirit that continually finds fault with others."[121]

"You to judge" (*ho krinōn*), an articular present participle standing in apposition to the emphatic pronoun, characterizes this individual as one who makes it his business to pass censorious judgment upon his "neighbor," the one next to him. "Your neighbor" seems clearly intended to recall the law of love cited in 2:8, "Thou shalt love thy neighbor as thyself" (ASV). It supports the view that by "law" James means this royal law of love. The reading "another" (KJV)[122] gives the rebuke a wider scope, but "thy neighbor," as the better attested reading, stresses that their close relationship as those living side by side demands a response of love rather than critical judgment.

NOTES FOR
James 4:1-12

1. In some manuscripts the second *pothen* was omitted as unnecessary. The Textus Receptus has the adverb only once.

2. M. F. Sadler, *The General Epistles of SS. James, Peter, John, and Jude, with Notes Critical and Practical*, pp. 55-56; James Macknight, *A New Literal Translation from the Original Greek, of All the Apostolical Epistles with a Commentary and Notes*, 5:382-83; and E. H. Plumptre, *The General Epistles of St. James*, The Cambridge Bible for Schools and Colleges, pp. 88-89.

3. A. T. Robertson, *Practical and Social Aspects of Christianity. The Wisdom of James*, pp. 192-93.

4. Douglas J. Moo, *The Letter of James*, pp. 138-39.

5. Philip Mauro, *James: The Epistle of Reality*, pp. 90-91.

6. Burton Scott Easton and Gordon Poteat, "The Epistle of James," in *The Interpreter's Bible*, 12:53.

7. Alfred Plummer, "The General Epistles of St. James and St. Jude," in *An Exposition of the Bible*, 6:607.

8. Spiros Zodhiates, *The Labor of Love. An Exposition of James 2:14—4:12*, p. 215.

9. J. Ronald Blue, "James," in *The Bible Knowledge Commentary, New Testament*, p. 829.

10. Luke 8:14; Titus 3:3; James 4:1, 3; 2 Pet. 2:13; and the compound form in 2 Tim. 3:4.

11. Gustav Stählin, "*Hēdonē, philēdonos*," in *Theological Dictionary of the New Testament*, 2:909.

12. William Barclay, *The Letters of James and Peter*, The Daily Study Bible, p. 116.

13. R. V. G. Tasker, *The General Epistle of James*, The Tyndale New Testament Commentaries, p. 85.

14. Robert G. Bratcher, "Exegetical Themes in James 3-5," *Review and Expositor* 66, 4 (1969): 407, n. 9.

15. H. Maynard Smith, *The Epistle of S. James. Lectures*, p. 219.

16. R. C. H. Lenski, *The Interpretation of the Epistle to the Hebrews and of the Epistle of James*, pp. 633-34.

17. Erasmus actually inserted this conjecture "in the second edition of his Greek Testament (1519). In his third edition (1522) he wisely returned to the true reading, although, strangely enough, he retained the false one, 'invidetis,' in his Latin version, whence it passed into that of Beza and others" (E. C. S. Gibson, *The General Epistle of James*, The Pulpit Commentary, p. 54).

18. John Calvin, *Commentaries on the Catholic Epistles*, p. 329.

19. James Moffatt, *The General Epistles, James, Peter, and Jude*, The Moffatt New Testament Commentary, pp. 56, 58; and Hugh J. Schonfield, *The Authentic New Testament*, p. 376.

20. "Thus Dibelius, 217-218; Adamson, 167-168; Laws, 171; Windsch, 27; Spitta, 114; and Cantinat, 197-198, among others opt for the conjecture." Peter H. Davids, *The Epistle of James*, p. 158.

21. E. C. Blackman, *The Epistle of James*, p. 125; Simon J. Kistemaker, *New Testament Commentary, Exposition of the Epistle of James and the Epistles of John*, p. 131; Joseph B. Mayor, *The Epistle of James*, pp. 130-32; C. Leslie Mitton, *The Epistle of James*, pp. 149-50; James Hardy Ropes, *A Critical and Exegetical Commentary on the Epistle of St. James*, p. 254; Richard Wolff, *General Epistles of James & Jude*, Contemporary Commentaries, pp. 66-67.

22. R. V. G. Tasker, *The Greek New Testament*, p. 355.

23. Brooke Foss Westcott and Fenton John Anthony Hort, *The New Testament in the Original Greek*; United Bible Societies, *The Greek New Testament*, 3d ed.; Nestle-Aland, *NOVUM TESTAMENTUM GRAECE*, 26th ed.

24. So RSV, NEB, TEV, Beck, Goodspeed, Lattey, Lilly, Weymouth, and Williams. See Bibliography.

25. Roy R. Roberts, *The Game of Life. Studies in James*, p. 118.

26. R. W. Dale, *The Epistle of James and Other Discourse*, pp. 122-23; Billy Simmons, *A Functioning Faith*, pp. 90-91.

27. Moo, p. 141.

28. Lenski, p. 633.

29. Plummer, 6:609.

30. Edward H. Sugden, "James," in *The Abingdon Bible Commentary*, p. 1336.

31. F. Blass and A. Debrunner, *A Greek Grammer of the New Testament and Other Early Christian Literature*, p. 227.

32. Edwin T. Winkler, "Commentary on the Epistle of James," in *An American Commentary on the New Testament*, p. 54.

33. In verses 2b-3 the verb *aiteō* occurs three times, the first and third time in the middle voice and the second time in the active. Some, like Ropes, hold that in the usage of James there is "no difference in meaning ... between the active and middle" (p. 259). But James Hope Moulton remarks, "It is not easy to understand how a writer like James could commit so purposeless a freak as this would be" (*A Grammar of the New Testament Greek*, 1:160). Mayor accepts a difference but concludes that the active suggests "using the words without the spirit of prayer," whereas the middle means asking with the spirit of prayer (p. 133). But how can one ask "amiss" or "basely" (v. 3) with a true spirit of prayer? It seems best to hold that the middle here retains its usual middle force, "to ask for your own selves." The purpose clause in verse 3 certainly involves this personal interest element.

34. Peter H. Davids, *James*, New International Biblical Commentary, pp. 99-100.

35. Rotherham.

36. Stählin, p. 921.

37. William F. Arndt and F. Wilbur Gingrich, *A Greek-English Lexicon of the New Testament and Other Early Christian Literature*, p. 170.

38. Davids, *The Epistle of James*, p. 160.

39. N. T. Caton, *A Commentary and an Exposition of the Epistles of James, Peter, John and Jude*, p. 42.

40. W. E. Oesterley, "The General Epistle of James," in *The Expositor's Greek Testament*, 4:458.

41. Quotes in Wolff, *General Epistles of James & Jude*, p. 68.

42. E. M. Sidebottom, *James, Jude and 2 Peter*, The Century Bible, new ed., p. 52.

43. The form is strictly an undetermined conditional relative clause, "he who if he may wish," but the vernacular Greek of the first century used *ean*, "if," instead of the classical *an*, which imparted vagueness and uncertainty in a sentence. The use of *ean* strengthened this vagueness with the subjunctive.

44. Moo, p. 144.

45. Frank E. Gaebelein, *The Practical Epistle of James*, p. 92.

46. J. B. Lightfoot, *Saint Paul's Epistle to the Galatians*, p. 147.

47. Winkler, p. 55; Blue, "James," in *Bible Knowledge Commentary, New Testament*, p. 830.

48. Dibelius, pp. 222-23, n. 82.

49. Passages suggested include Matt. 6:24; Gal. 5:17; 1 Pet. 2:1-3.

50. Blackman, p. 130.

51. See F. W. Farrar, *The Early Days of Christianity*, p. 341, n. 3; John Peter Lange and J. J. Van Oosterzee, "The Epistle General of James," in *Lange's Commentary on the Holy Scriptures*, 23:116; and Ropes, p. 262.

52. Sophie S. Laws, "Does Scripture Speak in Vain? A Reconsideration of James IV.5," *New Testament Studies*.

53. R. J. Knowling, *The Epistle of St. James*, Westminster Commentaries, p. 99; Mayor, p. 136; Curtis Vaughan, *James, A Study Guide*, p. 87; and Earl Kelly, *James, A Practical Primer for Christian Living*, p. 199; Stier, p. 409.

54. Laws, "Does Scripture Speak in Vain?" pp. 214-15.

55. So also the English edition of 1881.

56. See the Bibliography.
57. Arndt and Gingrich, p. 165. See also B. B. Warfield, "Scripture," in *A Dictionary of Christ and the Gospels*, 2:586.
58. Lenski, p. 641.
59. This is in accordance with the punctuation in the Greek texts of Nestle-Aland, *NOVUM TESTAMENTUM GRAECE*, 26th ed., and of Tasker. See also the margin in United Bible Societies, *The Greek New Testament*, 3d. ed.
60. Plummer, 6:611.
61. Robert Young, *The Holy Bible Consisting of the Old and New Covenants Translated According to the Letter and Idioms of the Original Languages*.
62. Marvin R. Vincent, *A Critical and Exegetical Commentary on the Epistles to the Philippians and to Philemon*, The International Critical Commentary on the Holy Scriptures of the Old and New Testaments, p. 10; and Zodhiates, p. 248.
63. Knowling, p. 100.
64. Ropes, p. 264.
65. Richard Chenevix Trench, *Synonyms of the New Testament*, p. 87.
66. Ropes, pp. 262-63.
67. T. Carson, "The Letter of James," in *A New Testament Commentary*, p. 579.
68. Moo, p. 145.
69. Martin, p. 150.
70. TEV and Moffatt regard it as a statement. Several versions that regard verse 5*b* as a quotation, by placing the question mark outside the quotation marks, imply that the quotation is viewed as a statement of fact.
71. Lenski, p. 640.
72. Robert Johnstone, *Lectures Exegetical and Practical on the Epistle of James*, p. 315.
73. C. Leslie Mitton, *The Epistle of James*, p. 156.
74. Davids, *James*, New International Biblical Commentary, p. 101.
75. Motyer, p. 87.
76. So in the following versions: NEB, NIV, TEV, JB, Goodspeed, Kleist, and Lilly.
77. So in KJV, Berkeley, Darby, Weymouth, Williams, and Young.
78. Henry Alford, *The Greek Testament*, 4:1, p. 315.
79. So in NASB, RSV, Beck, Lattey, Montgomery, Moffatt, Rotherham, Schonfield, 20th. Cent.
80. Zodhiates, *The Labor of Love*, p. 254.
81. Trench, p. 101.
82. Wolff, p. 69.
83. Wolff, p. 70.
84. Zodhiates, p. 261.
85. Plummer, 6:613.
86. Plumptre, p. 92.
87. Gaebelein, p. 97.
88. D. Edmund Hiebert, "Satan," in *The Zondervan Pictorial Encyclopedia of the Bible*, 5:282.
89. See ibid., 5:285-86, and the bibliography cited there.
90. Rudolf Stier, *The Epistle of St. James*, p. 413 (italics in original).
91. Stier, p. 414.
92. Alexander Ross, *The Epistles of James and John*, The New International Commentary on the New Testament, p. 80.
93. Moo, p. 148.
94. Ropes, p. 270.
95. Mayor, p. 142.

96. John Trapp, *Trapp's Commentary on the New Testament*, p. 701.
97. Trench, p. 238.
98. Zodhiates, p. 287.
99. In the New Testament the verb occurs in Luke 6:21, 25.
100. The Textus Receptus, following Aleph, A, K, L, and most minuscles, uses the more familiar verb *metastraphētō*, "change, alter."
101. Moo, 149.
102. The article here has a possessive force, "your joy."
103. Davids, *James*, New International Biblical Commentary, p. 104.
104. Some, like Martin, pp. 157-62, and Adamson, pp. 175-78, group these two verses with 4:13-17 as the beginning of a new section. But Davids, *The Epistle of James*, notes that in these verses "the author is ending a larger segment on the problem of community conflict," p. 169. On the other hand Moffatt transposes these verses to follow 2:13, "to what seems to have been its original place." But this transposition is devoid of all manuscript support and is unwarranted. See p. 172.
105. Ross, p. 82.
106. Ropes, p. 273.
107. Robertson, p. 212.
108. Wolff, p. 72.
109. Gerhard Kittel, "*Katalaleō, katalalia, katalalos*," in *Theological Dictionary of the New Testament*, 4:4.
110. The compound verb uses the genitive to indicate the person spoken against.
111. Kittel, pp. 4-5.
112. Zodhiates, p. 304.
113. The conjunctive view is supported by the reading *kai* in the Textus Receptus; the alternation makes clear the interpretation.
114. Friedrich, Büchsel, "*Krinō*," in *Theological Dictionary of the New Testament*, 3:939.
115. Wolff, p. 72.
116. Moo, p. 152. Moo's italics.
117. Oesterley, pp. 461-62.
118. Arthur Carr, "The General Epistle of St. James," in *Cambridge Greek Testament*, pp. 55-56.
119. Joh. Ed. Huther, *Critidcal and Exegetical Handbook to the General Epistles of James, Peter, John, and Jude*, p. 137.
120. The KJV follows the Textus Receptus which omits "and judge." For the textual evidence see Nestle-Aland, *NOVUM TESTAMENTUM GRAECE*, 26th ed.
121. Donald W. Burdick, "James," in *The Expositor's Bible Commentary*, 12:196.
122. So the Textus Receptus.

11

X. THE REACTION OF
LIVING FAITH TO PRESUMPTUOUS PLANNING

4:13-17   Now listen, you who say, "Today or tomorrow we will go to this or that city, spend a year there, carry on business and make money." [14]Why, you do not even know what will happen tomorrow. What is your life? You are a mist that appears for a little while and then vanishes. [15]Instead, you ought to say, "If it is the Lord's will, we will live and do this or that." [16]As it is, you boast and brag. All such boasting is evil. [17]Anyone, then, who knows the good he ought to do and doesn't do it, sins.

No expressed connection exists between this paragraph and the preceding section. Dibelius calls it "unquestionably an independent section" but admits that the author continues his warning to "people with a worldly mind."[1] Thus James marks a transition in passing from one form of worldliness to another. Worldliness does not always manifest itself in open enmity toward God; it also may reveal itself in an arrogant attitude of self-sufficiency in planning daily life activities in total disregard of God. It is possible to express one's dependence upon God in formal worship rites and then disregard Him in the restless pursuits of daily life. Men so engrossed in commerce and trade would be peculiarly liable to succumb to "the sin of side-stepping God's will while planning for the future."[2] James turns skillfully to this setting to expose and rebuke this form of worldliness. He does not suggest that commerce or trade is evil in itself, not does he imply that tradesmen and traveling merchants cannot be pious and God-fearing men. Although he used the activities of the traveling traders to rebuke presumptuous business planning, his rebuke is intended for all believers who are guilty of acting in self-willed independence of God in daily life.

James portrays and interprets the evil in this form of worldliness (vv. 13-14), indicates the attitude proper for believers (v. 15), and points out the sinfulness of their present attitude (vv. 16-17).

A. THE REBUKE OF THEIR SELF-SUFFICIENT ATTITUDE (vv. 13-14)

James first delineates this attitude (v. 13) and then exposes the arrogant presumption involved (v. 14).

1. The Delineation of the Attitude (v. 13)

"Now listen," an arousing interjection implying disapproval, marks the transition to a new form of worldliness. "Listen" (*age*) is in form a second person singular imperative, but it has become stereotyped and may be followed, as here, by a plural term of address. The added adverb "now" (*nun*) increases the sense of urgency. The expression, common in secular Greek, occurs only here and in 5:1 in the New Testament. Adamson calls it "the signal for an attack."[3]

"You who say" (*hoi legontes*), the articular participle used as the vocative of direct address, identifies the intended recipients of this rebuke. The present tense, "the ones saying," marks the statement that follows as characteristic, formulating the result of careful thought and planning on their part. Their words, identifying them as itinerant merchants, express graphically the type of worldliness James has in view. The picture fits the commercial Jews of the Diaspora. Since James in this paragraph does not use "brothers" as a form of address, some like Laws[4] hold that he is now addressing non-Christians, merchants who in view of their status and influence had not yet been attracted into the Christian community in such numbers as to constitute a distinct group. But Davids hold that his use of the articular participle (*hoi legontes*) implies that "James sees them as within the community rather than as outsiders."[5] Mayor holds that the appeal to knowledge in verse 15, "as above in 1:19, is a proof that the writer is addressing Christians."[6] Whereas the rebuke being administered is applicable to human beings generally, it is specially suited to professed members of the Christian community. The plan to which they here give expression is simply representative of their prevailing attitude.

"Today or tomorrow we will go to this or that city, spend a year there, carry on business and make money" vividly relates their fully developed plan. They have the whole thing settled in detail, even down to the profits from the year's trade. The language reflects assurance and self-confidence; they assume that its execution is entirely in their control. No thought is given to their dependence upon God or to the uncertainty of life. Behind it all James sees a reprehensible attitude.

"Today or tomorrow" seemingly suggests flexibility in their plan. The reading of the Textus Receptus, "today and tomorrow,"[7] indicates a two-day journey concerning which these restless travelers feel no uncertainty. The reading "or" is better attested and more probably original. Dibelius suggests that the copyists of the letter would desire "to place into the mouths of the planners as confident a declaration as possible."[8] Since "today and tomorrow" had apparently become a proverbial expression for the present and the immediate future (Luke 12:28; 13:32-33), the scribes would believe it was more appropriate. But Lenski, who accepts "or" as the correct reading, suggests that James wrote "or" to indicate that the plan here stated is simply representative: "Sometimes the thing planned is to start today; sometimes it is to start tomorrow."[9] This is in keeping with the fact that James is concerned with their habitual practice.

"We will go to this or that city" recounts the first stage of their plan. "We will go" expresses their self-assured completion of the journey, whereas "this or that city" marks the intended destination. The ASV rendering "this city" (*tēnde tēn polis*) regards the demonstrative pronoun as definite, but more naturally it is to be taken as representative: "into such and such a city."[10] The rendering "this city" would denote a predetermined city, in which the speaker may be viewed as pointing out on a map, whereas the rendering "such and such a city" is representative. Huther holds that, though each time the speaker has a definite city in mind, since James is speaking about a general practice, he "could only indicate it in an indefinite manner, and he does so by the pronoun each time a definite city is pointed to."[11] James is not concerned with a particular city but is rather thinking of the presumption involved in the typical assertion.

"Spend a year there," literally, "and do a year there," implies more than mere continuance; they intend to use the year actively. They presume that the whole year is at their disposal to use as they decide. Some manuscripts add the word "one," as though they already were beginning to contemplate what they would do the following year. This reading adds to the presumption, but it lacks sufficient authority to be retained.

"Carry on business" marks the intended activity. The verb (*emporeusometha*) means to travel into a region to get into the business there, to travel for trade, and then simply signifies "to do business, to trade." The term is used elsewhere in the New Testament only in 2 Peter 2:3, where it denotes deceptive exploitation. This significance is eloquent testimony to the cheating that too often attended ancient trade, but James's words do not imply this evil. James is not charging them with immoral activities but rather with presumption.

"And make money," make a commercial profit, states the goal of the whole program. The repeated "and" (*kai*) distinguishes the different steps in the plan, "which are rehearsed thus one by one with manifest satisfaction."[12] It pictures vividly these industrious and ambitious small businessmen who were constantly alert and eager to move to areas where business was most profitable. James is not condemning such trade or the acquiring of profits from legitimate trade. But clearly their hearts lay in their ability to reap rich profits, which was required as the mark of true success. For James, the fatal defect in their planning is their presumptuous self-centeredness, resulting in the effective exclusion of God from the practical affairs of their daily lives.

They were guilty of living a life of practical atheism. Zodhiates remarks that such practical atheism "is unfortunately far more common that reasoned unbelief, and we may well wonder what the judgment of God will be upon this practical atheism that plagues the Christianity of the twentieth century as it has apparently plagued the Christian church throughout the ages.[13] Christ's parable of the rich fool in Luke 12:16-21 confirms James's stern rebuke of the worldliness of these merchants.

2. The Presumption in the Attitude (v. 14)

James cuts into their worldly attitude by exposing a twofold presumption.

They were guilty of presumption because of their ignorance concerning the future: "Why, you do not even know what will happen tomorrow." James uses no word for "Why." He places this statement in apposition with "you who say" in verse 13: literally, "you who are such as [*hoitines*] know not." The qualitative relative pronoun marks them as belonging to a class of persons who by their very nature do not know the future. "Do not know" (*ouk epistasthe*) means that they have no sure and accurate knowledge concerning the morrow.[14] They were disregarding the scriptural warning "Do not boast about tomorrow, for you do not know what a day may bring forth" (Prov. 27:1). Their planning in bland disregard of God is the very essence of worldliness. But a living faith faces the unknown future with calm dependence on God as the true source of security concerning "tomorrow" (*tēs aurion*). The manuscripts are divided as to whether to include the neuter singular article or the plural before "tomorrow," or to read no article.[15] It seems better to include the neuter singular article and read "you know not the thing of the morrow" or, with the NIV, "you do not even know what will happen tomorrow." They forgot that they have no certain knowledge concerning the actual situation on the morrow.

They also are acting in presumptuous disregard of the uncertainty of human life. "What is your life?" There is a question of punctuation here. Should the period be placed after "tomorrow," or should this phrase be included with what precedes? Under the latter view, the NASB[16] renders it, "Yet you do not know what your life will be like tomorrow." This view assumes that they will be alive tomorrow but do not know what the day will bring. The separate question, however, is commonly accepted as preferable. It directs attention to the uncertain, fleeting nature of life itself. They do not even know that they will be alive tomorrow.

The interrogative pronoun "what" (*poia*)[17] conveys a depreciatory sense; it calls attention to the precarious nature of "your life." Zodhiates remarks that James does not say "our life" since "he could not possibly count himself as one with the merchants" in their presumption.[18]

"You are a mist that appears for a little while and then vanishes." The opening *gar* ("for"), not in the NIV, continues the depreciatory note and serves to confirm the precarious nature of their lives as individuals. Instead of "you are" (*este*), some manuscripts read "it is" (*esti*) or "it will be" (*estai*). The reading "you are" is rather unexpected after the preceding question, and it is more probable that the copyists would change the reading to the third person than the other way around. The metaphor "you are" is more vigorous and centers attention on the readers themselves. All that they have or engage in must therefore partake of their own instability. "Mist" occurs elsewhere in the New Testament only in Acts 2:19 as a quotation from Joel 2:30. It may denote a mist, a puff of smoke, or vapor, like the breath appearing momentarily in the cold air or steam from a hot pan.

James points out the import of this metaphor: "that appears for a little while and then vanishes." The present tenses denote that this occurs regularly. Vapor is visible "for a little while" (*pros oligos*) and is expected to remain visible for only a short duration; "then" (*epeita*), marking an event that is sure to follow, it "vanishes," totally disappears from sight. The popular wordplay in the original, like our English "appear" (*phainomenē*)—"disappear" (*aphanizomenē*), presses upon the readers the transitoriness of life. Mitton calls attention to the fact that the various figures that are applied to human life in the Bible—"the evening shadow" (Ps. 102:11); "a breath" (Job 7:7); "a cloud" (7:9); "grass" (Ps. 103:15)—all indicate its transitory and insecure character.[19] How foolish therefore to ignore the unchanging God and proudly plan for their life, which is as fleeting as a wisp of vapor! James is not implying that these busy merchants should carry on their daily activities with a sense of impending doom. "What he is requiring his readers to consider is that trust in God and not a well-thought-out plan for aggrandizement and gain is the only way to face the future. To live in the recognition that God —not the human being—is in control is to choose a Christian life of humility before God."[20]

B. THE INDICATION OF THE PROPER ATTITUDE (v. 15)

"Instead, you ought to say" (*anti tou legein humas*) is literally "Instead of your saying." The expression looks back to verse 13, "You who say," making verse 14 in effect a parenthesis that justifies his rebuke for their expressed attitude of practical atheism. Instead of their arrogant, this-world-oriented attitude, they should qualify all their plans and hopes with a conscious acceptance of God's sovereign will.

"If it is the Lord's will" expresses the believer's becoming attitude of mind, giving recognition to God as the One who has absolute authority and effectively controls all of life and its activities. "The Lord" expresses His ultimate sovereignty and is best taken to mean "God in His Absolute Unity, without any thought of the distinction of the Person."[21] Believers must be exercised about His will and desire to do it, since it is always good, acceptable, and perfect (Rom. 12:2). The conditional form (*ean* and the aorist subjunctive *thelēsē*) leaves open the question as to what God's will may be in a specific situation, but the believer expresses his willingness to accept it, knowing that God alone can make our plans prosperous. It is not merely adding "God willing" to the end of our formulated plans. "Each plan is evaluated by his standards and goals; each plan is laid before God in prayer with adequate time spent in listening for God's ideas."[22]

This expression does not occur in the Old Testament but appears on several occasions in the New (Acts 18:21; 1 Cor. 4:19; Heb. 6:3; cf. Phil. 2:24). But Paul on several occasions speaks of his plans for the future without using the expression (Acts 19:21; Rom. 15:28; 1 Cor. 16:5). That the biblical writers did not use it more often is, as Mitton suggests, "because this thought is so basic to their whole attitude that it is assumed rather than precisely expressed."[23] Obviously the early Christians did not regard "if the Lord will" as a ritual of piety that would validate the plans they made. Believers do well to avoid the rote use of the expression, but it is proper for them on appropriate occasions thus to give verbal testimony to their dependence on God when dealing with the future. Tasker questions whether the modern "refusal to say 'God willing' is really due to horror of hypocrisy or a failure to acknowledge the supremacy of God."[24] For the committed Christian, the conviction thus expressed is the true antidote against all feelings of fear and dread concerning the future.

The resultant expression of assurance is "we will live and do this or that." Both our lives and our activities depend on God's will for us. The two future indicative verbs assume that it is God's will for us that both our lives and deeds are to continue.[25] This recognition of our dependence upon God for the future is not an excuse for inactivity, nor should it discourage planning for the future. "We will . . . do this or that" rather implies that "we are directed to plan our future, but to do so in co-operation with God."[26] Having committed our all to Him, we may continue our planned activities under the encouraging sense of God's guidance and sustaining grace.

C. THE EVIL OF THEIR PRESENT ATTITUDE (vv. 16-17)

"As it is" (*nun de*, "but now"), "you boast and brag." The opening words "but now" turn the attention back to their present evil attitude in contrast to what they should be saying. In 1:9 the NIV renders the verb that it here renders "boast" as "take pride in." In 1:9 the verb, which basically means a feeling of pride or exultation in a certain condition, depicts the believer's reaction of exultation in view of God's grace, but here the term portrays a presumptuous sense of exultation; their language in 4:13 is a proud boast. Their present boasting is in sharp contrast to the proper submission to and confidence in God that should properly spring from a sense of the uncertainty of life. But as it is, their "pride has magnified the big 'I' in place of God's grace."[27]

As a result they continue to "brag," express their boasting in pretentious braggings. The expression used by James is not a finite verb but rather a prepositional phrase (*en tais alazoveiais humōn*, more literally, "in your pretensions" or "arrogance"). The NIV rendering accepts the phrase as modifying the verb: "boast and brag." But in sixteen instances in the New Testament where the verb "boast" (*kauchaomai*) is followed by the preposition *en* ("in"), the prepositional phrase expresses the ground of boasting (cf. Rom. 2:17; 2:23; 2 Cor. 10:17; 12:9). Thus we agree with Burdick that "it is best to understand that it was about their arrogant pretensions concerning the future that James's readers were boasting."[28] The noun in this phrase ("your pretensions") occurs only here and in 1 John 2:16 in the New Testament; it denotes a hollow pretension in word or deed, an ostentatious display that goes beyond that which reality justifies. The plural noun indicates that on repeated occasions they thus boastfully express themselves. They arrogantly assume that they can dispose of the future as they desire, gloating over the business deals to be made and the rich gains to be reaped. They act "as though human skill and cleverness were omni-competent."[29]

"All such boasting is evil." The simplicity of the verdict makes its severity all the more impressive. The correlative pronoun "such" (*toiautē*) suggests that there is a glorying that is good, like that in 1:9 or Paul's glorying in Christ Jesus (Phil. 3:3) and in His cross (Gal. 6:14). But this is glorying of a different kind and is "evil" (*ponēra*), "wicked," and pernicious in its results. In character it is morally akin to Satan, who is called "the evil one" (Matt. 6:13; 13:38; Eph. 6:16).

James concludes the paragraph with a summary maxim: "Anyone, then, who knows the good he ought to do and doesn't do it, sins" (v. 17). "Then" (*oun*, "therefore") indicates that the evil just exposed is comprehended in this general principle. Though broader than the particular case just dealt with, the principle explains why their boasting is evil.

The precise connection between this general statement and the preceding verses has been differently understood. Moffatt, who despaired of any direct connection, boldly transferred this verse to follow 2:26.[30] But this shifting of the verse to a different context has no manuscript support and is s gesture of despair. Others, like Mayor, view this verse as "a general summing up and moral of what has been said before," as far back as 1:22.[31] But if it was intended to serve as a general summary, it is difficult to see why James placed it here rather than at the end of the epistle. Mitton views the verse "as an independent saying which is slipped in at this point in the epistle, but without any pretense that it arises out of what has gone before."[32] He suggests that it should be treated as a separate paragraph. But in view of his *oun*, it is best to accept that James intends the statement to be understood as confirming the evil just rebuked.

It seems obvious that James intended the boasters to see themselves in this general statement: "Anyone, then, who knows the good he ought to do and doesn't do it, sins." The term "anyone" makes clear that James is holding up the picture of an unidentified individual characterized by knowledge of what he should do but failing to do it. This individual is portrayed by two dative participles without an article and connected by "and." The linear action in the two participles[33] makes clear that knowing and not doing are both true of this individual, characteristically united in him. As one who "knows the good he ought to do" he has an understanding of that which is "good" (*kalon*), that which is morally excellent and praiseworthy, the opposite of that which is morally malignant. The present active infinitive "to do" (*poiein*) makes clear that what is involved is not merely an intellectual understanding but an active doing of the good. As Jewish Christians, those rebuked well knew that they should be actively engaged in such activities in conscious dependence upon God's will. In pausing to reflect, they were well aware that their self-centered boasting was displeasing to God (Prov. 27:1; Isa. 56:12; Luke 12:19-20, 47).

The conclusion is inescapable: he "sins" (*hamartia autō estin*, "sin to him it is"). The original order stresses that their knowledge without obedience is nothing less than sin. As Moo notes, "They cannot take refuge in the plea that they have done nothing positively wrong; as Scripture makes abundantly clear, sins of *omission* are as real and serious as sins of *commission*."[34] Knowledge of what is right and the ability to do it creates the obligation to do so. Their failure to do what they knew was right leaves them without excuse. In light of the teaching of Jesus in Luke 12:27, "That servant who knows his master's will and does not get ready or does not do what his master wants will be beaten with many blows," they are openly guilty of sin. The merchants being rebuked thus display another of the inconsistencies that James rebukes in this epistle.

NOTES FOR
James 4:14-17

1. Martin Dibelius, "James. A Commentary on the Epistle of James," in *Hermeneia—A Critical and Historical Commentary on the Bible*, p. 230.
2. Lehman Strauss, *James, Your Brother. Studies in the Epistle of James*, p. 181.
3. James B. Adamson, *The Epistle of James*, The New International Commentary on the New Testament, p. 178.
4. Sophie Laws, *A Commentary on the Epistle of James*, p. 190.
5. Peter H. Davids, *The Epistle of James*, p. 171.
6. Joseph B. Mayor, *The Epistle of St. James*, p. 153.
7. Not here represented in the KJV.
8. Dibelius, p. 232 n. 9.
9. R. C. H. Lenski, *The Interpretation of the Epistle to the Hebrews and of the Epistle of James*, p. 649.

10. William F. Arndt and F. Wilbur Gingrich, *A Greek-English Lexicon of the New Testament and Other Early Christian Literature*, p. 555.

11. Joh. Ed. Huther, *Critical and Exegetical Handbook to the General Epistles of James, Peter, John, and Jude*, p. 139.

12. Alfred Plummer, "The General Epistles of St. James and St. Jude," in *An Exposition of the Bible* 6:620.

13. Spiros Zodhiates, *The Patience of Hope*, p. 16.

14. Stewart Custer, *A Treasury of New Testament Synonyms*, p. 112.

15. The Greek texts of Westcott and Hort, Nestle-Aland (22d ed.), and United Bible Societies (1st ed.) read no article. Souter, Hodges, and Farstad, Nestle-Aland (26th ed.), United Bible Societies (3d ed.), and Tasker agree with the Textus Receptus in reading *to*, the neuter singular article.

16. So also Goodspeed, 20th Cent., and TEV.

17. As a noun the term means "grass, herb, weed." Some early interpreters of James accepted this meaning here.

18. Zohiates, p. 25.

19. C. Leslie Mitton, *The Epistle of James*, p. 169.

20. Ralph P. Martin, *James*, Word Biblical Commentary, p. 166.

21. E. H. Plumptre, *The General Epistle of James*, The Cambridge Bible for Schools and Colleges, p. 95.

22. Peter H. Davids, *James*, New International Biblical Commentary, p. 113.

23. Mitton, p. 170.

24. R. V. G. Tasker, *The General Epistle of James*, The Tyndale New Testament Commentaries, p. 104.

25. Several Greek manuscripts make either the first or both verbs subjunctive. If the first only is subjunctive, "and we may live" could be taken with "if God may will," as in the Latin Vulgate and in Tyndale. If both are subjunctive, as in the Textus Receptus, the sentence must read, "If the Lord may will and we may live, let us do this or that." The subjunctives have less support and may have arisen from the misconception that they were still under *ean*.

26. H. Maynard Smith, *The Epistle of St. James. Lectures*, p. 269.

27. Roy B. Roberts, *The Game of Life, Studies in James*, p. 136.

28. Donald W. Burdick, "James," in *The Expositor's Bible Commentary*, 12:198.

29. Mitton, p. 172.

30. James Moffatt, *The New Testament, A New Translation*; and *The General Epistles of James, Peter, John, and Jude*, The Moffatt New Testament Commentary, pp. 45-46.

31. Mayor, p. 147.

32. Mitton, pp. 172-73.

33. The first participle, *eidoti*, is a second perfect with a present meaning; *poiounti* is a present tense.

34. Douglas J. Moo, *The Letter of James*, p. 158 (italics original).

12

XI. THE REACTION OF
LIVING FAITH TO INJUSTICE

5:1-11 Now listen, you rich people, weep and wail because of the misery that is coming upon you. [2]Your wealth has rotted, and moths have eaten your clothes. [3]Your gold and silver are corroded. Their corrosion will testify against you and eat your flesh like fire. You have hoarded wealth in the last days. [4]Look! The wages you failed to pay the workmen who mowed your fields are crying out against you. The cries of the harvesters have reached the ears of the Lord Almighty. [5]You have lived on earth in luxury and self-indulgence. You have fattened yourselves in the day of slaughter. [6]You have condemned and murdered innocent men, who were not opposing you.

[7]Be patient, then, brothers, until the Lord's coming. See how the farmer waits for the land to yield its valuable crop and how patient he is for the fall and spring rains. [8]You too, be patient and stand firm, because the Lord's coming is near. [9]Don't grumble against each other, brothers, or you will be judged. The Judge is standing at the door!

[10]Brothers, as an example of patience in the face of suffering, take the prophets who spoke in the name of the Lord. [11]As you know, we consider blessed those who have persevered. You have heard of Job's perseverance and have seen what the Lord finally brought about. The Lord is full of compassion and mercy.

In this two-part section James exposes further manifestations of worldliness. In the first part (vv. 1-6), James utters a stinging denunciation of the cruelty and oppression of the world, while the second part (vv. 7-11) aims at safeguarding believers against a worldly reaction to such experiences of injustice. The two parts stand in remarkable contrast. "There is a most vigorous and fierce indictment in the first part, and nothing else; while in the second there is gentle and affectionate entreaty."[1] That James intended a close connection between the two parts is clear from his use of "then" (*oun*) in verse 7. James's primary concern is not with the oppressive rich but rather with believers who are the victims of such unjust treatment. Yet the close connection makes clear the relationship between two very different aspects of the Christian message. Christianity is strongly opposed to all forms of social injustice, but it also urges believers to maintain a proper attitude and perspective amid such injustices (vv. 7-11).

A. THE JUDGMENT COMING UPON THE OPPRESSIVE RICH (vv. 1-6)

This passage reflects the spirit of the Old Testament in their fiery denunciation of social injustices (cf. Isa. 10:1-4; Amos 4:1-3; 8:4-10; Mic. 2:1-5; Mal. 3:1-5). Motivated by the reaction of his own faith to worldliness, James now makes a prophetic, cutting denunciation of the ungodly rich. He announces impending judgment upon them (v. 1), describes the coming judgment (vv. 2-3), and delineates the charges against them (vv. 4-6).

1. The Announcement of the Judgment (v.1)

"Now listen, you rich people" at once identifies the group to whom the announcement is directed. "Now listen," the identical formula used in 4:13, does not imply a continuation of the subject treated in 4:13-17; rather, it is a sharp call for the attention of the new group addressed. "You rich people" (*hoi plousioi*) denotes those who are materially wealthy. But James is not opposed to them simply because they are wealthy; the evils they are guilty of (vv. 4-6) establish their ungodly character. He is not denouncing rich men indiscriminately. The assertion of Barclay that "he aims to show the detestable character of those who possess riches"[2] is unwarranted. James should not be charged with the unscriptural view that wealth in itself is sinful,[3] but he well knew that its accumulation was often associated with evil practices. James is denouncing "the peril of unsanctified riches."[4]

James makes no reference to the religious profession of the rich being addressed. Some interpreters assume that "James is addressing those within the Christian community who have become entangled in the deceitfulness of riches."[5] But it is more probable that they are non-Christian Jewish owners of large estates in the communities where the readers live. Those addressed in verses 1-6 seem clearly to form a distinct class from the "brothers" addressed in verse 7. The term "brothers" does not appear in these six verses but occurs three times in verses 7-11. Those addressed are not called to repentance; nor is there any indication that they must amend their ways as inconsistent with their faith. Rather, he simply announces the fact that judgment awaits them. Calvin comments that "all that he says tends only to despair."[6] The attitude ascribed to these rich is not that of 1:10, where a rich believer is in view, but rather that seen in 2:6. Smith well observes that James "is not concerned with any economic theory, but with the sins of individuals."[7]

In thus addressing these guilty rich men outside the church, James employs the rhetorical device known as apostrophe, a turning away from his real audience to address some other group. He was well aware that his words would probably reach but few of those being addressed, but he does so for the benefit of his Christian readers. His primary concern is "to dissuade hesitant Christians from falling into a foolish attitude of envy toward the powers and privileges which wealth seems to confer on those who possess it.[8]

"Weep and wail because of the misery that is coming upon you" is an animated proclamation of impending doom. It is addressed "to the *poor rich*, who have nothing more than their riches."[9] "Weep and wail" is not a call for repentance, as in 4:9, but indicates the response of despair these rich men will have when the judgment strikes. "Weep" (*klausate*), "sob aloud, lament, weep bitterly," was used of wailing for the dead (Luke 7:13, 32; John 11:31-33); but it was also used of weeping for shame or remorse (Matt. 26:75; Luke 7:38). Here it denotes the emotional outburst of those who have disregarded God's claims and will be overwhelmed with the realization of their loss when He appears in judgment.[10] The use of the aorist tense, in view of the impending judgment, urgently summons them to do what they already should be doing in view of their fate. "And wail" (*ololuzontes*), or "howling," intensifies the scene of despair. This onomatopoetic verb, which occurs only here in the New Testament, was originally used of the cry of jubilation as well as of the wail of grief and pain; but in the Septuagint it occurs only in the expression of violent grief (Isa. 13:6; 15:3; 16:7; 23:1; Jer. 48:20; Ezek. 21:12; Amos 8:3; Zech. 11:2). The present tense participle pictures their audible sobbing being repeatedly pierced by their howls of agony at the return of the rejected Christ in judgment.

The catastrophe of coming judgment, "because of the misery that is coming upon you," justifies the call to lament. The noun "the misery" (*tais talaipōriais*, plural, "the miseries"), which occurs elsewhere in the New Testament only in Romans 3:16 as a quotation from Isaiah 59:7, pictures the resultant feelings of wretchedness, distress, and misery. The present participle, "the one coming" (*tais eperchomenais*), seems best taken as picturing these miseries as already approaching and about to strike. "Upon" (*epi* alone as well as with the participle) stresses that these miseries will fall upon them personally. Though it is quite possible to see a preliminary fulfillment of the picture in the destruction of Jerusalem, the reference is best understood as denoting the parousia, which the early church eagerly anticipated. "Like Isaiah (Isa. 13:6)," Davids notes, "James looks with divine foresight and sees the dark hurricane cloud of the Day of the Lord about to strike them down."[11]

2. The Description of the Judgment (vv. 2-3)

James first pictures the impact of the coming judgment upon their wealth: "Your wealth has rotted, and moths have eaten your clothes. Your gold and silver are corroded." The three verbs, all in the perfect tense, have been viewed as instances of the Hebrew "prophetic perfect," denoting future events "which to prophetic intuition are so certain that they can be spoken of as having actually happened."[12] But in view of the future tense of verse 3, it seems better to understand the perfects as denoting the abiding condition of their wealth as revealed in the Day of Judgment.

"Your wealth has rotted" may be understood in two ways. "Wealth" may be taken as a comprehensive designation for all forms of wealth that men accumulate. Then the verb "has rotted" (*sesēpen*), which literally means "has decayed, is rotten," must be understood figuratively to mean that their wealth has become worthless. Under this view the next two statements analyze this wealth as consisting of costly garments and precious metals. Others hold that the reference is to three specific forms of wealth: foodstuffs, garments, and metals. This view is in keeping with the natural meaning of the verb, "has rotted" or "is decayed," as implying that the form of wealth consists of perishable grain. Jesus' parable of the rich fool in Luke 12:16-20 illustrates such accumulations of vast quantities of grain as a common form of wealth. Oesterley notes that this view is in "harmony with the rest of the verse which speaks of literal destruction" and that "precisely the same idea . . . occurs in the eschatological passage *Enoch*, xcviii. 1ff."[13] The use of *kai*, "and," which coordinates this statement with the reference to moth-eaten garments, certainly denoting literal destruction, also favors the literal reference to perishable grain. The view that the reference is to three distinct forms of wealth is the more probable.

"And moths have eaten your clothes" pictures the worthless state of another form of their wealth. In the Orient "clothes" (*himatia*), the long, loose outer robes that often were richly embroidered and decorated, were a recognized form of wealth and were commonly passed on as heirlooms (cf. Judg. 14:12; 2 Kings 5:5; Job 13:28; Matt. 6:19; Acts 20:33). When such garments were stored in quantity in Oriental countries where there was a fairly high temperature during much of the year, damage by the larva of clothes moths was frequently extensive.[14] Garments that had become "moth-eaten" were practically worthless (cf. Job 13:28, the only other place in the Greek Bible where this adjective is used).

"Your gold and silver are corroded" (v. 3) declares the worthlessness also of this form of their wealth in that coming day. The verb "are corroded" (*katiotai*), occurring only here in the New Testament, is a compound form, the preposition *kata* giving it an intensive force, "are thoroughly or completely corroded or rusted." The application of this verb to their gold and silver is arresting, since these metals do not actually rust or corrode. The suggestion that James, as a poor man who did not handle stores of gold and silver, did not know this fact is unconvincing.[15] More probable is the suggestion that "the coins of that time were mixed with quite a large percentage of alloy, and did actually rust."[16] Most probable is the view that James intentionally applied this strong verb to their hoarded gold and silver to remind them that in the

Judgment Day this wealth would prove to be as worthless as rusted-out iron. Others, such as Davids, suggest a figurative meaning for the verb "corroded" by remarking that today "one might say, 'Your money is devalued by inflation.'"[17] But Blue points out that there is an element of literal truth in the term James uses: "Though they do not rust, they can become *corroded*. Gold can darken and silver tarnish."[18] And Roberts asserts that "even those of New Testament times were intelligent enough to realize that everything on this earth, including gold and silver, is in the process of *decay*."[19] Thus Peter makes reference to "gold which perishes even though refined by fire" (1 Peter 1:7). In regarding their hoarded wealth as a permanent source of security, these rich people, in the Day of Judgment, will find that their treasured wealth has disintegrated and lost all value.

The fury of the coming judgment also will strike the rich personally: "Their corrosion will testify against you and eat your flesh like fire." The use of *kai* ("and"), not in NIV, links this testimony concerning the worthlessness of their gold and silver in the judgment with the personal doom of the rich. It indicates how closely they linked their lives and aspirations with their wealth. "In the ruin of their property their own ruin is portrayed."[20]

In 3:8 the word rendered "corrosion" (*ios*) was used in the sense of "poison," but the context here clearly gives it the meaning of "rust" or "corrosion." The very presence of this rust upon their hoarded wealth "will testify against you," for in that day it will speak as a mighty witness whose testimony cannot be silenced. It will appear as a witness for the prosecution, bearing witness "against you" (*humin*), more literally, "to you," and all observers, declaring your undeniable guilt. The essence of the witness is not indicated. Ropes holds that the rust will be "the visible sign and symbol of the real state of the case—of the perishability of riches and hence of the certain ruin awaiting those who have no other ground of hope."[21] Winkler suggests that "the rust that had gathered upon the unused treasures would testify to the hard-heartedness of their possessors."[22] Instead of using their money to aid the poor and needy around them, they have hoarded it callously for their own selfish enjoyment in the future. Whatever the implied contents of its testimony, in the judgment the witness of the rust will verify their guilt.

In the Judgment Day the rust also will act to punish the selfish possessors "and eat your flesh like fire." The future verb (*phagetai*, "will eat") again refers to the time of the judgment. The corrosive action of the rust on their hoarded gold and silver is now symbolically presented as eating the "flesh" of the oppressive rich themselves in that day. The plural "your flesh" (*tas sarkas humon*)[23] probably was used to remind the rich that their chief concern had been to provide for their own physical comforts. Zodhiates suggests that the plural indicates that God will judge them individually and remarks, "This individual attention of God for man is indeed one of life's greatest mysteries. He saves people individually, He rewards them individually, and

He punishes them individually."[24] James warns them that in the Day of Judgment their rusted wealth, like a rusty chain, will eat into their pampered flesh like a festering sore. Its effect will be "like fire," torturing while it devours. Rust consuming iron is a slow process; but James greatly intensifies the terror of the process by likening it to fire, a familiar element in the biblical picture of the judgment. In this terrible picture of their doom, James seems to be echoing Jesus' teaching about the "whole body" of the wicked being cast into hellfire (Matt. 5:29-30; cf. 5:22; 10:28). Johnstone holds that the picture of James "seems most naturally to suggest the work of a remorseful conscience, . . . a gnawing or corrosion like that of rust."[25]

"You have hoarded wealth in the last days" (v. 3c) indicates the folly of their hoarding in view of the impending judgment. "You have hoarded wealth" renders a single verb in the original (*ethēsaupiste*), "to store up, to lay up treasure." In the context the verb implies its own object.[26] The aorist indicative simply states the historical fact with no reference to the duration of the activity, now viewed as terminated by the judgment. When the judgment falls, their efforts to accumulate further riches will be seen to have been foolish, for they failed to see that they were living "in the last days" (*en eschatais hēmerais*), days that bear the characteristics of being end-time days. Although the absence of the definite article with "last days" places emphasis on the quality of the days, the context calls for a reference to the days preceding the return of the Lord Jesus. The NEB renders it, "in an age that is near its close." The emphasis is on the crisis character of the times. The early Christians looked for the imminent return of the Lord, but, like us, they did not know when Christ Jesus would return. The exhortations in verses 7-9 make the reference to the second coming practically certain.

James's expression "in the last days" has been variously understood. The view that James here personalizes it to denote "the last days of their lives when these merchants will be grey and old and unable to work"[27] seems improbable. It may well be that these grasping merchants thus rationalized their greedy hoarding, but that does not seem to be the intended meaning here. If James intended to limit the expression to these merchants he could readily have indicated that by adding "your" to denote the precise relation. Without this restrictive pronoun it seems improbable that James was restricting the scope of this familiar biblical expression. Prophetically he viewed their activities as already overshadowed by the reality of the end-time judgment.

Others have taken "the last days" to refer to the impending destruction of Jerusalem in A.D. 70.[28] Huther agrees that these interpreters "are so far right, as the destruction of Jerusalem and the last judgment had not as yet been distinguished in representation."[29] The view that the reference is to the "last days" of the polity of Israel in the first century is possible but unlikely if an early date for the epistle is accepted.

Clearly James has the future Day of Judgment in mind. He was keenly aware that the attitudes and activities of human beings must be evaluated in the light of the future eschatalogical judgment.

James's words seem to echo the teaching of Jesus: "Lay not up for yourselves treasures upon earth, where moth and rust consume, and where thieves break through and steal: . . . for where thy treasure is, there will thy heart be also" (Matt. 6:19-21, ASV). But the rich men whom James castigates were not motivated by the spirit inculcated by Jesus. Their activity of heaping up earthly goods expressed a self-sufficient, this-worldly attitude that contradicted a vital sense of dependence on and accountability to God.

3. The Charges in the Judgment (vv. 4-6)

James now delineates the guilt of these rich men, previously only hinted at under the figure of rust and moths. His opening exclamation "Look!" marks his intense earnestness in proceeding with his formal arrangement. The charges deserve their serious attention. They are charged with oppressing the poor laborers (v. 4), living in luxurious self-indulgence (v. 5), and wantonly murdering the righteous (v. 6). There is a progression in these charges. Sin begets more sin.

a. *The oppression of the poor laborers* (v. 4). "The wages you failed to pay the workmen who mowed your fields are crying out against you. The cries of the harvesters have reached the ears of the Lord Almighty." The graphic scene is not drawn from their sharp business dealing with other rich men but from their fraudulent failure to pay the poor day laborers who have harvested their large estates. The scene centers on an unjust economic situation between an employer and his employees. James does not condemn the employer-employee relationship itself. What he does condemn is the *exploitation* of the employees by the employer. Zodhiates well remarks, "There is an established principle of justice and respect for the rights of each other. . . . The one should not steal from the other. . . . Here, since James deals with wealth and the capitalist, the condemnation of God falls upon him for injustice perpetrated."[30]

Here "the workmen," as generally in the New Testament, denotes agricultural employees, workmen dependent on their daily earning to meet their material need (Matt. 9:37; 20:1-10). They are further identified by an appositional construction, "who mowed your fields" (*tōn amesantōn tas chōras humōn*), "those who in-gathered your fields" (Young). "Mowed," a verbal form not used elsewhere in the New Testament, seems to have the primary meaning of "gathering in." The reference is to the wheat and barley harvests that were cut and shocked by hand. The aorist tense denotes that the work has been completed and "the wages," the stipulated pay for the labor, have been justly earned. "Fields" (*chōras*) here, as in the parable of the rich fool (Luke 12:16), implies the extensive fields of these rich landlords. The scene is placed at the time of the harvest when the ingathering of the new crop vastly increases the owners' wealth.

The joyous harvest scene greatly increases the landlord's callous cruelty because he has "failed to pay" the justly earned salary due the workmen. The salary, referred to at the beginning of the sentence, is further described by the appositional perfect participle *ho aphusterēmenos*, "the one having been withheld by you."[31] The compound verb indicates not just delay but complete default, apparently on the basis of some unwarranted technicality. The perfect tense indicates that the evil remains uncorrected. The verb occurs only here in the New Testament. This injustice toward day laborers was an evil of frequent occurrence from earliest times, one that the Mosaic law strictly prohibited (Lev. 19:13; Deut. 24:14-15) and the prophets vigorously denounced (Jer. 22:13; Mal. 3:5). "You failed" (*aph humōn*) charges the rich directly with the guilt of this sin. Most interpreters agree in connecting this phrase with the preceding participle, "the one having been withheld." Then the preposition (*apo*), which has the root meaning of "off, away from," is best understood not as denoting the direct agents of the action but rather "the quarter from which the action proceeds."[32] Then James charges the rich with being the kind of people who would perpetrate such an evil. Another interpretation is to connect the phrase with the following verb, "cries out from you." Thus Alford pictures the pay that "was kept back, and rests with you, cries out *from you*, your coffers, where it lies."[33] But this interpretation is quite improbable.

"Are crying out" (*krazei*), a present active verb, dramatically pictures "the wages" unjustly withheld as continually crying out for vengeance. It denotes a loud cry or scream, such as the cry of demons being expelled from their victims (Mark 9:26; Luke 9:39). But the verb also is used of inanimate things crying out in an appeal against injustice, such as the blood of Abel (Gen. 4:10) or the sin of Sodom (18:20; 19:13). The sin of the rich is an evil that cried to God for vengeance. "To condemn to hunger those whose labors supply us with bread is a crime that cries to heaven."[34]

With *kai*, "and," not in NIV, James adds another element to the picture: "The cries of the harvesters have reached the ears of the Lord Almighty." The needy victims also utter their "cries" (*hai boai*); the noun, which occurs only here in the New Testament, denotes a loud cry or shout. In the Septuagint it is used of the cry to God by the oppressed and downtrodden (Ex. 2:23; 1 Sam. 9:16; 2 Chron. 33:13; Isa. 15:8). The articular aorist participle "of the harvesters" (*tōn therisantōn*) pictures them as a specific group of workers who have completed the harvesting; but they cannot enter into the joy of the harvest because their hard labor remains unrewarded.

The cries of the economically oppressed receive God's attention. The cries of the needy harvesters do not gain the attention of the rich landlords, but they "have reached the ears of the Lord Almighty." The perfect tense verb "have reached," standing emphatically at the end of the sentence, assures that

God had already taken notice and that His judgment is being prepared. "Have reached" (*eiselēluthan*, more literally, "have entered in") is a vivid Old Testament anthropomorphism denoting that their cries have been heard by "the Lord Almighty" (*kuriou sabaōth*, "the Lord of Sabaoth"). *Sabaoth*, which occurs elsewhere in the New Testament only in Romans 9:29 as a quotation from Isaiah 1:9, casts "an Old Testament solemnity"[35] over James's words. It points to a Jewish author as well as to Jewish readers. It is one of the most majestic titles of the God of Israel, "expressing not only His majesty and power as creator and ruler of the world, but also as commander of the hosts of heaven."[36] The Septuagint transliterated the term or used such variants as "Lord of powers" or "Lord of Omnipotence." This distinctive Hebrew name for God "combines majesty and transcendence."[37] The NIV rendering "the Lord Almighty" conveys this concept but does not fully portray the picture of God as the Lord of the armies of heaven. The title, which occurs twenty-three times in the book of Malachi, stresses that the poor and the helpless have on their side the Lord of hosts, who can destroy the tyranny of the oppressors and punish their iniquities.

b. *The self-indulgence of the rich* (v. 5). "You have lived on earth in luxury and self-indulgence. You have fattened yourselves in the day of slaughter." Introduced without a connecting particle, this second charge sets the voluptuous living of the rich in sharp contrast to the hardships that they inflict on the poor. Three aorist indicative verbs summarize their self-indulgence from the standpoint of the Judgment Day.

"You have lived on earth in luxury" portrays their daily life as spent in soft extravagance. The verb (*etruphēsate*), which occurs only here in the New Testament, denotes a life of luxury and self-indulgence, although it does not imply wanton vice. It is the picture drawn by Jesus of the rich man who "was dressed in purple and fine linen and lived in luxury every day" (Luke 16:19). They lived in high style, indulging in the delights pertaining to the senses. "On earth" seems to indicate that their delights were limited to the things of this world; it was their portion and interest, the sum of their desires and aspirations. Apparently James intended it to remind these rich of the contrast between their enjoyment of their good things in this life and their lot hereafter (cf. Luke 16:25).

The second verb, "and self-indulgence" (*espatalēsate*), adds the thought of extravagant and unrestrained self-indulgence. If the preceding verb evokes the thought of the rich man faring sumptuously every day (Luke 16:19), this one recalls the conduct of the prodigal son, who spent his substance in riotous living (Luke 15:13).[38] This verb occurs also in 1 Timothy 5:6 in regard to the widow who lived in wanton pleasure. Moffatt renders it, "You have . . . plunged into dissipation."

The remainder of verse 5 lays bare the real significance of their life of luxury and wantonness: "You have fattened yourselves in the day of slaughter." "Fattened" (*ethrepasate*) here conveys the meaning "to fatten, to satiate with food." In Jeremiah 46:21 (which in the Septuagint text is 26:21) this Greek verb is used of fattened calves. It ironically implies that their life of self-indulgence may be compared to oxen being fattened for slaughter.[39] As applied to their manner of life, the expression portrays them as enjoying themselves on the day they slaughtered domestic animals for food. "Since the fresh meat was soon dried or salted, it was customary to have a big barbecue when one slaughtered animals."[40]

"Yourselves" is literally "hearts" (*tas kardias*), used figuratively to denote the seat of the inner life with its desires and affections. James suggests that their central concern in life is to indulge in the luxuries of earth and therein seek their satisfaction. But James intends the expression "in the day of slaughter" (*en hemēra sphages*) to convey a fuller spiritual significance. The preposition *en*, "in," does not mean "for," but here is best rendered "in connection with" a day of slaughter. The expression is indefinite, having the quality of a day connected with slaughtering, killing by slashing the throat. The expression is qualitative and need not be limited to the Day of Judgment; yet here it seems to be parallel with "in the last days" (v. 3). The imagery seems to be that of oxen being amply fed in preparation for their slaughter; they greedily continue to gorge themselves, even on the day they will be slaughtered. The NEB brings out this meaning with its interpretive rendering, "fattening yourselves like cattle—and the day for slaughter has come." Ironically the rich themselves are now the fattened cattle, with God's slaughter knife poised to strike.

Others, such as Blackman[41] and Adamson,[42] hold that the picture is rather that of warriors engaged in unrestrained feasting after a victory. Then the reference is rather to the callous indifference of those rich men in celebrating their victory when things turn out badly for the poor. But this does not seem to fit the scene, since the context implies that the rich themselves will be slaughtered. The imagery seems to be based on Jeremiah 12:3.

c. *The violence against the righteous* (v. 6). "You have condemned and murdered innocent men." The absence of any connecting particle again makes this stand out as an independent charge. "You have condemned" apparently looks back to what was hinted at in 2:6, indicating that these rich Jews controlled their Jewish courts or used their influence with pagan judges to secure an adverse verdict against the righteous.

"And murdered" (*ephoneusate*, "you have murdered") indicates that the condemnation secured has resulted in the death of the innocent. The absence of a connective "and" (cf. NIV) heightens the effect and "expresses the hastiness with which the murder follows upon the condemnation."[43] Whereas this verb was used to denote actual murder, Moffatt notes that in Jewish usage it had a wider significance and could mean murdering a man by depriving him of his living.[44] Thus Ecclesiasticus 34:22 declares, "*As* one that slayeth his neighbor is he that taketh away his living; and *as* a shedder of blood is he that depriveth a hireling of his hire." But the context makes the thought of judicial murder more probable. It seems clear that both verbs are to be taken literally. Thus "these wicked people did not merely condemn the just; they proceeded to execute the decisions of the puppet courts."[45] James does not pause to delineate the precise details; his purpose is to bear witness to the fact that these rich men perpetrate murder on innocent people. Thus, as Blue remarks, "What began as an interest in money ended as an insensitivity to murder."[46] The aorist tenses in this verse need not be restricted to an isolated event but seem best taken as making a summary statement of what has occurred repeatedly. History is replete with such judicial murders.

"Innocent men" (*tōn dikaion*, literally, "the righteous one") is not to be restricted to a particular individual; the article is generic, viewing the individual as representative of his class. His very character as "righteous," morally upright and just, would arouse the hatred of the unjust rich against him.[47]

On various occasions in the New Testament, Jesus is spoken of as "the Righteous One" (Acts 3:14; 7:52; 22:14; 1 John 2:1; 3:7; cf. also Matt. 27:19, 24; Luke 23:47; 1 Pet. 3:18). Some interpreters hold that James is referring directly to the death of Jesus. Plummer notes that "this interpretation has found advocates in all ages" but concludes that the context is against it.[48] James seems clearly to have in view a class sin, the evil of the powerful rich tyrannizing the poor. Even less likely is the suggestion that James, who came to be known in Jerusalem as "The Just,"[49] was anticipating his own martyrdom.[50] An early date for the epistle makes this highly unlikely. Blackman stamps this suggestion as "very far-fetched."[51]

"Who were not opposing you" (*ouk antitassetai humin*) is more literally, "he is not opposing you," in agreement with the singular "the righteous man" in the first part of the verse. Again the individual is pictured as representative of the class of righteous people opposed by the rich. In such a crisis situation each saintly soul must act on his own behalf. But, because they are righteous, there is a consistent pattern in their reaction. James presents the picture from the standpoint of such a representative individual. Mayor remarks that the use of the present tense "bring the action before our eyes and makes us dwell on this, as the central point, in contrast with the accompanying circumstances."[52] This righteous individual is viewed as making no move to place himself in active opposition to his murderers. Either the righteous man finds himself wholly unable to resist his oppressors and so must suffer at their hands, or the meaning is that the Christians under persecution were following the teaching of Jesus: "Do not resist an evil person" (Matt. 5:39).

The latter view is in keeping with James's constant stress on the need for patient endurance. The account preserved by Eusebius pictures James himself as practicing the teaching of Jesus at his own martyrdom. This is not a natural human reaction. As Roberts points out, "To be unresisting when one is committed to death, as an innocent victim, must demonstrate that one is controlled by the Holy Spirit."[53] The nonresistance of the righteous confirms the guilt of the rich, who remain unmoved by the patient sufferings they viciously inflict on their innocent victims. With this comment James reminds them that "the behaviour of the just under your persecutions is ever that of meekness and submission."[54]

Ropes, following the suggestion of the Westcott and Hort Greek text, takes these words as a question: "Does not he resist you?" He feels that reading these words as a statement of fact is "wholly unsuited to the context" and asserts that it ends "this powerful passage of triumphant denunciation" with an anticlimax.[55] But most other commentators do not feel the difficulty that Ropes alleges. Tasker rightly holds that the indicative "brings the section to an end on a note of majestic pathos."[56] The indicative is more natural and heightens the reader's sense of the guilt of the rich. The statement effectively serves as a transition to the exhortations to the saints in the next paragraph.

B. THE EXHORTATIONS TO THE AFFLICTED BRETHREN (vv. 7-11)

"Then" (*oun*, "therefore") marks the preceding prophetic denunciation of the rich oppressors as the foundation for this brotherly appeal to the readers. Following his fiery denunciation of the oppressors, James turns to counsel and encourage his afflicted brethren. He appeals for the needed steadfast endurance in view of the Lord's return, when their affliction will be terminated and they will be rewarded. As belonging to the class of nonresisting righteous (v. 6), let them exercise hope-inspired endurance while they refrain from unjustly blaming those around them.

This paragraph falls into three parts. James urges them to exercise patience in view of Christ's return (vv. 7-8), warns against the natural tendency of the afflicted to unjustly blame those around them (v. 9), and directs their attention to godly examples of suffering and constancy in the past (vv. 10-11).

1. The Call for Patience in View of the Parousia (vv. 7-8)

"Be patient, then, brothers, until the Lord's coming" (v. 7*a*). This is their urgent duty as his afflicted "brothers," marking their distinction from the oppressing world.

"Be patient" (*makrothumēsate*), used three times in these two verses, stresses the needed attitude as they confront the oppressive rich. The compound verb, used quite literally here, means being "long-tempered" as contrasted to "short-tempered." It does not call for a passive resignation to one's fate but an attitude of self-restraint that enables one to refrain from hasty retaliation in the face of provocation. The cognate noun is commonly rendered "long-suffering," which does not mean to suffer a while but to tolerate someone for a long time. It is a different term than that rendered "patient" (KJV; ASV) in 1:3-4, 12. The term used there (*hupomonē*) conveys the thought of patience or endurance in respect to the difficult circumstances of life; the term here used denotes the thought of being long-tempered or patient in relation to people who cause personal distress or suffering. Ropes notes that the term used here is rare in secular Greek.[57] It is a virtue that does not readily flourish in the heart of the natural man. It is quite common in the Septuagint, where it is mentioned as a commended virtue among men (Prov. 14:29; 15:18; 19:11), and it is used of God's attitude of forbearance toward the sins and faults of people (Pss. 86:15; 103:8; Jer. 15:15). The New Testament presents it as an attribute of God Himself (Rom. 2:4; 9:22; 1 Pet. 2:20) and urges its practice upon believers (Matt. 18:23-33; 1 Thess. 5:14; 2 Pet. 3:9). It is the opposite of an easily kindled wrath that readily lashes out in punishment. The aorist imperative here is best viewed as constative, demanding that this must be their unwavering attitude until the end.

Such patience will be necessary "until the Lord's coming." That event, held before them as a motive for patience, will terminate their subjection to oppression and injustice. "The Lord" here clearly refers to the Lord Jesus Christ in His second advent. James offers a scanty Christology in this epistle, but the expression, twice used in these two verses without further clarification, is a clear affirmation of the deity of Christ Jesus. He takes it for granted that His return is a living hope in the early church.

"The coming" (*tēs parousias*) denotes a specific event, a hope well known to the readers. "Coming" renders a compound noun composed of *para*, "alongside of, close to," and the substantival form of the verb *eimi*, "to be," hence, it literally means "being alongside of," or "presence." Papyrus usage shows that the term was common in secular Greek for a royal visit to a certain city or district.[58] The term does occur in the Septuagint[59] and was not used in connection with the Messiah until the time of Christ (Matt. 24:3, 27, 37, 39). In the New Testament epistles it is one of the most frequently used terms for the return of Christ (1 Cor. 15:23; 1 Thess. 2:19; 3:13; 4:15; 5:23; 2 Thess. 2:1, 8; 2 Pet. 1:16; 3:4; 1 John 2:28). The term may have the sense of "coming" as denoting His arrival, but its fuller significance centers attention on His presence with His people as the result of His coming. Hendricksen remarks that the term denotes "his 'coming' in order to bless his people with his presence."[60] In subapostolic times it was occasionally used of Jesus' advent in the incarnation,[61] but in the New Testament it always seems to be used of His return in glory.[62] The term, which is never used with an adjective or numeral in the New Testament, enshrines the distinctive Christian hope of the personal coming of Christ in glory. James has very little to say concerning the details of that eschatological hope, but for him it clearly was a hope that must have had a sanctifying impact on daily life.[63]

Aware of how hard it is to be patient, James undergirds his counsel with an illustration. "See" calls special attention to the illustration: "See how the farmer waits for the land to yield its valuable crop and how patient he is for the fall and spring rains" (v. 7b). The picture is very natural for a lifelong resident of Palestine.

"The farmer" (*ho geōrgos*), one who tills the soil, is here an independent landowner or a tenant farmer rather than a day laborer. Having sown
his field, the farmer looks forward to the harvest, but he knows that there
must be an interval of growth and development before he can expect to
receive the "valuable crop" of the land. The anticipated crop, the produce of
the soil, is valuable, that is, of great worth, because its production requires
hard work, and, in part, the maintenance of physical life depends on it. The
value of the harvest justifies his patient waiting. The compound verb "waits"
(*ekdechetai*) conveys the thought of looking expectantly for something that
comes to us from without; the farmer recognizes that the fruit is not simply
the result of his own personal activity but is dependent on forces outside
himself that he cannot control. The pious believer recognizes that the spiritual harvest that we anticipate also is dependent on the intervention of God in
human affairs.

The attitude of the farmer is further described by the observation "how
patient he is for the fall and spring rains." "How patient he is" (*makrothu-
mōn*) renders a present participle portraying his constant attitude of expectancy between seedtime and harvest, even when irregularities in the rainfall
may create uncertainty. The NIV rendering somewhat compresses James's
fuller statement: "having patience for it until it receive [the] early and [the]
later rain."[64] "For it" (*ep' autō*) denotes that the expected fruit is the farmer's
central interest, and his mental and emotional concerns are focused on it. He
confidently waits "until it receive" (*heōs labē*) the fall and spring rains. The
subject of "it receive" is not expressed. Some would render it "he receive,"
since the farmer is the subject of the sentence and the center of the illustration.[65] Others suggest that the intended subject is "fruit," indicated in the
preceding word "for it."[66] But most naturally the subject is the farmer's field.[67]
The farmer himself does not receive the rain, nor can he determine where
and when it will fall. Nor does the fruit produced actually receive the early
rain, since it is not yet in existence when the early rains fall. There is textual
uncertainty as to whether the original reading included the noun "rain" or
consisted instead only of the two adjectives "early and latter" (*proimon kai
opsimon*).[68] In the Septuagint the noun "rain" (*hueton*) always appears with
these two adjectives. Several important early manuscripts and versions have
only two adjectives here, but the majority of our Greek manuscripts include
the noun.[69] This variation in readings makes it more probable that the original did not have the word for rain in it and that the scribes added the noun to
eliminate ambiguity. The Palestinian setting of the picture makes it quite certain that James was speaking of the fall and spring rains, without which no
harvest could be produced. Jewish readers living north of Palestine would
understand the reference without the added noun.

"The fall" rains, generally arriving in a series of thunderstorms, come
in the latter part of October or in early November. They are anxiously awaited by the farmer since they are necessary to soften the hard-baked soil for

plowing and sowing. A serious delay of these rains diminishes the prospects for a crop; if they fail entirely, a crop failure results. The bulk of the rains come during December through February. The "latter," or "spring" rains fall during late April or May. These late rains, accompanied by warmer temperatures than in winter, are important for the maturing of the crops. The longer they continue, the greater the potential yield.[70]

The picture implies that James was personally familiar with these rains and their importance to the farmer. It supports a Palestinian origin for the epistle. Ropes observes, "The Apostolic Fathers and the apologists contain no reference to these terms for the rains of Palestine, and the names do not seem in any way to have become part of the early Christian religious vocabulary."[71] James intended his reference to these to be understood literally, and no allegorical meanings should be sought.

"You too, be patient and stand firm" (v. 8*a*) applies the illustration of the patient farmer to the readers. The aorist imperative verbs set forth two aspects of their urgent need. The original order, with the verb first, "You too, be patient" (*makrothumēsate kai humeis*, "be patient, also you") strengthens the call for patience by repeating the opening verb of verse 7, whereas the added "also you" underlines that they, like the farmer, need patience. Now the emphatic pronoun "you" (*humeis*) replaces "brother" of verse 7 but marks James's concern for them. Amid their experiences of oppression and injustices they must maintain and strengthen an attitude of longsuffering forbearance as they wait upon God to consummate His purposes with them.

"Stand firm" (*stērixate tas kardias humōn*, more literally, "make firm your hearts") urges them, as a decisive act, to strengthen and make firm their inner life. The verb conveys the thought of strengthening and supporting something so that it will stand firm and immovable. Instead of feeling agitated and shaken up by their experiences of oppression, they must develop an inner sense of stability. Williams paraphrases it, "You must put iron into your hearts," whereas the NEB calls upon them to be "stout-hearted." In other places this inner strengthening is spoken of as the work of God in the lives of believers (1 Thess. 3:13; 2 Thess. 2:16-17; 1 Pet. 5:10), but here James calls upon the readers themselves to take this matter in hand. It is their personal duty to develop an attitude of courage and firmness in facing their circumstances. And this can only be done by raising their gaze heavenward.

"Because the Lord's coming is near" (v. 8*b*) indicates that they must find this inner strengthening in their personal hope in Christ's return. His renewed reference to this hope (cf. v. 7*a*) indicates that it was a living reality for James. The lack of amplification implies that the readers were familiar with this thought. "Is near" (*enggiken*) renders the perfect tense, "has come near," and thus is at hand. It implies that the parousia is near but has not actually arrived. Whereas Christ's presence is now mediated to His saints through the Holy Spirit, His bodily presence with them is still a matter of the future.

His statement here leaves no doubt that James, like Paul, Peter, and John (Phil. 4:5; 1 Pet. 4:7; 1 John 2:18), looked for the personal return of Jesus Christ as imminent. And this attitude of expectancy was in keeping with the attitude that Christ had inculcated (Mark 13:32-37). The Lord had instructed His followers to be ready and watching; if they had believed that He would not return until centuries later, there would have been no occasion or need to watch for His return. "The Lord had laid it upon His people not only to believe, but to watch; not only to love, but to watch; not only to obey, but to watch; . . . and by the inspiration of the Holy Ghost they were in this state of mind."[72] But it is "wrong to assert that they were certain that they would live to see the Parousia; they were no more certain of it than we are today."[73]

Nor, we may add, were they certain that He would not come in their lifetime; neither are we. It is an undated event; each generation of believers is thus given the opportunity to live in the hope of His return. If the hope of the Lord's return is relegated to such a remote future that it has no present impact on our way of living, then this great Christian hope no longer exercises the vital influence upon Christian living that James and other New Testament writers present it as having (1 Thess. 4:18; 1 Pet. 4:7; 2 Pet. 3:11; 1 John 3:3). But the New Testament also makes clear that this hope of Christ's imminent return must not lead to fanatical excitement and unwarranted disruption of the duties of daily life (1 Thess. 4:10*b*-12; 2 Thess. 2:1-3).

2. The Warning Against Blaming One Another (v. 9)

"Don't grumble against each other, brothers, or you will be judged." The verb (*stenazete*) does not mean "murmur" but "sigh" or "groan" because of undesirable circumstances or oppression under which the individual suffers. Whereas the primary reference is to the inner feeling of dissatisfaction and personal irritation at another, rather than the expression of loud and bitter complaints, it involves a feeling of criticism and faultfinding directed against others. This personal feeling reflects itself in smoldering resentment that may display itself in an antagonistic expression of bitter groans. "Don't grumble" conveys the force of the original quite well. The present imperative with the negative *mē* indicates that such grumbling against fellow believers is taking place and must be stopped. Such a spirit threatens the inner unity of the brotherhood.

Before completing his warning, James stops to address the readers once more as "brothers." His prohibition is motivated by his brotherly concern for their spiritual welfare. He is not unsympathetic toward them amid their trying circumstances, which tend to make them irritable. But he is concerned about eliminating their tendency to grow sullen and exasperated "against each other" (*kat' allēlōn*). The preposition *kata* with the genitive denotes that their groaning is directed "down on" or "against" their brethren who are not responsible for their trying circumstances; the use of the reciprocal pronoun indicates that their half-suppressed feeling tends to be mutual. The warning is against the human tendency—when subjected to oppression and injustice—to give way to vexations by unjustly lashing out against those near and dear. "Brothers" appropriately stresses the incongruity of such a reaction.

> To walk above with saints we love,
> That will indeed be glory;
> To walk below with saints we know—
> Well, that's another story!

"Or you will be judged" (*hina mē krithēte*, "in order that you may not be judged") reminds them of the undesirable result to be avoided. Such mutual recrimination is both useless and sinful and evokes the Lord's censure. It violates the command of Christ (Matt. 7:1; Luke 6:37). They will be answerable to Him at the judgment seat (2 Cor. 5:10). The aorist tense suggests the finality of His judgment and implies that the evaluation will be adverse.

"The Judge is standing at the door!" James's opening exclamation, *idou*, "Behold," not in the NIV, calls attention not so much to the location of the Judge as to the imminence of the judgment. The heavenly Judge is fully aware of the relations among them, and His decision will determine the measure of their mutual guilt. "The Judge" is obviously the Lord Jesus Christ, whose return is viewed as imminent. That fact should stimulate the consciousness of their guilt in their feelings, thoughts, and reactions. His position as already standing "at the door" (*pro tōn thupōn*, literally, "before the doors") pictures Him as about to push the doors open to enter the judgment hall. It is "an expression indicating proximity, imminence, certainty."[74] The plural "doors" apparently denotes the double doors at the entrance to the stately judgment hall.[75] The realization of the nearness of the coming Judge should be both a comfort and a warning to them in their circumstances. "It is a shallow kind of Christianity that, seeing only God's grace in the Gospel, forgets inevitable judgment."[76]

3. The Examples of Suffering and Endurance (vv. 10-11)

Turning back to their adverse circumstances, James encourages his readers with a reminder of the experiences of God's saints in the past. He first recalls the multiple example of the Old Testament prophets (v. 10) and then the specific example of Job (v. 11).

a. *The example of the prophets* (v. 10). "Brothers, as an example of patience in the face of suffering, take the prophets." As "brother,"[77] James bids his readers turn their attention back to the religious history of their own people. James knew the value of an "example" (*hupodeigma*), an objective illustration that we can hold before us as a model to spur one to pursue the conduct desired. Though an example may be negative, showing us what not to do (Heb. 4:11; 2 Pet. 2:6), James here stresses the positive value of a good example. The term is emphatic as the first word in the sentence. Amid their suffering he bids his readers, as a definite act, to "take" (*labete*), hold before their minds, the example of the Old Testament[78] prophets. In the midst of their difficult circumstances they provide an example "of patience in the face of suffering" (*tēs kakopathias kai tēs markathumias*).

The exact force of these two nouns has been taken in different ways. The ASV rendering, "an example of suffering and of patience," denotes that the prophets presented a twofold example. The definite article with both nouns points to the specific experiences of the prophets, implying that they were well known to the readers as being similar to their own. The former noun, which occurs only here in the New Testament,[79] is a compound form meaning the experience of suffering what is base or evil, to suffer misfortune. The term may have a passive sense as denoting the suffering or miseries that come upon a person, but here it probably has an active force to denote the strenuous efforts made to endure the difficult situation.[80] The second noun (see the verbal form in v. 7 above) points to their brave endurance and steadfastness under affliction without succumbing.

Others view the expression as a *hendiadys*, the expression of one idea by two nouns.[81] Thus the NIV renders, "an example of patience in the face of suffering." Davids remarks that "it is not the suffering which forms the example but the fact that those who suffered did in fact endure patiently."[82]

Those offering this noteworthy example James identifies as "the prophets." This plural designation is not to be restricted to those prophets who penned one of the books of the Old Testament; it includes all those called to be God's messengers. In Matthew 5:12 Jesus encouraged His disciples boldly to face persecution, "for in the same way they persecuted the prophets who were before you."

The added designation, "who spoke in the name of the Lord," aptly reminds the readers that even the Lord's most eminent servants in the past were not exempt from ill-treatment. Although God honored them by using them as His spokesmen, they did not escape maltreatment. Rather, their very work provoked the world's opposition. If those who spoke "in the name of the Lord," delivering their messages as God's revelation to the world, did not escape persecution, those of lesser positions in His service should not expect to escape either. Jeremiah is an outstanding example of those who suffered such treatment as God's messengers. New Testament references to the persecution of the Old Testament prophets are remarkably frequent (Matt. 5:12; 21:35-36; 22:6; 23:29-37; Luke 13:33; Acts 7:51-52; Rom. 11:3; 1 Thess. 2:15; Heb. 11:32-38; Rev. 16:6; 18:24). Their very faithfulness to God amid such suffering for Him was a mark of their true character. He who speaks "In the name of the Lord" speaks with His authorization as His delegated messenger.

Davids remarks that with this identification James "both excludes false prophets and focuses on the true prophets' crucial characteristic."[83]

b. *The example of Job* (v. 11). In adding, "As you know, we consider blessed those who have persevered," James summarizes the general example of the prophets and prepares for the specific example of Job. "As you know" (*idou*, literally, "Behold," its last occurrence in this epistle) calls special attention to this matter of perseverance under testing. With his use of the first person "we" James united himself with his readers in expressing admiration for this virtue when displayed in others. The present tense verb "we consider blessed" declares that it was a common practice to admire a display of such brave perseverance, with the willingness to consider them "blessed," or "fortunate." Moo remarks, "'To be blessed' is not, of course, the same as being *happy*; . . . 'Happiness' normally suggests a subjective, emotional reaction; 'blessing' is the objective, unalterable approval and reward of God."[84] Does James imply that his readers were not making the same evaluation when their own endurance was involved?

"Those who have persevered" (*tous hupomeinantas*), an aorist articular participle, denotes a general class of sufferers who persevered and successfully completed their test.[85] They remained bravely under their siege of trials without losing heart and so faithfully endured until the end. It is the term that James used in 1:3-4 in describing the role of steadfastness in the production of Christian character and in 1:12 as necessary to receive the crown of life. Here he points to Job as an example of such steadfastness. This felicitation of such pious sufferers involves the common conviction that they will not remain unrewarded (Matt. 5:12). Job demonstrates not only the blessedness of such constancy under affliction but also the assurance of its blessed consummation.

"You have heard of Job's perseverance" implies that James expected his readers to be familiar with Job's story. This is the only place where Job is directly mentioned in the New Testament. (The only quotation from the book of Job in the New Testament is in 1 Cor. 3:19, where Job 5:13 is cited.) But the mention of Job in Ezekiel 14:14, 20, where he is named with Noah and Daniel as an example of personal righteousness, shows that he held an honorable place in Jewish thought. Oesterley notes that Job also "occupies a high place of honour in post-biblical Jewish literature."[86] Among early Christian writers, Clement of Rome made frequent quotations from the book of Job ("Corinthians," chaps. 17, 20, 26, 39, 56).[87] "Heard" is probably a summary reference to the fact that the readers had gained their knowledge of him from public reading and instruction in synagogue and church.

The point in the example that James stresses is "Job's perseverance." The familiar rendering, "the patience of Job" (KJV; ASV), does not seems to fit the picture of him as he appears in the book bearing his name. When reading his "impassioned outbursts against the shallow platitudes of his so-called 'comforters' (e.g., 3:1, 11; 16:2, etc.) or his distressed protests to God Himself (7:11-16; 10:18; 23:2; 30:20-23)," it is obvious that Job was not a model of stoic impassibility.[88] Fine asserts, "Honesty, not patience, is the real virtue of Job."[89] Although he did reveal remarkable patience in his initial acceptance of his calamities (Job 1:21; 2:10), Job's vehement protests against his sufferings can scarcely be described as "patient." But the term James uses here is not that found in verse 10 (*makrothumia*) but rather *hupomonē* (cf. the verb in 11*a*), which denotes endurance. (cf. 1:3-4, 12). In the face of all his unexplained sufferings, Job is a memorable model of endurance under tremendous testing, for under it all he remained unswervingly loyal to God (1:21; 2:10; 16:9-21; 19:25-27). Zodhiates remarks, "His imperfections and human weaknesses are scarcely remembered. Only his patience is spoken of. This is very characteristic of God's longsuffering towards His saints."[90]

As an encouragement to his readers, James also refers to the happy outcome of the story of Job: "and have seen what the Lord finally brought about." "And have seen" suggests that his readers followed with keen interest the outcome of the story as it unfolded scene by scene. "What the Lord finally brought about" (*to telos kuriou*, literally, "the end of the Lord") refers to the joyful end, or consummation, to which "the Lord" (genitive of agent) brought his sufferings. The outcome completely vindicated Job and crowned his sufferings with appropriate reward. Calvin remarks, "Afflictions ought ever to be estimated by their end."[91] The word "end" (*telos*) also can be used to denote the goal toward which a movement is directed.[92] Thus the RSV renders it, "you have seen the purpose of the Lord." Then the meaning is that the goal God had in view in allowing all Job's sufferings to come upon him has been revealed: to refute Satan's slander. (Job 1:11; 2:4-5) and to vindicate and strengthen Job's faith.

Augustine and others following him have suggested that "the end of the Lord" is a reference to Christ's death. This would give a double example of "perseverance." But this suggestion, while attractive, does not fit the context, which cites Old Testament examples. This view would require two different meanings for "Lord" in the same verse. Also, we would expect the article with "Lord" here if Christ were meant. "In that case," Ropes remarks, "not the mere death, but the triumph over death, would have had to be made prominent."[93] Mayor further observes,

> This, instead of giving one perfect illustration of the result of suffering rightly borne, gives two imperfect and barely intelligible illustrations. If *telos* [end] is supposed to refer to the Resurrection and Ascension, the main point of the comparison (suffering) is omitted: if it refers to the Crucifixion, the encouragement is wanting.[94]

It would have been more natural to bring in the example of Christ in connection with the prophets.

It is singular that James, unlike Peter (1 Pet.2:21-23), makes no mention of the example of Christ in His sufferings.[95] Probably the reason is that James, after having been brought to a belated realization of the true nature of Jesus Christ, instinctively shrank from placing Him on a level with other human sufferers. For him, Christ was uniquely "the Lord of glory" (2:1, ASV).

The consummation to which the Lord brought the case of Job demonstrates "that" (*hoti*, not in NIV) "the Lord is full of compassion and mercy." "The Lord" (*ho kurios*) here is obviously the Lord of the Old Testament, the common Septuagint rendering for the name "Jehovah" (YHWH, Yahweh). Men often fail to understand the true character of God as long as He permits them to endure oppression and injustice. James gently reminds his readers that, if they also will remain loyal to God amid their trials, they also will come to a personal realization of the kindly nature of God.

Two adjectives characterize God's dealings with His people: "full of compassion" (*polusplanchnos*) and "mercy" (*oiktirmōn*). James is apparently making a free quotation from Psalm 103:8. The former, a compound form meaning "very compassionate," is not found elsewhere in the New Testament or in the Septuagint and was apparently coined by James.[96] It was borrowed by Hermas in the middle of the second century (*Mand.* 4.3.5; *Sim.* 5.7.4) and always applied to Jehovah.[97] It declares that "God is not vicious; he does not love watching people suffer."[98] The second adjective occurs elsewhere in the New Testament only in Luke 6:36, where Jesus uses it of the divine mercy as the basis for an admonition to show mercy. The term is common in the Septuagint. His mercy has an external aspect as reaching out to mankind. The term here is plural, apparently "to express the concrete forms of expression taken" by God's mercy.[99] The God who revealed His abundant compassion and mercy in vindicating Job is the same today. The same spirit of steadfast loyalty to God under affliction will assuredly bring a fitting reward.

James has been concerned to help believers to overcome the tendency to react like the world to the injustices heaped on them by the world. The world, by its very nature antagonistic to God and His kingdom, will continue to oppose God's people. But if these truths grip the hearts of His people, it will enable them to overcome the spirit of worldliness by refraining from a worldly reaction to the world's injustices.

NOTES FOR
James 5:1-11

1. Charles Brown, "The General Epistle of James," in *A Devotional Commentary*, pp. 107-8.
2. William Barclay, *The Letters of James and Peter*, The Daily Study Bible, p. 135.
3. J. L. Kelso, "Wealth," in *The Zondervan Pictorial Encyclopedia of the Bible*, 5:911.
4. Theodor H. Epp, *James, the Epistle of Applied Christianity*, p. 223.
5. Billy Simmons, *A Functioning Faith*, p. 115.

6. John Calvin, *Commentaries on the Catholic Epistles*, p. 342.

7. H. Maynard Smith, *The Epistle of S. James. Lectures*, p. 276.

8. C. Leslie Mitton, *The Epistle of James*, p. 175.

9. Rudolf Stier, *The Epistle of St. James*, p. 434 (italics original).

10. Karl Heinrich Rengstorf, "Klaiō," in *Theological Dictionary of the New Testament*, 3:722-23.

11. Peter H. Davids, *James*, New International Biblical Commentary, p. 114.

12. E. C. Blackman, *The Epistle of James*, Torch Bible Commentaries, p. 142.

13. W. E. Oesterley, "The General Epistle of James," in *The Expositor's Greek Testament*, 4:467-68.

14. G. S. Candale, "Moth," in *The New Bible Dictionary*, p. 850; and W. M. Whitwell, "Insects of the Bible, Moths and Butterflies," in *The Zondervan Pictorial Bible Dictionary*, pp. 377-78.

15. Windisch as cited by Martin Dibelius, "James. A Commentary on the Epistle of James," in *Hermeneia—A Critical and Historical Commentary on the Bible*, p. 236 n. 34.

16. J. Nieboer, *Practical Exposition of James*, p.366.

17. Davids, p. 115.

18. J. Ronald Blue, "James," in *The Bible Knowledge Commentary, New Testament*, p. 832.

19. Roy B. Roberts, *The Game of Life, Studies in James*, pp. 144-45.

20. Alfred Plummer, "The General Epistles of St. James and St. Jude," in *An Exposition of the Bible*, 6:622.

21. James Hardy Ropes, *A Critical and Exegetical Commentary on the Epistle of St. James*, The International Critical Commentary on the Holy Scriptures of the Old and New Testaments, p. 286.

22. Edwin T. Winkler, "Commentary on the Epistle of James," in *An American Commentary on the New Testament*, p. 63.

23. Joseph B. Mayor, *The Epistle of St. James*, p. 151, asserts "The pl. *sarkes* is used for the fleshly parts of the body both in classical and later writers; . . . while the sing. *sarx* is used for the whole body." But Ropes, p. 287, declares, "The plural is used from Homer down, also by Attic writers and Plato, in a sense not distinguishable from that of the singular." John Peter Lange, "The Epistle General of James," in *Lange's Commentary on the Holy Scriptures*, 23:129, suggests that "the plural describes the life of the rich as exhibited in the carnalities or externals of religious, civil, or individual life, in which they take delight."

24. Spiros Zodhiates, *The Patience of Hope*, p. 57.

25. Robert Johnstone, *Lectures Exegetical and Practical on the Epistle of James*, p. 355.

26. Ropes insists that the verb requires an object and punctuates to connect "as fire" with this verb; he renders it, "since you have stored up fire" (pp. 287-88). This connection is adopted in the Greek text of Westcott and Hort. But other modern editors of the Greek text and most modern commentators prefer the punctuation connecting "as fire" with what preceded. With the NIV we accept the latter view as definitely preferable.

27. Zodhiates, p. 61.

28. See Joh. Ed. Huther, *Critical and Exegetical Handbook to the General Epistles of James, Peter, John, and Jude*, p. 145, for a list of advocates of this view.

29. Huther, p. 145.

30. Zodhiates, p. 64.

31. The more familiar term *apesterēmonos* used in the Textus Receptus means "having been robbed or deprived of" and suggests that the rich have underpaid the workers and so stolen part of the money justly due.

32. Mayor, p. 152.

33. Henry Alford, *The Greek New Testament*, 4:1, p. 321.

34. Winkler, p. 64.

35. Dibelius, p. 238.

36. R. J. Knowling, *The Epistle of St. James*, Westminster Commentaries, p. 122.

37. James B. Adamson, *The Epistle of James*, The New International Commentary on the New Testament, p. 186.

38. Richard Chenevix Trench, *Synonyms of the New Testament*, p. 202.

39. The comparative "as" (*hōs*) in the KJV follows the Textus Receptus, but it lacks adequate manuscript authority and is best omitted.

40. Davids, p. 117.

41. Blackman, p. 144.

42. Adamson, pp. 187-88.

43. Knowling, p. 125.

44. James Moffatt, *The General Epistles of James, Peter, John, and Jude*, The Moffatt New Testament Commentary, p. 70.

45. Zodhiates, p. 74.

46. Blue, p. 833.

47. The recent suggestion by D. Hill, "*Dikaioi* as a Quasi-Technical Term," *New Testament Studies* 11, no. 3 (April 1965):297-302, that *dikaioi* refers to teachers as a semidistinct class in the early church is improbable in this context.

48. Plummer, 6:625. Plummer names Cassidorus, Bede, Oecumenius, Grotius, Bengel, and Lange as supporting this view. See also Thomas Manton, *An Exposition of the Epistle of James*, pp. 416-18; and Smith, pp. 286-87.

49. Eusebius *The Ecclesiastical History Eusebius Pamphilus* 2.23.

50. Stier, p. 436, asserts, "So wonderfully prophetic is here the inspiration of the Holy Ghost—he is constrained unconsciously to prophesy of his own person."

51. Blackman, p. 146.

52. Mayor, p. 155.

53. Roberts, p. 149.

54. Alford, p. 322.

55. Ropes, p. 292.

56. R. V. G. Tasker, *The General Epistle of James*, The Tyndale New Testament Commentaries, p. 116.

57. Ropes, p. 293.

58. G. Adolf Deissmann, *Light from the Ancient East*, pp. 372-87; and James Hope Moulton and George Milligan, *The Vocabulary of the Greek Testament Illustrated from the Papyri and Other Non-Literary Sources*, p. 497.

59. It occurs in Codex A in Nehemiah 2:6 of Nehemiah personally. Paul also uses it of his own coming (Phil. 1:26; 2:12) or of some companions (1 Cor. 16:17; 2 Cor. 7:6-7). In 2 Thessalonians 2:9 it is used of the personal appearance of the eschatalogical man of sin.

60. William Hendriksen, "Exposition of I and II Thessalonians," in *New Testament Commentary*, p. 76.

61. William F. Arndt and F. Wilbur Gingrich, *A Greek-English Lexicon of the New Testament and Other Early Christian Literature*, p. 635.

62. Second Peter 1:16 can hardly be interpreted as Christ's first coming.

63. See Colin Brown, "The Parousia and Eschatology in the NT," in *The New International Dictionary of New Testament Theology*, 2:901-35, for recent scholarly treatments of New Testament parousia passages, together with a comprehensive bibliography.

64. Darby.

65. Ropes, p. 294. See the KJV, Moffatt, Williams, and Young.

66. Knowling, p. 128; Mayor, p. 156; Dibelius, p. 244.

67. E. C. S. Gibson, "The General Epistle of James," in *The Pulpit Commentary*, 49:69; Oesterley, p. 471.

68. The noun "rain" is omitted in the Greek texts of Westcott and Hort, Nestle and Aland, and the United Bible Societies. It is retained, with the Textus Receptus, in the texts of Souter, Tasker, and Hodges and Farstad.

69. See the evidence in the United Bible Societies' text, 3d ed.

70. J. H. Paterson, "Rain," in *The Zondervan Pictorial Encyclopedia of the Bible*, 5:27-28.

71. Ropes, p. 297.

72. M. F. Sadler, *The General Epistles of SS. James, Peter, John, and Jude with Notes Critical and Practical*, p. 69.

73. R. C. H. Lenski, *The Interpretation of the Epistle to the Hebrews and of the Epistle of James*, p. 665.

74. Zodhiates, p. 95.

75. In such figurative expressions, the plural may be equal to the singular. See F. Blass and A. Debrunner, *A Greek Grammar of the New Testament and Other Early Christian Literature*, p. 78; and Joachim Jeremias, "Thura," in *Theological Dictionary of the New Testament*, 3:174 n. 8.

76. Frank E. Gaebelein, *The Practical Epistle of James*, p. 113.

77. The pronoun "my" (*mou*) in the Textus Receptus (cf. KJV) lacks sufficient manuscript support. See the evidence in Nestle-Aland, *NOVUM TESTAMENTUM GRAECE*, 26th ed.

78. That James intended to include the Christian prophets (Eph. 2:20; 3:5) is highly unlikely since the reference in verse 11 to Job clearly limits the scope of reference to the Old Testament.

79. The cognate verb is used in James 5:13 and 2 Timothy 2:3, 9.

80. Arndt and Gingrich, p. 398; Deissmann, *Bible Studies*, pp. 162-63.

81. Ropes, p. 298; Dibelius, p. 245 n. 25.

82. Peter H. Davids, *The Epistle of James*, p. 186.

83. Davids, *James*, New International Biblical Commentary, p. 120.

84. Douglas J. Moo, *The Letter of James*, p. 171.

85. The present tense in the Textus Receptus lacks adequate manuscript support.

86. Oesterley, p. 472.

87. Clement, "The First Epistle of Clement to the Corinthians," in *The Ante-Nicene Fathers*, 1:5-21.

88. Mitton, p. 189.

89. Hillel A. Fine, "The Tradition of a Patient Job," *Journal of Biblical Literature* 74 (March 1955): 28.

90. Zodhiates, p. 106.

91. Calvin, p. 352.

92. Arndt and Gingrich, p. 819.

93. Ropes, p. 299.

94. Mayor, p. 159.

95. Burton Scott Easton and Gordon Poteat, "The Epistle of James," in *The Interpreter's Bible*, 12:67-68, appeal to this omission as support for the view that this section is Jewish, not Christian, in origin.

96. F. Wilber Gingrich, "Prolegomena to a Study of the Christian Element in the Vocabulary of the New Testament and Apostolic Fathers," in *Search the Scriptures, New Testament Studies in Honor of Raymond T. Stamm*, p. 177.

97. Knowling, p. 134.

98. Davids, *The Epistle of James*, p. 188.

99. Arndt and Gingrich, *A Greek-English Lexicon*, p. 564.

13

XII. THE REACTION OF LIVING FAITH TO SELF-SERVING OATHS

5:12 Above all, my brothers, do not swear—not by heaven or by earth or by anything else. Let your "Yes" be yes, and your "No" no, or you will be condemned.

The insertion of this injunction against swearing at this point in the epistle has been much discussed. Indeed, Sadler holds that it "has never been satisfactorily explained."[1] Some, like Oesterley, insist that "there is not the remotest connection between this verse and the section that has gone just before."[2] Minear explains this lack of connection as due to the fact that "we are dealing with an unorganized jumble of oral traditions which the editor felt no pressure to reorder into a smoother literary sequence."[3] But such a view is unsatisfactory to those who hold to the epistle's authenticity and unity. The use of the conjunction *de* indicates that some connection is intended.

Others hold that there is a close connection with what has gone before. Roberts sees in this verse "a continuation of the admonition on how to act in adversity."[4] Thus Reicke views the verse as intended "undoubtedly to emphasize the preceding instruction to be patient,"[5] whereas Harper connects the thought with verse 9.[6] Others suggest a connection with the larger subject of speech in the epistle. Thus Smith sees this verse as an afterthought by James, who realized that "after writing so fully on the perils of speech [he] had said nothing adequate on the sin of profane swearing."[7] But such an intended connection with varied prior portions of the epistle is not obvious.

It seems that the strong opening expression of this verse, "But above all" (ASV), is best understood as marking the conclusion of a line of thought that James has been pursuing and calls attention to this important concluding matter. Having censured three different manifestations of the spirit of worldliness (4:1–5:11), this verse concludes that discussion. This evil of swearing reflects the spirit of worldliness in one of its most reprehensible forms. James has in view the self-serving attempt to hide the truth by appearing to appeal to God to establish the truth. Such duplicity is totally inconsistent with Christian honesty.

The conjunction *de*, not indicated in the NIV, marks a connection with what precedes, but its intended force is not certain. It is rendered "but" when a contrast is intended. But a contrast is not obvious here. Rather, it seems intended to call attention to what follows. When simple continuation is intended, it may be rendered "and" or "now."[8] This seems preferable here. At times it is left untranslated.[9]

"Above all" (*pro pantōn*) may be understood in two different ways. Some, like Lenski, hold that its force "is temporal: before the readers do anything else they must cease using oaths."[10] Then the meaning is that James, aware that his readers have carried over this evil practice from their Jewish past, demands that they deal with this matter as their first duty. More probably the expression is to be understood as conveying the thought of importance, having the force of "especially" or "above all."[11] It is an evil about which James is especially concerned. "The oath," Adamson remarks, "is the commonest and most serious moral fault in speech, and James is hardly to be blamed for ranking it *pro pontōn*."[12] Mitton suggests, "Perhaps some bitter, recent experience has brought home to him how urgent this counsel is."[13] His injunction is so important because evil is so prevalent.

Before giving expression to his serious demand upon his readers, James indicates his tenderness and personal concern for them by addressing them as "my brothers." The fact of their common spiritual brotherhood justifies his insistence that this form of worldliness no longer be condoned in their midst.

His demand is stated both negatively and positively: "Do not swear— not by heaven or by earth or by anything else. Let your 'Yes' be yes, and your 'No' no." James's words are reminiscent of Jesus' teaching (Matt. 5:34-37; 23:16-22). It is difficult to resist the conclusion that James is reproducing in condensed form Jesus' teaching on oaths as given in the Sermon on the Mount. Either James himself had heard that sermon or had become acquainted with it as reported by others. But James gives no indication that he is quoting; he has made the teaching thoroughly his own.

"Do not swear" (*mē omnuete*) demands that this evil practice be stopped. The prohibition is absolute, agreeing with Jesus' teaching, "But I tell you, Do not swear at all" (Matt. 5:34). The reference is to the taking of an oath that involves invoking the name of God to ensure the truthfulness of what one says. Yet, paradoxically, "swearing is necessary only in a society where truth is not reverenced."[14]

Two examples of the kinds of oaths in view are immediately added: "not by heaven or by earth."[15] Zahn notes that these are Jewish oath formulas, "such as were in use among Jews, not among the Greeks and Romans."[16] James is content to employ only two of the four examples used by Jesus, nor does he mention the explanations that Jesus included (Matt. 5:34-36). "Or anything else" (*mēte allon tina horkon*, more literally, "or by any other kind of oath") is general, including all the other forms of oath used by the Jews. Roberts notes that in this last phrase the word "other" is *allon*, "another of the same kind," rather than *heteron*, "another of a different kind." Accordingly, he suggests that James means to prohibit all other oaths of the kind in view.[17]

Modern interpreters are not fully in accord as to just what James has in view when he says "Do not swear." Robertson, who entitles his discussion of this verse "Profanity," holds that the reference is to "the flippant use of oaths (profanity)" and comments that "few things are worse than sulphurous speech like the very fumes of hell."[18] But it is generally agreed that neither James nor Jesus is directly referring to what we call profanity, the impious practice of taking God's name in vain. Rather, the reference is to the practice, in the ordinary relations of life, of confirming a statement with an oath. Swearing an oath thus may be defined as making an appeal to God or to something held sacred to support the truthfulness of a statement, promise, or vow. This practice was common among the Jews to support almost every statement in life's daily relationships. But they had developed subtle distinctions between oaths that were held binding and those that were not. In Matthew 23:16-22, Jesus emphatically condemned the Jewish leaders for making hairsplitting distinctions between binding and nonbinding oaths.

In the Jewish *Mishnah*, a compilation of decisions made by the rabbis on the interpretation of various points of the law, a whole tract is devoted to the subject of oaths.[19] In the discussion of binding oaths it is asserted that oaths made "'by Shaddai' or 'by Sabaoth' or 'by the Merciful and Gracious' or 'by him that is long-suffering and of great kindness,' or by any substituted name, they are liable," but oaths "by heaven and by earth" are exempt.[20] Oaths in which the name of God was used were held to be binding, whereas those in which no direct mention of God was made were not held to be binding. Thus the force of an oath that to all appearances seemed binding could be evaded by minute inaccuracies in the formula used. They developed the fine art of hiding the truth behind their pious oaths. It was the use of such subtle distinctions to escape the binding obligations of their oaths that Jesus and James condemned. Such a practice of pretending to appeal to God to establish the truth while deftly framing an oath not considered binding was the worst form of worldliness. It is the hypocrisy of furthering personal advantage under the pious guise of appealing to God to establish the truth. Such verbal evasiveness is a close kin to the practice of profanity.

On the question of whether the teaching of Jesus, here supported by James, forbids the use of the legal oath by the believer, views have been divided down through history.[21] It is our conviction that this passage does not directly relate to that situation. Improbable is the suggestion of MacKnight that James forbade his readers, "when brought before the tribunals of their persecutors, to deny their faith with oaths; which some of them, it seems, thought they might do with a safe conscience, if the oath was one of those which were reckoned not binding."[22] But it would be difficult to disagree with the comment of Williams: "The use of oaths in court, to add reliability to what is said, is just what should be unnecessary if the words of Matthew and James were obeyed."[23]

Committed to the principle that his speech should be totally honest under all circumstances, the believer can maintain that court oaths become unnecessary. Clement of Alexandria held that a Christian should "maintain a life calculated to inspire confidence toward those without, so that an oath may not even be asked," and felt that it was an indignity for a Christian to be placed under an oath.[24] Fully conscious of the evils to which the practice of using oaths lent itself, the early church countered their use by its insistence on absolute truthfulness in all speech. This is clear from 2 Corinthians 1:15–2:4, where Paul defended himself against the charge of being less than completely truthful. In saying "I call God as my witness" (2 Cor. 1:23), Paul was placing himself under oath to establish his truthfulness. Epp remarks, "That all oaths are not entirely ruled out by the statements of Jesus and James is indicated by the fact that God Himself has occasionally bound Himself by oaths."[25] (See Genesis 22:16-17; 26:3.) The author of Hebrews, in 6:13-18, explains: God swore by Himself "so that, by two unchangeable things in which it is impossible for God to lie, we who have fled to take hold of the hope offered to us may be greatly encouraged" (v. 18). Aware of the proneness of fallen human nature to doubt God's simple promise, God added His oath to make doubly sure His promise to mortal man.

"Let your 'Yes' be yes, and your 'No' no," the positive aspect of his demand, indicates that James was essentially concerned with total honesty in speech on the part of Christians. The present imperative "let . . . be" (*ētō*)[26] marks this as the believer's unvarying duty. Their affirmative statement, "yes" (*nai*), is to be so transparently honest that no further confirmation is needed, while their negative statement, "no" (*ou*), will need no oath to assure its truthfulness. The addition of a confirmatory oath to his statement is an acknowledgment that the individual is conscious that his word is weak and ordinarily unreliable. "The use of oaths is an index of the presence of evil."[27] But a person known to be totally honest will have no difficulty having his plain declaration accepted.

The fact that our courts find it necessary to place a witness under oath to tell the truth is an obvious confession that they recognize that people are congenital liars. A Christian's reputation for rugged honesty in all relations of life should be such that no oath to tell the truth would be needed.

"Or you will be condemned" (*hina mē hupo krisin pesēte*, more literally, "that you may not fall under judgment") denotes that their use of such self-serving oaths left them culpable. Failure to heed his demand exposed them to the danger of falling under the adverse judgment of God. It is a reminder that "God's judgment strikes anyone who carelessly swears an oath and fails to uphold the truth."[28] Their continued use of such frivolous and unnecessary oaths would be to persist in a form of worldliness that stands under God's solemn judgment.

The text of Erasmus, not followed here or in the KJV, reads, "that ye fall not into hypocrisy."[29] Whereas this reading lacks adequate manuscript support,[30] it does witness to an understanding of James's words consistent with the evil condemned by Jesus in Matthew 23:16-22. But Tasker well notes that this reading, though "not unsuitable to the context, . . . is not really in keeping with the severity of the passage."[31] The ultimate concern of James is the acceptable standing of his readers before God.

NOTES FOR
James 5:12

1. M. F. Sadler, *The General Epistles of SS. James, Peter, John, and Jude, with Notes Critical and Practical*, p. 70.
2. W. E. Oesterley, "The General Epistle of James," in *The Expositor's Greek Testament*, 4:472.
3. Paul S. Minear, "Yes or No: The Demand for Honesty in the Early Church," *Novum Testamentum* 13 (January 1971): 7. Reprinted in Minear, *Commands of Christ*, p. 37.
4. J. W. Roberts, *A Commentary on the General Epistle of James*, p. 198.
5. Bo Reicke, "The Epistles of James, Peter, and Jude," in *The Anchor Bible*, 37:56.
6. A. F. Harper, "The General Epistle of James," in *Beacon Bible Commentary*, 10:244.
7. H. Maynard Smith, *The Epistle of S. James. Lectures*, pp. 315-16.
8. Among English versions, R. Young and Schonfield use "and"; Montgomery uses "again," whereas the RSV, NASB, Darby, Lattey, Lilly, Rotherham, and Weymouth use "but."
9. The conjunction is omitted by the NEB, NIV, TEV, 20th Cent., JB, Beck, Berkeley, Goodspeed, Moffatt, and Williams.
10. R. C. H. Lenski, *The Interpretation of the Epistle to the Hebrews and of the Epistle of James*, p. 668.
11. William F. Arndt and F. Wilbur Gingrich, *A Greek-English Lexicon of the New Testament and Other Early Christian Literature*, p. 708.
12. James B. Adamson, *The Epistle of James*, The New International Commentary on the New Testament, p. 194.
13. C. Leslie Mitton, *The Epistle of James*, p. 191.
14. Adamson, p. 195.
15. The use of the accusative *ton ouranon*, "by the heaven," to denote the person or object by which one swears, is in accord with common Greek usage. The use of *en* and the instrumental case in Matthew 5:34-36 is a Hebraism.
16. Theodor Zahn, *Introduction to the New Testament*, 1:91.
17. Roberts, p. 200.
18. A. T. Robertson, *Practical and Social Aspects of Christianity. The Wisdom of James*, pp. 248-50.
19. "Shebuoth" ("Oaths"). See Herbert Danby, *The Mishnah, Translated from the Hebrew with Introduction and Brief Explanatory Notes*, pp. 408-21.
20. "Shebuoth" 4.13; and Danby, p. 415.
21. Robert Johnstone, *Lectures Exegetical and Practical on the Epistle of James*, pp. 386-92; W. Ernest Best, "Oath (NT and Christian)," in *Encyclopaedia of Religion and Ethics*, 9:434-36; Christian Neff and Harold S. Bender, "Oath," in *The Mennonite Encyclopedia*, 4:2-4; and William Klassen, "Oath," in *The Mennonite Encyclopedia*, 4:6-8.

22. James MacKnight, *A New Literal Translation from the Original Greek of All the Apostolical Epistles with a Commentary and Notes*, 5:404.

23. R. R. Williams, "The Letters of John and James," in *The Cambridge Bible Commentary, New English Bible*, p. 137.

24. Clement "The Stromata" 8.8, in *The Ante-Nicene Fathers*, 2:537.

25. Theodor H. Epp, *James, the Epistle of Applied Christianity*, p. 242.

26. The imperative form *ētō*, rather than the usual *estō*, occurs elsewhere in the New Testament only in 1 Corinthians 16:22.

27. Alfred Plummer, "The General Epistles of St. James and St. Jude," in *An Exposition of the Bible*, 6:629.

28. Simon Kistemaker, *New Testament Commentary, Exposition of the Epistle of James and the Epistles of John*, p. 172.

29. This is the reading adopted by Zane C. Hodges and Arthur L. Farstad, *The Greek New Testament According to the Majority Text*.

30. For the manuscript evidence, see Nestle-Aland, *NOVUM TESTAMENTUM GRAECE*, 26th ed.

31. R. V. G. Tasker, *The General Epistle of James*, The Tyndale New Testament Commentaries, p. 125.

PART 4

THE RELIANCE OF LIVING FAITH ON GOD

14

XIII. THE RELIANCE OF LIVING FAITH ON GOD

5:13-18 Is any one of you in trouble? He should pray. Is anyone happy? Let him sing songs of praise. ¹⁴Is any one of you sick? He should call the elders of the church to pray over him and anoint him with oil in the name of the Lord. ¹⁵And the prayer offered in faith will make the sick person well; the Lord will raise him up. If he has sinned, he will be forgiven. ¹⁶Therefore confess your sins to each other and pray for each other so that you may be healed. The prayer of a righteous man is powerful and effective.

¹⁷Elijah was a man just like us. He prayed earnestly that it would not rain, and it did not rain on the land for three and a half years. ¹⁸Again he prayed, and the heavens gave rain, and the earth produced its crops.

In these five verses (5:13-18) James offers his final and basic portrayal of living faith. The life that is dominated by a living faith will turn to God amid the varied experiences and vicissitudes encountered. It is this constant turning to God in all circumstances that gives meaning, unity, and empowerment to the Christian life.

No connecting particle ties this paragraph to what has gone before. Views differ as to whether any close connection exists. Some, like Lenski, link this paragraph with the preceding prohibition of swearing as "closely associated with the right use of God's name in prayer."[1] But others, like Easton, find "no logical connection between" this paragraph and verse 12.[2] Stier more plausibly holds that in these verses James "speaks further of the right use of the tongue; yet he goes back at once to the heart, from the ground of which, as before men, so also before God, our speech should come in its sincerity and simplicity, according to the spirit of our mind. We say very properly that praying is the best and holiest use of our tongue."[3]

The absence of any connecting particle as well as the return to the interrogative form in verses 13-14 suggest that James intended this portion of the letter as an independent paragraph. The unifying theme of these verses is the place and power of prayer in the believer's life. Every verse in this para-

291

graph contains an explicit reference to prayer. James appropriately brings his tests of a living faith to a logical conclusion by insisting that Christian faith finds its center and power in a vital relationship with God through prayer in all the experiences of life. Through prayer the believer habitually lays hold of God's power for victory amid all these diverse experiences. Prayer constitutes the very heart of a vital Christian faith. Martin points out that "by concluding his work with an exhortation to prayer, especially for one another (v. 16*b*) in the apostolic circle, James follows a pattern that is common in the NT epistles (Rom. 15:30-32; Eph. 6:18-20; Phil. 4:6f; Col. 4:2-4, 12; 1 Thess. 5:16-18, 25; 2 Thess. 3:1f; Philem. 22; Heb. 13:18f; Jude 20)."[4]

James practiced what he preached. Eusebius quoted an ancient tradition saying that James spent so much time on his knees in the Temple praying for the people that his knees "became as hard as a camel's."[5]

The present passage has evoked much discussion, primarily because of its directives concerning prayer and healing. It is beset with difficulty due to the fact that several points are susceptible to different interpretations. James insists that the believer must resort to prayer in the diverse experiences of life (v. 13), sets forth its importance in times of sickness (vv. 14-16*a*), and asserts and illustrates the tremendous power of prayer in the affairs of life (vv. 16*b*-18).

A. THE RESORT TO PRAYER IN DIVERSE CIRCUMSTANCES (v. 13)

"Is any one of you in trouble? He should pray. Is any one happy? Let him sing songs of praise." This resumption of the interrogative form (2:5-7, 14-16, 20-21, 25; 3:13; 4:1, 4-5, 14) with the answering imperatives is fully in keeping with James's vigorous style. The rhetorical questions challenge the readers directly, while the singular verbs make this final test of a living faith an individual matter.

"Is any one of you in trouble?" challenges the readers to determine if being "in trouble" is the present lot of any "of you" (*en humin*), anyone in the local brotherhood. It is grammatically possible to punctuate this as a statement of fact,[6] but the question is more in accord "with that direct, stirring style of address which characterizes the whole Epistle."[7]

The Greek verb rendered "is in trouble" (*kakopathei*, more literally, "experience what is bad, suffer misfortune") primarily means to endure hardship, to experience misfortune or calamity. The occasion of trouble "can be physical, mental, personal, financial, spiritual, or religious—to mention no more."[8] *Kakopathei* is a general term and, in view of verse 14, is not here intended to indicate physical suffering. Thus the NIV appropriately renders, "Is any one of you in trouble?" Davids suggests examples of this kind of trouble:

persecutions, like those the prophets suffered (5:10; cf. 5:1-6); external misfortunes, like Job suffered (5:11); or being slandered by a community member (3:1-12; cf. 2:6-7. All of these are external misfortunes, which one could easily see as outside of God's will, for they stem from the evil in the world and are attacks upon the righteous.[9]

Michaelis suggests that the term here denotes "not so much the distressing situation as such, but the spiritual burden which it brings with it."[10]

"He should pray" (*proseuchesthō*), the present imperative, directs the sufferer to make it a practice to turn to God whenever he is in distress and emotional tensions assail. Instead of indulging in introspective self-pity, or complaining loudly to others of his terrible situation, let him turn to God for refuge and strength. His prayer may not change the situation, but it can give strength to bear it bravely as he submits himself to the divine providence. James began his message to his readers by setting before them the proper attitude to be taken amid trials (1:2-4) and reminding them of the availability of prayer to gain the wisdom needed to react rightly to their trials (1:5). The singular "he should pray" reminds them that this is the proper response of each individually to his own situation. Trouble should surely drive the believer to prayer.

"Is anyone happy?" depicts a contrasted emotional situation. The verb pictures an inner attitude of "good cheer," being "of good courage, in good spirits." It occurs elsewhere in the New Testament only in Acts 27:22 regarding Paul's efforts to cheer up his companions before their shipwreck on Malta.[11] It does not denote light and boisterous hilarity but an inner attitude of cheerfulness and elation. Moo offers the timely reminder, "When our hearts are comforted, it is all too easy to forget that this contentment comes ultimately only from God."[12]

"Let him sing songs of praise" directs that the believer's exultant feelings should appropriately find expression in sacred song. The rendering "let him sing psalms" (KJV) restricts the meaning of the verb too much. Whereas originally the Greek verb (*psalletō*), from which we derive our word "psalm," meant "to play the harp" and then "to sing to the music of a harp," in New Testament usage the term simply means "to sing," with or without musical accompaniment. The term leaves room for any kind of sacred song. In 1 Corinthians 14:15 and Ephesians 5:19 the term is used of singing praise to God in public worship, but here the reference is apparently to the individual expression of praise. James desires that God be remembered and praised in all situations, the good as well as the bad.

The two situations, "in trouble" and "is happy," form a strong contrast, designed to cover all the varied emotional experiences of life. Both verbs stand first in the two rhetorical questions and call attention to the nature of the situation. The gloomy valley and the sunny height can both be dynamic instruments in strengthening the believer's conscious relation to God.

Plummer suggests that the two imperatives might with equal truth be transposed: "Is any among you suffering? Let him sing praise. Is any cheerful? Let him pray."[13] Prayer should not merely be the plaintive cry of the sufferer; it is equally appropriate when exuberant feelings prevail. Songs of praise to God are suitable not only when the heart is glad but also when trials and distress engulf us. Paul and Silas sang hymns to God while in prison with bleeding backs and feet fastened in the stocks (Acts 16:25). A vital faith can both sing and pray, whether the circumstances are sad or glad.

B. THE RESORT TO GOD IN SICKNESS (vv. 14-16*a*)

Prayer is important in our Christian relationships. The prayer support of the brotherhood also can serve the physically needy brother. "Is any one of you sick?" centers attention on a particular form of "experience what is bad." The troubles in verse 13 relate to difficulties bearing down upon us from without, whereas here the trouble is internal. "Sick" (*asthenei*) means "to be without strength" and depicts the debilitating effect of sickness, incapacitating one for work. The verb is commonly used of bodily weakness, but it may denote any kind of weakness, be it mental, moral, or spiritual. Here the reference is primarily to physical weakness, but the sickness may have a spiritual aspect. Sickness often awakens a consciousness of sin in the sufferer. Some interpreters, like William Hoste, hold that "the sickness in this passage is that of a sick spirit in a sick body: and the latter the result of the former."[14] That all sickness is due to personal sin must not be assumed (cf. John 9:2-3). Even when it is simply a case of physical prostration, intercessory prayer is appropriate. James urges prayer for the sick person by the elders (v. 14*b*), asserts the impact of prayer (v. 15), and calls for mutual confession of sin (v. 16*a*).

1. The Calling of the Elders to Pray for the Sick (v. 14)

"He should call the elders of the church" indicates that the initial step is to be taken by the sick person. "Call" (*proskalesasthō*), an aorist middle imperative, places the duty on the sick person as a definite act to summon the elders to himself. Again prayer is the response to the need, but now the needy individual is directed to involve the elders in his need; they are called to come to him, confined by his weakness. At his summons the elders are to go to the home of the sick, rather than the sick person being brought to a healer at a public healing service. "It is not the business of the elders of the Church to go scouting for the sick."[15] The scene envisioned is in the privacy of a home. James is not introducing a new procedure, but is reminding his readers of the importance of prayer in time of a brother's need.

"The elders of the church" are obviously the leaders of the local assembly. The term "elder" (*presbuteros*) is a comparative form denoting one who is older than someone else (Luke 15:25); but here it is a designation of office.

Like the synagogues, the early Christian churches chose their leaders from among the older and more mature members. The plural is consistent with the New Testament picture of a plurality of elders in the local church (Acts 14:23; Phil. 1:1; 1 Thess. 5:12). Bornkamm well observes, "Obviously these are office-bearers of the congregation and not just charismatically endowed older men."[16]

"The church," mentioned only here in James, connects these elders with the local Christian community. In 2:2, James referred to his readers as assembling in their "synagogue." "In the very earliest period all Christians, both Jew and Gentile, used both expressions."[17] Among the Greeks, "church" (*ekklēsia*) was a common term denoting a consultative assembly, but for the Jews, familiar with the term from their Septuagint, it was a word that designated the Israelites assembled for religious purposes (e.g., Deut. 4:10). The compound noun, composed of *ek*, "out of," and the substantival form of the verb *kaleō*, "to call," denotes "a called-out assembly"; besides the idea of separation, it also has the thought of those called out as assembled to form a distinct group. In the New Testament the term at times includes all believers in Christ, the church universal (e.g., Matt. 16:18; Eph. 1:22; 3:10); but here, as usually, it denotes the Christians living in one place (e.g., Acts 5:11; 1 Cor. 4:17; Phil. 4:15). There is no need to regard the elders here called by the sick person as acting as the representatives of the whole church, as Lange suggests.[18] As the leaders of their local assembly, it was natural to call them as those who were spiritually mature and experienced in intercessory prayer.

Upon their arrival the elders are portrayed as engaging in a twofold activity, having a distinctly Christian character: "to pray over him and anoint him with oil in the name of the Lord." The NIV rendering might suggest that this depicts the contents of the call to the elders, but his use of the verb "they should pray" (*proseuxasthōsan*) makes clear that James is delineating the suggested procedure of the elders. As the central verb, prayer marks the specific activity of the ministry of the elders on behalf of the sick person. The aorist tense of the verb "hardly refers to a single invocation; it probably stresses urgency with the invocation."[19] "Over him" (*ep' auton*) seems best taken literally as picturing the elders standing by the bed of the sick and extending their hands over him while praying. It is, however, possible to understand the phrase to describe their prayer as in intent going out toward the sick man, that is, for his healing.

"Anoint him with oil" (*aleipsantes elaiō*), a participial phrase, denotes an activity subsidiary to the praying. The grammatical construction leaves undetermined whether the anointing is to be performed before or during the praying by the elders.[20] Probably the former. Tasker notes that "no mention is made of any previous 'consecration' of the oil,"[21] the common term for olive oil. The verb "anoint" (*aleiphō*), one of two Greek verbs so rendered, "is a general term used for an anointing of any kind."[22] Although generally used in connection with secular activities, in the Septuagint it also is used in a sacred sense of the anointing of priests (Ex. 40:15; Num. 3:3). The other verb (*chriō*) is commonly confined to sacred or symbolic anointings, but it is never used of literal anointing in the New Testament. In a papyrus document the cognate noun is used with a secular connotation of "the lotion for a sick horse,"[23] and the verb is used with reference to camels.[24] Contemporary usage thus invalidates the dictum of Trench that *aleiphō* is "the mundane and profane" and *chriō* "the sacred and religious" term.[25] This mixed usage thus renders questionable Lenski's claim that the participle used by James must be rendered "oiling him with oil" and can only have a medicinal significance.[26]

The practice of anointing the sick with oil is mentioned elsewhere in the New Testament only in Mark's summary of the preaching mission of the twelve in Galilee (6:13). Jesus Himself is never mentioned as using this medium in His healings. Whether the twelve adopted its use on their own initiative or at Jesus' direction is not known. In Mark 6:13 its use by the twelve was clearly in connection with miraculous healings. In Luke 10:34 the use of the oil obviously has a medical function. The practice of anointing the sick with oil was known among the Jews in Palestine and was used in connection with exorcism.[27]

The significance of this anointing of the sick by the elders is differently understood. Some view the act as the application of a healing remedy. The efficacy of olive oil as a medical agent was well known. But others view the anointing as symbolic, "to represent the healing power or presence of God."[28] Some, more precisely, view the oil as "a beautiful symbol of the Holy Spirit who lives in and watches over the saint (James 4:5)."[29] Davids holds that the anointing "is an outward and physically perceptible sign of the power of prayer, as well as a sign of the authority of the healer (Mark 6:13)."[30] That James did not regard the oil as the healing agent is clear from his assertion in verse 15 that the prayer of faith heals the sick. Mitton suggests that the use of the oil "was supplementary aid for awakening faith."[31]

That the anointing was performed "in the name of the Lord" was apparently announced by one of the elders as the oil was being applied. "The Lord" most naturally means Jesus Christ. The position of this phrase associates it with the act of anointing, but obviously the prayers of the elders also were offered in the name of Christ. The phrase implies that the elders were acting in trustful dependence upon Christ and His authority.

2. The Results of the Prayer of Faith (v. 15)

"And the prayer offered in faith will make the sick person well; the Lord will raise him up. If he has sinned, he will be forgiven." The initial "and" continues the picture and views the results as the anticipated sequence of what has just been done. James's statement does not contemplate failure. The future tenses leave open the matter of any time interval between the prayer and the results.

"The prayer offered in faith" (*hē euchē tēs pisteōs*, the prayer of faith") points to a specific prayer; the definite article with both nouns makes the expression very specific, not just any kind of prayer. "The prayer" is an unusual term[32] denoting a strong, fervent wish or petition (cf. the use of the cognate verb in Acts 26:29; 27:29; Rom. 9:3). The reference is to the prayer of the elders just offered. The precise expression, "the prayer of faith," occurs only here in the New Testament, and Sidebottom suggests that it "sounds like a technical term."[33] The genitive "of faith," describing the prayer, may be understood in two different ways. It may be understood as denoting "the body of truth known as 'the faith',"[34] but it is more probable that the reference is to the faith exercised by the elders in their prayer over the sick. Thus the NIV well renders "the prayer offered in faith." Davids characterizes it as "the prayer which expresses trust in God and flows out of commitment to him."[35] To achieve effective results such prayers must be grounded in the divinely revealed realities of the biblical "faith."

That the gift of healing (1 Cor. 12:9) was possessed by the elders in each local assembly is difficult to assume. Nor is it probable to assume that James envisions that everyone who is thus anointed and prayed for will be miraculously healed. We agree that such prayer for the healing of the sick should properly be offered with the condition "if the Lord will." But James's unconditional language seems best understood in accepting that "the prayer of faith" cannot "be prayed at will, but that it is given of God in certain cases, to serve His own loving purposes, and in strict accordance with His sovereign will."[36] Thus, it is not just an ordinary prayer for another, however good and sincere it may be, but the prayer prompted by the Spirit-wrought conviction that it is the Lord's will to heal the one being prayed for. But, as Moo remarks, "such faith cannot be 'manufactured,' however gifted, insistent, or righteous we are."[37] Whenever God in His wisdom does not grant immediate healing, such a service still has deep spiritual value for the believer in that it openly relates his illness to the will of God for him.

The indicated result—"will make the sick person well"—refers to his physical restoration. He will be rescued from his physical disability. The verb "will make well" (*sozō*, literally, "will save") is commonly used in the New Testament of physical healing (e.g., Matt. 9:21-22; Mark 6:56), and there is no reference here to the future salvation of his soul.[38] "The sick person" (*ton kamnonta*), a different term than that used in verse 14, renders an articular present participle that occurs only here in the New Testament with reference to physical illness. The verb primarily means "to be weary, fatigued" (cf. Heb. 12:3). Here it pictures the physical weariness and exhaustion that prostrating sickness produces. Perhaps it also includes the weariness of mind that commonly accompanies physical illness. Classical writers used the aorist and perfect participles in writing of the dead,[39] but the present participle here gives no ground for any claim that the reference is to one who is dying or is expected to die. James rather views the elders anointing one who is expected to live.

"The Lord will raise him up" clarifies the true source of the restoration. James thus excludes "any magical operation of the oil with which the sick is to be anointed."[40] "The Lord" is again best understood as denoting Jesus Christ, the One in whose name the anointing was done. As the Lord over the lives of His people, He heals according to His will. "Will raise him up" virtually repeats "will save" in the previous statement, meaning that the sick person will be raised up from his sickbed. Although the verb is used of the future bodily resurrection, that connotation is not involved here.

The added assurance, "If he has sinned, he will be forgiven," recognizes that the sickness *may* be due to sin. Mitton notes that whenever sickness strikes, this is a possibility that "haunts the human mind."[41] Whenever sickness does come, it is desirable for each believer to examine himself to determine before the Lord if the sickness is due to personal sin. But the construction used by James[42] makes clear that this is not always the case. It is wrong to assume that whenever a believer becomes sick it is due to sin in his life. But whenever that may be the reason, the words of James assure the sick person that the situation is not hopeless.

The periphrastic perfect verb "has sinned" (*hamartias ē pepoiēkōs*) supposes a condition where the sinner is now abiding under the consequences of his sins in the past. The plural "sins," standing emphatically before the verb, implies repeated occasions in the past where he missed doing the known will of God. But God will not withhold the needed healing because of the past. "He will be forgiven," literally, "it will be forgiven to him," as an impersonal construction, lumps together the sins in question and assures the sick person that forgiveness will be extended to him. "Forgiven," the standard New Testament term for forgiveness, pictures the sins as being "sent away" so that they are no longer held against him. The future indicative passive verb "means that this Christian did not free himself from his sins; but a power was needed that was outside himself, and that power was God. The same God who healed him also liberated him from the sins that bound him."[43] The promise implies that he has confessed his sins and has determined to turn from them because they are offensive to God.

3. The Duty of Mutual Confession and Prayer (v. 16*a*)

"Therefore confess your sins to each other and pray for each other so that you may be healed." "Therefore" (*oun*) establishes the thought connection with what precedes.[44] In view of the efficacy of intercessory prayer in the circumstances just described, James now appeals for its wider use. The two present imperatives, which might be rendered "make a habit of," call for a general practice. The imperatives, both in the second person plural and coordinated with "and," call for a group activity, whereas the reciprocal pronoun "each other" with both verbs stresses a mutual activity where the members are equal, regarded as brethren. The activity called for "is mutual and brotherly, not official or sacerdotal."[45] James's words offer no valid basis for the practice of auricular confession.

"Confess" (*exomologeisthe*) is a compound verb that conveys the thought of an open, frank, and full confession. The root form means literally "to say the same thing"; hence, it means that in confessing sin we agree to identify it by its true name and admit that it is sin. Compounded with the preposition *ek*, "out," the verb denotes a confession that is open and full in acknowledging personal guilt.

James calls for a confession of specific sins—not just a general confession of personal sinfulness but of "your sins" (*tas hamartias*), the definite sinful acts of which they are guilty.[46] The scene is not to be restricted to the sick chamber, nor does James seem to be thinking of a public worship service. It seems to be a smaller, private gathering where confidences are shared for the purpose of mutual help and intercession. The sins confessed seem naturally to relate to their wrongdoings "against other brethren, which spoil the fellowship one with another and make it difficult, if not impossible, for them to worship together as the people of God."[47] They also may include sins that burden the conscience of the one confessing and concerning which he feels the need for brotherly intercession for victory. Unconfessed sins have an upward as well as outward impact on the life of a believer. Such sins block the pathway of prayer to God and hinder interpersonal relations. Confession of sin is a Christian duty and a powerful deterrent to sin. But it should never be used in a way to bring injury to others. James's counsel is not to be construed as a call for an indiscriminate public confession of all sins. Purkiser well observes, "A sound principle is that the area of commission should be the area of confession."[48]

Such mutual confession must culminate in sympathetic intercession: "and pray for each other." Without this resultant intercession, confessions may prove to be harmful; but when they secure faithful prayer support from trusted, spiritual brethren, they can be of great value in furthering victory and spiritual maturity. The mutual confession must give stimulus and direction to the mutual intercession.

"So that you may be healed" states the true purpose behind all such confession and intercession. "You" denotes the readers generally and implies that in some sense all of them may stand in need of healing. The statement is potential, whenever that specific need arises. In view of the context, "be healed" (*iathēte*) should be understood to be primarily of physical restoration. Perhaps James means that in view of the efficacy of prayer for the sick, such praying should not be confined to the elders but should be common among the church members. But the word "healed" also is used figuratively of healing the diseases of the soul (Matt. 13:15; John 12:40; Heb. 12:13; 1 Pet. 2:24). "So that" (*hopōs*) may suggest that the result of intercession in the case of physical sickness implies that intercession for forgiveness of sins is also needed. The reference to the confession and forgiveness of sins in the context makes this broader scope of "healing" probable. For James and his readers, the thoughts of physical and spiritual healing were closely related. Modern psychosomatic medicine affirms the connection.

C. THE POWER OF A GODLY MAN'S PETITION (vv. 16*b*-18)

This part is distinguished from the previous injunctions by the absence of a connecting particle and its declarative contents. Following his calls for prayer (vv. 14-16*a*), James now encourages its use through his positive assertion (v. 16*b*) and a vivid illustration of the mighty power of prayer (vv. 17-18).

1. The Statement Concerning its Power (v. 16*b*)

"The prayer of a righteous man is powerful and effective." "The prayer" (*deēsis*), used only here by James, may be distinguished from the term employed in verse 15 (*euchē*), which was used exclusively of prayer addressed to God but included all types of prayer. The word now used is restricted to petitionary prayer, a petition for what is desired. Used without an article, the petition is left undefined; the noun centers attention on something personally desired. The nature of the desire is limited only by the fact that the petitioner is "a righteous man" (*dikaiou*). "Righteous" may be taken in a theological sense to denote a man who has confessed his sins and by faith stands acquitted before God.[49] But since James in this epistle is stressing that a living faith must manifest itself in daily life, the term more probably calls attention to his ethical character. The former truth is the foundation for the latter. Both are involved here. The singular is generic; the man is representative of his class. He is "the ordinary member in good standing, not just the elders or prophets."[50] He shows his justifying faith by his daily effort to conform his life to God's will. It does not imply personal sinlessness. When assured that his desire is not evil (4:3), a believer can confidently take his petition directly to God. "What is generally worth a Christian's time and efforts surely is worth his prayers."[51]

A godly man's petition "is powerful" (*polu ischuei*), more literally, "is strong, is able to do much." The words stand emphatically at the beginning of the sentence, "much availeth the supplication of a righteous man" (Rotherham). In Acts 19:20 the verb is used with the thought of prevailing over opposition: "So mightily grew the word of the Lord and prevailed" (ASV). Such prayer is an active power producing amazing victories.

"Effective" represents a single participle (*energoumenē*) standing at the end of the sentence. Etymologically this compound term denotes a power working inwardly; our English word "energy" is derived from the cognate noun. The exact force of the participle here has been variously understood. It may be taken as the practical equivalent of an adjective describing "supplication"; then it describes the prayer as actively accomplishing its task, as being energetic and effective. But more probably the emphatic participle does not describe the prayer but gives the reason why a righteous man's prayer is so strong. Thus others regard the particle as relating directly to the action of the verb. Its force may be either middle or passive.

Taken as passive, the meaning is "being made effective," that is, by God or the Holy Spirit. Thus Rotherham renders it, "Much availeth the supplication of a righteous man when it is energized." This is certainly in harmony with the biblical view of prayer, as for example in Romans 8:26. Thus Davids comments, "Prayer is not *itself* powerful; it is not magic. But its power is unlimited in that the child of God calls on a Father of unlimited goodness and ability."[52] A difficulty is that the context does not make mention of the empowering agent.

Others accept the voice as middle, meaning "when it is operating, is energizing." Thus Williams renders it, "An upright man's prayer, when it keeps at work, is very powerful."[53] "Keeps at work" well conveys the force of the present middle. Then the meaning is that the desire of the righteous man, expressing itself in his petition, keeps on putting forth its energy to get the petition answered.

Views are divided as to whether the form is middle or passive. Either view is possible; ultimately both truths are involved. Truly, "God 'rewards those who earnestly seek him' (Heb. 11:6), for his answers to prayer are indeed powerful and effective."[54] Both the Old and the New Testament provide varied examples of the power of prayer: Joshua's prayer and the sun standing still (Josh. 10:12-13); Elisha's prayer and the restoration to life of the Shaunammite woman's son (2 Kings 4:32-35); Hezekiah's prayer and the slaying of 185,000 Assyrian soldiers (Isa. 37:21, 36); the answer received by the importunate neighbor (Luke 11:5-8); the response to the persistent widow (Luke 18:1-8); and the answer received by the persevering Syrophoenician woman (Mark 7:24-30).

2. The Illustration of Its Power (vv. 17-18)

In illustration, James cites the story of Elijah, his fourth reference to an Old Testament character (Abraham, 2:21-24; Rahab, 2:25; Job, 5:11). "Elijah" (*Elias*),[55] whose name occurs thirty times[56] in the New Testament, held a prominent place in later Judaism. His prominence is in accord with his dynamic personality, but Jewish interest in him was especially stimulated by the prophetic announcement in Malachi 4:5 connecting his reappearance with the coming of the Messiah. He has been called "the grandest and most romantic character that Israel ever produced."[57] Numerous traditions grew up around him and exaggerated opinions developed, ascribing superhuman traits to him.

"Elijah was a man just like us" stresses his humanity. James thus disarms the natural reaction of his readers that common mortals like themselves could never expect to achieve the prayer results of a grand person like Elijah.

He was "a man" (*anthrōpos*), an ordinary human being, "just like us" (*homoiopathēs*), having the same nature and being subject to the same feelings and experiences of other men. The adjective rendered "just like us" does not mean that he was excitable or irritable or subject to corrupt passions, but rather that he was subject to the same weaknesses other men have. The adjective occurs elsewhere in the New Testament only in Acts 14:15, where Paul used it to persuade the people of Lystra that the missionaries also were ordinary mortals like themselves. Another translator renders it, "with feelings just like ours."[58] At times he also acted under the sway of his feelings. If God answered his prayers, why not ours?

James introduces his account of the prayer exploits of Elijah with a connective *kai* ("and"), not in the NIV, thus linking them closely with his assertion of this humanity, "just like us."[59] "He prayed earnestly that it would not rain, and it did not rain on the land for three and a half years." Although but an ordinary man, he prayed an audacious prayer, and that prayer brought about a crucial meteorological change.

"He prayed earnestly" (*proseuchē prosēuxato*), literally "with prayer he prayed"; the reduplication of the root term conveys an intensive force. Similar instances occur both in the Old and the New Testaments (Gen. 2:17; 31:30; Jonah 1:10; Luke 22:15; John 3:29; Acts 5:28). The intensification is generally understood to point to the inner attitude of Elijah and rendered "prayed fervently" or "earnestly." But it is possible to understand the intensification as relating to the activity described. Thus Adamson holds that James means "not that Elijah put up a particularly fervent prayer but that praying was precisely what he did."[60] Then the stress points out that in facing his situation, Elijah specifically resorted to prayer, giving himself wholly to it. Thus Hughes takes James to mean "that nothing else than *his prayer* produced the long drought."[61]

"That it would not rain" (*tou mē brexai*), an articular aorist infinitive, states the content as well as the purpose of his prayer. The aorist indicates that there should be no further occasion when rain fell. First Kings 17:1 does not record such a prayer on Elijah's part, but it is unjustified to claim that James read something into the story that was not there. His categorical announcement that there would be no further rain except at his word can only mean that he had prayed about the matter and had received God's assurance that his prayer was God's will and would be answered.

"And it did not rain on the land for three and a half years" states the amazing result of his prayer. "On the land" is best understood as meaning the land of Palestine; the punishment fell upon the idolatrous kingdom of Ahab and Jezebel. That period of no rain lasted "for three and a half years," more precisely, "for three years and six months." That precise duration is not expressly stated in the Old Testament, but Jesus in Luke 4:25 uses the same figure. First Kings 18:1 records that "in the third year" God told Elijah to go and show himself to Ahab; it resulted in the termination of the drought. But the date obviously marked the time Elijah had been in Zarephath and does not include the duration of the drought before his arrival there. Some, like Moffatt, suggest that "three and a half, being the half of the perfect number seven," has simply become symbolic of the duration of times of great calamity or distress.[62] Various scholars conclude that the expression should be taken figuratively.[63] But there is no indication that Jesus and James were using symbolic numbers. Lenski holds that the duration was "a well-known fact of history, one that was certainly not forgotten by the Jews."[64] Orr points out that the duration is fully consistent with the well-known weather conditions in Palestine.

> The ground had already been dry for six months—since the previous rainy season—when Elijah stayed the rain by his word at the commencement of the new rainy season. If the cessation lasted till the third year thereafter, the total period of drought would necessarily be about three years and six months. It was strictly true, therefore, that, as Jesus said, "in the days of Elijah," "the heaven was shut up three years and six months" (Luke iv.25).[65]

"Again he prayed" (v. 18) is a summary statement of the account in 1 Kings 18:41-45. Again it is pointed out that there is no mention of prayer in the account. The word, admittedly, does not occur, but the posture of Elijah in verse 42 implies an attitude of active prayer. His prayer was obviously grounded in God's promise to send rain (1 Kings 18:1).

Again his prayer achieved a tremendous result: "and the heavens gave rain, and the earth produced its crops." The drought was terminated, and the normal cycle of nature was restored. The personification "the heavens gave rain" is a reverential Jewish substitute for the name of God. The earth again produced "its crops," the normal yield of the ground.

This example of the tremendous power of prayer does not mean that Elijah could suspend the laws of nature at will. Rather, "the prophet's communion with God was so intimate that the Spirit could reveal to him not only the purposes of the Lord in these respects, but also the very time when they would come to pass."[66] Measured by the test of its resort to prayer, the faith of Elijah revealed itself vibrant with life and dynamic in impact. What does this test reveal about *our* faith?

NOTES FOR
James 5:13-18

1. R. C. H. Lenski, *The Interpretation of the Epistle to the Hebrews and of the Epistle of James*, p. 670.
2. Burton Scott Easton and Gordon Poteat, "The Epistle of James," in *The Interpreter's Bible*, 12:70.
3. Rudolf Stier, *The Epistle of St. James*, p. 470.

4. Ralph P. Martin, *James*, Word Biblical Commentary, p. 205.

5. Eusebius *The Ecclesiastical History Eusebius Pamphilus* 2.23.

6. Spiros Zodhiates, *The Patience of Hope*, pp. 114-15.

7. Robert Johnstone, *Lectures Exegetical and Practical on the Epistle of James*, p. 396.

8. Simon Kistemaker, *New Testament Commentary, Exposition of the Epistle of James and the Epistles of John*, p. 174.

9. Peter H. Davids, *James*, New International Biblical Commentary, p. 122.

10. Wilhelm Michaelis, "Kakopatheō, sungkakopatheō, kakopatheia," in *Theological Dictionary of the New Testament*, 5:937.

11. The adjective *euthumos* occurs in Acts 27:36, the adverb *euthumōs* in Acts 24:10.

12. Douglas J. Moo, *The Letter of James*, p. 176.

13. Alfred Plummer, "The General Epistles of St. James and St. Jude," in *An Exposition of the Bible*, 6:632.

14. William Hoste and William Rodgers, *Bible Problems and Answers*, p. 400.

15. Herman A. Hoyt, "What Is Scriptural Healing?" *Eternity* 9, no. 8 (August 1958): 29.

16. Günther Bornkamm, "Prebus, presbuteros," in *Theological Dictionary of the New Testament*, 6:664.

17. Karl Ludwig Schmidt, "Ekklēsia," in *Theological Dictionary of the New Testament*, 3:518.

18. John Peter Lange and J. J. Van Oosterzee, "The Epistle General of James," in *Lange's Commentary on the Holy Scriptures*, 23:138.

19. Martin, p. 207.

20. In relation to an aorist verb, the action of an aorist participle may be either antecedent or simultaneous with the action of the verb. See F. Blass and A. Debrunner, *A Greek Grammar of the New Testament and Other Early Christian Literature*, pp. 174-75; A. T. Robertson and W. Hersey Davis, *A New Short Grammar of the Greek Testament*, p. 379.

21. R. V. G. Tasker, *The General Epistle of James*, The Tyndale New Testament Commentaries, p. 130.

22. W. E. Vine, *An Expository Dictionary of New Testament Words with Their Precise Meanings for English Readers*, 1:58.

23. James Hope Moulton and George Milligan, *The Vocabulary of the Greek Testament Illustrated from the Papyri and Other Non-Literary Sources*, p. 21.

24. Ibid., p. 693

25. Richard Chenevix Trench, *Synonyms of the New Testament*, pp. 136-37.

26. Lenski, pp. 671-74.

27. Heinrich Schlier, "Aleiphō," in *Theological Dictionary of the New Testament*, 1:230; Paul Billerbeck, *Die Briefe Des Neuen Testaments Und Die Offenbarung Johannis Erläutert Aus Talmud Und Midrasch*, p. 759.

28. Harold S. Songer, "James," in *The Broadman Bible Commentary*, 12:137.

29. Hoyt, p. 29.

30. Davids, p. 123.

31. C. Leslie Mitton, *The Epistle of James*, p. 199.

32. It occurs three times in the New Testament; in Acts 18:18 and 21:23 it denotes a "vow." The verb, used six times, is generally rendered "I wish."

33. E. M. Sidebottom, *James, Jude and 2 Peter*, The Century Bible, new ed., p. 62.

34. Hoyt, p. 47.

35. Peter H. Davids, *The Epistle of James*, p. 194.

36. Guy H. King, *A Belief That Behaves. An Expositional Study of the Epistle of James*, p. 124.

37. Moo, p. 186.

38. This passage offers no exegetical basis for the Roman Catholic doctrine and practice of extreme unction. The Catholic scholar Jean Cantinat recognizes that "exegesis as such, and of

itself, would not suffice" to establish this sacrament from the words of James (A. Robert and A. Feuillet, *Introduction to the New Testament*, pp. 568-69).

39. Joseph B. Mayor, *The Epistle of St. James*, p. 168.

40. Heinrich Greeven, "Euchomai, euchē," in *Theological Dictionary of the New Testament*, 2:776.

41. Mitton, p. 201.

42. "And if" (*kan* with the subjunctive mode) states the condition hypothetically (third class) but with the probability of reality. See Robertson and Davis, p. 353.

43. Zodhiates, p. 144.

44. The KJV, following the Textus Receptus, omits the connective, but it has strong manuscript support, and modern editions of the Greek text include it as authentic.

45. W. Boyd Carpenter, *The Wisdom of James the Just*, p. 250.

46. The reading "your faults" in the KJV is based on the reading *to paraptomata*, "false steps, transgressions," that has inferior manuscript support.

47. Tasker, p. 135.

48. W. T. Purkiser, *Hebrews, James, Peter*, Beacon Bible Expositions, 11:163.

49. So Lenski, pp. 678-79; Donald W. Burdick, "James," in *The Expositor's Bible Commentary*, 12:204.

50. Davids, p. 196.

51. J. W. Roberts, *A Commentary on the General Epistle of James*, p. 222.

52. Davids, *James*, New International Biblical Commentary, p. 125.

53. Charles B. Williams, *The New Testament, A Private Translation in the Language of the People*.

54. Kistemaker, p. 179.

55. The KJV "Elias" transliterates the Greek spelling of the name, for the Greek can have an *h* only at the beginning of a word. "Elijah" goes back to the Hebrew form.

56. Including the variant reading in Luke 9:54. Outside the gospels, the name occurs only in Romans 11:2 and here.

57. Robert Young, *Analytical Concordance to the Bible*, p. 295.

58. Charles B. Williams, *The New Testament, A Private Translation in the Language of the People*.

59. In verses 17-18 James uses *kai* five times to connect each declarative statement with the preceding. Thus the whole prayer picture is closely linked to the fact that he was a real human being.

60. James B. Adamson, *The Epistle of James*, The New International Commentary on the New Testament, p. 201.

61. Joh. Ed. Huther, *Critical and Exegetical Handbook to the General Epistles of James, Peter, John, and Jude*, p. 161.

62. James Moffatt, *The General Epistles of James, Peter, John, and Jude*, The Moffatt New Testament Commentary, p. 82.

63. See Mayor, pp. 180-81; James Hardy Ropes, *A Critical and Exegetical Commentary on the Epistle of St. James*, The International Critical Commentary on the Holy Scriptures of the Old and New Testaments, p. 311; Sophie Laws, *A Commentary on the Epistle of James*, pp. 236-37.

64. Lenski, p. 682.

65. James Orr, *The Bible Under Trial, Apologetic Papers in View of Present-Day Assaults on Holy Scripture*, p. 193.

66. Herbert F. Stevenson, *James Speaks for Today*, p. 117.

15

XIV. THE ABRUPT CONCLUSION

5:19-20 **My brothers, if one of you should wander from the truth and someone should bring him back, [20]remember this: Whoever turns a sinner away from his error will save him from death and cover a multitude of sins.**

It is not certain whether these two verses connect with the final test of a living faith (5:13-18) or should be taken as a conclusion to the book as a whole. It is possible to connect them closely with the preceding passage and regard these verses as a return to the subject in verse 16. Then, in a manner characteristic of James, these verses may be understood as a reminder that their concern for the needy brother as expressed in their prayers is not a substitute for personal effort to restore the wanderer.[1] But others, like Easton, hold it is unnecessary to seek a close connection with what has just been said and feel that "this saying is complete in itself."[2]

Adamson concludes that the picture of the "wandering brother" in these verses is best understood as emerging "from the content of the Epistle as a whole."[3] Martin agrees and remarks, "The thrust of the entire epistle has been to prevent any Christian from wandering from the truth; if there is a lapse, he should be brought back."[4] Ropes notes that only here and in 2:1 does the direct address, "My brothers," stand first in the sentence (in the Greek) and asserts, "In both cases there is an abrupt change of subject."[5] There is no connecting particle that requires a close formal connection. It therefore seems more natural to assume that this reference at the very end to one who has erred is best understood in the light of the various evils that James has censured in the entire epistle.

"My brothers" (*Adelphoi mou*)[6] marks this concluding thought as expressed with loving warmth and sympathetic concern. James has the good of the Christian brotherhood at heart; he has spoken many sharp words of censure, but his aim is not to condemn but to restore. He is prompted by the obligations of brotherhood toward the erring brother. Knowling remarks that in this concluding exhortation from James "we may see an indication of his close following of the great Overseer and Shepherd of souls."[7] James concludes with a call to action.

James presents a hypothetical picture of an erring brother in their midst being restored (v. 19) and gives a stimulatimg assurance concerning its far-reaching importance (v. 20).

A. THE ASSUMED RESTORATION OF ONE ERRING (v. 19)

"If one of you should wander from the truth and someone should bring him back" presents a hypothetical situation, expressed in two coordinate statements.[8] The scene is not presented as a reality, nor is it regarded as inevitable; it is viewed as very probable, based on past occurrences. The statement is a flashing warning light. The frailty of human nature and the strength of the assaults of evil create the standing possibility that "one of you" (*tis en humin*) may thus succumb. The indefinite singular pronoun marks the danger as individual and not limited to any particular class. James gives recognition to "the infinite value of the individual soul."[9] "One of you" implies that this erring individual is a member of their local group. The majority of the brethren are in line, but they must have a clear feeling of responsibility for each individual in their brotherhood.

"Wander from the truth" suggests the familiar metaphor of a sheep wandering astray (Ezek. 34:4; Matt. 18:12; 1 Pet. 2:25). Although gregarious by nature, a sheep nibbling the grass among the rocks and crags could easily become lost. The aorist tense verb (*planēthē*) denotes an occasional rather than a habitual occurance. The verb may be interpreted as either passive or middle in force. If passive, the meaning is that the individual is deceived and led astray by others; if middle, he went off of his own will. Some, like Alford, hold that the force here is strictly passive and should be rendered "be seduced."[10] Then the power of worldliness and heretical or demonic allurements is prominent. But in classical writings and in the Septuagint the aorist passive also was used with a middle force, giving the meaning "to go astray, wander away." The force is probably middle, denoting personal accountability on the part of the erring. Under either view there is a serious departure from the path of rectitude, placing him in grave danger. Moo concludes that "wander" here "should not be restricted—as the English word could be—to an inadvertent or unconscious departure from 'the truth'; it was widely used to describe any deviation from the 'way of righteousness,' whether willful or not."[11]

"The truth" denotes the whole body of truth as contained in the gospel (cf. 1:18; 3:14). The expression contains no direct reference to Christ as "the truth" (John 14:6), but the truth of the gospel is inseparably bound to Him as the very embodiment of truth. To wander from the truth inevitably involves the loss of a vital relationship with Him. The gospel not only involves principles to be understood but also a life to be lived.

"And someone should bring him back" brings the scene to its Christian climax. The hypothetical statement is not an exhortation to the readers to carry out this important duty; it rather assumes that the task has been achieved by someone who cared. The verb (*epistrepsē*) literally means "to turn around, to turn back." While the term can be used to designate an initial turning to God for salvation (Acts 14:15; 15:19; 26:18; 1 Thess. 1:9), it here does not refer to making a convert to Christianity, as the familiar rendering "and one convert him" (KJV) might suggest. Jesus used the verb in His words to Peter in Luke 22:32: "When you have turned back, strengthen your brothers." The aorist tense simply states that the wanderer has effectively been turned back into the way of the truth. James gives no indication as to how this restoration of an erring brother is to be brought about. Fervent prayer as well as Spirit-empowered dealings with him surely seem involved.

The indefinite "someone" (*tis*) leaves the agent of the restoration unidentified, indicating that this important ministry is not the responsibility of the elders only. It must be the concern of all believers. "There is something fatally wrong about us if we have no strong desire to bring back sinners to God."[12]

The exact spiritual status of this wanderer has been differently understood. The suggestion that the picture is that of "soul-winning" in the modern sense of making new converts[13] is improbable. The meaning of the verb "convert" as well as the fact that the wanderer is "one of you," a member of the Christian community, makes this unlikely. Some, like Rodgers, suggest that the individual was "a mere professor, but who if rightly dealt with, may even yet be truly converted."[14] Tasker holds that "the erring brother is a converted Christian, and that he has only temporarily left 'the narrow way which leadeth unto life,' and has been brought back by personal contact."[15] Whatever one's theological presuppositions concerning his true status, it is clear that the wanderer had been estranged from the Lord and had deserted the Father's house, but in grace he had been brought back into a vital relationship with Him. His backsliding had been terminated.

B. THE ASSURED RESULTS OF THE RESORATION (v. 20)

"Remember this: Whoever turns a sinner away from his error will save him from death and cover over a multitude of sins." James approves and encourages this work of restoration by urging his readers to recognize its important results.

It is commonly accepted that the opening verb "remember this" (*ginōsketō*) is directed to "the converter and not the converted."[16] But there is considerable textual uncertainty as to the true reading of the verb. The manuscripts are divided between the plural and the singular imperative.[17] If the plural form of the verb (*ginōskete*) is accepted, the form may be either indicative, confirming a known fact, "you may be sure of that";[18] or an imperative, "remember this," addressed to the readers. If the singular is read (*ginōs-ketō*), it is a call to the one who has turned the wanderer back clearly to keep in mind the significance of what he has done. The textual editors are divided.[19] The singular form preserves the regular construction of the Greek sentence with its singular subject (*tis*, "someone") and two singular verbs. It also has better manuscript support. We accept the singular as more probably the original reading. The plural may have been introduced to conform to the plural "my brethren," or it may have been due to a desire to eliminate any question whether "let him know" referred to the converter or to the converted.[20]

"Whoever turns a sinner away from his error" by its repetition stresses this crucial point. But the use of the third person makes the statement objective and general. "Whoever turns" (*ho epistrepsas*, "the one who turned") renders an articular aorist participle and refers back to his successful work in verse 19 of having brought back a wanderer, "a sinner," one who missed the mark of God's will for him by wandering from the truth. "From his error" (*ek plenēs hodou antou*, more literally, "out of the error of his way") marks his former course as a way of "error" or delusion standing in contrast to God's truth. Truth and error are mutually exclusive. But the converter has turned him "away from" (*ek*), better, "out of," his erring way into the path of truth.

This work of restoring the erring one accomplishes two tremendous results: "will save him from death and cover over a multitude of sins." The future tenses state the assured results. "Of all philanthropists, the zealous, loving Christian is the greatest."[21] The converter, the subject of both of these verbs, is spoken of as doing what in reality only God can do. God works through his efforts and graciously credits him with the work. What an incentive to diligence in such work!

"Will save him from death" (*sōsei psuchēn autou ek thanatou*, more literally, "will save his soul out of death") depicts the result for the restored sinner. "His soul" here denotes the inner life of the individual in his responsibility before God. That he was saved "from death" stresses the seriousness of the condition from which he was rescued. While some would understand "death" here to mean premature physical death as punishment for sins (1 Cor. 11:30),[22] it is better to understand it as referring to spiritual death. Physical death does not seem adequate to satisfy the terms used. James does not say the wanderer was spiritually dead, or that he was dying, but he was saved from "death," which unmisatakably lies at the end of the path he was following. Sin is destructive, and unless its work in a man's life is broken, it will surely result in the death of the soul in eternal separation from God. See the picture by James in 1:13-15.

In some manuscripts the reading is "a soul,"[23] but whether the true reading is "a soul" or "his soul," the context points to the soul of the wanderer. Since in some Jewish writings it was held that meritorious deeds atoned for sin and saved from death,[24] some modern interpreters would attribute that meaning to James here as teaching that the good deed of reclaiming the wanderer saved the soul of the one who reclaimed him. While such a view was in keeping with Pharisaic Judaism, it is wholly alien to the New Testament teaching that forgiveness of sins is by grace alone. It is contrary to James's teaching in 1:21 (cf. 4:8; 5:15). Galatians 6:1 establishes that the work of restoring a sinner demands that the converter himself be a spiritual man; therefore, "the converter would scarcely be thought of as needing restoration from death or relief from the weight of unforgiven sin."[25]

"And cover a multitude of sins" states the second result flowing from the restoration of the wanderer. "Cover over" (*kalupsei*) is not to be taken in the sense of hiding the sins or keeping them secret. Rather the term is used in the Old Testament sense of securing their forgiveness (Pss. 32:1; 85:2). Our sins are covered and no more remembered by being placed under Christ's atoning blood. The erring individual may be guilty of "a multitude of sins," but he is assured that they all will be forgiven. Davids remarks, "The person is not branded in the church as someone who once went astray but is part of a company in which all are forgiven sinners."[26] Sin is a contagion that spreads rapidly, but the returning wanderer need not despair that his case is hopeless. Schweizer notes that logically this matter of the covering of his sins comes before the saving of his soul from death.[27]

There is debate concerning whose sins James thinks of as being covered. Ropes claims that to refer this statement "to the sins of the converted person makes a bad anticlimax" and holds that James means that the one who converts him thereby secures "forgiveness of one's own sins."[28] Mitton admits that this is not "the orthodox exposition of the verse," but in view of the teaching in Judaism and in the early church Fathers that good deeds atoned for one's sins, he thinks that this is James's meaning.[29] But it is difficult to believe that James espoused such a view. Would James encourage the good work of restoring an erring brother because thereby one secured the forgiveness of his own sins? Surely he must have been familiar with Jesus' teaching that before one can help a sinning brother, he must first cast the beam out of his own eye (Matt. 7:5). But Plummer observes that , according to this interpretation, "it is precisely those who have a beam in their own eye who should endeavour to convert sinners from the error of their ways, for in this way they may get the beam removed, or at least overlooked."[30]

A compromise view is that James means that there is a blessing for both the converted and the converter. There is no question that the one who is instrumental in restoring an erring brother thereby gains a blessing for his own soul (cf. Matt. 18:15). Dibelius, in supporting the view that the first assurance concerns the sinner and the second his mentor, remarks: "The nearest relative to the saying in James 5:20 probably is a saying in the *Epistola apostolorum* 39.10ff: 'Now if his neighbor [has admonished] him and he returns he will be saved; (and) he who admonished him will receive a reward.'"[31] But to say that the one who turns the sinner back into the way of truth will receive a reward is quite a different thing from saying that he thereby earns the forgiveness of his own sins. The view that his noble ministry will receive a reward, we readily accept; the view that he thereby earns—in whole or in part—the forgiveness of his own sins, we reject as unscriptural. That both parts of the double assurance are to be applied to the restored sinner offers no difficulty; he is not only rescued from death but alos receives God's blessing on his own soul.

With these beautiful words the book of James comes to an abrupt close. It has none of the usual closing features of a letter. That its ending was felt to be undesireably abrupt is evident from the fact that in various late manuscripts the scribes appended a concluding "Amen."

The abrupt ending is in keeping with the nature and purpose of the work of James. In applying his searching tests of a living faith to the lives of his readers, James has found it necessary to rebuke them for various inadequacies. But his motive has been not to condemn but to restore. In spite of their failures, he holds up before them the assurance that a living faith is vitally concerned for the welfare of those who have failed in life to measure up to the demands of such a faith.

> We're saved by faith, yet faith is one
> With life, like daylight and the sun.
>
> Unless they flower in our deeds,
> Dead, empty husks are all the creeds.
>
> To call Christ Lord, but not obey,
> Belies the homage that I pay.
>
> MAUD FRAZER JACKSON

NOTES FOR
James 5:19-20

1. C. Leslie Mitton, *The Epistle of James*, pp. 210-11.
2. Burton Scott Easton and Gordon Poteat, "The Epistle of James," in *The Interpreter's Bible*, 12:72.
3. James B. Adamson, *The Epistle of James*, The New International Commentary on the New Testament, p. 202.
4. Ralph P. Martin, *James*, Word Biblical Commentary, p. 218.
5. James Hardy Ropes, *A Critical and Exegetical Commentary on the Epistle of St. James*, The International Critical Commentary on the Holy Scriptures of the Old and New Testaments, p. 313.
6. The Textus Receptus omits "my," but the best authorities include it.
7. R. J. Knowling, *The Epistle of St. James*, Westminster Commentaries, p. 149.

8. The third class condition. See A. T. Robinson and W. Hershey Davis, *A New Short Grammar of the Greek Testament*, p. 353.
9. Knowling, p. 149.
10. Henry Alford, *The Greek Testament*, 4:1, p. 329.
11. Douglas J. Moo, *The Letter of James*, p. 189.
12. Alfred Plummer, "The General Epistles of St. James and St. Jude," in *An Exposition of the Bible*, 6:642.
13. Ronald A. Ward, "James," in *The New Bible Commentary, Revised*, p. 1235; and Louis H. Evans, *Make Your Faith Work. A Letter from James*, chap. 9, "Are You a Soul Winner?"
14. William Hoste and William Rodgers, *Bible Problems and Answers*, p. 400.
15. R. V. G. Tasker, *The General Epistle of James*, The Tyndale New Testament Commentaries, p. 142.
16. Joh. Ed. Huther, *Critical and Exegetical Handbook to the General Epistles of James, Peter, John, and Jude*, p. 162. But A. R. Fausett attributes the reference to "the converted" (Robert Jamieson, A. R. Fausett, and David Brown, *A Commentary, Critical and Explanatory, on the Old and New Testaments*, 2:494).
17. For the textual evidence see United Bible Societies, *The Greek New Testament*, 3d ed.; Nestle-Aland, *NOVUM TESTAMENTUM GRAECE*, 26th ed.
18. Charles B. Williams, *The New Testament, A Private Translation in the Language of the People*.
19. The plural appears in the texts of Wescott and Hort; United Bible Societies' text, 1st ed.; Nestle-Aland, 22d ed.; and Tasker. The singular occurs in the texts of Souter; Trinitarian Bible Society; United Bible Societies' text, 3d. ed.; Nestle-Aland, 26th ed.; Hodges and Farstad. The editors of the United Bible Societies text, in their 1st ed., on a scale of A to D evaluated their acceptance of the plural as D, while in their third edition they evaluate their acceptance of the singular as C. (See the Bibliography.)
20. Bruce M. Metzger, *A Textual Commentary on the Greek New Testament*, pp. 685-86.
21. Edwin T. Winkler, "Commentary on the Epistle of James," in *An American Commentary on the New Testament*, p. 74.
22. H. A. Ironside, *Expository Notes on the Epistles of James and Peter*, p. 63; and Lehman Strauss, *James, Your Brother. Studies in the Epistle of James*, p. 226.
23. See the evidence in the United Bible Societies' Greek text, 3d ed.
24. Cf. Ecclesiasticus 3:3, 30; Tobit 4:10; 12:9.
25. Knowling, p. 151.
26. Peter H. Davids, *James, New International Biblical Commentary*, p. 127.
27. Eduard Schweizer, "*Psuchē*," in *Theological Dictionary of the New Testament*, 9:652, n. 220.
28. Ropes, pp. 315-16.
29. Mitton, pp. 214-15.
30. Plummer, 6:641.
31. Martin Dibelius, "James. A Commentary on the Epistle of James," in *Hermeneia—A Critical and Historical Commentary on the Bible*, p. 259.

BIBLIOGRAPHY

I. BIBLICAL TEXT

The Greek Text

Aland, Kurt; Black, Matthew; Metzger, Bruce M.; and Wikgren, Allen, eds. *The Greek New Testament*. London: United Bible Societies, 1966.

Aland, Kurt; Black, Matthew; Matini, Carol M.; Metzger, Bruce M.; and Wikgren, Allen, eds. *The Greek New Testament*. 3d ed. New York: United Bible Societies, 1975. (Cited as the United Bible Societies' Greek text.)

Hodges, Zane C.; and Farstad, Arthur L. *The Greek New Testament According To The Majority Text*. Nashville, Tenn.: Thomas Nelson, 1982.

Nestle, Eberhard. *Hē Kainē Diathēkē*. 1904. Reprint. London: British & Foreign Bible Society, 1956.

Nestle, Erwin; and Aland, Kurt. *NOVUM TESTAMENTUM GRAECE*. 22th ed. New York: The American Bible Society, 1956.

————. *NESTLE-ALAND. NOVUM TESTAMENTUM GRAECE*. 26th ed. Stuttgart: Deutsche Biblestiftung, 1979.

Scrivener, F. H. *Hē Kainē Diathēkē. NOVUM TESTAMENTUM. Textus Stephanici A.D. 1550*. London: Cantabrigiae, Deighton, Elll Et Soc, 1867.

Souter, Alexander. *NOVUM TESTAMENTUM GRAECE*. 1947. Reprint. Oxford: U. Press, 1962.

Tasker, R. V. G. *The Greek New Testament, Being the Text Translated in The New English Bible 1961*. Oxford: U. Press, 1964.

Trinitarian Bible Society. *Hē Kainē Diathēkē. The New Testament, The Greek Text Underlying The English Authorized Version of 1611*. London: The Trinitarian Bible Society, 1977.

Westcott, Brooke Foss; and Hort, Fenton John Anthony. *The New Testament in the Original Greek*. Reprint. New York: Macmillan, 1935.

English Versions (with abbreviations)

Beck, William F. *The Holy Bible, An American Translation*. New Haven, Mo.: Leader, 1976. (Beck)

Berkeley Version in Modern English. Grand Rapids: Zondervan, 1959. (Berkeley)

Darby, J. N. *The "Holy Scriptures," A New Translation from the Original Languages*. Reprint. Kingston-on-Thames, England: Stow Hill, 1949. (Darby)

Good News for Modern Man. The New Testament in Today's English Version. New York: American Bible Society, 1966. (TEV)

Goodspeed, Edgar J. *The New Testament, An American Translation*. Chicago: U. Chicago, 1948. (Goodspeed)

The Holy Bible, American Standard Version. 1901. Reprint. New York: Nelson, n.d. (ASV)

The Holy Bible, King James Version. Reprint. Cambridge: U. Press, n.d. (KJV)

The Holy Bible, Revised Standard Version. New York: Nelson, 1962. (RSV)

Kleist, James A., and Lilly, Joseph L. *The New Testament Rendered from the Original Greek with Explanatory Notes*. Milwaukee: Bruce, 1956. Part 1, "Gospels," by Kleist; Part 2, "Acts-Rev.," by Lilly. (Lilly)

Lattey, Cuthbert. *The New Testament in the Westminster Version of the Sacred Scriptures*. London: Sands, 1947. (Lattey)

The Modern Language Bible, The New Berkeley Version. Edited by Gerrit Verkuyl. Grand Rapids: Zondervan, 1969. (MLB)

Moffatt, James. *The New Testament, A New Translation*. Rev. ed. New York: Hodder & Stoughton, n.d. (Moffatt)

Montgomery, Helen Barrett. *Centenary Translation, The New Testament in Modern English*. 1924. Reprint. Philadelphia: Judson, 1946. (Montgomery)

New American Standard Bible. Carol Stream, Ill.: Creation House, 1971. (NASB)

New International Version. The New Testament. Grand Rapids: Zondervan, 1973. (NIV)

The New English Bible. Oxford & Cambridge: U. Press, 1970. (NEB)

The New Testament of the Jerusalem Bible. Reader's Ed. Edited by Alexander Jones et al. 1966. Reprint. Garden City, N.Y.: Doubleday, 1969. (JB)

The New Testament. Revised Version of 1881. New York: Harper, 1881. (RV)

Phillips, J. B. *The New Testament in Modern English*. New York: Macmillan, 1962. (Phillips)

Rotherham, Joseph Bryant. *The Emphasized New Testament*. Reprint. Grand Rapids: Kregel, 1959. (Rotherham)

Schonfield, Hugh J. *The Authentic New Testament*. New York: New American Library, 1958. (Schonfield)

Stern, David H. *Jewish New Testament. A translation of the New Testament that expresses its Jewishness*. Jerusalem, Israel; Clarksville, Maryland: Jewish New Testament Publications, 1989. (Stern)

The Twentieth Century New Testament, A Translation into Modern English. Reprint. Chicago: Moody, n.d. (20th Cent.)

Weymouth, Richard Francis. *The New Testament in Modern Speech*. Revised by James Alexander Robertson. 5th ed. New York: Harper, 1929. (Weymouth)

Williams, Charles B. *The New Testament, A Private Translation in the Language of the People*. 1937. Reprint. Chicago: Moody, 1949. (Williams)

Young, Robert. *The Holy Bible Consisting of the Old and New Covenants Translated According to the Letter and Idioms of the Original Languages*. Reprint. London: Pickering & Inglis, n.d. (Young)

II. GRAMMARS, LEXICONS, WORD STUDIES

Arndt, William F., and Gingrich, F. Wilbur. *A Greek-English Lexicon of the New Testament and Other Early Christian Literature*. Chicago: U. Chicago, 1957.

Bengel, John Albert. *New Testament Word Studies*. A new translation by Charlton T. Lewis and Marvin R. Vincent, vol. 2. Reprint. Grand Rapids: Kregel, 1971.

Blass, F., and Debrunner, A. *A Greek Grammar of the New Testament and Other Early Christian Literature*. Translated and revised by Robert W. Funk. Chicago: U. Chicago, 1961.

Custer, Stewart. *A Treasury of New Testament Synonyms*. Greenville, S.C.: Bob Jones U., 1975.

Dana, H. E., and Mantey, Julius R. *A Manual Grammar of the Greek New Testament*. 1927. Reprint. New York: Macmillan, 1967.

Louw, Johannes P., and Nida, Eugene A., eds. *Greek-English Lexicon of the New Testament Based on Semantic Domains*. 2 vols. New York: United Bible Societies, 1988.

Moulton, James Hope. *A Grammar of the New Testament Greek*. Edinburgh: T. & T. Clark, 1908. Vol. 1, *Prolegomena*.

Moulton, James Hope, and Milligan, George. *The Vocabulary of the Greek Testament Illustrated from the Papyri and Other Non-Literary Sources*. 1930. Reprint. London: Hodder & Stoughton, 1952.

Robertson, A. T. *A Grammar of the Greek New Testament in the Light of Historical Research*. 5th ed. New York: Smith, n.d.

Robertson, A. T., and Davis, W. Hersey. *A New Short Grammar of the Greek Testament*. 1933. Reprint. New York: Harper, 1935.

Thayer, Joseph Henry. *A Greek-English Lexicon of the New Testament*. 1889. Reprint. New York: American Book, n.d.

Trench, Richard Chenevix. *Synonyms of the New Testament*. 1880. Reprint. Grand Rapids: Eerdmans, 1947.

Vincent, Marvin R. *Word Studies in the New Testament*, vol. 1. 1887. Reprint. Grand Rapids: Eerdmans, 1946.

Vine, W. E. *An Expository Dicitonary of New Testament Words with Their Precise Meanings for English Readers*. Reprint (4 vols. in 1). Westwood, N.J.: Revell, 1966.

III. NEW TESTAMENT INTRODUCTION

Barker, Glenn W.; Lane, William L.; and Michaels, J. Ramsey. *The New Testament Speaks*. New York: Harper & Row, 1969.

Baxter, J. Sidlow. *Explore the Book*. London: Marshall, Morgan & Scott, 1955. Vol. 6, *Acts to Revelation*.

Beasley-Murray, G. R. *The General Epistles, James, 1 Peter, Jude, 2 Peter*. Bible Guides. New York: Abingdon, 1965.

Dods, Marcus. *An Introduction to the New Testament*. London: Hodder & Stoughton, 1905.

Gloag, Paton G. *Introduction to the Catholic Epistles*. Edinburgh: T. & T. Clark, 1887.

Goodspeed, Edgar J. *An Introduction to the New Testament*. Chicago: U. Chicago, 1937.

Gromacki, Robert G. *New Testament Survey*. Grand Rapids: Baker, 1974.

Guthrie, Donald. *New Testament Introduction*. Rev. ed. Downers Grove, Ill.: Inter-Varsity, 1970.

Hadjiantoniou, George A. *New Testament Introduction*. Chicago: Moody, 1957.

Harmon, Henry M. *Introduction to the Study of the Holy Scriptures*. New York: Phillips & Hunt, 1878.

Harrison, Everett F. *Introduction to the New Testament*. Rev. ed. Grand Rapids: Eerdmans, 1971.

Heard, Richard. *An Introduction to the New Testament*. New York: Harper, 1950.

Hendriksen, William. *Bible Survey. A Treasury of Bible Information*. Grand Rapids: Baker, 1949.

Henshaw, T. *New Testament Literature in the Light of Modern Scholarship*. 1952. Reprint. London: Allen & Unwin, 1957.

Hunter, A. M. *Introducing the New Testament*. Philadelphia: Westminster, 1946.

Jones, Maurice. *The New Testament in the Twentieth Century*. London: Macmillan, 1924.

Kee, Howard Clark; Young, Franklin W.; and Froehlich, Karlfried. *Understanding the New Testament*. 2d ed. Englewood Cliffs, N.J.: Prentice-Hall, 1965.

Kümmel, Werner Georg. *Introduction to the New Testament*. Translated by A. J. Mattill, Jr. Nashville: Abingdon, 1975.

_____. *Introduction to the New Testament*. Translated by Howard Clark Kee. Rev. ed. Nashville: Abingdon, 1975.

Machen, J. Greshem. *The New Testament, An Introduction to Its Literature and History.* Edited by W. John Cook. Edinburgh: Banner of Truth, 1976.

M'Clymont, J. A. *The New Testament and Its Writers*. New York: Revell, n.d.

McNeile, A. H. *An Introduction to the Study of the New Testament*. Oxford: Clarendon, 1927.

Manley, G. T., ed. *The New Bible Handbook*. Chicago: InterVarsity, 1948.

Miller, Adam W. *An Introduction to the New Testament*. 2d ed. Anderson, Ind.: Warner, 1946.

Moffatt, James. *An Introduction to the Literature of the New Testament*. 3d ed. Reprint. Edinburgh: T. & T. Clark, 1949.

Robert, A., and Feuillet, A. *Introduction to the New Testament*. New York: Desclee, 1965.

Salmon, George. *An Historical Introduction to the Study of the Books of the New Testament*. 9th ed. London: Murray, 1904.

Scott, Ernest Findlay. *The Literature of the New Testament*. 1932. Reprint. New York: Columbia U., 1948.

Scroggie, W. Graham. *The Unfolding Drama of Redemption. The Bible as a Whole* (3 vols. in 1). Grand Rapids: Zondervan, 1970.

Shaw, R. D. *The Pauline Epistles, Introductory and Expository Studies*. 4th ed. Reprint. Edinburgh: T. & T. Clark, 1924.

Steinmueller, John E. *A Companion to Scripture Studies*. Rev. ed. Houston: Lumen Christi, 1969. Vol. 3, *Special Introduction to the New Testament*.

Wikenhauser, Alfred. *New Testament Introduction*. 1958. Reprint. New York: Herder & Herder, 1963.

Zahn, Theodor. *Introduction to the New Testament*. Translated from the 3d German ed. 3 vols. Edinburgh: T. & T. Clark, 1909.

IV. BOOKS ON JAMES

Adamson, James B. *The Epislte of James*. The New International Commentary on the New Testament. Grand Rapids: Eerdmans, 1976.

Alford, Henry. *The Greek Testament*. 4:1. London: Rivingtons, 1859.

————. *The New Testament for English Readers*. Reprint. Chicago: Moody Press, n.d.

Barclay, William. *The Letters of James and Peter*. The Daily Study Bible. 1958. 2d ed. Philadelphia: Westminster, 1960.

Barnes, Albert. *Notes on the New Testament, Explanatory and Practial— James, Peter, John, and Jude*. Edited by Robert Frew. Reprint. Grand Rapids: Baker, 1951.

Bennett, W. H. *The General Epistles, James, Peter, John, and Jude*. The Century Bible, A Modern Commentary. Edited by H. H. Rowley and Matthew Black. London: Blackwood, Le Bas, n.d.

Blanchard, John. *Not Hearers Only. Bible Studies in the Epistle of James*. London: Word, 1971.

Blue, J. Ronald. "James," in *The Bible Knowledge Commentary. New Testament*. An Exposition of the Scriptures by Dallas Seminary Faculty. Wheaton, Ill.: Victor, 1983.

Bowman, John Wick. *The Letter of James*. The Layman's Bible Commentary, edited by Balmer H. Kelly et al., vol. 24. Richmond, Va.: John Knox, 1962.

Brown, Charles. "The General Epistle of James." In *A Devotional Commentary*. London: Religious Tract Society, n.d.

Burdick, Donald W. "James," in *The Expositor's Bible Commentary*. Grand Rapids: Zondervan, 12:159-205. 1981.

Calvin, John. *Commentaries on the Catholic Epistles*. Translated and edited by John Owen. 1855. Reprint. Grand Rapids: Eerdmans, 1948.

Carpenter, W. Boyd. *The Wisdom of James the Just*. London: Isbister, 1903.

Carr, Arthur. "The General Epistle of St. James." In *Cambridge Greek Testament*. 1896. Reprint. Cambridge: U. Press, 1930.

Carson, T. "The Letter of James." In *A New Testament Commentary*. Edited by G. C. D. Howley. Grand Rapids: Zondervan, 1969.

Caton, N. T. *A Commentary and an Exposition of the Epistles of James, Peter, John and Jude*. 1897. Reprint. Delight, Ark.: Gospel Light, n.d.

Dale, R. W. *The Epistle of James and Other Discourses*. London: Hodder & Stoughton, 1895.

Davids, Peter H. *The Epistle of James. A Commentary on the Greek Text. The New International Greek Testament Commentary*. Grand Rapids: Eerdmans, 1982.

————. *James. New International Bible Commentary*. Peabody, Mass.: Hendriksen, 1989.

Dibelius, Martin. "James. A Commentary on the Epistle of James." In *Hermeneia—A Critical and Hisotorical Commentary on the Bible*. Revised by Heinrich Greeven. Translated by Michael A. Williams. Philadelphia: Fortress, 1976.

Dummelow, J. R., ed. *A Commentary on the Holy Bible by Various Writers*. 1909. Reprint. London: Macmillan, 1911.

Easton, Burton Scott, and Poteat, Gordon. "The Epistle of James." In *The Interpreter's Bible*. Edited by George Arthur Buttrick et al., vol. 12. New York: Abingdon, 1957.

Epp, Theodore H. *James, the Epistle of Applied Christianity*. Lincoln, Neb.: Back to the Bible, 1980.

Evans, Louis H. *Make Your Faith Work. A Letter from James*. Westwood, N.J.: Revell, 1957.

Farrar, F. W. *The Early Days of Christianity*. New York: Cassell, n.d.

Fulford, H. W. *The General Epistle of St. James*. London: Methuen, 1901.

Gaebelein, Frank E. *The Practical Epistle of James*. Great Neck, N.Y.: Doniger & Raughley, 1955.

Gibson, E. C. S. "The General Epistle of James." In *The Pulpit Commentary*, edited by H. D. M. Spence and Joseph S. Excell, vol. 49. Reprint. Grand Rapids: Eerdmans, 1950.

Gwinn, Ralph A. *The Epistle of James*. Shield Bible Study Series. Edited by G. R. Baker. Grand Rapids: Baker, 1967.

Harper, A. F. "The General Epistle of James." In *Beacon Bible Commentary*, edited by A. F. Harper et al., vol. 10. Kansas City, Mo., Beacon Hill, 1967.

Harrop, Clayton K. *The Letter of James*. Nashville: Convention, 1969.

Huther, Joh. Ed. *Critical and Exegetical Handbook to the General Epistles of James, Peter, John, and Jude*. Translated from the German. With a Preface and Supplementary Notes to the American Edition by Timothy Dwight. 1883. Reprint. Winona Lake, Ind.: Alpha Publications, 1979.

Ironside, H. A. *Expository Notes on the Epistles of James and Peter*. New York: Loizeaux, 1947.

Jamieson, Robert; Fausset, A. R.; and Brown, David. *A Commentary, Critical and Explanatory, on the Old and New Testaments*. Vol. 2, *New Testament*. Hartford: Scranton, n.d.

Johnstone, Robert. *Lectures Exegetical and Practical on the Epistle of James*. Reprint. Grand Rapids: Baker, 1954.

Kelly, Earl. *James, A Practical Primer for Christian Living*. Nutley, N.J.: Craig, 1969.

King, Guy H. *A Belief That Behaves. An Expositional Study of the Epistle of James*. 1941. Reprint. London: Marshall, Morgan & Scott, 1945.

Kistemaker, Simon J. *Exposition of the Epistle of James and the Epistles of John. New Testament Commentary*. Grand Rapids: Baker, 1986.

Knowling, R. J. *The Epistle of James*. Westminster Commentaries. London: Methuen, 1904.

Lange, John Peter, and Van Oosterzee, J. J. "The Epistle General of James." In *Lange's Commentary on the Holy Scriptures*. Edited by John Peter Lange. Translated from the German with additions by J. Isidor Mombert, vol. 23. Reprint. Grand Rapids: Zondervan, 1950.

Laws, Sophie. *A Commentary on the Epistle of James. Harper's New Testament Commentaries*. San Fancisco: Harper & Row, 1980.

Lenski, R. C. H. *The Interpretation of the Epistle to the Hebrews and of the Epistle of James*. Columbus, Ohio: Lutheran Book Concern, 1938.

McGee, J. Vernon. *James*. Pasadena, Calif.: Thru the Bible Books, 1978.

Macknight, James. *A New Literal Translation from the Original Greek of All the Apostolical Epistles with a Commentary and Notes*. vol. 5. 1821. Reprint. Grand Rapids: Baker, 1969.

Maclaren, Alexander. "Hebrews Chaps. VII to End, Epistle of James." *Expositions of Holy Scripture*. Reprint. Grand Rapids: Eerdmans, 1944.

Manton, Thomas. *An Exposition of the Epistle of James*. Reprint. Grand Rapids: Associated Publishers & Authors, n.d.

Martin, Ralph P. *James, Word Biblical Commentary*. Waco, Tex.: Word Books, Publisher, 1988.

Mauro, Philip. *James: The Epistle of Reality*. Boston: Hamilton, 1923.

Mayor, Joseph B. *The Epistle of St. James. The Greek Text with Introduction, Notes and Comments*. London: Melrose, 1911.

Mitchell, A. F. "Hebrews and the General Epistles." In *The Westminster New Testament*. London: Melrose, 1911.

Mitton, C. Leslie. *The Epistle of James*. Grand Rapids: Eerdmans, 1966.

Moffatt, James. *The General Epistles, James, Peter, and Judas*. The Moffatt New Testament Commentary. 1928. Reprint. London: Hodder & Stoughton, 1947.

Moo, Douglas J. *The Letters of James. The Tyndale New Testament Commentaries*. Grand Rapids: Eerdmans, 1985.

Motyer, J. A. *The Tests of Faith*. London: InterVarsity, 1970.

Nieboer, J. *Practical Exposition of James*. Erie, Pa.: Our Daily Walk, 1950.

Oesterley, W. E. "The General Epistle of James." In *The Expositor's Greek Testament*, edited by W. Robertson Nicoll, vol. 4. Reprint. Grand Rapids: Eerdmans, n.d.

Plummer, Alfred. "The General Epistles of St. James and St. Jude." In *An Exposition of the Bible*, vol. 6. Hartford, Conn.: Scranton, 1903.

Plumptre, E. H. *The General Epistle of St. James*. The Cambridge Bible for Schools and Colleges. Edited by J. J. S. Perowne, 1878. Reprint. Cambridge: U. Press, 1915.

Punchard, E. G. "The General Epistle of James." In *Ellicott's Commentary on the Whole Bible*. Edited by Charles John Ellicott, vol. 8. Reprint. Grand Rapids: Zondervan, 1954.

Purkiser, W. T. *Hebrews, James, Peter*. Beacon Bible Expositions. Edited by William M. Greathouse and Willard H. Taylor, vol. 11. Kansas City, Mo.: Beacon Hill, 1974.

Reicke, Bo. "The Episltes of James, Peter, and Jude." In *The Anchor Bible*. Edited by W. F. Albright and D. N. Freeman, vol. 37. Garden City, N. Y.: Doubleday, 1964.

Roberts, J. W. *A Commentary on the General Epistle of James,* Austin, Tex.: Sweet, 1963.

Roberts, Roy R. *The Game of Life. Studies in James*. Winona Lake, Ind.: BMH, 1976.

Robertson, A. T. *Practical and Social Aspects of Christianity. The Wisdom of James*. New York: Hodder & Stoughton, 1915.

Ropes, James Hardy. *A Critical and Exegetical Commentary on the Epistle of St. James*. The International Critical Commentary on the Holy Scriptures of the Old and New Testaments. Edited by C. A. Briggs, S. R. Driver, and A. Plummer. New York: Scribner, 1910.

Ross, Alexander. *The Epistles of James and John*. The New International Commentary on the New Testament. Edited by N. B. Stonehouse. Grand Rapids: Eerdmans, 1954.

Sadler, M. F. *The General Epistles of SS. James, Peter, John, and Jude with Notes Critical and Practical*. London: Bell, 1899.

Sidebottom, E. M. *James, Jude and 2 Peter*. The Century Bible, new ed. Edited by H. H. Rowley and Matthew Black. London: Nelson, 1967.

Simmons, Billy. *A Functioning Faith*. Waco, Tex.: Word, 1967.

Smith, H. Maynard. *The Epistle of S. James. Lectures*. Oxford: Blackwell, 1914.

Songer, Harold S. "James." In *The Broadman Bible Commentary*. Edited by Clifton J. Allen, vol. 12. Rev. ed. Nashville: Broadman, 1972.

Stevenson, Herbert F. *James Speaks for Today*. Westwood, N.J.: Revell, 1966.

Stier, Rudolf. *The Epistle of St. James*. Translated from the German by William B. Pope. 1871. Reprint. Minneapolis: Klock & Klock, 1982.

Strauss, Lehman. *James, Your Brother. Studies in the Epistle of James*. 1956. Reprint. Neptune, N.J.: Loizeaux, 1967.

Sugden, Edward H. "James." In *The Abingdon Bible Commentary*. Edited by Frederick Carl Eiselen, Edwin Lewis, and David G. Downey. New York: Abingdon, 1929.

Tasker, R. V. G. *The General Epistle of James*. The Tyndale New Testament Commentaries. Edited by R. V. G. Tasker. Grand Rapids: Eerdmans, 1957.

Thompson, R. Duane. "The Epistle of James." In *The Wesleyan Bible Commentary*. Edited by Charles W. Carter, vol. 6. Grand Rapids: Eerdmans, 1966.

Trapp, John. *Trapp's Commentary on the New Testament*. 1865. Reprint. Evansville, Ind.: Sovereign Grace, 1958.

Vaughan, Curtis. *James, A Study Guide*. Grand Rapids: Zondervan, 1969.

Ward, Ronald A., "James." In *The New Bible Commentary, Revised*. Edited by D. Guthrie and J. A. Moyter. Downers Grove, Ill.: InterVarsity, 1970.

Wesley, John; Clarke, Adam; Henry, Matthew et al. *One Volume New Testament Commentary*. Reprint. Former title: *The Methodist Commentary on the New Testament*, 1893. Grand Rapids: Baker, 1972.

Williams, George. *The Student's Commentary on The Holy Scriptures, Analytical, Synoptical, and Synthetical*. 1926. 5th ed. London: Oliphants, 1949.

Williams, R. R. *The Letters of John and James*. The Cambridge Bible Commentary, New English Bible. Cambridge: U. Press, 1965.

Winkler, Edwin T. "Commentary on the Epistle of James." In *An American Commentary on the New Testament*. Edited by Alvah Hovey. 1888. Reprint. Philadelphia: American Baptist, n.d.

Wolff, Richard. *General Epistles of James and Jude*. Contemporary Commentaries. Wheaton, Ill.: Tyndale, 1969.

Zerr, E. M. *Bible Commentary*. 1952. Vols. 5 and 6 (2 vols. in 1). Reprint. Raytown, Mo.: Reprint Publications, 1954.

_____. *The Labor of Love. An Exposition of James 2:14–4:12*. Grand Rapids: Eerdmans, 1960.

_____. *The Patience of Hope. An Exposition of James 4:13–5:20*. Grand Rapids: Eerdmans, 1960.

_____. *The Work of Faith. An Exposition of James 1:1–2:13*. Grand Rapids: Eerdmans, 1959. Also available in one volume, *The Behavior of Belief*, 1970.

V. MISCELLANEOUS WORKS

Adamson, James B. *James, The Man and His Message*. Grand Rapids: Eerdmans, 1989.

Andrews, Samuel J. *The Life of Our Lord upon the Earth*. 1862. Reprint. Grand Rapids: Zondervan, 1954.

Baer, Randall N. *Inside the New Age Nightmare.* Lafayette, La.: Huntington, 1989.

Billerbeck, Paul. *Doe Briefe Des Neuen Testaments Und Die Offenbarung Johannis Erläutert Aus Talmud Und Midrasch.* Vol. 3 in Strack and Billerbeck (see below). Munich: Beck'sche, 1926.

Bourne, F. W. *The King's Son; A Memoir of Billy Bray.* 20th ed. London: Bible Christian Book-Room. 1881. Reprint. London: Epworth, 1975.

Brandon, S. G. F. *The Fall of Jerusalem and the Christian Church.* London: SPCK, 1951.

Cadoux, Arthur Temple. *The Thought of St. James.* London: Clarke, 1944.

Clement of Alexandria. "The Stromata." In *The Ante-Nicene Fathers.* Edited by Alexander Roberts and James Donaldson, vol. 2. Reprint. Grand Rapids: Eerdmans, 1956.

_____. "The First Epistle of Clement to the Corinthians." In *The Ante-Nicene Fathers.* Edited by Alexander Roberts and James Donaldson. Vol. 1. Reprint. Grand Rapids: Eerdmans, 1950.

"Constitutions of the Holy Apostles" 1.3. In *The Ante-Nicene Fathers.* Edited by Alexander Roberts and James Donaldson, vol. 7. Reprint. Grand Rapids: Eerdmans, 1951.

Dana, H. E. *Jewish Christianity.* New Orleans: Bible Inst. Memorial, 1937.

Danby, Herbert. *The Mishnah, Translated from the Hebrew with Introduction and Brief Explanatory Notes.* 1933. Reprint. Oxford: Oxford U., 1964.

Deissmann, G. Adolf. *Bible Studies.* Translated by Alexander Grieve. Edinburgh: T. & T. Clark, 1903.

_____. *Light from the Ancient East.* Translated by Lionel R. M. Strachan. London: Hodder & Stoughton, 1910.

Dillenberger, John., ed. *Martin Luther, Selections from His Writings.* Garden City, N.Y.: Doubleday, 1961.

Douglas, J. D., ed. *The New International Dictionary of the Christian Church.* Grand Rapids: Zondervan, 1974.

Eadie, John. *Commentary on the Epistle of Paul to the Galatians, Based on the Greek Text.* 1894. Reprint. Grand Rapids: Zondervan, n.d.

Eusebius. *The Ecclesiastical History of Eusebius Pamphilus.* Translated from the Greek by C. F. Cruse. London: Bell, 1897.

Gingrich, F. Wilbur. "Prolegomena to a Study of the Christian Element in the Vocabulary of the New Testament and Apostolic Fathers." In *Search the Scriptures, New Testament Studies in Honor of Raymond T. Stamm.* Edited by J. M. Myers, O. Reimherr, and H. N. Bream, pp. 173-78. Leiden: Brill, 1969.

Hastings, James, ed. *Encyclopaedia of Religion and Ethics.* 13 vols. New York: Scribner, 1917.

James

Hendriksen, William. "Exposition of I and II Thessalonians." In *New Testament Commentary*. Grand Rapids: Baker, 1955.

Hoste, William, and Rodgers, William. *Bible Problems and Answers*. Fincastle, Va.: Bible Study Classics, 1957.

Howson, John S. *The Character of St. Paul*. London: Strahan, 1873.

Jerome. "Lives of Illustrious Men." In *Nicene and Post-Nicene Fathers of the Christian Church*. Edited by Philip Schaff and Henry Wace. Reprint. Grand Rapids: Eerdmans, n.d.

Josephus, Flavius. *Antiquities of the Jews*. Translated by William Whiston. Philadelphia: Winston, n.d.

————. *The Life and Works of Flavius Josephus*. Translated by William Whiston. Philadelphia: Winston, n.d.

Lenski, R. C. H. *The Interpretation of St. Paul's Epistles to the Galatians, to the Ephesians, and to the Philippians*. Columbus, Ohio: Lutheran Book Concern, 1937.

Lightfoot, J. B. *Saint Paul's Epistle to the Galatians*. 1865. Reprint. London: Macmillan, 1910.

Metzger, Bruce M. *A Textual Commentary on the Greek New Testament*. London: United Bible Soc., 1971.

Michaelsen, Johanna. *The Beautiful Side of Evil*. Eugene, Oreg.: Harvest House, 1982.

Miller, John. *Commentary on Paul's Epistle to Romans; with an Excursus on the Famous Passage in James (Chap. II. 14-26)*. Princeton: Evangelical Reformation, 1887.

Minear, Paul S. *Commands of Christ*. Nashville: Abingdon, 1972.

Montgomery, John Warwick, ed. *Demon Possession*. Minneapolis: Bethany, 1976.

Myers, J. M.; Reimherr, O.; and Bream, H. N., eds. *Search the Scriptures, New Testament Studies in Honor of Raymond T. Stamm*. Leiden: Brill, 1969.

Orr, James. *The Bible Under Trial. Apologetic Papers in View of Present-Day Assaults on Holy Scripture*. Edinburgh: Marshall, n.d.

The Oxford English Dictionary. 12 vols. 1933. Reprint. Oxford: Clarendon, 1961.

Peterson, Robert. *Are Demons for Real?* 1968. Reprint. Chicago: Moody, 1972. Original title, *Roaring Lion*.

Ramsay, W. M. *The Church in The Roman Empire Before A.D. 170*. 5th ed. 1897. Reprint. Grand Rapids: Baker, 1954.

Ramsey, Arthur Michael. *The Glory of God and the Transfiguration of Christ*. 1949. Reprint. London: Longmans, 1966.

The Septuagint Version of the Old Testament and Apocrypha with an English Translation. Reprint. Grand Rapids: Zondervan, 1972.

Sevenster, J. N. *Do You Know Greek? How Much Greek Could the First Jewish Christians Have Known?* Leiden: Brill, 1968.

Smeaton, George. *The Doctrine of the Atonement as Taught by Christ Himself.* 1871. Reprint. Grand Rapids: Zondervan, 1953.

Strack, Hermann L., and Billerbeck, Paul. "Das Evangelium Nach Matthäus Erläutert Aus Talmud Und Midrach." In *Kommentar Zum Neuen Testament Aus Talmud Und Midrach.* 1926. 5th ed. Munich: Beck'sche, n.d.

Unger, Merrill F. *Biblical Demonology. A Study of the Spiritual Forces Behind the Present World Unrest.* Wheaton, Ill.: Van Kampen, 1952.

_____. *Demons in the World Today.* Wheaton, Ill.: Tyndale, 1971.

Vincent, Marvin R. *A Critical and Exegetical Commentary on the Epistles to the Philippians and to Philemon.* The International Critical Commentary on the Holy Scriptures of the Old and New Testaments. Edited by C. A. Briggs, S. R. Driver, and A. Plummer. 1897. Reprint. Edinburgh: T. & T. Clark, 1950.

Westcott, Brooke Foss. *The Epistles of St. John, The Greek Text with Notes and Essays.* 1883. Reprint. Grand Rapids: Eerdmans, 1950.

_____. *The Gospel According to St. John, The Authorized Version with Introduction and Notes.* 1881. Reprint. Grand Rapids: Eerdmans, 1950.

Young, Robert. *Analytical Concordance to the Bible.* Reprint. New York: Funk & Wagnalls, n.d.

VI. DICTIONARY AND ENCYCLOPEDIA ARTICLES

Barabas, Steven. "Alphaeus." In *The Zondervan Pictorial Encyclopedia of the Bible.* Edited by Merrill C. Tenney, 1:118. Grand Rapids: Zondervan, 1975.

Bauernfeind, Otto. "*Haplous, haplotēs.*" In *Theological Dictionary of the New Testament.* Edited by Gerhard Kittel, translated and edited by Geoffrey W. Bromiley, 1:386-87. Grand Rapids: Eerdmans, 1964.

Best, W. Ernest. "Oath (NT and Christian)." In *Encyclopedia of Religion and Ethics.* Edited by James Hastings, 9:434-36. New York: Scribner, n.d.

Beyer, Hermann W. "*Episkeptomai, episkepeō.*" In *Theological Dicitonary of the New Testament.* Edited by Gerhard Kittel, 2:599-605. Grand Rapids: Eerdmans, 1964.

Blaiklock, E. M. "Ships." In *The Zondervan Pictorial Encyclopedia of the Bible.* Edited by Merrill C. Tenney, 5:410-15. Grand Rapids: Zondervan, 1975.

Bornkamm, Günther. "*Presbus, presbuteros.*" In *Theological Dictionary of the New Testament.* Edited by Gerhard Friedrich, 6:651-80. Grand Rapids: Eerdmans, 1968.

Brown, Colin, "The Parousia and Eschatology in the NT." In *The New International Dictionary of New Testament Theology*. Edited by Colin Brown, 2:901-35. Grand Rapids: Zondervan, 1976.

Büchsel, Friedrich. *"Krinō."* In *Theological Dictionary of the New Testament*. Edited by Gerhard Kittel, 3:933-41. Grand Rapids: Eerdmans, 1965.

Bultmann, Rudolf. *"Katakauchaomai."* In *Theological Dictionary of the New Testament*. Edited by Gerhard Kittel, 3:653-54. Grand Rapids: Eerdmans, 1965.

Candale, G. S. "Moth." In *The New Bible Dictionary*. Edited by J. D. Douglas, p. 850. Grand Rapids: Eerdmans, 1962.

Davies, R. E. "Gehenna." In *The Zondervan Pictorial Encyclopedia of the Bible*. Edited by Merrill C. Tenney, 2:670-72. Grand Rapids: Zondervan, 1975.

Dayton, Wilber T. "James." In *The Zondervan Pictorial Encyclopedia of the Bible*. Edited by Merrill C. Tenney, 3:391-95. Grand Rapids: Zondervan, 1975.

Forester, Werner. *"Eipenikos."* In *Theological Dictionary of the New Testament*. Edited by Gerhard Kittel, 2:418-19. Grand Rapids: Eerdmans, 1964.

Greeven, Heinrich. *"Euchomai, euchē."* In *Theological Dictionary of the New Testament*. Edited by Gerhard Kittel, 2:775-806. Grand Rapids: Eerdmans, 1964.

Harris, Charles. "Brethren of the Lord." In *A Dictionary of Christ and the Gospels*. Edited by James Hastings, 1:232-37. Edinburgh: T. & T. Clark, 1906.

Harrison, R. K. "Demon, Demoniac, Demonolgoy." In *The Zondervan Pictorial Encyclopedia of the Bible*. Edited by Merrill C. Tenney, 2:92-101. Grand Rapids: Zondervan, 1975.

Hauck, F. *"Markarios, Makarizō, Markaismos."* In *Theological Dictionary of the New Testament*. Edited by Gerhard Kittel, 4:362-70. Grand Rapids: Eerdmans, 1967.

Hayes, Doremus Almy. "James, Epistle of." In *The International Standard Bible Encyclopaedia*. Edited by James Orr, 3:1562-67. Grand Rapids: Eerdmans, 1939.

Hiebert, D. E. "Satan." In *The Zondervan Pictorial Encyclopedia of the Bible*. Edited by Merrill C. Tenney, 5:282-86. Grand Rapids: Zondervan, 1975.

Jacobs, H. E. "Brethren of the Lord." In *The International Standard Bible Encyclopaedia*. Edited by James Orr, 1:518-20. Grand Rapids: Eerdmans, 1939.

Jeremias, Joachim. *"Thura."* In *Theological Dictionary of the New Testament*. Edited by Gerhard Kittel, 3:173-80. Grand Rapids: Eerdmans, 1965.

Kelso, J. L. "Wealth." In *The Zondervan Pictorial Encyclopedia of the Bible*. Edited by Merrill C. Tenney, 5:909-11. Grand Rapids: Zondervan, 1975.

Keylock, Leslie R. "Brothers of Jesus, The." In *The Zondervan Pictorial Encyclopedia of the Bible*. Edited by Merrill C. Tenney, 1:658-66. Grand Rapids: Zondervan, 1975.

Kittel, Gerhard. "*Doxa*." In *Theological Dictionary of the New Testament*. Edited by Gerhard Kittel, 2:233-37, 242-51. Grand Rapids: Eerdmans, 1964.

_____. "*Katalaleō, katalalia, katalos*." In *Theological Dictionary of the New Testament*. Edited by Gerhard Kittel, 4:3-5. Grand Rapids: Eerdmans, 1967.

Klassen, William. "Oath." In *The Mennonite Encyclopedia*. Edited by Harold S. Bender and C. Henry Smith, 4:6-8. Scottdale, Pa.: Mennonite Publishing, 1957.

Koos, Harold D. "Mirror." In *Wycliffe Bible Encyclopedia*. Edited by Charles F. Pfeiffer, Howard F. Vos, and John Rea 2:1139. Chicago: Moody, 1975.

Michaelis, Wilhelm. "*Kakopatheō, sungakopatheō, kapopatheia*." In *Theological Dicitonary of the New Testament*. Edited by Gerhard Friedrich, 5:936-39. Grand Rapids: Eerdmans, 1967.

Michel, Otto. "*Ios, katieomai*." In *Theological Dicitonary of the New Testament*. Edited by Gerhard Kittel, 3:335. Grand Rapids: Eerdmans, 1965.

Neff, Christian, and Bender, Harold S. "Oath." In *The Mennonite Encyclopedia*. Edited by Harold S. Bender and C. Henry Smith, 4:2-6. Scottsdale, Pa.: Mennonite Publishing, 1959.

Paterson, J. H. "Rain." In *The Zondervan Pictorial Encyclopedia of the Bible*. Edited by Merrill C. Tenney, 5:27-28. Grand Rapids: Zondervan, 1975.

Rengstorf, Karl Heinrich. "*Apostolos*." In *Theological Dictionary of the New Testament*. Edited by Gerhard Kittel, 1:407-45. Grand Rapids: Eerdmans, 1964.

_____. "*Klaiō, klauthmos*." In *Theological Dictionary of the New Testament*. Edited by Gerhard Kittel, 3:722-26. Grand Rapids: Eerdmans, 1965.

Schlier, Heinrich. "*Aleiphō*." In *Theological Dictionary of the New Testament*. Edited by Gerhard Kittel, 1:229-32. Grand Rapids: Eerdmans, 1964.

Schmidt, Karl Ludwig. "*Ekklēsia*." In *Theological Dictionary of the New Testament*. Edited by Gerhard Kittel, 3:501-36. Grand Rapids: Eerdmans, 1965.

Schrag, Wolfgang. "*Sunagōfē*." In *Theological Dictionary of The New Testament*. Edited by Gerhard Friedrich. 7:798-841. Grand Rapids: Eerdmans, 1971.

Schrenk, Gottlob. *"Boulomai, boulē, boulēma."* In *Theological Dicitonary of the New Testament*. Edited by Gerhard Kittel, 1:629-37. Grand Rapids: Eerdmans, 1964.

Schweizer, Eduard. *"Psuchē.* The New Testament." In *Theological Dictionary of the New Testament*. Edited by Gerhard Kittel, 1:629-37. Grand Rapids: Eerdmans, 1964.

Seesemann, Heinrich. *"Orphanos."* In *Theological Dictionary of the New Testament*. Edited by Gerhard Friedrich, 5:487-88. Grand Rapids: Eerdmans, 1967.

————. *"Peira, peiraō, perrazō, peirasmos."* In *Theological Dictionary of the New Testament*. Edited by Gerhard Friedrich, 6;23-36. Grand Rapids: Eerdmans, 1968.

Stählin, Gustav. *"Hedonē, philēdonos."* In *Theological Dictionary of the New Testament*. Edited by Gerhard Kittel, 2:909-26. Grand Rapids: Eerdmans, 1964.

————. *"Orgē.* The Wrath of Man and the Wrath of God in the NT." In *Theological Dictionary of the New Testament*. Edited by Gerhard Friedrich, 5:419-47. Grand Rapids: Eerdmans, 1967.

Straham, James. "Mirror." In *Dictionary of the Apostolic Church*. Edited by James Hastings, 2:42-43. Edinburgh: T. & T. Clark, 1918.

Sweet, Louis Matthews. "Demon, Demoniac." In *The International Standard Bible Encyclopaedia*. Edited by James Orr, 2:827-29. Grand Rapids: Eerdmans, 1939.

Warfield, B. B. "Scripture." In *A Dictionary of Christ and the Gospels*. Edited by James Hastings, 2:584-87. Edinburgh: T. & T. Clark, 1906.

Whitwell, W. M. "Insects of the Bible, Moths and Butterflies." In *The Zondervan Pictorial Bible Dictionary*. Edited by Merrill C. Tenney, pp. 375-80. Grand Rapids: Zondervan, 1963.

VII. JOURNAL AND MAGAZINE ARTICLES

Bratcher, Robert G. "Exegetical Themes in James 3-5." *Review and Expositor* 66, 4 (1969):403-13.

Cabaniss, Allen. "A Note on Jacob's Homily." *The Evangelical Quarterly* 47, 4 (October-December 1975):219-22.

Cranfield, C. E. B. "The Message of James." *Scottish Journal of Theology* 18, nos. 2, 3 (June, September 1965):182-93; 338-45.

Elliott-Binns, L. E. "James I. 18:Creation or Redemption?" *New Testament Studies* 3, 2 (January 1957):148-61.

————. "The Meaning of *Hulē* in Jas. III. 5." *New Testament Studies* 2, 1 (September 1955):48-50.

Evans, George E. "The Sister of the Mother of Jesus." *Review and Expositor* 44 (October 1947):475-85.

Fine, Hillel A. "The Tradition of a Patient Job." *Journal of Biblical Literature* 74 (March 1955):28-32.

Gundry, R. H. "The Language Milieu of First-Century Palestine." *Journal of Biblical Literature* 83 (1964):404-8.

Hill, David. "*Dikaioi* as a Quasi-Technical Term." *New Testament Studies* 11, 3 (April 1965):296-302.

Hodges, Zane C. "Light on James Two from Textual Criticism." *Bibliotheca Sacra* 120, 480 (October-December 1963):341-50.

Hoyt, Herman A. "What Is Scriptural Healing?" *Eternity* 9, 8 (August 1958):27-29, 47-48.

Johanson, Bruce C. "The Definition of 'Pure Religion' in James 1:27 Reconsidered." *The Expository Times* 84 (January 1973):118-19.

Laws, Sophie S. "Does Scripture Speak in Vain? A Reconsideration of James IV.5." *New Testament Studies* 20, 2 (January 1974):210-15.

MacArthur, John F., Jr. "Faith According to the Apostle James," in *Journal of the Evangelical Theological Society*, 33, 1 (March 1990), pp. 13-34.

Minear, Paul S. "Yes or No: The Demand for Honesty in the Early Church." *Novum Testamentum* 13 (January 1971):1-13.

Scanzoni, John. "The Man with the Gold-Ringed Finger." *Eternity* 14, 8 (August 1963):11-13.

Shepherd, Massey H., Jr. "The Epistle of James and the Gospel of Matthew." *Journal of Biblical Literature* 75 (1956):40-57.

Songer, Harold S. "The Literary Character of the Book of James." *Review and Expositor* 66 (Fall 1969):379-89.

Travis, Arthur E. "James and Paul, A Comparative Study." *Southwestern Journal of Theology* 12, 1 (Fall 1969):57-70.

Ward, Roy Bowen. "Partiality in the Assembly: James 2:2-4." *The Harvard Theological Review* 62, 1 (January 1969):87-97.

Wenham, John W. "The Relatives of Jesus." *The Evangelical Quarterly* 47, 1 (January 1975):6-15.

SCRIPTURE INDEX

* Italicized pages numbers indicate consecutive passages of the commentary; subdivisions within each of these passages are not listed in the index.

Jude	
1	14, 17, 24, 26, 30, 52, 127
8	144
20	292
23	195
24	127

Revelation	
2:10	85
2:22	228
5:13	104
8:9	105
16:6	275
18:15	239
18:24	275
19:20	197
20:10, 14, 15	197
21:1	104

TOPICAL INDEX